The Politics of Reception

Northwestern University Press
Studies in Russian Literature and Theory

Founding Editor
  Gary Saul Morson

General Editor
  Caryl Emerson

Consulting Editors
  Carol Avins
  Robert Belknap
  Robert Louis Jackson
  Elliott Mossman
  Alfred Rieber
  William Mills Todd III
  Alexander Zholkovsky

The Politics of Reception

CRITICAL CONSTRUCTIONS OF
MIKHAIL ZOSHCHENKO

Gregory Carleton

NORTHWESTERN UNIVERSITY PRESS / EVANSTON, ILLINOIS

Northwestern University Press
Evanston, Illinois 60208-4210

Copyright © 1998 by Northwestern University Press.
Published 1998. All rights reserved.

Printed in the United States of America

ISBN 0-8101-1609-X

Library of Congress Cataloging-in-Publication Data

Carleton, Gregory.
    The politics of reception : critical constructions
of Mikhail Zoshchenko / Gregory Carleton.
       p. cm. — (Studies in Russian literature and theory)
    Includes bibliographical references and index.
    ISBN 0-8101-1609-X (cloth : alk. paper)
    1. Zoshchenko, Mikhail, 1895–1958—Criticism and
interpretation. 2. Criticism—Soviet Union—History.
I. Title. II. Series.
PG3476.Z7Z57   1998
891.73'42—dc21   98-29222
                                                                              CIP

The paper used in this publication meets the minimum requirements of the American National Standard for Information Sciences—Permanence of Paper for Printed Library Materials, ANSI Z39.48-1984.

*He has a sense of humor—
a decidedly rare quality these days.*
—Innokenty Oksenov on Zoshchenko, 1923

Contents

Acknowledgments — ix

Introduction   Anatomy of a Legacy   1

Chapter One   Parameters of Text and Reception   15

Chapter Two   *Skaz* and Mimesis   31

Chapter Three   "Controlling" Parody   59

Chapter Four   Fiction as Documentary:
Youth Restored and *The Blue Book*   81

Chapter Five   Authorizing Interpretation:
The Co-optation of the Mass Reader   111

Chapter Six   Writer as Reader: The Paradox of
Resolution in *Before Sunrise*   140

Conclusion   Reading Soviet Writers
after Socialist Realism   161

Notes — 172

Bibliography — 204

Index — 221

Acknowledgments

The debts incurred in writing this book are many, and words here do not do justice to what I truly feel. My deepest gratitude and respect I extend to my graduate adviser at the University of Michigan, I. R. Titunik, for teaching me how to read literature. To him I am indebted as well for the second R, writing. As he often noted, it's easy not to make sense, and thus under his tutelage clarity and coherence became my watchdogs. (As for the third R, math, that I'll never get.) He toiled countless hours on my behalf and in recompense demanded the highest of standards. I hope that this book, the roots of which were begun under his guidance, does not betray the confidence he placed in me. Unfortunately, "Ti" passed away before *The Politics of Reception* saw print, but I know he'll recognize something both from and for him in it.

I am grateful as well to many others who have read various parts of the manuscript and offered much welcome advice and a (very) patient ear as I made the transition from graduate student to professor: Katerina Clark, Evgeny Dobrenko, Herbert Eagle, Michael Gorham, Vida Johnson, Thomas Lahusen, Michael Makin, Piotr Michalowski, Gary Saul Morson, and David Sloane. I am especially grateful to Caryl Emerson and Alexander Zholkovsky, who read the book for press and provided detailed commentary and criticism. Their open-mindedness and professionalism are truly commendable. The same extends to Northwestern University Press, where I would like to thank especially Susan Harris, Editor-in-Chief; Rachel Drzewicki, Assistant Acquisitions Editor; and Ellen Feldman, Managing Editor. Specializing in early soviet literature left me little time to specialize in computer technology, and I very much appreciate their support and patience in dealing with the many questions and snafus that attended the book's revision and publication. I alone, however, take full responsibility for any errors or omissions in the text.

I also want to extend my sincere gratitude to the members of the Department of German, Russian, and Asian Languages and Literatures,

Acknowledgments

Tufts University, for their encouragement during my years here. Vida Johnson and David Sloane deserve special mention in this regard. They truly exemplify the colleague who is both a mentor and friend, and I am privileged to have worked with them. I want to thank in particular as well Christiane Zehl Romero, who as chair was (and remains) a tireless source of support. In 1996 Tufts University graciously provided a semester grant, funded by the Mellon Foundation, which was instrumental in allowing me to complete the book. I am also indebted to the Mellon Foundation for funding my graduate study at the University of Michigan. In 1993 IREX provided a travel grant that allowed me to conduct invaluable research in Russia. The Davis Center for Russian Studies at Harvard University kindly allowed me the opportunity to present and receive commentary on my work. Staffs at the following institutions have been very helpful in assisting me track down the more arcane items of Zoshchenko's critical legacy: Harlan Hatcher Library, the University of Michigan; the Slavic and East European Library, University of Illinois at Urbana-Champaign; Widener Library, Harvard University; the Institute of Russian Literature (Pushkinsii dom), St. Petersburg; and the Lenin State Library, Moscow.

Finally, I dedicate this book to my parents, Diane and Richard Carleton, who for over three (no doubt trying) decades have always supported me in my endeavors—no matter how wrongheaded, simpleminded, or Gogolian they might have been. Often they wonder what I do in the library; I hope that what follows helps answer that question.

Introduction

Anatomy of a Legacy

> It would be difficult to find in soviet literature anything more repulsive.
> —Andrei Zhdanov on Zoshchenko

AT FIRST, Mikhail Zoshchenko's fate would seem a familiar entry in the log of Stalinist repression of the arts: a writer, persecuted by the state, dies in official disgrace. Yet the contradictory claims made upon his name and work and the varying ways in which he has been typed "anti" or "pro" on both sides of the Atlantic suggest that all is not so simple. As one of the most popular and politicized Russian writers of the postrevolutionary period, Zoshchenko has been enlisted by critics to fight the cultural conflicts of the early Soviet Union, the cold war, and, posthumously, even the glasnost era. This book seeks to understand why his writing became, and still remains, a battleground for competing ideological interests and what this fracturing of critical opinion can tell us about ourselves as readers and about the interpretive practices of our field.

THE UNMAKING OF A WRITER

Rarely has a children's story ignited such fury among heads of state, gained the international stage, and entered history as a cultural landmark.

Early in the summer of 1946, when Zoshchenko's "The Adventures of a Monkey" appeared in the widely circulating journal *Zvezda,* no one could have known that in August a Party resolution would pronounce him, alongside Anna Akhmatova, the "scum of literature" and label his story a "vulgar lampoon," a "monstrous caricature," which "slanderously depicts the soviet people as primitive, uncultured, and stupid." Nor could anyone have anticipated that Stalin's cultural spokesperson, Andrei Zhdanov, would thereafter single them out as heads of a veritable conspiracy to defile soviet literature; that in the emerging conflict with the postwar West, Zhdanov would then launch on their backs a program for an intensely nationalist and puritan reconstitution of the arts and sciences, thereby making them the first targets in the cultural battles of the cold war; or that twelve years later, with Stalin and Zhdanov dead and the Thaw five years old, Zoshchenko would die, his productivity crushed and his health shattered.

All for a mere four pages? A monkey escapes from the zoo after German bombs overturn its cage, steals food "without paying" (since it "doesn't understand what's what" in the human world), and is chased by an astonished crowd. When a dog snaps at its heels, the monkey thinks that leaving the zoo might have been a mistake and entertains the idea (which became fateful for Zoshchenko) that "it's easier to breathe in a cage." A boy befriends the monkey, but an old drunk takes it to sell for beer money. The monkey runs away and again is pursued. The boy rescues it once more and domesticates it into a well-behaved individual that can stand as an example for children and "even some adults."

Harmless enough, it would seem. Yet for Zhdanov it was simply monstrous that anyone, a year after the Second World War, would enlist a monkey to judge the Soviet Union. Its view of the human world exuded a "noxious poison of zoological enmity" that culminated in "the vile, venomous, antisoviet belief that it is better to live in the zoo than in freedom and that it is easier to breathe in a cage than among the soviet people."[1] Comments such as these brought a "stormy applause" and paved the way for Zhdanov to drag Zoshchenko through Russian's wealth (unfortunate in this case) of pejoratives. How the writer painted soviet society was, in truth, only a window onto his own loathsomeness: he was "vulgar," "simple-minded," "scum," a "philistine," a "preacher of immorality and vulgarity," an "unprincipled and shameless literary hooligan," exhibiting (as if doubt remained) a "rotten and corrupt sociopolitical character." He had committed, no less, the gravest of cultural sins: violating the sacred pact of "soviet literature living for the interests of the people." At a time when the Soviet Union enjoyed unprecedented stature in the postwar world, when its citizens matured so rapidly that "today we are not who we were yesterday and tomorrow we will not be who we are today," Zhdanov behaved as if he had uncovered a plot to corrupt the whole of society. Despite its brevity, "The Adventures" was nothing less than "an attempt to deprive literature of its elevated standing and progressive social function and dump it into the swamp of reaction." More to the point, Zhdanov charged that if the country had let writers such as Zoshchenko educate soviet youth, the war would have been lost. After all, what was Zoshchenko but a magnet for all the "manure" (to borrow from Stalin's critical vocabulary) that had fouled soviet literature. He not only betrayed the tradition of social edification as enshrined by Belinsky, Chernyshevsky, and Lenin but was guilty of treachery of Darwinian proportions. If Akhmatova's acmeism was an exhortation (via Osip Mandelshtam) "back to the Middle Ages," then Zoshchenko had sounded a call "back to the monkey." From here it was a short step for Zhdanov to raise Zoshchenko's delinquency to a global scale. If Western culture was the heart of bourgeois decadence, then Zoshchenko only "kowtowed" to such tastes, and his work, consequently, aided those on the "other side" of the "iron curtain" whose sole desire was to slander "the truth of the Soviet Union." (Churchill's metaphor was obviously very fresh.)

These were no small stakes when in the same breath a writer was cast against a country, a world war, international rivalry, and the future of human civilization. The ever-higher standards Zhdanov invoked made Zoshchenko's writing appear all the more misguided, trivial and yet at the same time all the more injurious. How could he have been so blind to his own culture and deaf to his people and, worse, how could he mock both? What made such effrontery even more incredible—and painted the crime as all the more brazen—was that the charges hurled by Zhdanov were not the first Zoshchenko had heard. Fair warning, in a sense, had already been given in 1943 when *Before Sunrise*, Zoshchenko's last major work, was pulled from publication only after half of it had appeared in the journal *Oktiabr*. The chorus of printed responses lambasting this earlier work had only primed the stage for Zoshchenko's damnation three years later: "crap," "disgusting to read," a "vulgar, unartistic work alien to the feelings and sentiments of our people" that gave "an extremely distorted picture of life." It was an "immoral" work, "garbage that is of use only to our country's enemies."[2] And, in the model conclusion given by four "workers" in an open letter to the journal *Bolshevik*, *Before Sunrise* was a glob of "filthy spit in the face of our reader."[3]

Records now substantiate that the attacks in 1943 and 1944 on *Before Sunrise* were instigated by both Stalin and Zhdanov and that the latter personally edited the above letter.[4] But by openly committing his own voice and position in 1946, Zhdanov provided what others critics could not: an immediate imprimatur for all future denunciations. Since his words graced a Party resolution, they became inviolate, outliving Zhdanov (who died in 1948) and Stalin (1953).[5] This stamp of disapproval, as it were, led directly to ritualistic, knee-jerk calumniation familiar from the 1930s. In "Preacher of Immorality," Lev Plotkin's follow-up article to Zhdanov, we find nearly verbatim the same charges arrayed against Zoshchenko. Once again he was a "malicious ignoramus," harboring "cold contempt for his people"; *Before Sunrise* was unprecedented for its "sinister, dark tones" and so forth.[6] Repetition here was not only a sign of an expected unified front against the enemy but was inherently sycophantic as well. What better praise was there than taking a superior's charge and passing it along? Hence Stalin's behind-the-scenes description of Zoshchenko as a "preacher of immorality" entered the Party resolution as "of *putrid* immorality," picked up steam with Zhdanov, who added "of immorality *and vulgarity*," and finally was crowned as the title of Plotkin's article.

Of course a criminal of this magnitude demanded an equally villainous biography. No time was lost in locating the roots of Zoshchenko's corruption in his very first writings. His stories of the early 1920s had appeared under the aegis of the Serapion Brothers, a group of young writers who were known (and notorious) for experimentalist-modernist fiction and proclamations of artistic nonallegiance to politics. Neither reputation boded well. By the 1930s the term "Serapion," often wedded to that other bastion of corruption, "formalism," had entered official vocabulary as a synonym for "antisoviet." Needless to say, such an auspicious beginning played directly into the hands of Zhdanov and his acolytes. (Akhmatova's case required no linkage; her pre-revolutionary prominence as an acmeist poet already guaranteed postrevolutionary disloyalty.) Since Zoshchenko had matured in an environment of decadence and individualism, who could he become but a depraved writer? Logic such as this inflated him into a lasting representative of all "bourgeois-aristocratic literary schools" and automatically made him a paragon of reaction, behind whom the monsters of counterrevolution (i.e., the West) could rear their heads. To cement this connection, critics reduced Zoshchenko's life to these two poles, the early 1920s and the present-day 1940s, so that the career of this vulgarian-extraordinaire evinced a clear descent from Serapion machinations to the antisocial "biologism" of "The Adventures." Bound to this frame, the biography that emerged was a model of villainy and hence worthy only of reprobation. As a person, Zoshchenko was nothing more than a misanthrope; as a citizen, he was nothing less than a coward for spending most of the war in Alma-Ata; as a writer, he remained a slave to his ego, yearning wherever possible to "turn his pitiful soul inside out" and shout "look what a hooligan I am"; as a thinker, he was simply "ignorant," "narrow-minded," and possessed of "pseudo-scientific" beliefs. To summarize his work we can defer to Stalin, who—again displaying that special critical acumen of his—declared it an "emetic" and reportedly outlined Zoshchenko's future in no less uncertain terms: "It's not for society to reform itself according to Zoshchenko, but for him to reform, and if he doesn't, then he can go to hell."[7]

If such a biography was eminently sufficient for the Party's needs, its verity for the public record lay in its concision. The caustic trail burnt through Zoshchenko's past left no space for refutation or alternate interpretation. It also left a lot out. Gone were the published accolades of many soviet critics in the 1930s and early 1940s. For then—no quiet time in the Soviet Union—Zoshchenko was celebrated as a master of irony, a great satirist, charged with "dynamite," who displayed (as a plus) "no sympathy for philistines and the petite bourgeoisie."[8] Indeed, his narratives of contemporary life, by exposing negative elements of society, made him a true "realist."[9] At the same time, he was proclaimed an optimist, exhibiting "belief in the socialist future."[10] Unlike that of many of his Serapion colleagues, his writing was accessible to all, even the "marginally literate." He maintained a personal correspondence with Maksim Gorky, the official mentor of soviet literature, who read and praised Zoshchenko's work. We also hear of a "stormy ovation" given him at a public reading in 1932, where his most faithful readers were identified as "the working youth" of Moscow.[11] For the twenty-first anniversary of the Revolution, he was showered with ritualistic approbation in another "spontaneous" open letter from students wishing him strength and health in order to continue his "remarkable work"—an uncanny, though reverse, foreshadowing of the workers' spit rebuke.[12] Ignored as well were the 1939 awarding of the Order of the Red Banner of Labor by the Supreme Soviet and, most glaringly, the fact that Zoshchenko was one of the most widely read authors in the country, besieged with thousands of letters from readers who often addressed him endearingly as "brother."[13] Print runs for his work were enviable; in 1926 alone they exceeded half a million copies.[14] His stories had been staged countless times, had been broadcast over the radio, and had become a fixture of contemporary culture. In short, to maintain the image of Zoshchenko's unbroken descent into a "literary hooligan," nothing of an ascent could remain.

To be sure, there was one person who objected to these omissions. In letters to Stalin, Zhdanov, and the orthodox critic Vladimir Ermilov, Zoshchenko rebutted point by point the new interpretation of his life and work.[15] This "traitor" had volunteered for the Red Army during the civil war, and in the Second World War he had been evacuated from Leningrad during the siege and therefore did not "flee" to Alma-Ata. In 1946 he even received a medal for his plays and stories during the war. *Before Sunrise*, far from being antisoviet, antiartistic, and pseudoscientific, had been favorably reviewed before publication by academics, scientists, and other writers. Moreover, "The Adventures" was, in truth, nothing but a simple story. It had first been published the previous year in the children's magazine *Murzilka* and later reprinted in *Zvezda* without his knowledge (where he admitted it might look strange if read through an adult eye).[16] In his letter to Stalin, Zoshchenko ended on a personal note, deferentially couching his refutation in a denial of the same:

> Please believe me—I'm not looking for anything and am not asking for any improvement in my fate. And if I'm writing to you now, then it's with the single purpose to relieve something of my pain. I never was a literary scoundrel, a base person, or someone who dedicated his work to landowners or bankers. That is a mistake. I assure you.

With Zhdanov he sharpened this point by literally numbering the blank spots from the 1930s:

1. The fact of Gorky's praise
2. His overwhelming popularity among soviet readers
3. His 1939 award
4. Comments from editors detailing the utility of his work

The Politics of Reception

For Ermilov he reserved the counterpunch. He explicitly contrasted the unimpeachable authority of the above four institutions with Ermilov's criticism, thereby making the latter's attack seem all the more reprehensible for its obvious sycophancy. Noting the fact that in the 1930s Ermilov himself had praised Zoshchenko, he wrote:

> I guess that you, a critic, made a grave mistake by valuing my work so highly then. I guess that Gorky was mistaken as well. . . . I guess that in 1939 the administration of the Writers' Union made a mistake too when they awarded me the Order of the Red Banner of Labor for my literary accomplishments. I guess that thousands of readers, whose letters are piled in my cabinet, were also mistaken. Yes, I guess that these were all monstrous mistakes which for decades aided me in producing my own defective work.

Zoshchenko was one of the more astute readers of his own biography, and the underlying sentiment of these defensive postures, one that was hinted at but never expressly stated, posed the question that Zhdanov and others had to leave unasked: If Zoshchenko was a bastion of reaction, if he had flaunted his hostility to the state for more than two decades, why only in 1946 had he been discovered? How could Zhdanov, who became the authority in cultural affairs in 1934, or countless others have been so blind, so lax, and—to use a watchword of the period—so unvigilant? In fact, if one were to accept the script offered by Zhdanov, one could only wonder how such a writer could have survived the purges of the 1930s.

Just as this question was not directly asked, it was never answered. Zoshchenko's appeal to recover his name and ability to publish failed. As both his letters and witnesses attest, this led to an accelerated attack of the melancholy that he had suffered periodically since adulthood. He still wrote when energy and spirit permitted, but his output was of diminished quality (as he himself recognized) and nearly impossible to publish. (A few stories were printed sporadically, and two tame anthologies appeared in 1956 and 1958). Much of his time was consumed with personal affairs, since the loss of his professional standing caused immediate financial difficulties. To ensure some income he returned to shoemaking, a profession learned before writing, and did translation work as well. Nevertheless, he and his wife were forced to sell their possessions and borrow substantial sums.

The combined material and psychological pressures ravaged his mind and body. In a letter three years before his death, he poignantly declared: "I've become tired and lost the capability of making sense of the complex paths of our life. It turns out that it's not so good to live long!"[17] The last comment, a reference to his controversial quasi documentary on aging, *Youth Restored* (1933), put in relief his inability, even at a personal level, to escape his work of the past. Indeed, it seems that nearly all the psychological and physical ills that he had explored, mocked, and feared in his writing—

self-doubt, depression, the debilitating effects of age, chronic fatigue, frail nerves, a weak heart, and hypochondria—converged after 1946 to incapacitate him. What remained was an almost suicidal resignation. Though claiming that an "improper eating regimen" impaired one's creative abilities, he would explicitly refuse food. Four months before Zoshchenko's death in 1958, Kornei Chukovsky, a friend and one-time mentor, described him behaving incoherently, like a "corpse in which someone has stuck a speaking machine."[18] What Chukovsky saw was the twelve-year accumulation of Zoshchenko's inability and, finally, unwillingness to understand what had happened to him. Notably, in both prescribing and following a recipe for a writer's death, Zoshchenko (consciously?) reenacted the suicidal behavior of Gogol, reportedly the only person with whom he would allow himself to be compared.

THE MAKING OF A NAME

What spelled Zoshchenko's demise in the Soviet Union became the single most important factor in his rise in the West. Along with Akhmatova, he emerged in Western eyes as an icon for the tragic fate of soviet literature. The year 1946 immediately became a watershed, much like 1928 and the cultural revolution, 1934 and the inauguration of socialist realism, and 1953 and the Thaw. Zhdanov's speech and the Party resolution signaled that the Soviet Union was reentering an insular, fiercely ideological period, not as physically destructive but more aesthetically debilitating than the 1930s. Official efforts would now be directed at purging soviet culture of all "decadent" and "ideologically impure" elements. Virulent xenophobia and, in equal dose, Russophilic nationalism fueled the engine of this campaign, known broadly as Zhdanovism. Sweeping quickly through literature, theater, cinema, and music, it spilled over into the fields of science, history, economics, linguistics, and agriculture. Its uncompromising hyperbole has left us such gems as the denunciation of Dostoevsky as "useful only to the lackeys of Wall Street" or of T. S. Eliot as an author whose works "hyenas could have written."[19] Equally dramatic was the appropriation of many scientific discoveries and inventions (wireless telegraphy, the lightbulb, penicillin, the radio) under the rubric of specifically Russian achievements. Such animosity translated into a massive outpouring of anti-Western literature and film that only amplified the Soviet Union's retreat into a shell of isolationism and intolerance. With war scares a frequent phenomenon in the early years of the cold war, Western observers in the media imparted a special meaning to events of 1946: they were the harbinger of a new "Dark Ages," which for the arts marked the final and absolute subordination of creativity to ideology— a move that represented nothing less than an attempt "to destroy one of the most precious values in our Western civilization."[20]

The Politics of Reception

The fact that Zoshchenko first gained widespread attention during this most heated and confrontational period played no small role in his Western legacy. What was initially reported and prognosticated by the media received later confirmation from academia. For the nascent yet rapidly growing field of soviet-Slavic studies, Zoshchenko provided immediate, intensely personal, and (for the time) still living illustration of what state control of the arts meant. In his fate could be found the moral coordinates that gave the field its sense of purpose and direction. Zhdanov's tirade and the subsequent pillorying of Zoshchenko, the denigration of an all-popular author into an all-purpose villain, his expulsion from the Writers' Union, the resultant personal hardship and his struggle for redemption, and the evident downward cast in his work all gave to a new generation of scholars a clear, decisive picture of what a totalitarian state could do to the writer. It readily defined that unfortunate feature of the soviet literary environment: *travlia*, the "hounding" or extended bullying in the media of a writer who had fallen into disfavor. The ad hominems of 1946, which grafted disparate and stunningly simplistic lines of biography and literature, fact and fiction, amply reinforced soviet criticism's reputation for hackwork. Zoshchenko's fate essentially offered Western scholars irrefutable and still pulsating proof that fools, assassins, and bootlickers populated their counterparts' ranks, that ineptitude and ignorance dominated the field, that expletive and invective had replaced analysis, and that artists' reputations were bound to a highly visible, yet incorrigibly elastic, ideological procrustean bed. Zoshchenko's name thus became automatically and irrevocably identified with "The Winter" of soviet culture, which was soon typed in the West as one of the "bleakest and most sterile periods,"[21] a "monotonous plain" of mediocrity, a "desolate scene,"[22] where originality and experimentation were driven out wholesale under the pledge of a "conflictless literature," a contest between "the good and the better."

The forward position Zoshchenko naturally assumed in the West's attempts to comprehend this new phase of soviet culture gave scholars a ready-made schematic frame to locate the import of his life and work. The first major survey of Zoshchenko (1953) was expressly titled "The Tragedy";[23] a decade later, another appeared with the title "The Condemned Humorist."[24] The vocabulary of his introduction to the field was intimately tied to the contemporaneity of his fate and its utility in helping to understand soviet conditions. Western critics' recurring and understandable themes in these first studies were those of loss and destruction: "merciless persecution," "broken backbone," "erased as if he had never lived";[25] "mortally wounded," "a literary execution";[26] the "crushed" work of "one of the most promising and brilliant writers of Soviet literature";[27] the death of "an outstanding master of letters" without whose talents Russian literature would be incomparably "impoverished";[28] the "exemplary victim of this new onslaught on creative freedom."[29] Before the landmark confrontations over Boris Pasternak and

Alexander Solzhenitsyn, Zoshchenko's *travlia* and death embodied all (except the camps) that was to be abhorred in the new, postwar soviet culture. Critical attention, therefore, was given as much to defense as to analysis; its goal via interpretation was to preserve and uphold, just as a foreign-émigré press would, what soviet literature had itself officially expunged.

With the dissolution of the Soviet Union, the cold war-Zhdanovian catalyst to understanding Zoshchenko has only become more prominent. As Russia tries to reclaim its past from soviet obfuscation, manipulation, and denigration, Zoshchenko and the events of 1946 occupy a key place in the historical-cultural canon. Among the widespread efforts to come to grips with the monumental legacy of Stalinism, much of the focus has understandably been on the 1930s as the time of collectivization and the Terror. Yet nearly equal attention has been paid as well to the postwar years, since they combined the peak of the Stalinist cult with the nadir of Russian arts and because more witnesses (and participants) from this period are still alive. With Zoshchenko, the industry of recovery—the publication of memoirs, archival notes, commentaries, and revelations—has therefore had two major targets, both of which center on 1946: uncovering the behind-the-scenes, intra-Party details of the Stalin-Zhdanov attack and documenting the personal side of the writer's fall.

Research into the first—where the "why Zoshchenko" question resonates most often—has produced a clearer picture of Stalin's and Zhdanov's direct role in orchestrating the writer's persecution, of editors' and critics' duplicity (privately approving of Zoshchenko's work but publicly disavowing it), and of Zoshchenko's own attempts to avoid confrontation.[30] Speculation here has even catapulted Zoshchenko to the center of Kremlin intrigue, casting him as an unknowing victim of internecine struggles between Stalin's lieutenants.[31] The second effort reexamines the final twelve years of Zoshchenko's life through letters, diaries, and eyewitness observations. These illuminate his thought, behavior, and relations in much more detail and are directed primarily at removing the stains of 1946. At the same time, the official treatment of Zoshchenko has given this material added meaning, as lines (expressly or not) are sometimes drawn on culpability: Who helped him? Who joined the official silence? Who is to blame?

Significantly, as much as Zoshchenko has served the West as an icon in the cold war, in Russia these combined recovery efforts, by taking 1946 as their defining point, have also made him a symbol of the turpitude of the Zhdanovist period. Since the initial stirrings of glasnost he has become a martyr, and this, more than anything, has shaped recent interpretations of his life and work. From the first years after the Revolution, Zoshchenko rises as a pillar of truth and compassion, fighting against the lies of the state. In a major glasnost reprint (1987) of his work, Iurii Tomashevsky introduced Zoshchenko as a defender of the "poor," common, everyday person.[32] Though born before the Revolution in relative security and "on clean sheets," Zoshchenko "understood the life of these people and dedicated his labor to bring them real help." No simple writer, he was a person invested with a mission. Even in childhood "the future writer already knew . . . that the world into which he had arrived was unjust, and at the first opportunity he set out to study this unjust world," and it was his express role to "open the people's eyes." Stanislav Rassadin has extended Zoshchenko's vision by finding in his characters' voices of the 1920s precursors of Stalin's own words in the 1930s. For this reason Rassadin awards Zoshchenko the titles of "authority on the human soul" and "savant of human nature."[33] In similar fashion, if Zhdanov consigned the writer to oblivion, Dmitry Moldavsky returned in 1987 to immortalize him (demonstrably in the very same journal, *Zvezda,* over which the controversy in 1946 exploded). Zoshchenko's work breathes not only with the "traditions of the Russian classics" but with the "traditions of world classics" as well. *Youth Restored* reminds us of scientific tracts of the Renaissance and *The Blue Book* of prose of the same period, and *Before Sunrise* is simply "unique" in world literature.[34]

In the vocal efforts to reclaim Zoshchenko, investigation and analysis have often given way to unfettered adulation.[35] One is no longer surprised to hear Moldavsky's defiant challenge to Zhdanov that "Mikhail Zoshchenko lives and will live." These are the expected words by which a culture resurrects its victims, but there is more to these sacral tones than just a reversal of the Leninesque formula and more than just a need to make Zoshchenko something of an angel in the hell of the past. For many, his authority as historian, judge and teacher did not diminish with his death; instead, as Rassadin subtitles his essay, Zoshchenko "belongs in our time." His work, consensus holds, speaks to Russia's moral dilemmas and thereby illuminates its present condition. His very words, characters, observations, and themes permeate today's society as it lurches from perestroika to an unknown future. As M. Z. Dolinsky announced in an introduction to a 1991 reprint of Zoshchenko's lesser-known work, the same concerns, the same difficulties, the same tensions, even the same individuals have not disappeared. What Zoshchenko saw in his life, Russia still experiences. "Wherever one looks [in his work]," Dolinsky has observed, "one finds a striking similarity between personal and social behavior of people in the 1920s and 1980s."[36] Rassadin, too, compares Zoshchenko's early stories with economists' reports on Russia during perestroika. By endowing him with such proleptic vision critics have only heightened his symbolic value today. As Dolinsky concludes, Zoshchenko's legacy embodies the vicious turns of his country's history, and the writer continues to serve as its conscience: "How have we lived all these decades, if the same problems that burden Zoshchenko's characters burden us, that is, if we today are still located in the same place which we wanted to leave? Running in place may be good for morning calisthenics but not for society's advancement."[37]

Sentiments such as these have made the stakes of Zoshchenko's reception as far-ranging as those of the criticisms by Zhdanov. Interpretations in both the West and postsoviet Russia have made Zoshchenko a vehicle through which to personify and pass judgment on the heritage of soviet literature—a sentence, needless to say, that is unfailingly negative. His legacy is unconditionally set against the official shadows of his time: Zoshchenko is the voice of Truth, and, as Zhdanov's actions showed, the victim for it. This impression has made the events of 1946 seem inevitable; that is to say, given Zoshchenko's artistic and political predisposition, it was clear that sooner or later the ax would fall. For this reason, scholarship has generally assumed the task of bringing his transgressions to light and answering the question Zoshchenko implicitly posed before: How was it that he escaped persecution for so long? This goal has frequently turned critics into literary detectives. Rebecca Domar symbolically appended to her 1953 essay the subtitle "The Case of Zoshchenko." What was implied here was that the prosecutor (Zhdanov), the victim (Zoshchenko), and the sentence (silence) were already known; only the particulars of his "criminal" behavior needed to be explicated.

THE DIFFERENTIALS OF A REPUTATION

As they have unfolded since 1946, Zoshchenko's fate and critics' subsequent reconstruction of his writing and biography make for a compelling and convincing story. It is also a familiar one. The nature of Zoshchenko's confrontation and downfall offers us a model of the writer-versus-the-state conflict that has characterized so much of Russian literature. In this model the need for clarity in political axes is paramount, and against the likes of Stalin and Zhdanov it generally is not difficult to uphold such distinctions. In Western and contemporary Russian redactions of Zoshchenko's career, the lines of pro- and antisoviet, of ally and enemy, run deep and clear.

Yet this tendency only masks a more problematic condition: the contradictory ways in which his work has been enlisted as antisoviet. Representative here would be the difficulty often faced in reconciling the multiplicity of his narrative postures with a uniform image of author. Many, for example, have interpreted his narrators as portraits of the newly ascendant proletarian (a.k.a. the "soviet vulgarian") and thus the exclusive targets of his satire. Turning the scales, others have defined them as victims; their daily struggle for existence exposes the tragedy of life under the soviet system. Here Zoshchenko's irony, instead of mocking his narrators, "gives expression to their pent-up bitterness" and thereby makes him nothing less than "the spokesman of the masses of plain insignificant people." Still others, in a kind of compromise position, fluctuate between seeing the narrator as a target and viewing him as a mouthpiece in which wry and ingenue-like comments constitute the writer's real voice.[38] In short, all three approaches find a proper place for Zoshchenko's presence in the text, and each operates with the assurance that it has located the real writer within. After this, however, allegiance ends. In the first narrative voices are to be rejected; in the second they are to be embraced; whereas in the third they are split: positive and optimistic soviet statements are assigned to the target, and skeptical and pessimistic tones are advanced as the author's true sentiments.

Such pronounced confusion marks Zoshchenko's "case" as different from others that in the West make up the canon of antisoviet writers—different, for example, from Solzhenitsyn, with whom there is little disagreement as to where the writer's polemic is.[39] And the vacillation evident in Zoshchenko's critical legacy cannot be dismissed by the simple fact that readers bring different expectations to bear, for it directly impinges on the assumed political dominant of his efforts. If anything, Zoshchenko's alleged antisovietness is the precise point where continuity fractures. Where one senses hostility, another hears sympathy; where one locates target, another sees Zoshchenko's compatriot or the author himself; what one highlights, another conceals or discards.

To be fair, what we witness here is not exclusive to Western interpretations. To a marked degree the above dissension parallels the twists and turns of Zoshchenko's reception in the Soviet Union. His unusual characters in unusual situations, his unusual authors "writing" unusual texts have always caused consternation and have always annoyed, irritated, or amused readers. In the Soviet Union in the 1920s, the search for clarity, for the "real Zoshchenko," was greatly facilitated by the interpretive practice of identifying all voices—both narrators' and characters'—directly with the writer's. Essentially anything in the text, therefore, could be tacked onto him. He quickly became known as a propagator of "philistine-bourgeois" values, and his texts were decried as mirrors of and thus platforms for negative social types—that is, the prerevolutionary elements that the state had not yet succeeded in eliminating. Indeed, the words that greeted his first story collection, *The Stories of Nazar Ilich, Mr. Sinebriukhov*, would have made Zhdanov proud: "In absolutely no way should these first steps have seen print or been put on sale."[40]

However, by the end of the decade—precisely when Boris Pilniak and Evgeny Zamiatin were hoisted as the archvillains of soviet literature and one would have expected the same treatment for Zoshchenko—his critical reputation shifted. Now, in a reversal of a most shocking degree, critics began to claim him as a pro-soviet satirist. Far from supporting philistines or the petite bourgeoisie, Zoshchenko was seen as always having attacked and vilified these enemies. His strategy was to castigate deficiencies in society, expose corruption, and point his readers to the proper path—only he did it from behind, by assuming the voice of the enemy.

This interpretation remained dominant until the 1940s, when Zhdanov and others resurrected, more or less, the temperament of the 1920s. But after his death in 1958, Zoshchenko regained his reputation as a pro-soviet satirist. In a series of articles and monographs in the 1960s and 1970s, his texts were once again celebrated as exposés from within of the philistine-bourgeois mind-set, and this status continued until the onset of perestroika-glasnost launched his reputation, as we have seen, to unprecedented heights.[41]

Where does this leave us? Zoshchenko was a "political" writer and has become an overtly "politicized" figure. In fact, he has had the unusual yet illuminating fate of being cast in all the roles that the soviet experience offers the investigator: hero, martyr, villain, and dupe. However, politics, as the point of inquiry, does not necessarily account for the interpretive somersaults and backflips that attended his life and have accumulated after his death. Critics in the West or contemporary Russia may share a similar ideological posture, but the Zoshchenkos that emerge from under their antisoviet label are decidedly inconsistent. Likewise, a marxist orientation, broadly understood, may unite soviet critics, but continuity among them, needless to say, has been conspicuously absent. If Hugh McLean's admission that with Zoshchenko "we cannot be sure" finds a crosscultural echo in the profusion of terms like "ambiguous," "unclear," and "opaque" that littered soviet readings, and if political claims on the writer exhibit the same contradictions as the "opposition," this should encourage us not to join in the exchange of ideological labels but to try to make sense of what has occurred at all levels. In fact, the one constant in his reception, regardless of whether we are speaking of soviet, Western, or Russian critics, is pronounced indecision about how Zoshchenko's intentions manifest themselves in the text.

In describing the fate of literature in the Soviet Union, the West often mobilizes the writer-versus-the-state theme. But this tradition automatically assumes that all is clear for us, as if a given writer was a problem (whether politically or aesthetically) for them, as if only then and there were readers baffled or confused. In no uncertain terms, the vicissitudes of Zoshchenko's reputation compromise this conviction. Indeed, the fracturing of critical opinion only puts in relief the fact that the Zoshchenko phenomenon is broader than the sum of his work and fate in the Soviet Union. At a primary level, the problem we face is that of making meaning: to understand how his texts have been read as viable statements on or satires of soviet reality, as documents of the "philistine" condition, and as catalogs of and for the "masses."

Zoshchenko's legacy suggests that he operates with themes and conventions in an unorthodox manner, one that upsets critics' attempts, regardless of the ideological motives at hand, to make his texts a cohesive platform or vehicle through which to comment upon the soviet environment. Critics have long acknowledged the difficulties that his masks, evasions, and hyperboles cause; many as well have produced valuable studies on the originality and humor of his writing. What has remained absent is a study of how readers on all sides have sought to resolve these complications. My intent therefore is not to provide a history of Zoshchenko's reception but to analyze the ways in which readers of different backgrounds—official, popular, Russian, Western—have handled literature that deviates from ideological and aesthetic norms. The question motivating this study can be summed up as follows: What is the interconnection between how he writes, how he has been read, and how, in the end, he sought to read himself? Its goal is to elucidate, in concrete terms, the strategies by which we generate meaning from such texts and how, in turn, these same texts operate upon us. This objective automatically intersects with key issues of soviet literary culture—the notions of realism, reference, genre, parody, and readerships—and can also help illuminate how these same phenomena have been understood in the West. This is a primary concern of mine and is, I believe, the compelling point of Zoshchenko's legacy, for it casts light not only on what occurred then but also on our own interpretive assumptions, needs, and prejudices.

The first chapter discusses interpretive paradigms most often employed, with emphasis on the shared realist expectations of soviet and Western readers. The second and third focus on how, commensurate with these expectations, readers have sought to fix Zoshchenko's classic short stories and novellas within specific political paradigms that are anticipated and parodied by the texts themselves. The fourth centers on his two most controversial works, *Youth Restored* and *The Blue Book,* which played upon a contemporary drive to merge fiction with documentary. The fifth, drawing upon "unofficial" responses of soviet mass readers, details how Zoshchenko dealt with critical opposition by crafting a special image of reader. I concentrate on the conflict between this and official images of the reader and consider how this impacts his mythic status today as "writer for the people." The last chapter introduces Zoshchenko himself as a reader and his attempt in *Before Sunrise* to resolve the very same interpretive problems that have troubled his readers. His own "critical construction" of self provides important insight into others' efforts to do the same. In the conclusion I argue that the paradoxes of his reception illuminate some of the problems inherent in the tradition of viewing soviet authors through a writer-versus-the-state paradigm—one that might seem dated with the passing of socialist realism but that, in key respects, has remained dominant.

Chapter One

Parameters of Text and Reception

> Literary realism is a tantalizing contradiction in terms.
> —Robert Alter[1]

THE PURSUIT (AGAIN) OF REALISM

One hesitates to begin with a term that, perhaps more than any other in literary studies, has caused eyes to roll. With realism characterizing—often simultaneously—a period, genre, writer, text, style, narrative mode, or epistemology, presumably no phenomenon has escaped its grasp. It might be tempting to rid ourselves of this gadfly by adopting any number of structuralist or post-structuralist positions that highlight the "fallacy" and "illusion" behind claims of realism. We now can safely (and slavishly) assert that realism is but a construct: no text can suppress its own mediating influence; no text is adequate to the world to which it gestures; the world, as experienced by humans, is itself made up of texts; no text therefore can refer to anything but another text; humans, in sum, are imprisoned in a discursively mediated and defined world. So much, then, for any confidence we may have harbored about what a "realistic" portrayal is. Anyone brave (or foolish) enough to argue for mimetic accuracy is cast into the purgatory of tautology.

Still, no matter what our theoretical convictions, we are fated to remain in its company. Even if claims of realism seem misguided, obsolete, or impossible, this does not mean that texts automatically lose their authenticity, authority, or "realness" in the field of cultural interaction. What theory says is out there and how readers tend to behave are often quite different. We might hesitate or refuse to accept that a given text reflects some external reality, but this does not mean that readers cannot cite it, employ it, believe it, or attack it with the perception that it does.

In fact, if we turn to early soviet literature, there is no other word—not even the Party labels of marxist, Leninist, Communist—that we meet with more frequency in critical discourse. Régine Robin's characterization of the term as a "virtual obsession" at the time would seem a most accurate description in light of the formidable pile of realisms the short period of 1917–34 has bequeathed us: proletarian, critical, revolutionary, romantic, psychological, naturalistic, socialist.[2] Essentially no group or writer could pretend to any authority without first planting a stake in this issue. The immediate fallout was, of course, the cascade of modifiers that realism bore as factions scrambled to protect their *realizm* as the only true one. And though as a consequence of this imbroglio the term was predictably rife with imprecision and inconsistency, it remained the yardstick to gauge allegiance and the club to quiet opponents.

No less than their soviet counterparts, Western critics have staked much of their practice on the principle of realism as well. Here it takes on different colors, but its value is similar. It serves to distinguish those (realist) writers who have presumably told the truth about the soviet experience from those (propagandistic) ones who have deliberately covered up or, worse, falsified it. Though of course not reflective of all Western criticism, this premise is dominant in Zoshchenko's critical legacy. Even the addition of qualifiers like *ironic* or *satiric* does not infringe upon what has been his central value for the West: finding the authentic Soviet Union in his writing. Consensus holds that he illuminated for the reader everything propaganda left out or, more often, tried to hide. In Marc Slonim's exemplary summation, Zoshchenko "reveals the ruts and rot of daily existence with its vulgarity and stupidity behind the facade of magnificent slogans."[3] For Viktor Sven he became the "only Soviet satirist who with his pen drew an accurate picture of the life that the Soviet citizen lives, of a life that is monstrous."[4] Gleb Struve, too, has argued that Zoshchenko gives us "a true picture of Soviet weekdays, stripped of all romantic and heroic varnish, of all pretension and make-believe."[5] In short, ample room has been found for Zoshchenko among the ranks of other explicitly antisoviet writers. His motivation was the same; the only difference is that he approached the target from below. If, say, a Zamiatin or Bulgakov aimed at the overarching theoretical, ethical, and ideological failures of the Bolshevik Revolution, then Zoshchenko provided a microscope for its day-to-day ones.

If our objective, then, is to understand what readers do and have done in concrete circumstances, the task we face regarding realism is somewhat different: not to define what (the illusion of) realism is, but to elucidate what its application as a term means and how it impacts reading strategies. The same year as Zoshchenko's debut as a writer, Roman Jakobson offered some prescient observations on its function.[6] Arguing that nearly every artistic movement has claimed realism as its raison d'être, despite antithetical approaches to art and wide variations in genre, he demonstrated that its main critical value has been as a polemical tool to promote one artistic current over another. The importance of being able to claim "fidelity to life" and denounce opponents for its violation is for political, social, and aesthetic reasons undeniable. Consequently, as Jakobson shrewdly noted, even an artistic movement that is antireferential or celebrates chaos and disorder generally sanctions its approach by claiming greater accuracy with respect to the "true state" of the world (the absurdist text reflecting an absurdist world is a familiar wording). This points to why realism persists in our own critical vocabulary and why it, no matter what turn theory may take, will undoubtedly remain. It has been and is primarily an axiological tool that signals cultural relevance: what a readership can learn from a text. What is "realistic" is most often what is able to serve the reader as the purveyor of socially valid meaning. Only in a limited scope, with nineteenth-century prose as the canon, has realism designated a style or type of text.

My attention in this chapter will be focused more on the Western use of realist notation for the very reason that it is the least commented upon, even among its own practitioners. For every dozen questions, accusations, and charges leveled at soviet critics—especially if the subject is Zoshchenko—we direct perhaps one to ourselves. Almost a decade after the onset of glasnost, we remain curiously resistant to metacritical examinations of our own practices. This is not to say that debate hasn't occurred, that objections haven't been made, or that paradigms haven't "shifted." But we seem to pay less direct attention to the contents of our own interpretive canons—assuming a pose almost as if we have nothing to learn from ourselves.

Motivation for the West's parallel "obsession" with realism can be found in classic statements from the field's formative period. In *The Captive Mind*, Czeslaw Milosz embeds invitation in indictment:

> "Socialist Realism" is much more than a matter of taste, of preference for one style of painting or music rather than another. It is concerned with the beliefs which lie at the foundation of human existence. In the field of literature it forbids what has in every age been the writer's essential task—to look at the world from his own independent viewpoint, to tell the truth as he sees it, and so to keep watch and word in the interest of society as a whole.[7]

His is not a call, of course, for the writer to abandon the "essential task" but to approach it covertly. Against the manifest grip of censorship and persecution, the writer must labor carefully. Perhaps he or she will suffer keeping "watch and word," but the risk has to be taken. In one stroke Milosz thus joins ethics and aesthetics and elevates the writer willing to accept this charge to a sanctified position, one impregnated with the truth that the state has consciously forsworn. Equally important, the counterworld created by the writer is recast as well: no matter what its fictional origins, it is closer to the "real world" than any generated by the official clichés of socialist realism.

Directives of this kind are inherently directives to readers, for the truth produced by this literature is lost if not received and understood. The reader's implicit but essential role is to translate the writer's counterworld back into the terms of the real one. This is not neutral behavior; decoding the text "properly" makes one complicit with the author's (criminal) act of truth telling. It also raises the reader (critic, scholar) to nearly the same height as the writer—which is not an unflattering prospect. As Leo Strauss once noted in *Persecution and the Art of Writing*, if we uncover this truth, or if we assume we do, we join a select group of "trustworthy and intelligent readers."[8] Arguably, the personal incentives in making sure we discover the "forbidden fruit" can be as strong as the moral ones.

In his 1982 study of Andrei Platonov, a writer whose legacy is no less volatile than Zoshchenko's, Mikhail Heller has acutely demonstrated how such precepts translate into practice. To gain the privileged status of purveyors of the (antisoviet) truth, Western critics first need to recognize the special ground they have entered: "In studying pre-soviet Russian literature or the literature of other countries, a scholar may or may not include the social context in his scope of attention. The scholar of soviet literature has no such choice."[9] What is significant in this statement is not the relevance/non-relevance of social context per se, but the exceptionality reserved for the study of soviet literature. Not only is inquiry into affinities it might share with other literatures precluded from the start, Heller assumes that it should be evaluated in an exclusive manner because of exigencies not in force in other cultural contexts. For him soviet literature has existed in such unique circumstances that its study mandates presumptions, processes, and, most important, an objective specific to it and only it. What this endpoint is, what constitutes the nature of the "social context," Heller enumerates without hesitation: "Any work of every soviet writer, by necessity, should be analyzed as the result of an artist's single-handed combat against a machine."[10]

Heller drapes the critic's chair with the same cloak of ethics that Milosz extends to writers. It is a seat, no doubt, that most of us would like to occupy (for who wants to side with the machine?), but in so doing we surrender a good measure of independence and flexibility. We have "no such choice"; "by necessity" our task is preordained. We assume a moral imperative that places the pursuit of truth, defined as confirmation of the abject nature of soviet reality, at the head of the interpretive mission. At the same time, though, the desideratum is liberating in that it validates a wide scope of inquiry. The writer's counterworld can take myriad forms, and since some, as in any combat, are highly camouflaged, we should cast the net as far as possible.

Where the moral imperative places constraint is in how we use any text caught in this manner. If the truth is located in the writer's counterworld, then its accession calls for us to assign it real-life accuracy, no matter what its formal or fictional propositions and no matter how unconventional its shape. Ultimately, as the pursuit of truth and that of realism merge, the moral imperative asks us to leave fiction altogether. With the assertion "Platonov didn't exaggerate or invent anything," Heller negates the imaginative side of literature. Its specific devices, what causes us to accept it as fiction, do not impede its capacity to interpret and transmit the soviet experience. This active, conscious effort to read fiction as the equivalent of that reality abolishes any functional distinction between it and documentary statements. For Heller, both permit direct, authoritative access to an extratextual phenomenon. If anything, the former can do the job better because the narrative freedoms that fiction allows are often the only guarantee of referential accuracy.

If accepted, this precept empowers the critic to turn literary distortion and obfuscation inside out. However opaque the writer's lens may seem, we can reclaim opacity in and of itself as a confidential servant of clarity. In Heller's view, if the Soviet Union was so "fantastically" horrific, then only a narrative with an equal dose of fantasy and hyperbole can adequately capture its essence. Directly naming Zoshchenko along with Platonov, he declares that the hallmark of an accurate portrait of their society can only be a "distorted mirror," for this is what "reflects the actual state of soviet reality."[11] His confidence in redefining distortion as a mimetic intensifier makes the following assertions nonoxymoronic: unconventional language can "depict the fantasticality of reality and the reality of fantasticality"; a character can be simultaneously "grotesque and as realistic as possible"; or, if one accepts the totalitarian United State of Zamiatin's dystopia *We* as the standard for the Soviet Union, then "the real and therefore fantastic world depicted by Platonov begins to resemble the fantastic, and consequently real, world of the United State."[12] In sum, the original—and false—distortion is the corruption inherent in the Soviet Union; artistic counterdistortion only rights the picture and, as a result, deserves the laurels of verisimilitude.

I do not question why Heller and many others have read writers like Zoshchenko and Platonov as windows onto soviet conditions. The fears expressed by Milosz rang all too true to be taken lightly, then or now. Censorship, bloodshed, exile, and the camps leave little room for neutrality. What concerns me in this study are the methodological practices that issue from this principle. Put simply—if we allow for a provocative question—why is it that interpretations in the West sometimes sound like Engels when he made the celebrated claim that he "learned more" about French society from Balzac's *Comédie Humaine* "than from all the professional historians, economists and statisticians of the period together?"[13] No doubt Heller would have recoiled at the comparison, yet however divergent their ideological orientation, the questions they ask and the answers they expect to find in literature are not substantively different. In effect, both define narrative on one plane, the representational-referential, to which other factors and features are subordinate. They adhere to an interpretive procedure, what I would deem a *referential condition*, that is engaged prior to and, significantly, irrespective of genre. In using this term, I do not wish to muddy even more the idea of realism but seek to clarify the differences Jakobson had in mind between realism as a label of genre and as an interpretive-evaluative mode. Western and soviet usage, admittedly, offers little help in this regard since one term encompasses both meanings, but the two are not synonymous. The former directs attention more to constituent narrative components (what conventions or tropes signal, in Roland Barthes's words, the "reality effect" in a given discursive environment), whereas the latter reflects what is done with a text and occupies the field of cultural authority.[14] As a performative designation, the referential condition points to which texts can be made into repositories of socially relevant meaning regardless of their formal trappings. For this reason, it embraces a wide range of discourses, any of which can deviate substantially from "naive" or "classical" realism. In fact, taken to its full potential, for which Heller serves as but one example, the referential condition makes texts functionally homogeneous. Any kind of writing can afford the reader adequate foundation for accessing external reality, and, equally important, its "realistic" value or cultural utility is predicated on that capacity.

The referential condition allows us to connect soviet, Western, and postsoviet Russian interpretations of Zoshchenko. As will be in evidence throughout this study, *the* central precept in critical constructions of his literary profile has been the drive to make his texts a valid simulacrum, model, or record of actual or putative reality. Here lies the refrain of his work's capacity—even for texts that stylistically violate the genre of realism—to "show," "reveal," "illustrate," "affirm," "prove" the truths of his time. The coincidence of such expectations, which defy chronological, cultural, and ideological differences, is striking, and it means that what Barthes identifies as the illusion of transparency is, in fact, the reader's chore. It becomes his/her task to make the text achieve this effect, which is something Zoshchenko's readers have never hesitated to do. This practice puts before us a number of questions that generally have been left off the table in studies of soviet literature: What are the strategies readers employ to make texts "realistic"? How in concrete terms do readers seek to resolve the boundaries between text and world? How are fictional texts, particularly unconventional ones, made into repositories of authoritative, culturally valid meaning?

MAKING SENSE OF THE TEXT

These objectives leave us having to take seriously the meanings with which readers endow texts. It is understood, I would assume, that this prospect neither condones nor ignores what may have been done in the name of those values (Zhdanov is never far from the scene), but is aimed at the conditions of their realization. The goal is to reverse attention, to avoid yet another formulation of what a "realistic" text is. Broadly speaking, at issue is not the relative adequacy of a text's representation of the world but how assumptions of adequacy in the reader's mind delineate what textual components are recognized as semantically relevant, what meaning they are given, and how they are perceived to interrelate. For this reason, there will not be in this study a comparison between Zoshchenko's fictional world and the "actual" composition of soviet society; the matter instead is one that in various degrees engaged Zoshchenko's formalist contemporaries: how the same text can perform different functions in varying interpretive environments.[15]

Petr Bogatyrev, a later adherent of theirs in the Prague School, has left us a lucid illustration, albeit nonliterary, of what is at issue semantically. An article of clothing projects a variety of latent significations; it may serve as practical or defensive cover, as aesthetic ornament, or as a distinguishing mark of nationality, social rank, profession, gender, marital status, political allegiance, and so forth. No category alone, whether ideological, social, aesthetic, or sexual, defines the totality of the item; its potential meanings exist in a competitive field. What is deemed purely ornamental in a ceremonial context, for example, can signify economic status, sex, and so on in another. Each "reading" of the clothing hierarchizes different possibilities; each necessitates a shift in our recognition of the value of the apparel's constituent components:

> A military uniform, for example, has on it certain details that indicate the rights of the wearer and his rank in the army. When a private sees a uniformed officer, he knows that he is obliged to obey his command; in this case the quality of the material or the aesthetic value of the uniform is irrelevant. If we take a rich soldier's uniform, made of better material than the officer's uniform [in the days when soldiers outfitted themselves], and send it to a second-hand dealer who does not know about military distinctions, he may attach higher value to the uniform of the rich soldier. Or, if there is no difference in the quality of material, the dealer might assess the uniforms as equal, despite the fact that in the army these uniforms differ substantially as signs.[16]

As the features of the rich soldier's uniform acquire a different value in each context (braid as rank, braid as wealth), the clothing effectively changes form. The actual material, of course, stays the same. Whether a property is "visible" depends on the meaning ascribed to it. Under one dominant it may become the signifying center; under another it may be defined in relation to a different center; under a third it may be ignored and disappear. Its deletion in this last case is not literal (the braid is not cut off) but a result of semantic relevancy. Similarly, a textual feature can bear a number of meanings, just as one meaning can be shared by a number of features. Yet in all these circumstances, differences are of a functional nature; what distinguishes features is what is *done* with them. They have no inherent value except when perceived in a specific discursive context.

The semiotic ground mapped by Bogatyrev in 1936 is well trodden by now; yet it is important that this process can be expressed in relatively neutral terms such as his. In order to relate various readings, we have to understand their enabling strategies on equivalent grounds. At first we might hesitate to consider any equivalency between soviet and Western interpretations, given the reputation soviet critics of Zoshchenko have had in the

West. Yet, as will become clear, how the West has "clothed" Zoshchenko can be no less problematic, no less self-serving, and, finally, no less wrought with politicization, reductionism, and the host of other interpretive demons that generally have been reserved for soviet critical activity. The point is not to substantiate this fact but to address circumstances of interpretation in the terms outlined above: how Zoshchenko's uniform has been cut, its fabric dyed, and its buttons sewn and, most important, what to do with that which doesn't seem to fit the current fashion.

What is at stake can be illustrated by the response to one of Zoshchenko's first publications, "About Myself, Ideology and Some Other Stuff as Well," which appeared in 1922 alongside a series of Serapion "autobiographies" in the journal *Literaturnye zapiski*. Since his contribution has had a decisive influence on his reputation and because it has rarely been printed in full in either the Soviet Union or the West (for reasons which will become clear), I include it below. (Ellipses are in the original.)

About Myself, Ideology and Some Other Stuff as Well

My father's an artist, my mother an actress. I'm saying that because in Poltava there are other Zoshchenkos. For example: the tailor Egor Zoshchenko. In Melitopole there's also Zoshchenko the male midwife and gynecologist. But for the record, I'm in no way related to them, never met them and don't want to.

On account of them, no bones about it, don't even want to be a famous writer. They're sure to come visit. They'll read something and head on over. Just like one of my aunts from Ukraine already did.

Overall it's really a problem being a writer. Take ideology. . . . Today everyone's demanding ideology from a writer.

Here's what Voronsky (a decent fellow) writes:

. . . Writers have to "identify themselves more precisely in terms of ideology."

Oh God, what a headache!

You tell me what kind of "precise ideology" I can have if not one party as a whole appeals to me?

These party types think that I'm an unprincipled person. Let them. As for myself I'll say outright: I'm not a communist, not an SR, not a monarchist, I'm just a Russian and politically indifferent at that.

In all honesty, I still don't know, let's say for instance, Guchkov. . . . What party is Guchkov in? Who the hell knows what party he's in. I do know he's not a bolshevik, but whether he's an SR or a kadet—that I don't know and don't want to. And if I do find out, I'll still love Pushkin just as before.

This will upset a lot of people. (What innocence, they'll say, he's preserved after three revolutions.) But that's how it is. And that ignorance is, nevertheless, a comfort to me.

I don't have any hostility for anyone—that's my "precise ideology."

Even more precise? All right, more precise. In a general sense I'm closer to the bolsheviks. And I'm willing to bolshevize with them.

Parameters of Text and Reception

Yes, and who should be a bolshevik if not me?

I "don't believe in God." It's funny, even incomprehensible how
an
educated
person
goes to the Church of Paraskeva Piatnitsa and prays there to a painted-up picture.

I'm not a spiritualist. Don't like old women, don't accept my own family and I love old-fashioned Russia.

And that's where the bolsheviks and me have something.

But I'm not a communist (more likely not a marxist) and don't think I'll ever be one.

I'm 27 years old. By the way, Olenka Ziv thinks I'm younger, but that's the way it is.

In 1913 I entered college. In 1914 went to the Caucasus. At Kislovodsk I fought in a duel with the lawyer K. After that I immediately felt that I was an unusual person, a hero, an adventurist—and went to war as a volunteer. Was an officer. I won't say any more or else I'll start stealing from myself. Right now I'm writing *Notes of a Former Officer,* which is not about myself of course, but everything will be in there. Even the time during the revolution when I got locked up with the quartermaster Khorun in the city's refrigerator.

After the revolution I went about to a lot of places in Russia. Was a carpenter, went on a hunting expedition to Novaia Zemlia, was a shoemaker's apprentice, worked as a telephone operator, a policeman, worked at the Ligovo railroad station, was a criminal investigator, card player, clerk, actor and then again was at the front as a volunteer in the Red Army.

I've never been a doctor. Well, that's not exactly true. Was a doctor once. In 1917 after the revolution the soldiers picked me as their senior doctor, though at the time I was commander of the battalion. This happened because the senior doctor in the regiment was kind of stingy in giving out sick leave to the soldiers. I seemed more compliant to them.

I'm not joking. I'm speaking seriously.

Here's a bare-bones sketch of events in my life:
- arrested—6 times
- sentenced to death—1 time
- wounded—3 times
- tried to commit suicide—2 times
- beaten up—3 times

All that happened not out of a sense of adventure, but "just because"—wasn't lucky.

Now I've given myself heart trouble and probably for that reason became a writer. Otherwise, I would've been a pilot as well.

Well, that's about all.

Wait, I almost forgot: wrote a book too. They're stories, *Poking Around.* (I haven't published them; maybe I'll publish some). Another book of mine on sale is *The Stories of Nazar Ilich, Mr. Sinebriukhov.* I think it's being sold in the Food Trust because I haven't seen it in the window of any bookstores.

> The book went in two copies. Zoia Gatskevich, a nice person, bought one; the other Mogiliansky probably bought. For a review. Guber wanted to buy a third but changed his mind.
> I'm finishing up.
> Among contemporary writers I can read only myself and Lunacharsky.
> Among contemporary poets I like most of all, dear editors, Olenka Ziv and Neldikhen.
> And about Guchkov I just don't know.[17]

Few personal statements offer such wealth of detail, breadth of vision, and, to put it mildly, flights of fancy in compressed form. Yet however garbled its foci, however jocular its tone, it is biographical. With a journalist's scalpel (and a grant of latitude) we can extract the essential, expected facts. From description of family, age, profession(s), and ideological (non)views to major events, it's all there. Zoshchenko includes the Revolution and civil war, acquaints us with the political landscape, and introduces us to an impressive roster of names. A running count would give (in order of appearance) Voronsky, noted editor of *Krasnaia nov'*; Guchkov (we can answer for Zoshchenko), head of the prerevolutionary Octobrist party and the first minister of war during the Provisional Government; "Olenka" Ziv, poet and future journalist; the lawyer K., suspected to be fellow Serapion, Veniamin Kaverin; Khorun, quartermaster; Zoia Gatskevich; Mogiliansky, critic who later reviews Zoshchenko's collection *Poking Around;* Guber, literary scholar; Neldikhen, poet; Lunacharsky, playwright, critic, and commissar of education.[18] Zoshchenko also includes—as we would hope to find in an autobiography—the curios that normally escape the biographer: the duel, the refrigerator incident, hints of work in progress, the adoring aunt. And who else can boast such a rich "bare-bones sketch" or employment résumé?

This summary is not meant to be entirely facetious. "About Myself" has served readers as an authentic document of Zoshchenko's person and position; in fact, it has been acknowledged almost exclusively in this capacity. The most famous instance is Zhdanov's speech of 1946. In order to show that the slanderous angle of "The Adventures of a Monkey" had roots leading back to Zoshchenko's first years as a writer, Zhdanov returned with vengeance to this text:

> Who was Zoshchenko in the past? He was one of the organizers of the literary group, the so-called "Serapion Brothers." What was Zoshchenko's social-political profile during the period of the Serapion organization? Let's take a look at the third issue of the journal *Literary Notes* for 1922, in which the groups' founders expressed their credo. Among other admissions, there's Zoshchenko's "symbol of faith," a short piece with the title "About Myself and Some Other Stuff as Well [sic]." Zoshchenko, with no shame whatsoever, publicly bares himself and openly pronounces his political and literary "views." Let's listen to what he said there:

"Overall, it's really a problem being a writer. Take ideology.... Today everyone's demanding ideology from a writer.... Oh God, what a headache."

"You tell me what kind of 'precise ideology' I can have if not one party as a whole appeals to me?"

"These party types think that I'm an unprincipled person. Let them. As for myself I'll say outright: I'm not a communist, not an SR, not a monarchist, I'm just a Russian and politically indifferent at that."

"In all honesty, I still don't know, let's say for instance, Guchkov.... What party is Guchkov in? Who the hell knows what party he's in. I do know he's not a bolshevik, but whether he's an SR or a kadet—that I don't know and don't want to" etc., etc.

What would you say, comrades, about such an "ideology?" Twenty-five years have passed since Zoshchenko submitted his "confession." Has he changed since then? Not much. For two dozen years not only has he not learned anything but he hasn't changed in any way. Quite the contrary, with cynical bluntness he continues to be the advocate of ideological corruption and vulgarity as well as an unprincipled and shameless literary hooligan.[19]

Homing in on these key phrases (one can imagine the tone he used in their citation), Zhdanov left little room for equivocation. In 1946 any one of the following would have been sufficient to damn Zoshchenko irrevocably: reveling in ignorance of contemporary politics, contempt for the ideologized public atmosphere, the inability to distinguish between ally and enemy, the reduction of the Revolution to a mishap with an appliance, the establishment of bolshevik credentials via atheism, antispiritualism, and dislike for old women. And from this perspective, it would be hard—if we were to place ourselves in Zhdanov's audience—to deny the substance of his charge: this writer is an implacable enemy of the state.

For all his virulence, Zhdanov has not been alone in finding the "hooligan" within Zoshchenko. Of all the places, it is in the West that we find concurring voices. In his 1958 valediction, "Whose Friend and Whose Enemy Is Zoshchenko" (an answer to Chumandrin's 1930 article, "Whose Writer Is Mikhail Zoshchenko"), Sven heartily accepted "About Myself" as the writer's ideological "passport." It placed him squarely on Sven's side as antisoviet. Bolstering his conclusion with the following excerpt from "About Myself," Sven celebrated that here, in full and open view, was proof that a writer "had distanced himself once and for all from 'them,' the party building communism":

> These party types think that I'm an unprincipled person. Let them. As for myself I'll say outright: I'm not a communist, not an SR, not a monarchist, I'm just a Russian. This will upset a lot of people. (What innocence, they'll say, he's preserved after three revolutions.) But that's how it is. I don't have any hostility toward anyone—that's my precise ideology ... I'm not a communist ... and I think I'll never be one.[20]

In fact, as Sven triumphantly continued, if there were a "super-Nobel prize" for soviet writers, one that rewarded openness and sincerity, no one could beat Zoshchenko. In Sven's words, such a victory could be drawn up as a three-point program based on this document:

1. No party appeals to me . . .
2. I don't accept any ideology . . .
3. I'm not a communist and will never be one . . .[21]

While Sven embraces what Zhdanov spits out, they are joined by a common effort: to secure a unified portrait of the writer. It is not a coincidence, therefore, that they share the same quotes. For them "About Myself" gains its legitimacy as authorial credo because of its clear, undivided focus: these are Zoshchenko's political views. Yet this unidirectionality is due precisely to an interpretive operation, a critical reshaping of "About Myself" so as to trim its edges and flatten its topography. It succeeds as autobiography, whether positively or negatively charged, because it is limited in both cases to a select body of evidence. Reciprocity in conclusion, evidence, and emotion (the hostility of one balanced by the enthusiasm of the other) stems from how each critic, in the most basic sense, sees the text. In their hands, what is peculiar about it disappears. The text is no less and *no more* than an incendiary political document—for Zhdanov as proof of treason, for Sven as proof of opposition.

Yet peculiarity is, in these circumstances, no small matter. However it was read in 1946 or 1958, "About Myself" was and remains a highly unusual text. Most striking, no doubt, is what gains admission in Zoshchenko's review of his "life." He displays a pronounced appetite for extremes; nothing seems left untouched. As reflected in the title—"other stuff as well"—the most recondite, personal, and (presumably) even fictitious person or incident can find itself in the company of vaunted individuals and events. And within the text there are no apparent criteria to make sense of the collision of the trivial and the grand. Where we would expect elaboration, as with any of the categories of the "bare-bones sketch," we face silence; where amplification would appear unnecessary, as with his stint as a doctor, details accumulate. Components seem cobbled together as if all are of equal importance; its transitions occur more through whim than reason.

The absence of a logical order makes "About Myself" top-heavy in unconventional areas. In a sense it offers the reader too much, yet this excess is not duplicative (one element supporting another) but disruptive. Indeed, the only consistency in this text seems to be on the level of treatment: whatever is mentioned is subject to the same ironic penetration. This is important given that its ideological potential alone has engaged most readers. Yet however irreverent the political gestures are in "About Myself," this same spirit animates *all* levels of the text, from personal life, to the composition itself (the fractured punctuation and visual structure) to the status of his professional reputation: "Wait, I almost forgot: wrote a book too." Regardless of their political significance, all clichés of autobiography—the past, family, friends, ideology, profession—are available for ironic deflation, including the author's own voice itself. Conspicuously absent is the conviction that would presumably underlie any attempt at autobiography. Instead, we are immersed in indecision and self-contradiction: his "I won't say anymore" comes halfway and precedes the most "biographical" section, his fear of revealing the contents of an upcoming project, *Notes of a Former Officer* (something Zoshchenko actually was working on), only spurs additional commentary.

Appearances, as always, are deceptive. "About Myself" wraps this axiom in an additional layer: we are caught between two interpretive possibilities. If read as a straightforward autobiographical statement, the text would present us with an author who possesses a good measure of political daring but is also somewhat unbalanced. And while certain elements (the names, professions, titles of books, etc.) can be checked through other texts, we are never released from uncertainty as to the verity of all its contents. If we accept from the evidence in the text that the writer is twenty-seven or has written a book *The Stories of Nazar Ilich, Mr. Sinebriukhov* (both actually true), then by the same criterion (we have accepted these statements at face value) we should also expect to find a gynecologist by the name of Zoshchenko in Melitpole and should assume that the author does not actually know who Guchkov is (a proposition few would believe). Conversely, if we take "About Myself" as an extended ironic joke, we are left at odds with a certain empirical truth of the text (the very same names, professions, and books). Neither possibility, in and of itself, gives us satisfactory grounds to understand the text. It all may be true; it all may be false. The text does not provide a consistent frame of reference to resolve this.[22]

In short, the norms by which we recognize and interpret autobiographies, by which we accept as legitimate the opinions and data contained within, are invoked but never adequately realized by "About Myself." It is this quandary that renders problematic the authority not only of the biographical facts (did the refrigerator incident really happen) but also of the political statements. If we authorize as "autobiographical" only that which we feel is true, we enter a hermeneutic trap by validating that which we want to see. Yet to move in the opposite direction immediately begs the question, where does incredulity begin? After the first line with the reference to Egor? Where then do we draw the line after that?

Given this perplexing duality, the brevity of Zhdanov's and Sven's citations is perhaps not surprising. It is decidedly not a move to economize on space. What we see in their interpretations is that clarity—here the ability to identify the text as projecting a coherent authorial identity—cannot be achieved without reduction or, to be more precise, expurgation. For this reason the nature of Sven's ellipses is most revealing. Gone are the entanglements in which political notes appear; no bathetic interruptions—"don't like old women, don't accept my own family"—remain; and visual disruptions, such as the odd placement of "an educated person," are muted. Through these deletions we can better understand the underlying interpretive motive. By isolating political gestures in his Nobel triplet (a mirror of Zhdanov's four points), Sven removes them from their narrative environment to a more context-neutral, irony-free stage, where they are more readily acceptable as Zoshchenko's uncompromised voice. The literality Sven and Zhdanov seek in "About Myself" thus becomes self-fulfilling: the text is the writer's authoritative declaration of position because these statements, in and of themselves, are all that the two work with. Without the original, who could deflect Sven's one-two-three punch or gainsay the direction of Zhdanov's attack?

What drives the two to such radical surgery is an inordinate amount of what David Bordwell terms "recalcitrant data" (or in Iurii Lotman's coinage, "noise"): that which initially impedes, inhibits, or otherwise complicates direct access to what the reader perceives as the text's (message's) semantic core.[23] Depending on the text and the reader's understanding of normalcy, such "data" can take many forms, but they are usually understood as any narrative elements that are excessive, superfluous, redundant, and contradictory and that in some way resist accommodation within the reader's conceptual scheme for the text. No text is without some degree of recalcitrancy since nothing is an exact duplicate of expectation, norm, genre, or model. This means that every interpretive act must deal, in some way, with textual overflow.

Needless to say, with its inflated contradictions, "About Myself" presents an extreme case of recalcitrancy, and Zhdanov and Sven show us the most concise (yet arguably effective) way to render it a meaningful whole: remove from the text that which interferes. This holds as well, it should be noted, for my initial summary. My request for a "scalpel" and a "grant of latitude" is no less an appeal for a minimalized text. To treat "About Myself" within the bounds of autobiography, to accept it as "fact-giving" to any degree, requires the dilution of its preposterous accents—regardless of the reader's political aims. If these accents cannot be accepted as the normal asides of a narrating persona, then another place must be found for them that is satisfactory to the reader. My efforts, along with those of Zhdanov and Sven, suggest that a zero-meaning—the complete abnegation of a semantic role for a sizable quantity of textual properties—is equally possible and, given our respective needs, even necessary.

THE ZOSHCHENKO CANON

In short, readers of diverse political orientations have faced essentially the same task in order to assert their rights over authors like Zoshchenko: restoring referential coherency to the text. This need puts our current infatuation with textual instability, indeterminacy, polyphony, and so forth in a different light. While texts may not inherently be monologic, Zoshchenko's reception illustrates that readers often seek for them to be. Bordwell's recent quip to this effect, that audience response can make *Psycho* "seem as univocal as a shopping list or a telephone book," is timely because it points to what actually does occur in the readers' (audiences') minds: in assimilating, using, and "consuming" texts, readers tend to and, in fact, need to constrict meaning.[24] To this extent, absolute polysemy is more of a hypothetical potential, to which we can always have recourse, but which exists in a preinterpretive state. In practice, whether in the hands of critic, censor, marginally literate, or even the most deconstructivist reader, a text is always made to bear some concrete meaning (even if we toss it out or use it as a paperweight). Consequently, though we can always declare texts to be indeterminate, once we speak of actual interpretation, the reader never remains in an indeterminate state. Often confused, no doubt; sometimes frustrated, of course. But as readers we never encounter a text, regardless of its condition, accessibility, or internal complexity without trying to reduce or account for these factors in order to make some sense of it.

In an interpretive environment overtly politicized (as we of course have here), Bordwell's observation constitutes a maxim. A central lesson to be confirmed by Zoshchenko's critics is that ideological imperatives have little patience for the opacity that, in Barthes's term, "writerly" texts occasion. Clarity of purpose—what the writer is for or against—becomes the primary goal of interpretation. What cannot be made to fit within this requirement is generally seen as irrelevant and thus often ignored.

In the West, the constancy with which critics have held to this zero-sum template of literary value has injected two invariants into the traditional treatment of Zoshchenko's anomalous sides. First, nothing less than the canon of his writing has been defined by the need to contain him within politically digestible lines. Until very recently few in the West—notable exceptions would be Krista Hanson, Linda Hart Scatton, and Alexander Zholkovsky—have accepted anything he wrote in the 1930s as more than requisite obeisance to "the times" or, in Hugh McLean's colorful expression, as "bones to the critics." These works, it was argued, were not true products of the writer's pen but reflected official dicta and could be treated accordingly. This opinion gained such currency that in 1986 Mikhail Kreps lumped together such disparate works as *Youth Restored* and *The History of a Life* in the bin of "defeats." For all their expressed concern for the human side of Zoshchenko, arguments such as these are curiously depersonalizing. Even if we make (as we should) allowances for outside pressure, the vocabulary of capitulation only discourages individual attention to texts of this period. One need merely acknowledge the time of publication to pass judgment, as if a text's meaning had already been set by the hand of Stalin.

Second, with Zoshchenko's "authentic work" so tightly bound, it has not been difficult to validate his profile as an inveterate antisoviet. A vital component of this impression is an ipso facto condition prominent in many Western analyses of soviet literature: the occurrence of persecution is taken as proof of a writer's hostility to the state, regardless of when or how such persecution took place. What this has meant for Zoshchenko is that the last twelve years of his life are often accepted as the script for the preceding twenty-five, as if from his first stories until his dying day he disbelieved in the Revolution and sought at every opportunity to malign the soviet state, and that his relation with the establishment was therefore one of unbridled confrontation.

We might notice in this scenario a peculiar symmetry with the very course Zhdanov had plotted for Zoshchenko. In an illuminating though no doubt uncomfortable way, the Party "hatchetman" has contributed more to our assumptions and understanding of Zoshchenko than most would care to admit. In fact, the more we accept conventional readings of Zoshchenko, the more Zhdanov emerges as a kind of *ur*-reader of him. The reason, simply, is that the thrust of Zhdanov's charge has proven to be the most acceptable interpretation for the West and contemporary Russia. Indeed, many studies do not move outside the lines set by his script. This overlap holds no small irony in that as a result nonsoviet critics, while condemning Zhdanov, have often provided the most consistent support for his claims. Just as Zhdanov found it practical to bypass Zoshchenko's work of the 1930s and the praise given him by soviet critics, so has the main current of Western readings. Where Zhdanov read all of his literature into exclusively oppositional, plus-minus compartments, many in the West have followed suit yet reversed the tags. Anything in Zoshchenko's work or life that could be marshaled as evidence of the writer's antisoviet designs is so enlisted, but what for Zhdanov was antisoviet negative is realigned now as antisoviet positive.

Ultimately, the strange dance between Zhdanov and the West points to a common concern held by both sides: noise in the channel of myth. Once a writer has been crowned anti or pro, then any disparity or graying tends to be disavowed. And today, despite the counterbalance of less political approaches to Zoshchenko, this tendency has not abated. Zhdanov's impact is too strong for a single, crucial reason. He has given us an unimpeachable license, a fail-safe map, as it were, to mine Zoshchenko's work for all ostensibly antisoviet features. This is the chain that runs throughout nearly all variations of his Western-Russian canon and, as we will see, still continues, though in new theoretical colors. Whether co-opted by deconstructionists or by adherents of post-structuralist subversion theory, the script of Zoshchenko as an icon of uncompromising dissidence endures.

Chapter Two

Skaz and Mimesis

> This is what concerns us: Which flag is Zoshchenko fighting under?
>
> —Mikhail Chumandrin

REFERENCE AND TABOO

The idea of taboo has proven to be one of the most valuable in Western discussions of how soviet writers have tried to "beat the system." It rests on the premise that manifold ideas, events, actions, and characters—in short, the warts of soviet life—were a priori hidden or excluded from public discourse. This is why critics, almost as a rule, have marked as subversive any text that delves into or gestures to negative elements of soviet society. For many, this feature alone has become irrefutable proof that Zoshchenko's intention was, in Richard Chapple's concise summary, to "demonstrate the harmful effects of the Revolution and communism on mankind."[1] Consensus on this account is not hard to find. For Mikhail Kreps, Zoshchenko's self-ordained "task" was to "reflect the new character of his time: the nearly universal criminality and corruption that is typical of periods of great economic difficulty and sharp deficits of food and other goods."[2] Sven supports this with the contention that here we finally have pictures of "life unvarnished," or, as A. B. Murphy asserts, of "the crushing squalor" of soviet reality.[3] Such conclusions have secured for Zoshchenko the reputation of being a kind of revelatory writer, one who thrusts before us, in Hugh McLean's opinion, the "disparities between official mythology and the stubborn facts of everyday life" and thus brings the reader into intimate contact with precisely the kinds of people and events that were assumed absent in the public domain.[4]

A logical result of this belief has been to fix content, in and of itself, as the target of investigation, as if it alone offers a reliable guide to adjudicate authorial intent and pronounce a text "for" or "against" the state. However, a primary reliance on subject matter alone to measure a text's cultural impact carries with it some problematic weight. No doubt, for example, the domain of taboo would include any number of the following topics that Western critics have drawn upon to indict soviet conditions: the threat to artistic creativity posed by institutional mandate and regimentation; the butchering of texts to make room for ideological formulas and consequent reduction of art to political slogan; a literature ruled by ignorant, sycophantic critics who regurgitate labels with no regard for aesthetic criteria; the slavish obedience to ritual; and indoctrination to the point where citizens become automatons, mouthing only knee-jerk, ideologically correct statements.

Holding to the notion of taboo, we would expect that any text addressing such material would be condemned or censored outright. But what if these very same topics appeared on the pages of key organs such as *Pravda* or *Literaturnaia gazeta* during one of the most politically heated periods, the first half of the 1930s? What, too, if their appearance was repeatedly praised as opportune and beneficial, leading even to their republication during the purges later in the decade?

It is to Ilia Ilf and Evgeny Petrov that we owe this distinction.[5] And their extended treatment in feuilletons and stories of what would seem forbidden topics cannot be dismissed as a mistake, fluke, or oversight. Instead, it suggests that content by itself does not tell us enough and thus compels us to ask different questions. Under what conditions could such phenomena enter public discourse? How can we account for what would seem a most egregious violation of taboo?

The key lies in motivation, the relation between prevailing modalities of representation and interpretation or, to put it simply, between what a text "offers" and what a reader sees, needs, or wants it to do. What made the content of Ilf and Petrov's work acceptable—indeed, proper—was the context in which it was read: as an attack against the dogmatic extremes of RAPP and other orthodox proletarian groups during their ascendancy in the cultural revolution. Since by 1932 these groups had been discredited and officially disbanded, critics could locate in Ilf and Petrov's feuilletons (which were published mainly in the years 1932–35) an ideologically satisfactory motivation for attention to decidedly negative cultural phenomena.[6] Of course, this is not to suggest that the post-1932 environment was free of similar tendencies or that Ilf and Petrov themselves sought to limit their concerns to the target that critics identified. But the publication of these feuilletons does point to the fact that the presence of apparently taboo-breaking phenomena, in and of themselves, is not necessarily indicative of (and was not accepted as) a subversive intent. For how, along such lines, could we ever predict or understand that this subject matter would appear under the aegis of Stalin?

The same holds true for Zoshchenko. That his stories of the 1920s and 1930s treat with the mundane details of soviet life, or *byt,* is not at issue; one can readily agree with Domar's statement that he "describes everyday incidents which take place in an overcrowded community apartment, in the street, public garden, or park, restaurant, cinema, theater, store, tavern, streetcar, office, village—wherever there are people."[7] Where one should be cautious, however, is in assuming that descriptions of *byt* or, more specifically, of less favorable social conditions could occur only under an antisoviet mantle. To do so is to read Zoshchenko against a limited background of either Party pronouncement or canonical fiction. This is where, for example, Cathy Popkin in a recent study locates his antiauthoritarian, antiregime orientation. If soviet critics in the 1920s made extensive appeals for an "epic" literature as personified by Lev Tolstoy, then this call, needless to say, was not to be found in Zoshchenko's stories. For Popkin, therefore, their "insignificant" content makes his writing a "proto-deconstructive project . . . [one that] focuses precisely on the minuscule to destabilize the authorized version, dismantle its oppositions, and re-empower its readers."[8]

How, exactly, the minuscule nature of Zoshchenko's referential world was to "re-empower" readers remains unclear. The environment in which he was read then was manifestly broader than most now recognize; readers of the 1920s did not necessarily confine themselves to just those texts that interest scholars today. If we compare his work with what was published and/or circulated at that time, it becomes evident that the themes, events, or character types held to be the exclusive province of writers hostile to the state were, in fact, common enough features of public discourse. It need not be stressed that in varying densities nearly all major writers of the 1920s incorporated elements of negative *byt* in their work. More important, media organs themselves readily included condemnations and exposés of the entire spectrum of behavior—crime, stifling bureaucracy, greed, drunkenness, philistinism, egoism, ignorance—that is most often cited as Zoshchenko's particular domain. An instructive example can be taken from the marxist (Komsomol) journal *Molodaia gvardiia*, which in its section "Life Today" (*Otdel byta*) included articles on poor living conditions, red tape, social offenses, and violations of the law. Its illustrated cousin, *Smena,* liberally informed readers of the evil doings and hooliganism of soviet citizens. Key newspapers such as *Vecherniaia Moskva* and *Leningradskaia pravda* regularly published chronicles of the "day's events," which included, in detail, graphic events such as arsons, murders, suicides, beatings, thefts, and even a "killer goose" that reportedly scared a child to death.[9] *Krasnaia gazeta* offered readers a "complaint book" that told of the maddeningly humorous incidents and idiocies of contemporary soviet society.

In a 1928 description of cases commonly heard in the judicial system, "Philistinism before the People's Court," we gain a concise picture of precisely the kinds of characters who have now become famous through Zoshchenko's fiction.[10] Litigants more often than not expose their own guilt, crass intentions, or plain stupidity when they plead their cause in their own words. Inane attempts to formulate arguments in what they presume is proper bureaucratic-legalese rival those of "Monkey Language" (*Obez'ianyi iazyk*), and the accounts of their intra-apartment clashes seem a direct echo of the celebrated fight among communal tenants in "Nervous People" ("*Nervnye liudi*").

Neighbors literally tear at one another's hair; a doctor, accused by his complainant of kicking him, is identified in court as "the butting doctor." A forestry specialist continually howls like a dog in order to drive out his neighbor, a pianist who practices in the next room. Likewise, two newlyweds haul their aunt to court for giving them as dowry a calf instead of a promised cow and so on. Indeed, in numerous articles on soviet culture no less a figure than Leon Trotsky offered something of a primer in much that was wrong with contemporary society and where it had deviated from or failed to meet its goals. These problems, to be sure, may not have been solved, but in no way were they hidden or ignored. As Trotsky admitted (regretfully, one assumes), to find evidence of social "disorder," "you don't have to search at all; just look around."[11]

Unfortunately, we have been less prone to "look around"—a habit born from the tendency to project the more restrictive phases of Stalinism (i.e., post-1934) onto the decidedly more chaotic 1920s and, consequently, to assume that the sum of soviet cultural expression breaks down into two mutually exclusive planes: the official one that is by definition sanitized and a covert one where one can find all the dirt.[12] What needs to be recognized is that the standard fare of available reading, particularly in the 1920s, made explicit use of, had recourse to, ridiculed, and entertained with these images. I am not implying that treatment was equal or unidirectional; my point is more to demonstrate that at a number of levels—fiction, press, Party—these phenomena circulated widely. To be sure, in soviet discourse there were topics, in and of themselves, that were forbidden: disparaging images of the Party, explicit sex, graphic violence, the mention of specific individuals after they had become "nonpersons," natural disasters occurring in the Soviet Union, and so forth. Yet for the most part, representation in soviet literature was not as simple as fixed exclusion versus permissibility. One cannot automatically assign an explicitly antisoviet orientation to the inclusion of something objectionable or trivial in a text. Instead, events and characters making up the content plane that informed soviet literature preexisted strict positive-negative categories. The value of a given referent (the philistine, criminal activity, daily mishaps, etc.) was, one could say, substantively neutral *before* its perception in a literary structure. As V. Veshnev, a harsh critic of Zoshchenko in the 1920s, made clear on more than one occasion, content per se was not at issue. "What's there to say? Our reality overflows with failures and dark—often horrific—spots." What counted, he argued, was how an author such as Zoshchenko treated these "spots" and what was the nature of the "critical-social approach."[13]

Thus, however profitable the notion of taboo is to describe certain conditions of soviet culture, it can be somewhat misleading. A far more relevant question to ask is what the operative strategies were by which textual contents could be perceived as acceptable and ideologically secure, no matter what their origin and what value they may hold for us now. In the case of Ilf and Petrov, the suitability of their work for the 1930s environment lay in critics' success in (1) locating in the text an obvious, unequivocal target that was within the given bounds of villain, (2) identifying an authorial attitude toward it (whether stated directly or given via other gestures), and (3) determining from the first two factors whether the proper approach-treatment was present. The same procedure applied as well to the aforementioned philistine litigants. The logic, as it were, that justified publishing these diverse "tidbits of life" lay in their shared sense of waste; they poignantly demonstrated the personal and social energy consumed by such petty (especially against revolutionary standards) affairs. In this way the text offered the reader a reason (and remedy) for these societal affronts and offenses. No doubt was left as to the distance that separated these types from the progressive elements in society; they were the products of the past, the remnants of a prerevolutionary mind-set that would disappear when socialism triumphed. Likewise, most other accounts of the dirt in soviet society had clean, tidy conclusions much like those of a TV detective series. The section "Justice and Daily Life" in *Vecherniaia Moskva* even gave prisoners' sentences in bold print, in case the reader had any question as to what their fate would be.

These cases further illustrate that the relevance of issue, event, or character was not just a question of its politics. Rather, there were interlocking ideological *and* discursive sides. Determining who or what was to blame for these transgressions was contingent on the clarity of their textual representation. Before one could assign responsibility for action or words, one had to be able to delineate their source. Was it the villain, narrator, author, or something extant in the system itself? This meant, of course, that the reader needed to be able to distinguish and define domains of represented speech, thought, and behavior. Clarity was thus not simply something "of the text"; it constituted as well the axis of evaluative norms, describing how critics handled a given representation and the aim of their interpretive efforts. In sum, the value of a text, whether fiction or journalism, was a function of how it could be made to support extant paradigms.

THE CHARACTER OF *SKAZ*

Nowhere else are the discursive conditions of motivation and voice more acutely felt than in *skaz*. The *skaz* effect is most commonly seen as a kind of stylized monologue where the author turns the reins over to another who assumes the task of narration. This illusionary shift of responsibility dramatically heightens the palpability of the narrative itself by amplifying two key features. The first is the individuality of this new mediating presence, as described by McLean: "[T]he lights are thrown on the narrator, and his is the star performance."[14] The second is the consequent subjectivity or spin that modulates everything the narrator passes on to the reader. Such, for example, are the immediate impressions when we meet Zoshchenko's most famous *skaz* persona, Nazar Ilich Sinebriukhov, who, claiming he "can do it all," takes command of the writer's first story collection and delivers himself thus:

on history:

> Then they began, of course, askin' me about the revolution. What's what.
> "I," I say, "am not a lightened-up person. But the February Revolution, I say, has happened. That's for sure. The overthrow of the Czar and the Czarina.
> What's gonna be later on, again, I repeat, not lightened-up. But there'll be, I think, something good for people in it."

on friends:

> I had this dear friend, a terribly educated guy, I'll tell it to you straight—gifted with qualities. Had the rank of valet and traveled through a lot of foreign powers, he even understood, perhaps, in French and drank foreign whiskey, but was just like me, just the same, a private in a guard's infantry regiment.

on medicine:

> There once lived this miller. Had this sickness, would you believe—pox is his sickness. That miller I cured. How'd I do it? Maybe I just took a look at him. Took a look and I say: Yup, I say, your sickness is the pox, but don't you be worried or get scared, no danger in that sickness, and I can say it right now—kid's stuff.[15]

With Sinebriukhov, the act of reporting, of the transmission of events, is foregrounded. The "lights thrown" on his (attempted) descriptions outshine what actually concerns him and give full picture to a host of narrator-narrating hijinks: bias, inanity, error, unreliability, repetition, idiocy, egocentricity, marginal literacy. Nothing we read is exempt from Sinebriukhov's contamination in the fullest sense of the term. What actually ails the miller? We never know for sure. Sinebriukhov, not the most convincing diagnostician, pronounces *zhaba*, which can mean both a throat infection (literally, quinsy) and the decidedly more serious angina pectoris. The term is colored as well with tinges of the occult through its usual meaning of "toad." (I have translated it as "pox" to retain ambiguity of seriousness—"chicken" v. "small"—and its superstitious flavor.) Initially Sinebriukhov seems to lean to the first, quinsy, by labeling it a "kid's" sickness; later we come to suspect the more serious *zhaba*, given the miller's telltale "blue fingernail" and his stepdaughter's belief that he will die soon. But since this evidence is filtered through Sinebriukhov (who also uses *zhaba* to castigate rich Americans and, still later, to disparage a rival), the confusion must remain.[16]

In the end it makes no difference to the miller, since he dies from a bullet. But it does to us. Fiction has certainly accustomed us to the regulation of information by narrators or characters. We might see or know X only because a personage in the text sees or knows X. With Sinebriukhov, however, the prism extends to linguistic, psychological, and ideological planes. We face, as David Oulanoff points out, nothing less than a "grotesque verbal medium" that necessarily imparts to us an "irresistibly hilarious impression."[17] What is important for Oulanoff, though, as he reminds us through repeated emphasis on the affected oral spontaneity of Sinebriukhov's speech, is that no matter how deficient or ludicrous this narrating medium may be, the *skaz* frame is not an impediment to mimesis. Instead, it is a special way of producing certain mimetic effects. The illusion of reality is transferred from the more usual features of setting or event onto the narrator's own shoulders. The modes by which Sinebriukhov regulates his transmission of events and people function for us as icons of his world. His visibility and audibility, in and of themselves, become the essential loci of "real life" in the text. His idiosyncrasies, as reflective of speech, mind-set, and behavior normally excluded from authorial position, become the vehicle to impart the image of a "lively, happy-go-lucky fellow, somewhat glib, rather poorly educated and with a smattering of knowledge," and hence for us they become the primary means for accepting the plausibility of the fictional text. As Oulanoff concludes, "at every turn" we feel ourselves in the *"presence of the living narrator."*[18]

What Oulanoff describes is the common ground where scholars have most often sought to locate the artistic and rhetorical significance of *skaz*. Its vaunted oral cues and use of nonliterary language serve as a particular form of characterization that, at the same time, carries with it the rights to narration. The effect that Boris Eikhenbaum identified in one of the first studies of *skaz*—"making the narrator as such a real personage"—was echoed fifty years later by Ekaterina Mushchenko, Vladislav Skobelev, and Lev Kroichik in *The Poetics of Skaz* and has crossed the ocean with Oulanoff, McLean's analysis of Nikolai Leskov, and the *skaz* study of Martin Rice.[19] What links these diverse scholars is the understanding that the *skaz* voice sounds like a character yet behaves like a narrator. By ceding a character this status, the writer of *skaz* minimizes his/her own diegetic obligations (and potential) in the text. We learn of these personages not from outside descriptions, but from the inside, from their own mouths, as it were. As narrative, *skaz* inherently becomes, in I. Sats's words, a "means of autocharacterization."[20]

To a significant and revealing extent, this understanding of the *skaz* effect is very much akin to what Erich Auerbach has identified in *Mimesis* as a signal development in representations of reality: the use of an individual, distinct from author, as the speaker, who offers not "objective reality" but a "subjective image" of it "as it exists in the mind of the speaker."[21] Citing the feast scene (chapters 37–38) of Petronius's *Satyricon,* where we are introduced to characters through the highly colored views of one of the guests himself, Auerbach argues that such "raw" subjectivity, far from complicating or distorting what we read, constitutes an exercise in self-revelation. "The speaker portrays himself: his language, and the standards of value which he applies, give a clear idea of his personality."[22] And from this we gain, in the end, a qualitative step in accuracy:

> This procedure leads to a more meaningful and more concrete illusion of life. Inasmuch as the guest describes a company to which he himself belongs both by inner convictions and outward circumstances, the view-point is transferred to a point within the picture, the picture thus gains in depth, and the light which illuminates it seems to come from within it.[23]

As an archetypal description of how a writer can employ another personage to limit point of view and thus introduce the reader to an unconventional perspective, Auerbach outlines the essential coordinates from which the above expectations for *skaz* originate. Whatever its distortions, artifices, and projected illusions as a narrative medium, it serves to open a new window onto reality through the personages in whose name we receive it.

Notably, it is precisely the understanding of *skaz* as character-oriented that played *the* fundamental role in Zoshchenko's rise in soviet literature in the 1930s. Earlier in the 1920s, marxist critics either identified Zoshchenko directly with Sinebriukhovian-type antics or saw *skaz*'s inherent opacity as a suspicious act in and of itself. There was express concern that substituting another voice for "author" could serve the writer as a cover through which to make insidious comments on soviet society (an interpretation that would later be enshrined, as we have seen, in the West). Typical were the fears of Georgii Gorbachev: "The most important thing in the *skaz* method is the author's opportunity to hide his own face from the public and express his own thoughts without personally taking responsibility for them." For him, employing the "mask of a philistine" could only signal a desire to shield similar inclinations:

> A mask can serve as well to hide the absence of an [authorial] face. Cannot a story in the guise of a philistine at times simply help camouflage one's own philistine essence? Don't the Serapions, who have announced that they don't know and don't want to know "what party Guchkov belongs to," have considerable reason to hide behind Sinebruikhovs?[24]

Yet starting in the late 1920s with Evgeniia Zhurbina's introduction to Zoshchenko's collected works, a new wave of critics (including Tsezar Volpe, Anna Beskina, and I. Sats as the major architects) turned such objections on their head.[25] For them, the narrator, as representative of a philistine, and the narrating voice as a whole constituted Zoshchenko's target. As Volpe argued in a 1941 discussion of the Sinebriukhov cycle, Zoshchenko's "task is to present the reader with a psychological portrait of the narrator," who, in turn,

Skaz and Mimesis

"is first and foremost one of the negative characters of that time."²⁶ By cutting a clear and (so it would seem) incontrovertible line between the narrating voice and Zoshchenko, critics could sanction his place in the canon of official literature.

The power of this critical shift is readily apparent in that essentially anything—even that which was directly at odds with soviet standards—could be motivated by recourse to the narrator. Who was responsible for the farrago Sinebriukhov mouths? Not Zoshchenko but Sinebriukhov himself and the social milieu that spawned him. From this identification of narrator as both character and target arose the standard conclusion that Zoshchenko's stories are exercises in *samorazoblachenie*—that is, how narrators self-destruct, how they unwittingly display their own ignorance and corruption in their very attempts to make sense of life. Zoshchenko's fictional world equals a laboratory that intentionally delivers up specimens offensive to soviet society. The latter would, as soviet critics assured themselves, teach the reader how not to act, think, and speak.

Put simply, the matter was one of voice attribution: the narrator should not be confused with the actual author. The need for keeping discursive channels separate in one's mind became a central concern for Western critics as well. It is no coincidence, therefore, that Leskov has often served as the backdrop to such discussions of *skaz*. Why this is so can be seen in how Leskov himself once answered the criticism that his narrators spoke in an unorthodox, unliterary, and thus unsatisfactory manner:

> [A]ll characters have to speak in a language that corresponds to their position. If characters speak in a language that doesn't match it, then who the hell knows who they actually are and what their social class is. The writer's modulation of speech consists of the ability to master the voice and language of a character and not let oneself slip from alto to bass. As for myself I've tried to develop this skill to the point where, I feel, my priests speak like members of the clergy, nihilists like nihilists, peasants like peasants. . . . For many years I've listened closely to the accent and pronunciation of Russians at different social levels. In my work they all speak *in their own way*.²⁷

Leskov's explicit recourse to a mimetic rationale is significant because it sets the stage not only for how his characters but also how his narrators behave in the text. As we are accustomed to find in *skaz*, the narrator often renarrates the speech of others, telling us what someone said on a specific occasion at which the narrator was most likely present. Since in these renarrated situations the narrator, in effect, assumes control of characters' voices, there is ample room for ambiguity as to the exact nature of what was said. Notably, therefore, in Leskov's exemplary works of "realistic" *skaz* ("Night Owls," "The Sealed Angel," "At the Edge of the World") attention is given to preserving distinct channels of voice.²⁸ Hence, even if the narrator is minimally educated and thus prone to mistakes or is identified as coming from a specific sociolinguistic group, his/her individuating malapropisms and dialectal traits can disappear when relaying the speech of others. In "Night Owls," for example, the speech of Maria Martynovna manifestly shifts when she relays the conversation of a priest and Tolstoyan Christian. Her typically semieducated argot gives way to a cleaner, more constrained and formal Russian. Of course, the point is not that Maria suddenly and for that instance only "learns" how to speak and transmit speech correctly or in a different dialect. Rather, as McLean notes, we see the hand of Leskov himself as he "reach[es] around his narrator and straighten[s] out the language of his more cultured characters."[29] Interestingly, this maneuver reveals that Leskov was willing to break one illusion, the integrity of narrator as the controller of narrative, in order to maintain another, the relative autonomy and individuality of certain characters present. In short, the concerns of portraiture took precedence, with the result that a "faithful" transcription of the narrator's speech yielded to the interests of narrative clarity.[30]

Significantly, Leskov's statement of purpose stands at the center of Eikhenbaum's and McLean's respective analyses of *skaz*, and it encapsulates the effect for which *skaz* is best known and usually defined. The narrator functions at a level equivalent with that of other characters; all serve to project individual identities. The essential difference is that by virtue of the nature of the text we receive more information on the narrator (who very often is the protagonist as well). What we observe in these circumstances, both in the text and accompanying critical expectation, is the underlying conviction that *skaz* texts should and must yield to the discursive conditions we have become accustomed to via traditional realism. That is to say, critical investigation is motivated by the assumption that the text provides a cohesive and consistent hierarchy of voice through which the reader can make secure judgments regarding character and action, can accommodate the mediating influence of the narrating lens, and can postulate the intentions of the authorial eye—all so as to come to some conclusion as to the nature and import of this fictional world. Yet what has remained conspicuously absent amid the pursuit of character in *skaz*, regardless of the ideological motives behind it, is consideration of the problems this kind of narrative form may pose for the very effects that are most often cited as its raison d'être.

THE CONTOURS OF *SKAZ*

In *Problems of Dostoevsky's Creative Art*, Mikhail Bakhtin introduced certain narrative principles that can help us elucidate the semantic and hermeneutic peculiarities of *skaz*.[31] Narrative discourse can be divided into two categories, single- and double-voiced. Single-voiced discourse exhibits one semantic orientation and manifests itself in two key ways: (1) as "direct authorial speech" that strives for maximum adequacy with regard to its functional intentions and that we accept as the "ultimate semantic authority" in the text, and (2) as the direct speech of characters that operates in the narrative as an autonomous whole. Though direct character speech is ultimately subordinate to the authorial-appropriating context, it still retains its semantic integrity since, internally at least, it is not subject to penetration by other voices. To borrow Bakhtin's example, it is "objectified" speech that behaves "like a person who goes about doing his own thing and doesn't know that he's being watched."[32] As we see with Auerbach, direct character speech plays a key role in the mimetic effect by allowing us to experience firsthand, as it were, the illusion of an unmediated picture of a person's behavior, thought, and speech. Conversely, double-voiced discourse is that which exhibits two orientations within itself: toward a referent like single-voiced discourse *and* toward another discourse, to someone else's speech. Here an author appropriates another's voice but "introduces into it a new semantic orientation."[33] Consequently, in double-voiced discourse we recognize two speech centers, two intentions, which may either harmonize or clash.

Six years after Bakhtin, though without reference to him, Anna Beskina argued that double-voicing stands at the heart of Zoshchenko's *skaz*:

> In every word and every gesture of the character-narrator we receive not only a portrayal, a disclosure, of [his] philistine essence but the author's own attitude toward him as well. . . . Zoshchenko's *skaz* is not just the stylized language of the urban philistine. It is dramatically deformed by the author's own intervention.[34]

Two essential points emerge from Beskina's statement that, with little exception, exemplify the post-1930 critical consensus, both soviet and Western, regarding Zoshchenko's *skaz*. First, Zoshchenko always operates from "within" Sinebriukhov, and this interiority sets in motion critics' efforts to divide the text into such readily identifiable and, most important, relatively inviolate domains: those of narrator and writer. In fact, while the claimed portrait of whom Sinebriukhov actually represents in real life has often changed, what has remained constant is the drive to preserve separate channels of speech and identity between the two. Second, whatever the nature of Zoshchenko's authorial presence, Sinebriukhov's voice at one and the same time must function in the interests of autocharacterization—that is, reinforcing his image as a distinct sociopsychological entity.

It is the second that will occupy us for now. Most critics focus on cataloging the narrator's individuating features: Who is Sinebriukhov? What does he "sound" like? How does he think? These questions necessarily cast critics' eyes and expectations toward the objectified speech of single-voiced discourse, as if Sinebriukhov is a distinct, definable identity. However, this is where they inherently find themselves in a complicated situation: arguing, on one hand, for the relative autonomy of a voice so as not to violate, in Oulanoff's terms, the "picture [of] a *living concrete* and *strongly characterized subject of speech*," and, on the other, for the manifest interpenetration of author into this same voice.³⁵

In and of themselves, these expectations are not automatically incompatible. Leskov shows how in *skaz* a writer can incorporate concerns for single-voiced clarity within a double-voiced context by subordinating narrative shenanigans to the interests of textual coherency. ("The Sealed Angel" is a good illustration.) A problem arises when a text deliberately plays on the demarcation of speech domains. Sinebriukhov provides a noteworthy example when he describes a conversation with an officer in the Imperial Army:

> The company commander, has the rank of lieutenant in the Guards and is your highness a prince, calls me over. All right. A decent guy.
> So he calls me. Such and such, he says, you, Nazar, I respect a lot, you really are a charming person. . . . Do for me, he says, just one more little thing.
> The February Revolution, he says, has happened.
> My father's pushing the years and I'm awful worried on account of my immovable property. Go, he says, to the old prince at the home estate, deliver this here very note into his very own, that is, hands, and wait to see what he says.
> And to my, he says, wife, the beautiful Pole, Victoria Kazimirovna, pop down low, make it a good bow and cheer her up with some words and such. Do that, he says, I'm asking you please, and I'll, he says, put a smile on your face with a tidy sum and hand you an indefinite furlough.
> "Okay," I answer, "prince your highness, thanks for the kind gesture, only maybe I'm not worthy of these words of yours."³⁶

A prince? Where?! Lexically and dialectally his reported speech veers sharply and almost irrevocably to Sinebriukhov, what with its colloquial dimunitives (*sluzhbishka, pis'mishko, ruchki*), unexpected glosses ("the beautiful Pole"), substandard locutions (*niz'ynko*), fractured syntax, and the Sinebriukhovian tag phrase "the February Revolution has happened." Moreover, a broad swath of the prince's own words is replaced by the token "such and such." In fact, the reported speech's very status as a character's voice is tenuous given the complete absence of proper punctuation to distinguish direct speech from its reporting context. Only pronominal distinctions (I-you), imperatives, and the wildly random attributive "he says" stand as some kind of cue for when the prince is supposedly speaking. As a result, the boundaries between him and Sinebriukhov are highly contestable, which leads to substantial fluidity between two important contexts: (1) what the prince actually said and what Sinebriukhov says he said; and (2) what speech and thought are expressed then, at the time of the conversation, regardless of their source, and what speech and thought are expressed now, at the time of narration. To wit, is a "beautiful Pole"—though it ostensibly "belongs" to the prince—Sinebriukhov's addition? Most would presumably agree. But does it reflect what he was thinking to himself then, does it represent what he adds only now in the act of renarrating, or both? What then as well of a "charming person" or of the claimed "respect"?

The accumulation of question marks hampers our efforts to measure the identity of any personage in the text. Little, if anything, remains uncontaminated from which we could make some conclusion regarding the prince and his attitude toward Sinebriukhov and others. For this reason, Kreps's assertion as to the nature of Sinebriukhov's personal relations is problematic: "His 'friends' are a rather dubious lot, and even his 'bosom buddies' Rylo and Utin do not really care about him. He is not welcome anywhere, and nobody has any use for him. In short, he is a loser."[37] Yes and no. Their profiles always appear in contexts that, like the prince's, are highly questionable:

> I've amazed quite a few people. The instructor Rylo, this is still in the city police, he was also really amazed. Sometimes he'll come to me, well, like to his dear friend:
> "Well, what about it," he'll say, "Nazar Ilich Comrade Sinebriukhov, you wouldn't have some baked bread stored up, would you?"
> I'll give him, for example, some bread and he'll sit down, I remember, at the table; he'll chew and eat, and stretch out his arms like this.
> "Yup," he'll say, "when I look at you, Mister Sinebriukhov, just can't find the words. Get the shakes at what a guy you are. You, he says, probably could even run a country."[38]

What is the source of these superlatives? Rylo's own desire to weasel some bread or Sinebriukhov's own ego? Once again clear answers are not forthcoming. What do stand out are the signs of Sinebriukhov's intrusion, the most obvious being the collocation, "Nazar Ilich Comrade Sinebriukhov," which echoes how Sinebriukhov refers to himself elsewhere.

The Sinebriukhov stories immerse us in a bald play on voice attribution that holds in check easy conclusions as to characters' sociopsychological identity and the exact nature of the fictional world they inhabit. What we essentially lose is the key, to continue McLean's metaphor, by which to "straighten" out dialogue and direct speech. This absence vibrates through Zoshchenko's writing of the 1920s and early 1930s and impinges directly upon those factors—expressions of belief, thought, motivation—that are fundamental to the projection of an individual portrait. The result is to force upon the reader the responsibility for clarifying channels and hierarchies of voice.

It is this tension between textual conditions and critical need that shapes the arena where readers have fought over Zoshchenko's *skaz*. In *Zvezda* in 1933, Volpe declared Zoshchenko's discursive web "one of the largest and most complex problems of contemporary literature."[39] The words are admittedly hyperbolic, but, given the writer's popularity and reach, they nonetheless are apt. Significantly, Volpe's own efforts to untie this knot demonstrate how "complex" the matter truly is. The centerpiece of his analysis is Zoshchenko's 1929 story "The Lady with the Flowers," where the narrator takes as his charge the exposé of the postrevolutionary intelligentsia.[40] What serves as the ostensible basis for his study is the relationship between an engineer and his wife, her death by drowning, and his subsequent liaison with a new lover. This subject sends the narrator into a two-page (out of nine total) preamble where he justifies attention to such "serious" matters by claiming that they prove the verity of a materialist epistemology:

> At times there are those minimally humorous snippets that come right out of life. Say, a fight, head-bashing, vicious murder or somebody's property got ripped off.
> Here, in truth, there's not much to laugh at or amuse the most honorable public. And I would like, so to speak, to accommodate the reader in this respect, but circumstances do not permit it.
> Or, for example, this story. A decidedly sad one. About how one lady of the intelligentsia drowned.
> In other words, can't get a lot of laughter out of this fact.
> So the author most humbly begs his pardon for such impudence and for launching into these really distressing quasi-intellectual reports. . . .
> Although, it ought to be said, even in this story there are certain funny aspects. You'll see for yourself.
> Of course, I wouldn't think of troubling today's reader with this not overly sensationalist story, but you know, it's an important snippet for these times. About materialism.
> In a word, it's a story about how once 'cause of an accident it finally became clear that all this mysticism, all this idealism, and all such celestial love and so on and so forth is a straight pack of lies and nonseneism. And that in life only a genuine materialist approach counts and nothing else, unfortunately. . . .
> What's more, to repeat, where's the humor if a lady drowned. She drowned in the river. She wanted to go swimming. So she stepped onto the boards. By the shore at the river there were some floats. Rafts and such. And she was in the habit of going out far from the shore on these boards for some peace and taking in some nature. And, of course, she drowned.
> But that's not the point.

The narrator then introduces us to the protagonists' "bourgeois" lifestyle with, for example, a description of the husband's return from work each day:

> He's the first to jump from the boat. He's carrying somethin' in his hands. There's either presents or underwear for her or some newfangled brassiere.
> He gives it to her right there and claps her on the back, jokes around, hugs her. What's it to him! The main thing is he doesn't pull any weight for society and is all shut up in his own horizons and tender thoughts.

Describing the wife's daily activities, he adds: "In a word, she was a poetic figure, able to sniff flowers and nasturtiums all day or sit on the shore and look out, as if somethin' concrete is hangin' out there like fruit or liver sausage."

To say the least, these passages leave us with a wealth of divergent and dissonant accents: the preamble's confusing relay of "it is but it isn't"; tautologies ("presents" and "underwear," "flowers and nasturtiums"); contrasting pitches (from the highly formal "most humbly begs" to "ripped off" and "snippets"); neologistic malapropisms ("nonsenseism"—*erundistika*); alogical juxtapositions (the inclusion of "unfortunately" following "a genuine materialist approach"; the collocation of "fruit" and "liver sausage"); and a coarse, fractured cadence generated by a plethora of incomplete and run-on sentences.

Into the heart of such daunting verbosity Volpe places a banner of cohesion by dividing the text into two narrative "planes." The first, which he labels the "obvious" one, equals what the narrator himself claims to present: the falsehood of that idyll the husband and wife appear to live:

> The narrator-"author" unmasks the engineer Gorbatov's "celestial love" for his wife. Engineer Gorbatov's wife has drowned. The engineer is distraught. But the tragedy of his love turns out to be illusionary. The end of the story categorically demonstrates the insincerity of the engineer's feelings [referring to the fact that he is seen with another woman after the death of his wife].[41]

The second constitutes Zoshchenko's satiric attack against the narrator, who, given his "inane understanding of materialism," reveals himself to be no better than the subjects of his story. In all, then, the text yields two targets, the narrated and the narrating, and this allows Volpe to recover a referential dominant on the first plane while, on the second, accommodating all the defects, quirks, and flukes of its presentation.

Dividing the narrative into two autonomous spheres—the plane of the fictional world as opposed to the narrator's embellishment and/or distortion of it—represents one of the most concise and frequently employed ways that readers have sought to inject order into Zoshchenko's verbal sprawl. Containment offers a straightforward means to maximize clarity, since author, narrator, and character are held to operate detached from one another. This is where, however, Zoshchenko's *skaz* strikes its most problematic chord. Volpe accepts the narrator's opinions and Gorbatov's own statements as the primary evidence for the latter's philistine essence. But these two contexts run circles around each other and share remarkable similarities:

> He wasn't in step with the times. 'Course, he was about forty and living all in the past. Point being that he liked his past bourgeois life with its little pillows, consommé and so on.

Didn't see anything in current life today except banality and kept his face clear of all of it. And 'cause she, spouse you know, wasn't gonna put the drop on him, he let her in about all his reactionary thoughts and opinions.

"I, he says, am a man of profound intellect, got a handle, he says, on a lot of those mystical and abstract facets of my childhood. So I, he says, can't reconcile myself with this banal life, specialist-baiting, labor reductions, rent and so on. I, he says, was raised on all sorts of pretty things and knickknacks, understand genteel love and see nothing decent in banal embraces and so on and so forth."

So you see, on account of all this, he broke with the masses and fully shut himself up in his family and love for that precious thing of his with the flowers.

Much of Gorbatov's own vocabulary and intonation—"mystical," "banality," "pretty things and knickknacks"—seems to have transferred directly (and at times verbatim) from the narrating context and offers little, if anything, from which to construct his psychological-ideological disposition. Any expected singularity of voice gives way to an intersection of voices. Significantly, Volpe offers tacit acknowledgment that this evidence is tainted when he argues that in the end we need not bother with distinguishing speech contexts since all personages speak the same: "Zoshchenko's narrator speaks the same urban-philistine jargon as do the other characters. It is one replete with bureaucratic locutions, officialese, dry journalistic phrases and clichés, and is mixed up with unexpectedly archaic and 'bombastic' words." The exceedingly broad terms in which Volpe allows for overlap do not resolve the issue. In truth, they only void a larger problem. What critics seek to divide, the text pushes and mixes together. The conditions of the second plane do not merely sit above the first, awaiting separate interpretation; they have an immediate and decisive impact on the text as a whole. How Volpe tries to get around this is—almost by necessity—slippery. All distortion is assigned to the second plane (the narrating) without consideration of how it might interfere with the first (the narrated). Not surprisingly, this maneuver forces Volpe to maintain two contradictory positions. By confirming the narrator's claims regarding the first plane as legitimate, he validates the narrative's capacity at this level (i.e., it does present us with a coherent story). Yet he also argues for the narrative's predominant absurdity at the other (the narrator as a satiric target who continually "misfires" in his telling of the story). In short, Volpe asks us to accept the narrator's performance as competent in the first but reject it as deficient in the second.

All these twists and turns bring to center stage what I. R. Titunik has identified as the central problem of *skaz*. The narrator's voice is, first and foremost, fulfilling *authorial function*. As such it affects the reader's experience of the text in a number of fundamental ways beyond that which is accountable in narrator-as-character formulations. Working from Bakhtin and Valentin Voloshinov, Titunik argues that *skaz* represents a special form of double-voiced discourse, one that operates as authorial speech yet displays and, as its distinguishing trait, is dominated by features of object speech. What creates this impression is the intersection of two normally distinct discursive contexts, that of reported and reporting speech. If, as a norm, authorial-reporting speech is more restricted in terms of the tense and person employed, its stylistic range, its lexical fund, its avoidance of metalinguistic gestures, and so forth, then reported speech displays a wide range of grammatical, situational, expressive, allocutional, dialectal, and semantic features that are usually excluded from the former.[42] That which marks the narrative voices of the Sinebriukhov stories or "The Lady with the Flowers"—their mélange of stylistic aberrations (from oral gestures to colloquialisms, substandard usage and solecisms), the bump-jolt rhythm, the interjections and asides, the slip-ups, repetitions, overcompensations and diversions, the inclusion of the "reader-audience" into the here and now of the narrative world, and their presumption of allegiance with this same audience—is what one would typically expect to find not in the guise of author but, more likely, in the direct speech of a character, where such idiosyncrasies are more apt to make sense. In *skaz*, therefore, the normally distinct planes between speech at the level of character and that at the level of author appear to intermix, and features peculiar to the first (the reported) begin to fulfill the function of the second (reporting). This explains why, in answer to the observation continually made of Zoshchenko, people in his stories "all talk the same."[43] As Titunik demonstrates with direct reference to Zoshchenko, no speech source, whether nominally author or character, remains inviolate.[44]

By identifying the extended discursive conditions through which we perceive *skaz*, Titunik lays the ground for us to recognize its full multidimensionality. It emerges from a complex interaction of factors (of which the often-cited "oral flavor" is but one) and thus confronts us with a host of potentially unconventional features. Its dislocating effect can contaminate essentially all levels of the text: linguistic, characterological, narratological, hermeneutic. And while Leskov reveals how such contamination might be contained so that a *skaz* text still projects a reasonable fictional world and even explicitly aids the reader in its comprehension, Zoshchenko's texts point to an opposite tack.

The crucial factor, as Titunik underscores, lies in the troublesome position of author in the text. Given its fluid discursive boundaries, in *skaz* the point is not only that "another's speech [is] manipulated by the author but that the author's speech itself is manipulated as well, . . . at the basis of skaz lies a reciprocal relationship, an interpenetration and interaction of both these speech contexts."[45] Nowhere else is this "reciprocal manipulation" more evident than in a text like "The Lady with the Flowers," where there is no cohesive authorial anchor. Indeed, that which claims this function is decidedly inadequate. The text is introduced as a profile of negative

The Politics of Reception

social phenomena, and all strings are pulled on what its plot could be or do: it is tragic, has contemporary relevance, and can serve as substantive proof for the favored ideological line. But what comes out is decidedly not what is promised at the beginning. Instead of a decisive lesson, the final lines sputter to an anticlimax in which the story's own importance is expressly dismissed:

> And after that [the discovery of the wife's body] N. N. Gorbatov left for Otradnoe and from there to Leningrad.
> And not long ago he was seen walking on the street with some other lady. He had her by the elbow and was laying it on thick.
> So that's the whole story.
> With our deepest respects to the drowning victim and to the engineer's impassioned celestial love for her, we'll move on to current events. Especially as now's not the time to linger on drowned citizens and use them to show up all that psychology, physiology and so on.

The simultaneous declaration and revocation of the plot's significance are echoed repeatedly in the refrain "but that's not the point," an assertion that generally follows what would presumably be important material. What, actually, is "the point" remains exceedingly vague. In fact, a most peculiar description of the drowning itself—an event where one would expect the narrative to come together—leaves the distinct impression that there is no consistent story beyond discussion of its potential:

> But, in a word, she drowned. It's of course very sad, a real tear-jerking fact, but you can forget bringing her back to life, especially with our doctors.
> Of course if back then she had at least done some regular exercising, she'd of recovered at the last moment and swam up. But now she fell in with her flowers and went straight to the bottom, offering no resistance to nature.
> What's more, she was walking on slippery boards. That's the way she always went to go swimming. But now after the rain she slipped on her French heels and lost it. Only her undies remained on the deck.
> Maybe she jumped in the water on purpose. Maybe she had lived, had lived enough with that backward element [her husband] and up and jumped in. What's more, maybe he drove her batty with his mysticism.
> Only that's doubtful of course. Most likely, if it had to be explained psychologically, she slipped on the boards and drowned.

The ludicrous attempt to understand (and even get on paper) the circumstances of this central event and to establish the reasons behind the character's death (especially the "psychological" one, slipping!) gives us nothing short of a breakdown in narrative logic and linearity.

These examples illustrate how the problems of narration are not, as Volpe is wont to argue, of a strict political-ideological orientation (i.e., the gross misunderstanding of "materialism"). When the identity, behavior, and mentality of characters are always circumspect, when the narrating voice only generates confusion, and when little concrete can be gleaned from the plot beyond a basic skeleton that (1) the wife dies and (2) the husband is later seen with another woman, the viability of the narrative structure as a whole comes under question. Needless to say, such conditions only complicate a search for the "real" Zoshchenko among the myriad voices and accents. At first Volpe is adamant in the assertion that the narrating voice is but the target of Zoshchenko's ire. When the sensitive issue of ideology is posed by the text, Volpe emphatically declares, "So who is this speaking about materialism? Zoshchenko himself?! Of course not!," and he continues to caution the reader, "It is important to underscore this [distinction]. It would truly be a mistake to equate Zoshchenko's narrator with Zoshchenko himself, even when the story is conducted in the name of the 'writer.'"[46] Yet when he seeks to accredit the pseudo-lachrymose scene of the discovery of the wife's body with a deeper "philosophical meaning" that originates in Zoshchenko himself, Volpe doubles back. "On the other hand, it would be incorrect to reduce the objectives of Zoshchenko's narrative to that of discrediting the 'authorial mask,'" he argues, since here the writer "shows that his plan is *not funny* and profoundly sentimental" (emphasis in original). With this passage, Volpe assures us, the reader "is no longer laughing." Perhaps not. But what Volpe fails to mention is that this scene is marked by idiosyncratic gestures similar to the others and that immediately following it we find ourselves in the denouement, quoted above, with its flippant dismissal of all that has preceded.

MASK–CHARACTER–VOICE

Volpe's equivocation puts in relief how Zoshchenko's prose diverges sharply from traditional, quasi-realistic *skaz*. The conviction that underlies McLean's ability to find the true Leskov amid double-voicing is lost with Zoshchenko's anarchic argot: "If the narrator's attitude toward the events recounted is different from the author's own, a correctional factor must be provided so that the reader can draw the 'right' conclusions without explicit statement. . . . This Leskov carefully prepares us to do."[47] Why Zoshchenko differs—the marxist formula is difficult to resist—reflects a quantitative change effecting a qualitative one. If *skaz* presents us with a range of possible abrogations of narrative standards (not just orality or overt subjectivity of the narrator), then in Zoshchenko's hands this potential reaches an absurd extreme. Speech boundaries and hierarchies are the first to go; hence from behind each name or identity issues, more often than not, a profusion of incongruent voices. Using one of the more salient examples, Titunik points out that "professionals" possess the most unusual speech habits. Doctors, for instance, give prognoses of the following kind:

The Doctor says:
"Obesity is the principal reason for your immobile life. Or it's the other way around. You've got," he says, "to walk back and forth more and maybe 'cause of that fact you'll get thinner."[48]

Discursive incompatibility figures prominently as well in situational contexts. In "A Tragic Event," we find that narrator-character speech displays a remarkable ability to shift tone irrespective of its presumed source or context. When movie viewers object that Nikolai Ivanovich is vomiting in the theater—"going to Riga"—their reported speech (in a collective voice at that!) is rendered most ludicrously as:

Suddenly the sober public began to express its dissatisfaction on account of, you know, Riga.
"Comrade, they say, for that purpose you might go to the foyer only because, they say, you're diverting the attention of those who are watching the drama toward other ideas."[49]

The representation of Nikolai himself holds to similar, convoluted logic, as in the example of his inebriated thought:

Hey, he thinks, you know what—I'll go to the movies. I'm a guy, he thinks, who's cultured, something of a quasi-intellectual. Why the hell should I crap around on the streets and bug these passers-by. Hey, he thinks, I'll watch a movie in an intoxicated state. Never seen anything like it.

The collision of semisophisticated stylistic rises ("intoxicated state," "passers-by") with liquored drawl produces a fractured image of character, and this impression is amplified by Nikolai's two contrasting requests for his money to be returned following the "trip to Riga":

"Ma'am, he says, the ticket that was just purchased here, could you please return the money. The reason is I just can't look at the picture—the darkness gets to me."
"Listen you pig, he says, I didn't see any of your movie. Hand over, I'm telling you, my dough."

Likewise, in "Nervous People" during the famous fight in the communal apartment over the wire brush, Ivan Stepanovich declares his property rights in one amazing breath:

So this Ivan Stepanovich appears and says:
"I, he says, well, work like an elephant in the cooperative for thirty-two rubles plus change, I smile, he says, at the customers and weigh them sausage, and from that, he says, on my labor pittance I buy myself brushes, and in no circumstances that is will I ever let some unknown foreign personage use these brushes."[50]

Skaz and Mimesis

Ivan's credibility-defying performance is outdone only by the police: "A copper appears. He shouts: 'Stock up on the coffins, bastards, I'm gonna shoot!'"

Unmotivated, seemingly random shifts in speech are one of the most common features of Zoshchenko's early prose. The absence of a consistent pattern behind speech mutation means that diverse gestures of optimism and pessimism, conformity and deviance, lucidity and madness, pathos and bathos meet and vie for dominance. The effect, to say the least, is unsettling. And while the West has generally focused its attention on debased political slogans and soviet critics highlighted "bourgeois-intellectual" corruptions, such violations of linguistic norms and hierarchies do not restrict themselves solely to what may be termed a denigration of these high, authoritative discourses.[51] Any lexical item, no matter what its perceived social domain, is subject to this deformation.

In such an environment what takes charge, what fuels the text, is the macaronic in and of itself. Voices that permeate Zoshchenko's *skaz* tend not to adequacy of expression; instead, they compromise their own expressive potential. The noted beginning of "A Fluke of Nature," which describes (I use the verb hesitantly) an attack of spring fever, serves as a poignant example:

> Of course city living's not for everybody. There's, for instance, some folks living all homelike at the Rybatsky station.
>
> Got less of course of the comforts than in the cities. No big avenues, say. Just hop off the station and shuffle on down the tracks. Don't want to go down the tracks—just sit your life then at the station.
>
> One of our pals, born and lives in Rybatsky, just couldn't hold back and popped out once for a walk. This was still in the spring.
>
> So he left the station and is walking down the tracks. During spring. In April. Right before Easter.
>
> He's walking down the tracks. And the road, you know it's these ties. But there's also this spring slush, puddles. Slip to the side and, no joke, curtains. Could drown. Because it's spring. Nature's melting. Blooming.
>
> So our pal's walking down the line. He's walking and dreaming off about something. And this, as I've been saying, was during spring. After Easter. End of April. Birds flapping about. There's chirping everywhere. Air all around's going crazy.
>
> So there's our pal walking, you see, and thinking: birds got it good chirping up there, but take one and test his noggin on these here rails, money down, he's a goner.
>
> That's what he thought and right then stepped to the side. Now this, keep in mind, was still during the spring. Easter. Wet out.[52]

The coordinates of setting—something that by expectation would complement the creation of a fictional world—become a springboard to disrupt and compromise this process. Normally, redundancy helps clarify. Here the patently illogical repetition of references to time, place, and action only congests narrative linearity. The convoluted attempt to establish "what" and "when" turns on itself with arresting obstinacy, as successive layers of overcompensation and non sequitur threaten to displace the motivating event itself. Very often, this "interference" issues from what would normally be the least obtrusive elements in composition: words performing modal, phatic, conative, or metalinguistic functions such as "maybe," "he says," "so," "that is," "well," and so forth. Though "auxiliary," as Marietta Chudakova terms them in *The Poetics of Mikhail Zoshchenko*, these words compete with and often drown out the story proper.[53] As a result, what dominates his early *skaz* are acute breakdowns in transmitting an adequate referential world (something that he attempts to rectify two decades later in *Before Sunrise*). And this can occur no matter what the alleged social or ideological value of the content at hand. Such breadth is noteworthy given the tendency, especially in the West, to assume that Zoshchenko's attention is directed only to weighty sociopolitical targets or ideological sloganeering. This argument ignores the fact that anything that enters the text can be made macaronic, even something as trivial as a drunk vomiting in a theater:

> He bought a ticket with his dough. And he sat in the front row. So he's sitting in the front row, watching in orderly and decent fashion.
> He saw, maybe, just one credit and went straight to Riga. It's really warm in there, the public is breathing; and darkness has that kindly effect on the psyche.
> Straight to Riga went Nikolai Ivanovich, all in orderly and decent fashion—not touching anyone, not grabbing at the screen, not pulling out the lights, but just sitting there by himself, quietly on the road to Riga.[54]

as the loss of one's teeth:

> Of course, years are collecting, goes without saying. Organism, so to speak, is falling apart. Bones, might be a weakness here of prewar material, is taking a breather.
> Point being, Ivan Egorych Kolbasev, who lives in our building, s'been seeing his teeth bust and fall out.[55]

as the death of a pig:

> So this pig left the yard, oinky-oinky, it's looking up at the tracks and lumbers its ass to that there same embankment. Hell knows how it got itself up on the rails with those hams. Was getting near fourish, train's coming. Engineer sees that things on the track not okay, something's pokin' its nose up there, he whistles.... That sow, doesn't give a damn, lying around like a queen, sniffing the rails. Splat, got her in the side and snout, halved her in three, pieces flying every which way. Didn't even oink.[56]

or as serious as murder:

> A tragedy occurred in our building. Murder. Out of jealousy a husband killed his authentic young spouse and her juridical mother.[57]

or as grim as war:

> Aaa, I'm thinking, dammit—gas. . . .
> All calm I take my mask (the rubber one) and haul up into the trench.
> Me: such and such, I shout, prince your highness, breathe through the mask—it's gas.
> All hell breaks in that there trench.
> The broad, this nurse—plop—down she goes. One dead corpse.
> But I dragged our prince your highness out in the clear and made a fire just like in the rules.
> I light it. We're lying, not a peep . . . waiting . . . breathing.
> Gas still around. . . . The German's a clever bastard, but of course, we know something too: 'gainst the law for gas to sit itself down on fire.[58]

TEXT AND CRITICAL NEED

Given the fecundity of voices and dispositions that propel Zoshchenko's *skaz*, we would be justified in celebrating again, as many have done, the reign of polyphony in literature. But the farcical, unfathomable inconsistency of expression that rains down on the reader makes for something qualitatively different. If polyphony describes a multivoiced text, with each voice contributing to an intratextual (and ultimately intertextual) dialogue, then the cornerstone of this effect lies in the fact that the participating voices are, relatively speaking at least, distinguishable and have some measure of authority (i.e., can be traced to a specific source). What we encounter with Zoshchenko, however, shatters any such foundation. And the resulting shards give us precisely that: cacophony, a profound confusion of voices with chaotic—and wildly comic—results.[59]

The distinction is crucial because of the tendency to identify the narrating agent or mask in *skaz* with only one voice. Yet assertions of narrating monovocality preclude or at least make highly problematic the appearance of other, unmotivated voices that are stylistically, semantically, or sociologically at odds with the perceived mask. Significantly, the complications inherent in reading a single identity into Sinebriukhov are evident in the earliest critical responses. In his 1922 review, Aleksandr Voronsky objected to rapid mutations in Sinebriukhov's language. He felt such "dislocations" (*sryvy*) were expressly out of place since they "do not correlate with Sinebriukhov's overall style. Sinebriukhov speaks differently."[60] This is a curious yet most revealing comment. Does Sinebriukhov "speak differently?" Can we point to where "he" actually is so as to cast off all the rest as obfuscating embellishment? To carry the issue further, has Zoshchenko failed to provide an accurate (and by extension realistic) linguistic portrait of a narrator by making Sinebriukhov the fount of all and sundry? Or are diffusion and incongruity the heart of the matter? (We can only imagine Voronsky's consternation when "Sinebriukhov" reappeared in 1923 and 1924 at the head of compositions that, in stylistic terms, departed dramatically from his original *Tales*.)[61]

Voronsky's criticism resonates throughout those analyses of *skaz* that seek to distill the whole of the narrating medium down to an individual, real-life personage. When Bakhtin argued that in most cases *skaz* has been employed for the sake of introducing someone else's (generally nonstandard) voice into literature, many seem to have taken his use of the singular literally. Yet monovocality is, of course, not a sine qua non, since *skaz* is not an actual recording of speech but a created effect. It issues from a writer's manipulation of convention, and convention, after all, can be defied. If *skaz* can create the illusion of a specific, individuating mask, then it can also effect the opposite. As Viktor Vinogradov pointed out in one of the earliest studies devoted to *skaz*, the narrating agent may constitute—rather than a single character or person—a "pronoun," in which a variety of dispositions collide:

> The writer's "I" is not a name but a pronoun. Therefore anything at all can be hidden behind it. It is capable of embracing forms of speech issuing from various literary genres and verbal-dialectal sources. Psychological cohesion is also optional for a writer. He has always enjoyed the right to transform himself. Therefore, in the game of literature a writer can freely change stylistic masks within a single work of fiction.[62]

More than anything else, this pronominal capacity has wrought havoc with readers' attempts to locate the real Zoshchenko in the text and, by extension, decipher authorial intent. During the 1920s, as attested to by the comments of fellow author Panteleimon Romanov, orthodox marxist critics reproached anyone who did not "show his face" in a literary work. "What is wanted from him [the writer]," Romanov continued, "is that all should be explicitly clear: what he favors, what he's driving at, and what his attitude is to that which he's describing."[63] Zoshchenko turned this charge on its head. Instead of silence (of which Romanov himself was accused), here we have the opposite: excess. Zoshchenko's garrulous "I" embraces essentially all ideolects, including the (essentially endless) realm of malapropism and solecism, and, importantly, it offers too many faces—grimacing, glowering, smiling, and deadpan—to the reader. What is more, since stylistic-semantic orientations are not bound to set speech domains, within one authorial persona or between "narrator" and "character," varying and often incompatible linguistic competencies may fluctuate. We essentially lose the means to distinguish voice and point of view and to differentiate among direct, indirect, and free or quasi-indirect discourse (*style indirect libre*)—all of which are necessary to elucidate the province of character, narrator, and implied author and, in the end, to clarify what the writer is driving at.

Seven decades hence have not left us in an appreciably better position. N. Popova, in one of the most recent attempts to elucidate Zoshchenko's true voice in works of the 1920s, retreats, perforce, to the broadest of generalizations, asserting that (we hope) his is the voice of decency.[64] Anything more specific would necessarily rebound against imbalance and irregularity. This has not stopped others, however, from declaring the issue resolved. (Acknowledged frustration is one of the least common entries in a critic's vocabulary.) As Lev Kroichik has argued, no matter what the quantity or quality of voices that permeate Zoshchenko's *skaz*, attaining the desideratum, clarity, is still not a formidable task:

> In satire what the author affirms is easily distinguishable from the "opposite." The clearer the satirist's ideal, the more profound and complete is his analysis of negative phenomena. The satirist always endorses the opposite of what he disparages in his work. Such are the dialectics of affirmation in satire. The more active the characters in M. Zoshchenko's stories, the more diverse their comments upon and appraisal of all that is happening, the more palpable becomes the writer's true position. The narrator's perspective is not only not that of the writer's, but, on the contrary, helps us understand the actual depth of his [Zoshchenko's] opinions and the nature of his perspective.
>
> M. Zoshchenko counterposes the narrow-mindedness and pettiness of the philistine's views with his own clear and broad-minded vision of the surrounding world.[65]

Since satire admits a recognized degree of illogic, hyperbole, humor, and the like, it has become a kind of critical panacea employed by all political sides of the Zoshchenko debate to explain his singularity. Only in this way, so it seems, can we accommodate the unusual, discordant, and unorthodox aspects of his writing. But even if we rush to claim satire, do we escape the pronounced elasticity with which Zoshchenko's writing confronts us? Are we not in full rights to ask exactly where Zoshchenko's "clear vision" is? It is no small matter that the facility with which Kroichik locates "Zoshchenko" is belied by the very fact that critics have advanced decidedly contradictory images of author. Indeed, along the roller coaster of his legacy, the most observable consistency comes not in his writing but in critics' lasting yet incompatible conviction of the clarity inherent in his *skaz*.

Most often, univalency has been discovered by reducing the text to a plus-minus spectrum of meaning. Filtered through an ideological lens, such concision yields the predictable result that Western and postsoviet Russian critics have identified skeptical, pessimistic, and otherwise "antisoviet," gestures with Zoshchenko himself, whereas soviet critics of the 1930s and post-1960s advanced positive, optimistic, or otherwise reasonable sentiments as the writer's own. Yet this circumscription of meaning has compromised, intentionally or not, the most commonly valued aspect of his *skaz:* its richness and colorfulness. As Beskina's conclusion reveals (and she is by no means alone), political need essentially dictates that in functional terms Zoshchenko's discursive world must be monochromatic. Author and narrator serve as preset categories that subsume and ultimately consume any multiplicity of voice: "In all of Zoshchenko's work, the narrator is always one and the same. The authorial attitude to that narrator also remains unchanged. In him [narrator], Zoshchenko denigrates the philistine, the petit bourgeois, the vulgarian."[66] Beskina's insistence on uniformity bears witness to the inadmissibility of any ambiguity, of any nuances or features, that might lie outside a critic's political scope. Her drive to infuse Zoshchenko's writing with symmetry and predictability exemplifies critics' tendency, as it were, to "finish writing" Zoshchenko. And we should not forget, of course, that it is precisely the need for univalency that in the 1950s led—literally—to the rewriting of certain stories so that they would be more ideologically and discursively palatable for a soviet audience.[67]

THE MANY FACES OF *SKAZ*

What do these exercises of the critic and censor reveal? If Zoshchenko employs the common stuff of early soviet writing—its typical themes and characters—then he does so in an uncommon way. His stories are most certainly infused with *byt*, with the reality of the early Soviet Union in all its rich linguistic, social, and human density. Yet it is not the presence of *byt* alone that has fueled controversy but the context and modes of its appearance. Far from replicating standard rhetorical strategies in the portraiture of villain and protagonist, the good and the bad, or the trivial and the monumental, Zoshchenko's *skaz* explicitly disparages its referential authority. While most of his texts pose as cohesive narratives, whether in the guise of true accounts, homiletic exercises, or conventional satires, in nearly all instances we encounter a narrative that runs wildly astray.[68] Indeed, when we look across the entire spectrum of critical response, the enduring point of contention is not that Zoshchenko highlights the trifles, deficiencies, mishaps, and absurdities in postrevolutionary society. Rather, it is that his approach impedes normative motivation. In fact, it is in the very diffusion of voices and dispositions that emerge from Zoshchenko's narrative mask that we may recognize the number of identities that have been promoted as its source, whether ideological deviant, social misfit, tragic hero, idiot, or camouflaged mouthpiece for Zoshchenko himself.

This range, more than anything else, suggests that not all *skaz* texts are created equal. As with any narrative form, *skaz* can uphold an illusion of traditional realism and, conversely, can work to the opposite. It behooves us not to forget this flexibility, given the tradition of defining *skaz* primarily (and often exclusively) as a mimetic exercise. Such, for example, is the conclusion of Mushchenko, Skobelev, and Kroichik, who argue in *The Poetics of Skaz* that it is an inherently "democratic" gesture—a narrative form that reaches out to the neglected "common" or "mass" reader by highlighting nonliterary discourses. From assertions like this issues the refrain that *skaz* represents "speech from the streets" and therefore serves as a vehicle for the "little guy" (in all its various redactions) to gain a voice in literature. While not discounting that this may be, at times, an author's intent, we should hesitate before reducing *skaz* to this functional possibility, since such a designation a priori restricts the linguistic fund upon which it may draw. To claim that a writer's use of *skaz* is always "democratic" assigns a presumed intention to a potential result. As Vinogradov and Titunik have pointed out, since the heart of the matter is the contravention of literary norms, any discourse may function in this capacity whether it is substandard, colloquial, professional, dialectal, archaic, or even foreign in origin. The wealth alone of Zoshchenko's verbal diversity illustrates this as does others' use of arcane discourses to produce the *skaz* effect. (Vsevolod Ivanov, Zoshchenko's Serapion colleague, provides another notable example in *The Tales of Brigadier-leader M. N. Sinitsyn, as Told by Him in the Days of the First Five-Year Plan* with its prominent technoindustrial jargon.)

More to the point, to define *skaz* strictly as socioideological in origin is to canonize select elements of it (its supposed facilitation of the reading process through nonliterary speech) while disregarding how in other ways (as double-voiced discourse) it interferes with conventional procedures for interpreting texts. Whether *skaz* "democratizes" literature, whether, in Bakhtin's words, it motivates the inclusion of "alien discourse," whether it offers literature new characters and identities, and whether it serves to limit narrative point of view, the tensions inherent in the foregrounding of "reportage" can be either muted or subject to display. Both engage us in different ways—one encourages the reader to attend to narrated events as such; the other makes the conditions of narrative impede upon the narrated event. And it is Zoshchenko's indulgence of the latter that fuels critical dissension, for it confronts us with the very norms by which we could construct an adequate fictional world. This is the condition that led Iurii Tynianov to the conclusion in 1924 that Zoshchenko's *skaz* "introduces into prose not character but the reader."[69] Notably, however, Tynianov made no mention of where we, as readers, are to go, of what to grant *auctor* status once "inside." Do we still not chew on the same question once posed to Zoshchenko in 1928 on a postcard from one of his millions of "unnamed" fans? "I would be very grateful if you could answer the following question for me: Why do you laugh? Do you laugh from grief, from sorrow; do you laugh from happiness, or do you laugh simply to get some bread?"[70] No doubt, in varying degrees all four apply to Zoshchenko. But to fathom one, and only one, in his writing casts us back onto the horns of vacillation or tendentiousness.

With typical brevity and opacity, Viktor Shklovsky offered another way out of this impasse: "Zoshchenko is precisely that which you read."[71] To be sure, instead of resolving the question, these words only underscore the circularity that often marks interpretive efforts to whittle Zoshchenko down to some uniform size. But in shorthand they capture a salient point: the Zoshchenko "problem" lies as much in readers' expectations as it does in the nature of his prose.

Chapter Three

"Controlling" Parody

> All this is in the highest degree nihilistic and artistically unjustified, and it's not clear with what purpose it's being done.
> —K. Loks

WITH THESE WORDS Loks, a soviet critic, dismissed the Serapion almanac in which the Sinebriukhov story "Viktoria Kazimirovna" first appeared.[1] His outrage underscores what has become the critic's goal when encountering such texts: justify the "unjustifiable" and clarify the "purpose" behind the "nihilistic." As seen with Zoshchenko's *skaz*, the task is made easier through recourse to a term like *satire* because it immediately evokes the image of political dissidence, arguably the single most important metaphor for the field of soviet literature. As a consequence, it also resolves the thorny question of authorial intent and simultaneously assumes that the contemporary impact of such literature was consistent with our present ideological needs.

A similar explanatory power attends parody, another term employed in most interpretations of Zoshchenko. With few exceptions its value has been seen as a subset of satire. Whether we turn to the early Soviet Union, the cold war West, or Russia today, tradition has it that Zoshchenko used parody as an instrument, albeit one of many, to magnify the sins of his real-life targets. He deliberately distorted characters' and narrators' speech in order to cast them in a negative light. Their manifest inability, for example, to understand and properly use bureaucratic and political locutions stood as proof of their arevolutionary, unsoviet disposition.

Decidedly less attention has been given to the question of how parodic factors, operating at a different level, might interfere with readers' attempts to accommodate his texts within a mimetic paradigm. This neglect, notably, figures as well in the growing number of theoretical studies of parody in the field as a whole. As an artistic mode exploring and interrogating extant conventions, it finds full favor in a post-structuralist environment that celebrates quotation and meta-ironic approaches. Thus two of the most influential writers on the subject today, Margaret Rose and Linda Hutcheon, champion parody for the unique insight it offers into the reception and sense-making process of literature.² At the same time, they, like others, do not confront two primary questions raised by their theoretical postulates: What, in actuality, have readers done or sought to do with parody, and how might they try to combat or overcome its interpretive difficulties? Instead, they substitute descriptions of presumed textual effects for empirical investigations, and here we can see an enduring gap in studies of parody. The field suffers not from a want of theory but from an unwillingness to engage the problems real readers have faced with convention-breaking literature. The silence is telling and keeps us from a closer understanding of what impact in actual terms parodic texts have had on their contemporary environment. In *The Boundaries of Genre*, Gary Saul Morson has made the relevant observation that sometimes a culture "'needs' to take it [parody] as a 'serious' work."³ If we allow the notion of culture to denote a body of specific reading habits, then we come to the central issue in critical treatment of Zoshchenko's parodies: Do readers always allow (or want) parody to show its true colors and thus transgress or interrogate accepted norms? Or do readers seek to reread it, as it were, so as to remove its troubling edges and accommodate it within traditional literary forms and, by extension, within established political conventions?

SENTIMENTAL TALES

The first five texts of Zoshchenko's cycle, "The Goat," "Apollon and Tamara," "A Terrible Night," "What the Nightingale Sang," and "A Happy Adventure," were published between 1923 and 1926 without direct reference to their possible interrelation. In 1927, they were anthologized along with two more stories, "Wisdom" and "People," under the collective title *What the Nightingale Sang: Sentimental Tales*. In 1930, "Lilacs in Bloom" and *M. P. Siniagin* appeared and can be considered additions to the cycle since they follow the original seven in their narrative persona, stylistic flavor, and thematic register.

What most strikes readers of the series is Zoshchenko's apparent turn to the despondent and lugubrious. Contemporaries such as Abram Lezhnev voiced surprise at this "unexpected side" of the writer.⁴ Elsewhere concern was raised that the writer was in danger of "losing his gift" since on these pages once-cheerful smiles had turned sour.⁵ Western critics as well fixed attention on the seemingly qualitative change evident in the *Sentimental Tales*. Though they were written concurrently with Zoshchenko's more popular short stories, the "gay humor" of the latter was markedly absent, as von Wiren noted, and had given way "to almost bitter irony and sarcasm."⁶

At first glance readers' fears would seem well grounded. Zabezhkin's dream that marriage to a landlady with a goat will provide quiet security in life is crushed when he learns that the goat belongs to another suitor. Apollon Perepenchuk returns from the war to discover that his fame as a ballroom piano player has passed; shortly before his death he finds employment as a gravedigger. Kotofeev, a triangle player in the orchestra, goes temporarily insane over the suggestion that his skill could be replaced by an automated instrument. Ivan Belokopytov, a member of the intelligentsia who had displayed liberal inclinations before the Revolution, returns from voluntary exile after 1917 only to learn that his training as a philologist is of no use in his native town. Abandoned by his wife, fired from his job, he survives in the woods, sleeping in animals' burrows. Siniagin, a failed symbolist poet, lives as a "parasite" off his aunt's property and is finally reduced to beggary. In a final scene of "optimistic reconciliation," he dies just as he begins to work in the administration of a cooperative.

Loss and despair were not the period's most favored topics. Predictably, initial reaction was hostile. In 1927 no less an organ than *Izvestiia* challenged Zoshchenko's effrontery in a six-columned review, "Philistine Alert." Here M. Olshevets upbraided Zoshchenko for his alleged contempt for the world and lack of faith in its future. *Sentimental Tales*, Olshevets asserted, was nothing more than a "crooked mirror" held to all that was bright and promising in the Soviet Union.[7] The same year *Molodaia gvardiia* confirmed that Zoshchenko was a writer of limited scope, of limited range, and of a limited world; he could offer nothing but characters enslaved by "their own bestial interests and [who] writhe like maggots in a pile of manure."[8] Four years later the judgment remained. Can there be any hope for him? inveighed a representative of the "Karl Marx Factory." No, came the conclusion. Zoshchenko still "cannot find his way out of the swamp of philistinism"; he is nothing but the "chronicler" of its putridity.[9]

However, as we might expect, the tables could turn quickly. Only three years after *Izvestiia*'s thunder, new voices championed the series as a concentrated attack against the enemies of the Soviet Union. In a speech at a Leningrad meeting of proletarian writers, Mikhail Chumandrin declared that these stories "only support the fact that Zoshchenko detests philistinism and attacks it without mercy."[10] At the same meeting Iurii Libedinsky offered still higher praise. If Lenin had recognized that the weight of the past would be one of society's most resilient enemies, then, Libedinsky argued, Zoshchenko would go down in the history of literature as having accomplished "significant work": "The Revolution has placed a great task before Zoshchenko and he is fulfilling it."[11] It is rare indeed to move so quickly from censure by the state's official organ to allegiance with the father of the Revolution—especially since at this time Zamiatin, one of the Serapion mentors and now an enemy of the state, had been pilloried in the press and was soon to leave the country. Even more surprising, though, is that the chorus of approval, sustained as well by Zhurbina, Volpe, and others, lasted until the early 1940s. As an incisive demonstration of the bankruptcy of the old culture, *Sentimental Tales* served in their eyes as a collective "obituary" for the past and thus proved the writer's allegiance to socialist ideals.[12] Demonstrably, in 1938 I. Sats proclaimed Zoshchenko a "true realist" for detailing his protagonists' demise and supported the writer's efforts by providing a sociohistorical background to confirm the texts' veracity.[13]

With an obviously different political motive, the West has offered the most consistent support for the earlier soviet version. Portraits of individuals unable or unwilling to cope with postrevolutionary conditions confirmed standing opinion that Zoshchenko's intentions were strictly antisoviet. Von Wiren emphasized that the writer had finally withdrawn all masks and begun "more or less openly to question the validity of the social system."[14] And Domar, by holding up these novellas as proof that Zoshchenko "does not think highly of human beings in general," inadvertently gave full voice to earlier soviet accusations of his incorrigible misanthropy.[15] The insistence on Zoshchenko's animosity has been so strong that it leaves the impression that *Sentimental Tales* is an exemplary piece of traditional critical realism. Indeed, Blair's introduction to an English reprint of *People* prepares us to enter the world of Zola:

> It is a story about despair and decay, about the collapse of illusions, about the struggle for existence, and about the animal in man. It is interspersed with humour, but the humour is often savage and leaves a bitter taste. . . . Little by little his [Belokopytov's] illusions are shattered, he finds no place for himself in society, and comes to see life as a cruel and forlorn struggle for existence. He becomes more and more obsessed with the animal side of his nature until in the end he is hardly recognizable as a human being.[16]

The topicality of Zoshchenko's subject matter—what the Revolution ostensibly holds for the newly disenfranchised—has consequently sparked a primary interest in the documentary potential of *Sentimental Tales*. The texts' inherent fictionality notwithstanding, the overriding critical objective has been to explicate how they illustrate accepted truths of postrevolutionary life. In fact, amid the clouds of political conflict, no doubts have been voiced as to their accuracy in transmitting some bona fide empirical state, whether taken as laments for or tirades against the bourgeoisie. What is relevant here is not whether fiction can serve readers in the capacity of historical proofs. Zoshchenko's own legacy and the whole of the mimetic tradition provide abundant evidence that readers have believed it can. Instead, such a concern prompts consideration of how this goal is to be achieved. This question, introduced earlier with reference to Bogatyrev's description of a tailor "reading" clothes, takes its most dramatic turn with *Sentimental Tales*. For in their reception the metaphor of cutting cloth is literalized. Zoshchenko the documentarian emerges via one of two semantic operations: deletion of what does not fit or restoration of what should presumably be there.

"Controlling" Parody

THE "SENTIMENTAL" EFFECT

In all this the guilty party is not necessarily critics' dogmatism or tendency to oversimplify. If any "blame" is to be assigned for their handling of the texts, then we should first look to Zoshchenko's narrative persona, the garrulous, frightfully contradictory aspiring writer whom in later editions he identified as I. V. Kolenkorov.

What is significant is that Kolenkorov himself figures as the most vocal advocate for mimetic readings of *Sentimental Tales*. Indeed, no writer would be more pleased at the referential authority with which critics have endowed his work. Throughout the series he professes to be a "naturalist," translating onto the page "real-life" experiences without any invention, embellishment or, we can add, manifest fiction:

> The author assures his esteemed readers that in no way will he misconstrue or color events; on the contrary he will reconstruct them exactly as they occurred. (AT, 42)[17]

> The author simply doesn't want to lie and why should he when, ultimately, all he wants to see is life as it really is, without fabricating or playing up anything. (WNS, 86–87)

> We will not distort reality. (TN, 66)

> Here there won't be any fancy phrases, clever twists or ecstatics over the grandeur of nature. Here there will simply be a life told truthfully. (MPS, 4)

And it is by this very insistence on fidelity to the world around that Kolenkorov justifies attention to marginal topics and people. Since *Sentimental Tales* is but a mirror to what he has lived and witnessed, critics cannot hold him accountable, even if the subject matter conflicts with contemporary demands for grandiose or ideologically responsible literature.

> It'll happen again. They'll rail at the author for this new work. Once more, they'll say, it's a blatant slander on people, out of touch with the masses and so forth.
>
> You know, we'll hear them say, these ideas are not of the shattering kind. Nor are the characters moving any mountains as, of course, might want them to be. Their social significance, they'll say, is hardly turning any heads. What they've been doing is not, then, going to be winning any votes from the laboring masses. Nobody'll follow them unconditionally.
>
> Of course what's there to say—these characters, I'll admit, are not the tops. Certainly no big guns. They're just, so to speak, other citizens with their own little habits and concerns in life.
>
> About the slander on humanity, well that's simply not here. . . .
>
> The author is not out of touch with the masses. On the contrary he lives and limps right in the middle of that, could say, stew of people. He's not describing stuff you'll find on Mars but on our damned little planet in our eastern

hemisphere, right where there is the communal apartment, in which the author takes his abode and where he, so to speak, sees everybody with his own eyes. No curtains, frills or polish. (LB, 43–45)

While simultaneously an ironic response to actual criticisms leveled at Zoshchenko, Kolenkorov's myriad qualifications and assertions also place concerns of mimesis on center stage. His chronicles of love and loss are to be just that—chronicles. His discourse should (and does, he insists) constitute a transparent window on extratextual events. Therefore, its coherency, univocality, and referential authority are above reproach. And this is where he falls on his face.

Kolenkorov "unknowingly" demonstrates the fallacy of these very same claims. Another side of him, one typically absent from critical attention, is bent on fouling the best intentions of the other. Character and setting, two features that he often advances as primary evidence for the empirical accuracy of his narratives, are likely to fall prey to Gogolian distortions or Sternian paradoxes. In "What the Nightingale Sang," the heroine's brother and mother create unusual problems of portraiture, the first because of narrative's inevitable lag time from the subject's real-life existence and the second because of literature's inherent lack of interest in certain topics:

> Mishka Rundukov, her little brother the komsomolets, is already slipping from memory. The little brat was just an ass and a bully. As for appearances, was a towhead and had kind of a pig face.
> Oh, forget it. The author doesn't want to go on about what he looks like. The brat is at that transitional age. Describe him and he, that son of a bitch, will be grown up when the book is done and then try to figure out who this Mishka Rundukov is. Where did he get the mustache if he didn't have it when you were describing him.
> Regarding the old lady, that is to say Mama Rundukov, well, no reader's going to complain if we just pass her by. All the more, making art out of old women is mighty hard. Old is old. The hell if we can tell them apart. And who even needs a description, say, of her nose? A nose is a nose. Details aren't going to make the reader's life on this planet any easier. (WNS, 88–89)

The same pathological inability to place narrative components in logical and hierarchical order (a condition born in Zoshchenko's Serapion autobiography) extends even to the weightiest of topics, the period covering the First World War and the October Revolution.

> Tremendous changes occurred during this time. Social ideas gave quite a shake to the former way of life and down it tumbled. Many exceptional people joined their forefathers in eternity. You have, for example, Kuzma Lvovich Goriushkin, the former school administrator, a truly decent and cultured individual. Typhus did him in. Off went Semen Semonovich Petukhov, also a most outstanding person and a hell of a drinker. The death of Fedor Perepenchuk, the medical assistant, dates from this period as well. (AT, 46)

Yet just as in Zoshchenko's stories, breakdowns in clarity and coherency are not restricted to specific themes, characters, or events. When Kolenkorov might careen, lose control, or grind the narrative to a halt is amusingly unpredictable. His hand can lie tantalizingly dormant, only to launch the text into quagmires of muddle and retreat. At the climax of "People," where Belokopytov hopes to die fighting his wife's lover, he grapples instead with "Babka" Pepeliukha's dog—a turn of events that perplexes Kolenkorov.

> The author's somewhat put out and feeling a little strange for having to talk about this event. Ivan Ivanovich's action has even given him cause for some grief. Of course, the author couldn't care less for the Pepeliukhan beast, what a bitch that dog, the author's just troubled that his action's kind of fuzzy, a bit silly, and it's just not clear whether his mind was going round in circles or cutting a straight path or whether it was just some game, chance or a real bad case of nerves. Whatever. It's still really fuzzy and psychologically inexplicable. (P, 188)

Authorial ignorance and indecision deflate pathos, and any sentimental tears we might be tempted to shed dry up as the bewildered Kolenkorov seeks to relay his protagonist's psychological motivation. For an entire page he continues in an inquisitive mode, refusing to lie in order to cover his ignorance (like "Jack London would do"), and reports how other witnesses perceived Belokopytov's state. Any lingering hope that Kolenkorov can steer the narrative back on its ostensibly verisimilar course dissolves when he again mixes up the reality of the narrated event with the progression of the narrative itself:

> Auntie Pepeliukha, for example, crossed herself and swore that Ivan Ivanovich went nuts, what with his tongue hanging out and drooling all over. Katerina Vasielevna [Kolenkorov's sister], no less devout a lady, also felt this way. On the other hand, the station guard and hero of labor, Eremei, argued the opposite. He stated that Ivan Ivanovich Belokopytov was healthy as an ox and that the sick and crackpots are usually placed in special homes. Egor Konstantinovich Yarkin was also convinced that Belokopytov was in his right mind and thinking straight. As for the esteemed comrade Sitnikov, well, Sitnikov wasn't going to jump to any conclusion, saying, that he could, only in the case of absolute necessity, strike up a correspondence with a certain Moscow psychiatrist. But that's a long and unsure thing. By the time comrade Sitnikov gets to pen, and by the time that Moscow psychiatrist lets slip an answer, no doubt after a nip of the strong stuff, so what's the point of the Moscow bit, he'll just spew such gibberish that if you put it in print, then go try to prove later on that you're clean. Seems better to leave it all on the reader's conscience; this author's going to go on. (P, 188)

What Kolenkorov claims to offer and what emerges from his pen never coincide. The "raw data" with which he works (the individual displaced by revolution) travels a confused, illogical path at essentially all levels of the text. On a linguistic level, colloquialisms and substandard deviations collide with

The Politics of Reception

formal locutions, with the result that (attempted) lyric flights are distended by soviet jargon. At the level of discourse, we find the trademark breakdown between boundaries of direct and indirect speech, which leaves characters expressing themselves in astoundingly tortured ways. On a thematic level, traditional sentimentality and melodrama vie with slapstick puppetry. The resulting tenor, both within and across the texts, is maddeningly inconsistent. Gogolian excesses of "The Goat" are tempered by the relatively restrained chords of "Wisdom"; despondent brooding in "A Terrible Night" finds its supposed antidote in "A Happy Adventure."

Ultimately Kolenkorov's own commentary, flights of whimsy, memoiristic interjection, and discussion of descriptive possibilities only confirm the impossibility of his self-ordained task. Indecision over which "real-life" individuals or facts are necessary to his chronicles only highlights that mediation—what enters the text, why, in what order, in what context—is inescapable. Confused at what constitutes realism, confused at the proper constitution of literature, confused over the border between text and world, Kolenkorov collapses under the choices narrative imposes. Facts come neither "as is" nor with some preset discursive coating, and his manic intrusions serve to underscore that representation necessitates manipulation. Kolenkorov hopes to sweep such responsibility under the carpet through recourse to his mantra, fidelity to extratextual reality, but in his very struggle to render the narrative as such he defeats himself.

As a writer, Kolenkorov's ancestral roots extend not just to the Russian intelligentsia or bourgeoisie, as is usually noted, but to a Spanish knight as well. His frustration echoes the enduring Quixotian paradox: there is no neutral or natural way of narrating an event or life. It can only be portrayed through convention (artifice); yet it is precisely the presence of convention that militates against the mimetic accuracy of a given portrayal. As Kolenkorov is unable to write or argue his way out of this circle, pressure builds across the series. His narratives become top-heavy with the accumulated detritus of authorial claim, proof, pose, and counterpose. Something of a critical mass emerges, with implosion an ever-present possibility, as evident in the perplexing account of Belokopytov's struggle. This passage only encapsulates in microcosm the broader narrative demons that plague Kolenkorov. In each of his assumed roles—sociologist, historian, psychologist, literary critic, biographer, and, finally, writer—he trips himself up, with the result that alleged chronicles of love, loss, or ruin turn into failed attempts of the same.

Nevertheless, ineptitude, at least for us, still has its rewards. Each "failure" reveals a different route, another way to tell what are—on the basis of the "facts"—essentially similar stories. Through such transpositions, we get a glimpse of the yawning, and thus for Kolenkorov, terrifying freedom of representation that any narrative enjoys. If the same theme can serve both tragic and comic ends, if the author can easily assume a voice of sympathy or derision, distance or allegiance, then no one treatment can be seen as standard for or inherent to the given material. Kolenkorov unwittingly signals as much in "Lilacs in Bloom" when he pauses to try his hand at "true art" and launches into a three-page excursion through the modernist palette, complete with symbolist sound play, imagism, a futurist's staircase, a dose of hyperrealism and Pilniakian exhortations ("*Rasseia!*"). The sheer flood of narrative possibilities leaves Kolenkorov exhausted, and he finally calls for mercy:

> Oh, the hell with it! It's not working. The author is courageous to admit that he just doesn't have the gift for so-called belles lettres. You got what you got. The good Lord gives one a crude, simple tongue; another can turn artistic tricks all day.
> But this author is not setting himself up as any distinguished master and is returning with his raw language once more to a description of events. (LB, 58–60)

Of course, Kolenkorov's hasty retreat back to the comforts of his "raw language" only betrays that the latter is as artificial a medium as the rigmarole that precedes. It is not as if Kolenkorov's prose obeys some pure, unadulterated model; rather, its cultivated roughness and vulgarity are but part and parcel of the essentially infinite complement of rhetorical devices and positions available to the writer.

CRITICAL RESPONSE

It is little wonder, then, that the series bedeviled contemporaries. Chumandrin's warning in 1930 that Zoshchenko is often "vague and difficult to pin down" reminds us that obfuscation earns few allies in highly charged environments. Indeed, what links antithetical interpretations is the compelling need to restore the univocality and referential authority that Zoshchenko has failed to uphold, whether, as is variously given, because of oversight, ill health, incompetence, psychological trauma, or a desire to avoid censors. If Zoshchenko couldn't do it himself, then it has been up to critics to rescue him, so to speak, from his own ambiguity.

Fortunately, Chumandrin has shown us one of the most steadfast ways of securing harmony amidst dissonance: excise offending parts. In his hands *Sentimental Tales* assumed a singularly impressive shape: there was no narrating frame. Gone were Kolenkorov and with him any mention of the maddening antics and hijinks that litter the series; only descriptions of the texts' contents remained. "Apollon and Tamara," for example, functioned solely as a catalog of that "typical philistine trait: the desire to hide one's true intentions behind cheap romantics." By boiling each text down to the mechanics of plot, he easily discovered a document worthy of sociological extrapolation and sufficient to prove—in answer to the title of his speech—"Whose Writer Is Mikhail Zoshchenko?" If each tale introduced a protagonist doomed to extinction, then what was being reflected but the "death knell of the petite bourgeoisie"? Chumandrin's confidence even allowed him to introduce empirical evidence, the current state of soviet society, to corroborate the accuracy of Zoshchenko's fictional studies. If a "philistine" was to blame when workers protested a lengthened day or if during a recent flood in Yaroslavl a certain Ivan Ivanovich (!) refused to help save equipment but "built a raft and paddled around to his neighbors to drink tea," then did this not prove the strength of Zoshchenko's exposés?[18] Did his writing not confirm the malignancy of this "scum" while simultaneously hastening its eradication?

Chumandrin operated as if writers' intentions can be distilled directly from their protagonists' fate. Such a maneuver was perhaps stunning in its simplicity but cunning in its effect, for it left little room for argument—that is, until two decades later, when Sven answered Chumandrin in kind in the article "Whose Friend and Whose Enemy Is Mikhail Zoshchenko?" Most striking in Sven's refutation is that though the politics were reversed, essentially the same methodology was retained. Here, too, Kolenkorov posed no problem because for Sven no such fictional persona existed. All voices in the text were flattened to one plane of expression. "It's not important if a character is looking through Zoshchenko's eyes or Zoshchenko through a character's. What's important is that the reader has someone in these stories who, along with him, looks soberly on life. Here no illusions remain."[19] In truth, though, Sven was not interested in all voices; only those that were despondent, melancholic, or otherwise negative were allowed to serve as "eyes" for the reader. In fact, by freeing narratives from the context of their presentation, Sven was then himself free to turn Chumandrin's conclusions on their head and return Zoshchenko to the antisoviet fold. Where Chumandrin saw a necessary distance between author and character, Sven found unwavering allegiance: Zoshchenko was defending the victims of the state. And where Chumandrin saw fit to cite the real-life "crimes" of philistines to substantiate Zoshchenko's ostensible vision, Sven followed suit but unloaded both barrels with a litany of the Soviet Union's bloody past: starvation, execution, imprisonment, and exile.

Symptomatically, even when Zoshchenko's stylistic peculiarities have been acknowledged, the same mimetic argument can be heard. In 1928, in one of the first and darkest émigré portraits of the writer, Iulia Sazonova argued that authorial disruption, intrusion, and commentary were to be expected given the nature of the postrevolutionary environment. For her, sincere Russian writers can only oppose what they see in the Soviet Union. Therefore, breaks in linearity, retardation, and hyperbole do not impede the transmission of a fictional world; instead, they serve as clear signals of its "hopelessness." "Zoshchenko's style is deliberately inconsistent. As if to strengthen the impression of general despondency, he chooses words that are out of place, clouds his speech with a number of intrusive words, and never gives definitive answers."[20] Sazonova's conclusion demonstrates how narrative noise can be made to complement mimesis. It amplifies and thus clarifies the true nature of an extratextual world by delineating its salient features. Hence, to use the popular example, Kolenkorov's confusion over Belokopytov's climactic fight with the dog does not detract from the potential pathos of the event but intensifies its impact on the reader. "This symbolic scene, which strays from the realistic flow of the story, defines the internal law of that terrible world constructed by Zoshchenko. . . . [Belokopytov] has no use for that life, that fatal struggle for a right to exist on this earth, in which one 'must grapple bare-handed with an animal.'"[21] Needless to say, the discovery of a "law" gave Sazonova a powerful critical tool. With it she could move Zoshchenko's writing onto determinate grounds, with cogency and regularity the immediate offspring. At the same time it allowed her to seal his work within predetermined and unchanging limits: "Zoshchenko creates a closed circle in which everything is subject to his law; anything incompatible with it cannot penetrate."[22]

It is in Sazonova's rush to pronounce a kind of hermetic finality that we can see the effect of the ideological warrant under which Zoshchenko's critics have operated. "Incompatibility" was, in truth, more a reflection of Sazonova's needs than evidence of uniformity in Zoshchenko. It betrayed the parameters within which she, Sven, Chumandrin, and others defined the writer. Only those elements of his writing that seconded their beliefs regarding the Soviet Union were subject to illumination and explication. Each was secure in what constituted the "true" Soviet Union, and it was only this "truth"—however contradictory—that Zoshchenko was permitted to reflect in his work.

On both sides selective amnesia has gone far in carving Zoshchenko's work down to politically digestible portions. Critics have sought to remove the textuality of the text by expressly ignoring it or by legitimating its presence through recourse to some real-life disposition. Either course allows one to dispense with questions of narrativity and thus deal directly with the assumed reality of the represented. Of course, this only parallels what Kolenkorov so desperately seeks in his determination to write his narratives as "faithful reflections" of the world. Critical need and "authorial" intention thus come head to head, and the irony is both rich and revealing: *Sentimental Tales* has been read in the very terms in which Kolenkorov offers it, with the result that critics' mimetic expectations have collided with a parody of the very same.

NARRATOR VERSUS AUTHOR

If this collision has fostered critical reductivism, then its immediate and most prominent casualty has been Zoshchenko himself. How, where, and to what degree is his actual voice evident in the series? Generally speaking, his found presence vacillates between two poles with respect to Kolenkorov: (1) Kolenkorov equals Zoshchenko (though the latter "naturally" does not express himself in this manner, the narrator's views cannot but be those of the real writer); (2) none of Kolenkorov's speech reflects Zoshchenko's true disposition; instead it serves as the target of his ridicule.

To a large extent, these poles reflect the problematic rise of Kolenkorov himself. He first appears by name not in any of the individual stories but in successive prefaces to the later anthology *What the Nightingale Sang: Sentimental Tales*. As a latter-day creation, he postdates that which is attributed to him, and the "facts" of his life emerge retroactively, after critics had responded to *Sentimental Tales* themselves. From the most expanded description Zoshchenko provided, we learn that Kolenkorov was born in 1882 (over a decade before Zoshchenko), is the brother of one of the characters in "People," and grew up in the petit bourgeois family of a tailor.[23] (We remember that this is the same profession given to "Egor Zoshchenko" in Zoshchenko's Serapion autobiography.) Exhibiting something of his creator's rich professional background, Kolenkorov worked as a shepherd in his youth and then became an actor. Now, after five years of study in a literary circle under the direction of "M. M. Zoshchenko," he is fulfilling his dream: writing poetry and fiction. Though he belongs to the "right wing" of fellow travelers, he is reeducating himself. Perhaps in the future he will become a noteworthy writer of the naturalist school. Zoshchenko himself, it is stated, has assumed only the task of correcting orthographic mistakes and "straightening out" (!) Kolenkorov's ideology. Royalties will, of course, remain with Kolenkorov.

Before we begin to treat Kolenkorov as a developed character with a distinct psychological-sociological profile, it should be kept in mind that he was born under and because of a cloud. Many readers of the 1920s saw fit to identify Zoshchenko directly with his narrating voice; the most notorious example of this confusion was Olshevets's attack on the pages of *Izvestiia*. Understandably then for Zoshchenko, a separate name and biography would presumably wake his readership up to the fact that narrator and writer are distinct entities; they need not share the same voice and views. Kolenkorov thus became a buffer for the writer, and, notably, his very identity grew in direct proportion to critical opposition.

More often than not, however, such efforts proved to be in vain. When Zoshchenko wrote that Kolenkorov belongs to the "right wing" of fellow travelers, Viacheslav Polonsky unhesitatingly turned this statement back onto the writer himself and placed Zoshchenko in the unenviable company (from the marxist point of view) of Bulgakov, Zamiatin, and Bely as representatives of the "bourgeois right wing."[24] Such were the conditions in the 1920s, when a fictional persona could owe its biography and very existence to official condemnation. Indeed, only Lezhnev seemed to lament the fact that a writer should have to resort to this tactic in order to assuage critics. Recognizing that some of Kolenkorov's complaints regarding contemporary expectations were legitimate, Lezhnev argued that critics should be more tolerant and temper their language. He recalled the abuse meted out to Babel and with uncanny prescience (as Babel was shot fifteen years later) warned that critics should not destroy Zoshchenko as well.[25]

True to form, Zoshchenko could not resist the opportunity to pay critics back in kind. If they had forced him, in effect, to create a negative foil, then Zoshchenko made sure it would be a decidedly slippery one.[26] Like the other authorial masks in Zoshchenko's stories (Gavrilych, Sinebriukhov, and of course "Zoshchenko" himself), Kolenkorov does not embody a single disposition or voice. What emerges from his pen is the same kasha that defies accommodation within a single linguistic, psychological, or political register. Moreover, in his editorial asides, Zoshchenko deliberately toys with the boundary between "narrator" and "writer." The opening lines of "Lilacs in Bloom" would seem an emphatic protest against critics' tendency to identify him with his narrator. Yet even here Zoshchenko cannot resist muddying the water:

> In light of past misunderstandings the writer wishes to inform critics that the individual in whose name these stories are narrated is, so to speak, an imaginary person. He's the average intelligentsia type who's had to live at the threshold of two epochs.
> Neurasthenia, political wavering, a heap of contradictions, melancholy—that's what we've had to endow our *vydvizhenets* with.
> Now the author-writer M. M. Zoshchenko, a son and brother of these unhealthy types, pulled through all this a long time ago. At the present time he's free of contradiction. Inside it's all crystal clear with roses popping out. And if they ever droop and the heart gets the shakes, then it'll be because of a lot of reasons, and the author will talk about them sometime later.
> As for right now this is a literary device.
> Therefore the author beseeches his most respected critics to remember this special circumstance before lashing out at a defenseless writer.
> Nevertheless the author considers it his duty to calm the reader: notwithstanding the fact that the person who narrates the work is an invented one, the story itself is far from invented. Everything is taken straight from life, and the major events literally unfolded before the author's eyes. (LB, 43)

Each step to clarify the relation between Zoshchenko and his narrating voice is always held in abeyance. The initial paragraph, employing the technical language of the literary craft, underscores distance. Zoshchenko admits that here we have a textbook example of a fictional stand-in for the author. However, once we learn of its identifying characteristics, we sense a resemblance with the writer's own person. Neurasthenia speaks to Zoshchenko's own troubled disposition (his depressions and melancholy were already in full swing), and ideological wavering, of course, draws from his public profile. It echoes those marxist critics who excelled in reading sinister motives into his verbosity. Zoshchenko then tosses out a most daring statement, a direct equation with "son and brother." But he immediately switches gears and checks this with the face-saving "pulled through." Contemplation of this new twist is then upstaged by banter on "roses." When a hint of seriousness returns, we hear again of a "literary device," which resurrects a formal distance between the two and sets up a final appeal for a more sophisticated treatment of his writing. But the final lines add another dose of mystification by once more suggesting a certain closeness between the narrating and authorial eye.

So where are we to begin? While acknowledging the central "problem" in his writing, Zoshchenko immediately derails readers' attempts to resolve it. Instead of using the opportunity and authority of a preface to demystify his relation, he ups the ante. Predictably, an equivalent vacillation has graced critical assessment. In order to prove that the narrator is Zoshchenko's target, Volpe cited just the following lines from the above passage: "Now the author-writer M. M. Zoshchenko, a son and brother of these unhealthy types, pulled through all this a long time ago. At the present time he's free of contradiction."[27] Conversely, Sven restricted his attention to one line and added the necessary verb "is" so as to join narrator with author: "Now the author-writer M. M. Zoshchenko is a son and brother of these unhealthy types."[28] For both, only calculated deletion could guarantee clarity.

As might be expected, the pursuit of uniformity can often snap back with amusing yet revealing results. In the scramble to identify the authentic Zoshchenko in *Sentimental Tales,* Domar and Murphy were quick to point out how soviet critics "made fools of themselves" by taking the stories seriously and reading Zoshchenko into Kolenkorov's own voice. (Olshevets was usually fingered on this account.) Haste, however, got the better of them. Both had recourse to the same evidence as the "fools" and adopted verbatim much of Kolenkorov's disposition as Zoshchenko's own. In fact, if any group is to be singled out for the "mistake" of accepting Kolenkorov at face value, then we need go no further than the heart of Zoshchenko's Western reception. Sazonova continually allowed for "Zoshchenko" to substitute wherever she quoted Kolenkorov's negativisms; Alexandrova easily slipped between the two as well, transferring Kolenkorov's title of "naturalist" to the writer himself: "According to Zoshchenko's own classification, he belonged to the 'naturalist' school. In his view this school was the 'only honest one,' to which 'the entire future of Russian literature' belonged."[29] Similarly, Sven, having proved that Zoshchenko and his narrator are siblings, essentially let no page go by without a citation from the latter to corroborate the writer's virulent hostility to the Soviet Union. And with no hesitation von Wiren declared that finally here "the author himself intrudes as a social philosopher expressing his disillusion on the contemporary state of affairs."[30]

THE PARODIC CONDITION

In 1928 Zoshchenko stepped forward to alleviate, so it would seem, the confusion surrounding *Sentimental Tales* and to defuse the emerging controversy. Reflecting a newfound tendency to publish nonironic authorial declarations (a defensive move we can attribute as much to outside antagonism as to an ingrown, personal desire), he prefaced the first critical anthology devoted to him with the brief exposition "About myself, critics and my work." The collection consisted of three articles by Shklovsky, Vinogradov, and A. G. Barmin and represented the most favorable and detailed discussion of his writing to date. Notably, Zoshchenko's introductory statement embraces the self-referential, metafictive current in his prose:

> I want to make one comment. Perhaps it may seem strange or unexpected but the point is I am a proletarian writer. More precisely, in my work I parody that imaginary yet authentic proletarian writer who should exist in today's conditions and atmosphere. Of course, at least for now there is no such a writer. But when he appears, society and life will be significantly improved in all respects.
> I only parody. I'm a temporary replacement for the proletarian writer. That's why a simplistic philosophy permeates my stories; it's exactly what my readers are looking for.
> In larger pieces again I'm just parodying. My target is the clumsy, ponderous (Karamzinian) style of a contemporary Red Tolstoy or Rabindranath Tagore and the sentimental vein characteristic of it. I'm parodying the writer from the intelligentsia who, perhaps, doesn't exist but would, if he sought to fulfill the social dictate not of publishers but of that segment of society which now occupies center stage.[31]

To be sure, his allegiance to the articles that followed was very guarded.[32] While they dissected and expounded Zoshchenko's comic exuberance, he expressly discounted a humor-by-design approach. In his words parody came as a last resort, a necessary yet temporary measure born of readers' demands rather than of authorial whim. If a new literature was needed to match unique, postrevolutionary concerns, then the contemporary press placed salvation in a "Red Tolstoy"—that is, a writer who could capture the same epic range, artistic mastery, and pedagogic force as the godfather. However, for Zoshchenko the time for such a classic style had passed; its themes, characters, and language could no longer command the authority they once enjoyed. Therefore, any attempt to merge today's subjects with yesterday's narrative modes would by default yield a cumbersome and, for the newly literate, inappropriate work.

Needless to say, in *Sentimental Tales* Zoshchenko offers up Kolenkorov as sacrificial proof. Never will he join Tagore in the ranks of Nobel Prize winners. Instead, Kolenkorov's inability to produce a cohesive narrative in traditional registers only marks their inadequacy for the depiction of contemporary *byt*. Each step by him into the past—as Dostoevskian psychologist, symbolist memoirist, Tolstoyan chronicler—drives another nail into their collective coffin of obsolescence. Herein lies Zoshchenko's much celebrated tendency to quote classic plot motifs of Russian literature and critics' subsequent habit of searching *Sentimental Tales* for intertextual references. "The Goat" issues from Gogol's "Overcoat"; "A Terrible Night" was obviously written with Dostoevsky's "Mr. Prokharchin" in mind; "Apollon and Tamara" reminds us of, among other works, Pushkin's *Eugene Onegin*. Likewise, *M. P. Siniagin* evokes the (now discredited) symbolist heritage both through Blok, whose lyrics, as Volpe first pointed out, appear in slightly disguised form as the protagonist's work, and through Bely, whose claims about the difficulties of writing in soviet times are echoed, as Chudakova has shown, by Kolenkorov himself.[33]

The most penetrating and exhaustive study of Zoshchenko's parodic orientation in this direction is Chudakova's *The Poetics of Mikhail Zoshchenko*.[34] Framing his intentions in Bakhtinian terms, she argues that Zoshchenko's narrative contortions stem directly from the post-1917 destruction of stylistic hierarchies in public discourse. In the whirlwind of competing voices and linguistic registers that were unleashed by the massive social upheavals of the revolution and civil war, any authoritative expression or stable authorial "I" was an impossibility. Such confidence would only be a patina, a false security. To be faithful to the times and to new (often barely literate) readers, a writer could only tread gingerly, with irony and parody a conscious sign of cautionary indecision.

Chudakova makes the crucial connection between Zoshchenko's parodies and problems of interpretation by highlighting his evasive authorial profile. In this respect, she has done much to raise our understanding of Zoshchenko above plus/minus categories of satirist. Yet even with this welcome attention to his metafictive dominant, she, too, finally seeks to define textual ambiguity as necessarily dependent on and reflective of some concrete, extratextual state. Though I would not discount the sincerity of Zoshchenko's intentions in answering readers' concerns (a matter to be addressed in chapter 5), the questions posed by his work extend beyond the parodic revelation of obsolescent or otherwise impractical discourses. Chudakova's conclusion does not give us adequate grounds to understand fully how his texts produce and sustain dramatically different readings. Clarity of purpose and singleness of impression—all has been done for the new reader—are precisely what his texts defy. If anything, the extent of ironic play in his texts bespeaks a near-absurdist approach to verbal art that cannot be explained solely as a form of literary satire or as a quasi-mimesis of linguistic anarchy in the 1920s. Indeed, the fact that neither side can be excused from appearing the "fool" goes a long way in suggesting that his texts are more complex than parodies of the proletarian writer "who should but does not yet exist."

Critics' own beguilement points us to where this complexity might be. As much as Kolenkorov embodies analogues of writing, he, too, constitutes models of reading—models, it quickly should be added, that are no less tainted than what he offers as "author." To continue with Bakhtin, all discourses that permeate Kolenkorov's world enjoy absolute object-oriented authority. He accepts the texts that make up his experience—fiction, newspaper, political tract, street speech, substandard dialects—as functionally equivalent. His pronounced faith in the authority of all discourses "allows" him to intermix stylistic registers with full conviction of their adequacy. In fact, far beyond any laments for the past, mimetic extremism is his single domineering characteristic, a condition that defines (and dogs) him both as processor and transmitter of information. What is said, what is read, what is heard, regardless of origin or context, is for him what *is*. As he reveals how texts enter his world and what use he makes of them, he emerges as a passive, incautious, naive reader, one whose expectations move only in one direction and reflect only one perspective: erasing the distinction between fiction and nonfiction and closing the gap between text and world.

As exemplary reader, Kolenkorov again follows the path of Don Quixote, with their kinship being qualitative in nature. The significance of Quixote's habits is not really the quantity of his reading (though perhaps he did read too much) but what beliefs are in display. Kolenkorov, too, is locked in the grip of an expanding, all-consuming referentiality. In this way both serve as vehicles to inscribe in the text strategies for its interpretation. Of course, any such guidelines are false models, distinct clues of how *not* to read. Not only do both engage in lengthy discussions regarding narrative accuracy, but both—to their detriment and our amusement—act upon their faith. Quixote's plane of action is physical; belief in uncompromised discursive authority compels him to draw his sword against wineskins. Kolenkorov's is distinctly literary. His delusions are put in relief via the assumptions he holds regarding pure mimesis and the governing position this condition occupies in his mind.

Whether aspiring knight errant or aspiring writer, both in functional terms objectify literalist modes for understanding texts. But whereas readers of Cervantes have learned from Quixote's mishaps and thus remain circumspect regarding textual propositions, many of Zoshchenko's have not heeded the same warning. And it is for those readers that he reserved his final punch. In the last text of the series, *M. P. Siniagin*, the narrator dutifully sets out to record—what else?—the life of a failed poet. His manifest zeal to be as accurate as possible is admirable; after all, as he declares, he will speak only of events to which he bore personal witness. The accoutrements expected of an objective history quickly follow: "Mikhail Polikarpovich Siniagin was born in the year eighteen eighty-seven on the estate of Pankovo in the province of Smolensk. His mother came from an aristocratic family; his father was an honorable gentleman" (MPS, 16). However, concern for precision soon overtakes him. Alongside documentary topoi of person, place, and chronology, we find not merely detailed descriptions of individuals' appearance and personal habits and not just commentary on their character—we have their photographs as well. (Presumably Cervantes and Sterne would have jumped at the same if the technology had been available.) Who knows, in truth, who they actually are? But here, in the text, we have the most explicit documentation available for Siniagin, his relatives, wife, and lover. "True to life" was never offered with greater hope and never fell flatter. And, we should add, it never put the mimetic reader in a tighter spot. If elsewhere we have accepted Kolenkorov at face value, then by the time we encounter *M. P. Siniagin*, we have walked into a trap. The single-voiced authority by which we have matched Kolenkorov with Zoshchenko leaves us with two equally unattractive exits once we *literally* see Siniagin's visage. Either we accept that photographs are a normal method of characterization, or we adopt the impossible position (it is, after all, patently fiction) of arguing for the characters' real-life existence.

In truth there is a third option: ignore the pictures. And this last route has been the most common. Of all the reviews and critical studies of Zoshchenko over the past sixty years, not one treats with the exceedingly peculiar status of referentiality in *M. P. Siniagin*. Perhaps we ought to accept this silence as symptomatic of readers' reluctance to question their own mimetic needs. In fact, nowhere else does Zoshchenko parody the mirroring illusion of fiction in such bold and challenging terms; nowhere else are the hazards of approaching his texts as referentially adequate in such striking display.[35]

Zoshchenko's inclusion of photographs encapsulates the greater paradox that runs throughout the series. Fiction, conceived and presented as history, uses the tools of the documentary to play up and accentuate its very own fictionality. The game shares common ground with Shklovsky's famous article "Literature Outside the Plot," an analysis of Vasily Rozanov's anomalous hybrids *Solitaria* and *Fallen Leaves*.[36] Here, demonstrably, Shklovsky discusses the tension between facts and the conditions of their appearance on the basis of Rozanov's ground-breaking use of photographs in these two works. Devoid of inscription or the darkened border that usually separates picture from printed page, they appear as if an afterthought, as if taped directly into the book. For Shklovsky, the artifice involved "lays bare" that the texts' structural looseness and their apparent randomness and unmotivated status are part of a conscious, aesthetic decision. Photographs now serve a new purpose beyond documentary illustration. In his words, they raise "a biographical fact to the level of a stylistic one."[37]

"Controlling" Parody

The photographs in *M. P. Siniagin,* appearing after Shklovsky's article, represent a literary (and literal) enactment of his treatise. In the novella, the material nature of the photographs is not altered. Celluloid is still celluloid; image is still image. But by crossing the border into a new context, the photographs are now subject to a different semantic condition, and this shift necessarily endows them with a value that they do not possess in their home environment, the album from which Zoshchenko presumably took them. Significantly, the new value is actually the loss of whatever authority they originally enjoyed. We know that they still constitute real photographs, but the normative relation between sign and referent is severed. While convention would therefore direct us to respond to them as authentic representations of their referent, the nature of the text as fiction precludes this possibility. In short, whereas Rozanov evades motivation, Zoshchenko willingly provides it but with a twist: we cannot accept it.

RED TOLSTOY AND THE "FACTS"

As much as his overt parodying of nineteenth-century plot motifs, Zoshchenko's challenge to referential sensibilities also made him a special participant in the Red Tolstoy polemics. Of course, his voice was not the only one that sounded the futility of resurrecting the acknowledged master. Much more militant were the futurists centered around the journal *LEF*. From its first issues in 1923 to the culminating anthology *Literature of Fact,* they lambasted classic realism as "an opium for the people."[38] In their opinion readers should cease such noxious genuflecting to the past, a practice that Sergei Tretiakov memorably likened to a cat "which habitually returns to the same corner of the room even though the litter box has been moved."[39] What could such nostalgia offer now? he asked rhetorically. Its conventions were stagnant and outdated, and repetition would dull a reader's mind and cognitive powers. Only facts could release the reader from this narcotic; only clear, unadulterated documentaries could effect in cultural terms the same revolution that had transformed society. Citing the newspaper as an exemplary form, Tretiakov proclaimed it "our Bible," communicating an existence far richer than what the count's heavy tomes could offer: "What *War and Peace* are we to speak of when every morning, newspaper in hand, we turn page after page of that amazing novel, the title of which is life today."[40]

One of the more pointed and, for our purposes, relevant explications by LEF of why the Tolstoyan heritage needed to be excised comes in Osip Brik's 1927 article "Closer to the Facts."[41] Fiction, he argued simply, had disqualified itself by being unfaithful to "facts." Narrative had corrupted and polluted their natural, edenic state. Only a person who believed that reality was in need of some cosmetic enhancement would favor such embellishment or "staging" (*instsenirovka*). "One should love facts," he championed, "and one should therefore keep them free of contaminating invention. The two must not be mixed." Facts deserved better than some vulgar literary formulation; they required a discursive mode that respected their sovereignty and, in effect, allowed them to speak for themselves. For Brik, only *protokol*, a genre embracing biography, memoir, and history, offered such a crystalline form; therefore, it should be what the culturally advanced soviet citizen preferred.

Litterboxes and narcotics aside, LEF's arguments run parallel with Zoshchenko's narrating pose in *Sentimental Tales*. The key targets of LEF's broadsides—invention (*vymysel*) and imagination (*fantaziia*)—are the very same devils Kolenkorov hopes to exorcise. In his efforts to produce a fully transparent narrative he echoes nearly verbatim the battle cry of LEF's campaign. Only "facts" enter his writing and this alone makes it "true" and "authentic." Imagination and fantasy, he continually reminds us, are the heralds of distortion, artifice, and interference, and, as such, are the antithesis of the cold, hard truth.

Coincidences, however, do not stop here. Notably, both Kolenkorov and Brik trip over the same wire that brings Quixote down. Challenged by the canon to explain why he, "a reasonable man," accepts "all the extravagant absurdities in these ridiculous books of chivalry as really true," the knight presents what seems to him irrefutable proof:

> Books which are printed by royal license and with the approval of those to whom they are submitted, and which are read with universal delight and applause by great and small, poor and rich, learned and ignorant, plebeians and gentlefolk—in short, by all kinds of persons of every quality and condition—could they be lies and at the same time appear so much like the truth? For do they not specify the father, the mother, the family, the time, the place, and the actions, detail by detail and day by day, of this or that knight?[42]

What escapes Quixote is that which Zoshchenko's formalist contemporaries had long recognized: even though a text may draw exclusively upon actual characters or events from the real world, authenticity is not automatically conferred upon the text just by virtue of their inclusion. The value of facts does not precede their textualization; rather, it is dependent on their narrative environment and the interpretive conditions brought to bear. The central lesson Cervantes has bequeathed us is that pure, objective mimesis is an illusion, no matter what cloth—fiction or *protokol*—the text comes in. The photographs in *M. P. Siniagin* (where, as Quixote wishes, we have the "mother," the "family," and so forth) put this in dramatic light. A photograph cannot function as a fact (in the sense of ontological proof of some empirical entity) absent a structure that allows it to "perform" as such. Despite Brik's belief, no expression presents it uncompromised or "free of contaminating invention."

"Controlling" Parody

With *M. P. Siniagin* we can best see that the attention Zoshchenko pays to realism in his writing has less to do with achieving a traditional, realistic effect than with playing up the very procedures by which such a potential could be claimed. Along with the other *Sentimental Tales,* this text afforded him a double-barbed parody, one that targeted epigons of the nineteenth-century canon and, simultaneously, problematized the solutions championed by LEF. Perhaps this was indirect payback for Mikhail Levidov's derisive comments in the journal's first issue, where he dismissed Zoshchenko with a stroke of a pen: "[He] can't find a damn thing [to write about] in the war or Revolution except simple anecdotes."[43] More important, however, by objectifying the processes by which narratives function as authentic representations, Zoshchenko furthered Serapion experimentation with the paradoxes inherent in using texts as structural guides to life and history. With the observation that "[e]ven in the real world we live in an illusion. We are convinced that features of our daily life exist in the precise form that we perceive them," Ilia Gruzdev set the stage for Zoshchenko and other Serapions to play with the myriad shapes, qualitatively distinct and quantitatively infinite, that "form" can take.[44] Tradition holds that the Serapions' conflict with their peers was due to their overt calls for an "apolitical" literature. But this was only part of what was at stake. By casting repeated attention to how a text interacts with the world, the Serapions, as the most spirited and conscious heirs to Sterne in soviet literature, assumed a unique role in the polemics over realism in the 1920s. If contemporaries argued that reality governs the text, then they worked in the opposite direction, questioning this hierarchy by explicitly marking the distance between the two as well as the formative role a text has in shaping its referent. Lev Lunts's celebrated charge that "art is as real as life itself" was, of course, an appeal that literature not be subordinated to political agendas (coming as it did at the end of the 1922 Serapion autobiographies).[45] Yet inherently and alongside this, it is was also a direct call that a text be seen *as text.*

Though such an assertion may seem commonplace, even clichéd today, for that time it was a radical departure from contemporary literary doctrines, all of which, regardless of ideological affiliation, sought to eliminate the functional distinction between text and world. Readers actively located and understood texts within a one-to-one relationship with the world, as if the data of that real world were immanently accessible through fiction without appreciable infringement. The point is not that fiction was read as historically true (there were no actual Don Quixotes among soviet critics) but that it could be accepted and cited as if it were as credible as a documentary account. Here lies Chumandrin's ability to draw upon "real-life" philistines to corroborate the veracity of character portraits in *Sentimental Tales,* but here too, we should not forget, lies Zoshchenko's ironic answer to readers' search for photographic realism in his work.

The Politics of Reception

If moving the text outside its boundaries into life has been the central concern of Zoshchenko's critics, then exploring the very nature of this border and the consequences of transmission is a prior condition of his writing. This tension allows for a more empirical grounding of Bakhtin's theory, later developed by Morson and Hutcheon, on parody's inescapable open-endedness.[46] Critical treatment of Zoshchenko suggests that precisely because parody is an instantiation-illustration par excellence of a text's ability to evade final interpretation, readers have struggled to provide closure. In a recent study of soviet metafiction, David Shepherd has commented on soviet critics' antagonism towards this kind of writing;[47] here we see that they are not alone. On both sides of the Atlantic the traditional way of reading Zoshchenko's parodies has been, in fact, to de-parodicize them. In this respect appeals to realism are more than just an evaluative statement; they seek to ground the text by shifting attention away from its own ambivalent postures to the more solid frame of satiric, social commentary.[48] Needless to say, such monologic imperatives fracture when they hit Zoshchenko's writing, and critics' search for a cohesive fictional world and consistent image of author can be met only through the tendentious promotion of select textual components. If, as Kolenkorov quips in the story "People," "strange things" can happen in literature, it has fallen to his readers, in a reversal of the formalist edict, to make the strange familiar.

Chapter Four

Fiction as Documentary:
Youth Restored and *The Blue Book*

> This book will probably bring us grief and trouble.
> —*Youth Restored*

ON THE BORDER OF FICTION AND HISTORY

Kolenkorov's "bewilderment" at the strange face of literature would only have mounted over the next four years during the cultural revolution. In fact, by the turn of the decade his travails over fiction's expressive capacity seemed premonitory. Imaginative literature as we know it was experiencing something of a crisis. When the playwright Vladimir Kirshon declared in the summer of 1930 at the Sixteenth Party Congress that reality was "more interesting" than and had actually "eclipsed" whatever a writer could dream of, he was giving voice to a growing sense that fiction had exhausted itself.[1] Under the aegis of the first Five-Year Plan (introduced in 1928) the Soviet Union had begun its militant, violent lurch forward to socialism. In its wake foundered the debris of the past—all the cultural practices and beliefs, classes and peoples that had failed to keep pace. And literature, the mere product of one individual and one creative impulse, found itself among the first victims. Raw revolutionary reality had grown impatient with its dawdling fantasies, make-believe, and inevitable lag time. No fiction, epic or not, could presume to chronicle the whole of the new age, its feverish pace, its tremendous heroes, and especially the twin pillars of "progress": industrialization and collectivization. The fire and fury with which soviet society hurled itself into the race for modernization demanded an equivalent outlet of expression, an uncompromising lens through which to gauge itself, mark its achievements, and plot its future victories.

More ominous were the words Kirshon reserved for writers themselves, especially fellow travelers, who by the onset of the cultural revolution had extinguished the last remaining tolerance of orthodox Party critics and proletarian groups. The Shakhty affair of 1928 had whipped up suspicion against all intelligentsia-bourgeois specialists working for the state and put further conciliation and accommodation in doubt. Its literary echo was the campaign against Pilniak and Zamiatin, who immediately became the poster villains for this period. Sounding the alarm, Kirshon warned that "the class enemy is active in literature." Its supporters were nothing less, he continued, than "agents both of the kulaks and bourgeoisie within our borders, and of the émigrés and imperialists abroad." Therefore, the time for compromise had passed; no longer could there be an excuse for those not on the "right track." After all, Kirshon declared, "no other age has offered writers such tremendous material as ours." What, he then ventured, was their problem? They suffered from that most frequent of ills, the cancer of the Ivory Tower. They had distanced themselves from the proletariat, from the new reality of the Soviet Union; they had blinded themselves to the brilliance of this "most remarkable epoch," and now they had "to decide once and for all whether they are on our side of the barricade or if they will become deadweight, an obstacle in our path."[2] The cure offered by Kirshon left little room for equivocation. Either they, like all bourgeois remnants, should be "mercilessly liquidated," or they had to "reorganize themselves" and break from all individualistic and "caste-based" artistic traditions. How might writers awaken to this new reality? Kirshon triumphantly presented a one-way ticket: "They need to plunge into the thick of it all; they need to quit their city offices and literary clubs and go to the country; they need to visit construction sites so that side by side with the proletariat they can obtain new material for their writing and, thenceforth, reeducate themselves."[3]

Needless to say, when the opportunity presented itself, most took the latter route. The cultural revolution witnessed an unprecedented effort by writers to experience firsthand "socialist construction" and then report back to the country on their findings. As recorder, observer, or laborer—such as in the striking example of Marietta Shaginian, who worked a year and a half in Armenia building a hydroelectric station—many sought to integrate themselves directly into soviet life. Whether they were spurred on by the likes of Kirshon's browbeating or motivated by a genuine desire to aid the country's social-economic development, contact with the "masses" became de rigueur. Some made personal journeys; others joined "writers' brigades," a practice culminating in the 1933 trip by 120 writers (including Zoshchenko) to the White Sea–Baltic Canal. The results, as Shaginian discovered in Armenia, could be miraculous. This was the "happiest period" of her life, from which she emerged cleansed, with a new sense of social commitment and, for all intents and purposes, a new identity.[4]

Such ideological epiphanies (publicly stated or not) were no doubt somewhat rare, but the campaign's impact on genre, narrative, and interpretive norms was dramatic. It was quickly acknowledged that merely documenting the "facts"—in the journalistic sense of who, what, when, where—was insufficient; it lacked the capacity to dramatize the experience and communicate its essential meaning, whether for the writer personally or for society as a whole. Conversely, an overtly fictional rendition based solely on hypothetical actions and people would seem to betray the legitimacy of an actual event, since relevancy and topicality were the desiderata. What emerged from this tension was the frequent, yet pronounced, dissolution of the boundaries between nonfiction and fiction. Authors were inclined to bolster their plots with documentary apparatus, detailing the historical, political, technological or scientific premises behind their "story." Such additions, imbedded in a fictional narrative (and not always adequately motivated), were seen as added bonuses, for they drew attention to the work's practical application.

Here lie the roots of the period's two most important genres: reportage/"production" novels and the *ocherk* (a dramatized, essayistic sketch). The former generally attest to the writer's own conversion, the country's economic development, and/or its citizens' ideological advancement. Titles alone are sufficient to indicate the material at hand: Shaginian's *Hydrocentral,* Iakov Ilin's *The Great Conveyor,* Fedor Gladkov's *Energy,* Vasily Ilenkov's *The Driving Axle.* Given their overt political agenda, today they are usually placed in the family of strict propaganda or "agitlit" (a term, interestingly, that was often a pejorative at that time as well). Yet it would be wrong to reduce the whole of this drive to such generalizations. How individual writers responded to the call to participate in socialist construction took a variety of forms: from Shaginian's beatific description of personal salvation, to Kataev's impressionistic and colorful paean to technological revolution in *Time, Forward!* to Ivanov's tongue-in-cheek, *skaz* version of his labor-enlightening trip in *The Tales of Brigade-leader M. N. Sinitsyn as Told by Him in the Days of the First Five-Year Plan,* to Pilniak's *The Volga Flows to the Caspian Sea,* a reluctant attempt to graft dam building onto his earlier work *Mahogany,* a novella that had earlier earned him the title of traitor.

The *ocherk,* which flooded journals in 1930 and 1931, exhibited similar elasticity. An essayistic, on-the-spot report, it served to acquaint readers with the sights, sounds, and smells of change, and was favored for its immediacy and brevity. Though in generic terms the *ocherk* was nonfiction, since it was an account of a real-life event or location, the writer enjoyed wide latitude of expression and often borrowed fictional devices to render atmosphere. The effect was not unlike human interest documentaries that, through a proportional mix of scene, dialogue, and rote fact, seek to make the reader an invisible witness to the action at hand. Some *ocherki* approached a straightforward journalistic description (with photographs and so forth), whereas others made no exact record of "who, when, where" and thus denied the possibility of checking the referent's true status. What was important were not facts used to verify but facts used to dramatize people and places of the Soviet Union. This flexibility was reflected as well in the choice of subject matter. It could be of minimal or major importance and, notably, need not contain an ideological moral or lesson (in contradistinction to the assumption that all was slave to propaganda).[5] Indeed, the range of thematic and narrative options makes it difficult to pin down the distinguishing characteristic of the *ocherk* beyond the fact that, if so desired, it could deviate widely from documentary and use fictional apparatus. This potential seems to differentiate it from strict journalism and history, since it would not necessarily answer the questions that a reader would typically ask of the latter two. This freedom of representation and rendition, coupled with its short length and topicality, made the *ocherk* the ideal form for the thousands of workers and peasants who were hastily promoted to the rank of writer during the cultural revolution and, sometimes with the barest of training (and education), charged with the task of establishing a "proletarian hegemony" in literature.

Fiction, in short, could prove the "fact" of social progress, just as journalism could reach for the dramatic and emotional impact of fiction. Together, they served as sourcebooks for the period, and it was not uncommon (with the notable exception of Pilniak) for officials to cite both genres as documentary evidence for the achievements of the early 1930s. This did not mean, of course, that there was a direct call for the death of the novel (as we heard, for example, with LEF). The effort was not to turn fiction into fact or eliminate literature as a unique species but to effect a kind of hybrid, so that if a text appeared more fictional (like Kataev's *Time, Forward!*), it would still have an accurate base; if it took a more documentary line, it would still retain the flavor of a story well told. The *intended* result of much of this writing might be likened to the New Journalism of the 1960s and 1970s, as exemplified by writers such as Gay Talese, Truman Capote, and Norman Mailer, who presented historical events in a narrative form more typical of fiction though replete with and based on real life. Here the reader supposedly gained the legitimacy of fact with the appeal of literature, and the success of these writers, whether measured by sales or by their influence on later journalism, would be difficult to deny. Regarding the soviet attempt, however, few would be so charitable. Common opinion holds that its fact-fiction hybrids failed both as entertainment (being aesthetically barren and soporific) and as documentary (the facts presented were less than adequate and less than accurate). Given the 1933 conclusion of Robert de Saint Jean, a more scornful dirge has probably not been sounded: these "fountain-pen robots" produced nothing but "a monstrous literature of reportings interrupted by political hymns."[6]

For a good majority of the works published during the cultural revolution one might be inclined to agree with de Saint Jean. But more important is the impact of this writing and attendant proclamations on the course of interpretive norms. Put simply, what made literature valuable was its edifying, informational capacity. As Leopold Averbakh charged in "The Cultural Revolution and the Mission of Proletarian Literature," the immediate and most essential task facing writers was to help convert readers into a "new type of person," one whose "culturedness" would be defined not merely by the use, say, of "toothbrushes and handkerchiefs" but by their high ideological principles and commitment.[7] It should be kept in mind, as Averbakh made clear, that "proletarian" referred not to an author's socioeconomic class but to a text's perceived value in the ideological struggle. Hence every text could be evaluated as contributing to (or detracting from) this common goal. What knowledge it could give readers, how it could raise their consciousness, how they could use it to improve their minds and lives were the questions literature should answer, regardless of its generic branches. Crucial for the times, this sentiment crossed political camps. Though no ally of Averbakh, Anatoly Lunacharsky argued as well that all writing should be seen as functionally equivalent: "[T]he *ocherk*, story, novel and poem constitute different ways of giving the reader a clear picture of what is going on in the country, providing the appropriate evaluation of various aspects of reality, and allowing him to penetrate deeper into their meaning."[8] And a tidy circuit was formed when the published voice of mass readers echoed this mandate. In fact, the ability and willingness to interpret all texts, of whatever genre, according to the same referential standards were hailed as the distinguishing features of the new, class-conscious soviet reader.[9]

In sum, by this period we witness not only the textual manifestation but the official institution of referential maxims as the standard of value. As socialist realism later made evident, the specific nature of referential norms could change based on fluctuating needs. Yet, referentiality would henceforth be canonized as the cornerstone of evaluation. Readers from all levels of society would be expected to hold all modes of writing to the same yardstick: their capacity to transmit a coherent and accessible represented world.

ZOSHCHENKO'S CONTRIBUTION

In his own idiosyncratic way, Zoshchenko both joined and confounded the campaign to make literature an integral part of soviet readers' lives. The opportunities for writers to chronicle the New Age were by no means limited, what with the trumpeted victories of collectivization and industrialization. But Zoshchenko did not follow the path of his compatriots to the field or factory. Instead he went to the laboratory, a homemade one. From his first appearance as a writer, we know that he suffered from debilitating attacks of melancholy and depression that often alternated with sweeping bouts of arrogance and self-obsession. This infamous neurasthenia, the collective term under which he lumped such mood swings, became a constant, behind-the-scenes struggle hidden from his reading public until the ill-fated publication of the first half of *Before Sunrise* in 1943. Nonetheless, in earlier personal correspondence his health and own efforts to cure himself was a—and often *the*—major topic. "I'm an extremely sick person," he wrote Gorky in 1930, "suffering terribly from insomnia, depression and who the hell else knows what."[10] "Who the hell else knows what" is indeed a sizable affair, something of a blank check for illness that any hypochondriac would envy. Yet Zoshchenko took this license a step further and became his own doctor. A year later in a letter to Shaginian, he claimed victory by having discovered both the cause and the cure of his troubles. Mental exhaustion and overwork, he argued, destroy the body; they upset natural rhythms and shatter the nerves. The usual result is an early death, generally at mid-life. The answer, therefore, is simple enough: rest and careful "regulation of the organism" restore body and mind to harmony and hence guarantee long life. The technological metaphor is Zoshchenko's own. Indeed, while basking in the glory of his self-discovered cure, he cheerfully proclaimed that his body ran like "a machine," and he was its sole pilot and engineer: "It is in my power to control this mechanism." "So now when neurasthenia hits," he concluded, "I simply give a little twist to the nuts and bolts."[11]

It is perhaps inevitable that the hypochondriac's self-absorption can easily spill into an overbearing ego. His letters to Shaginian (who at that time was undergoing her own personal transformation but in a decidedly more orthodox way) display a burgeoning penchant for preaching and didacticism, underwritten by a sense of his own infallibility. Only in such a state of mind would he have had the effrontery to declare—while chiding Shaginian for her own failure to acknowledge the "truth"—that "*not one person* on this earth could have survived the condition I had been in."[12] Zoshchenko's home cure gave new meaning to Averbakh's call for writers to reform their readers. But it spoke to the energy and personal commitment with which he launched his next project, the one that was to cause more distress and confusion yet at the same time garner more praise than any of his preceding works—*Youth Restored*.

With the less-than-welcome response to *M. P. Siniagin*, his first attempt at a "documentary" (which, it should be remembered, was published the same year as Kirshon's speech), we might expect a different approach. The exclamation in 1931—"Who needs this book? Definitely not the advanced soviet reader"—could not have failed to impress upon Zoshchenko that his writing, for all its popularity, continued to beguile and frustrate critics.[13] The Kolenkorov cycle had made his narratives seem only more opaque, his meaning still impenetrable. Recognition in the 1930 *Encyclopedia of Literature* was grim: both he and his work were "petit bourgeois" and "philistine."[14] With *Youth Restored*, therefore, we find Zoshchenko for the first time laying the ground *before* publication as to what his intentions were. An article appearing in April 1933, under the auspicious title "The Writer at His Manuscript," described him at work on a "story about health, happiness in life, the thirst for life, and the struggle for prolonging it."[15] Emphasis was placed on Zoshchenko as a historian surrounded by piles of research and lists of famous people who had died in their prime, the mid- to late thirties. (Coincidentally Zoshchenko himself was just entering this age.) "Chance deaths do not occur," he declared here. Pushkin's death in a duel and Mayakovsky's suicide were, in a sense, foreseeable. After all, the former (the "cured" Zoshchenko now feels comfortable pointing the finger of blame) was a "terrible neurasthenic," whereas the latter drove himself to the grave, never knowing a moment's peace.

On the basis of this research, Zoshchenko planned to offer readers something of a self-help guide, a work that would direct their attention to the power of the mind in alleviating illness and preventing the debilitating effects of aging. In the foreground would be the "message," which the artistic medium would bring to life and thus make more palatable. To achieve such a goal he had designed a most unusual work. Instead of integrating fiction and fact like many of his contemporaries, he would keep the two separate. The primary narrative, a fictional story about a soviet citizen struggling for happiness in life, was to be supported by historical commentary and observation.

On the surface it all seemed quite simple. Clarity and credibility were to be his guiding points. After all, these were two features that critics had found glaringly absent in his previous work and thus would presumably help Zoshchenko free himself from the barrage of negative criticism in the 1920s. Indeed, by the turn of the decade his reputation had finally begun to climb. The proletarian writers Chumandrin and Libedinsky had already claimed—though with qualification—Zoshchenko as one of their own. Likewise, Evgeniia Zhurbina's preface to his six-volume collected works, which had begun to appear in 1929, finally brought to critical awareness the need for separating Zoshchenko from his narrators and characters. (Of course, Vinogradov and the formalists had pointed this out before but were not given credit.) Nevertheless, the 1930 charge "which flag is Zoshchenko fighting under" had lost none of its poignancy or threat, especially in this most heady of times. Many fellow travelers (and the critics who had supported them) had been hounded out of print; others, conversely, had been co-opted by the establishment. The stakes were high when Zoshchenko's most problematic text appeared. For no matter what he claimed, no matter what his personal conviction, his response to the times was decidedly unorthodox, in terms of both subject matter and form. He did not choose the route of realistic, fact-based fiction or that of documentary with a fictional feel. He bonded strict fiction to, in his eyes, straight fact. Yet, as critics were to make painfully aware, lucidity and intelligibility seemed to have ended with his declaration of intent.

Curiously, the first lines of *Youth Restored* suggest that little had truly changed in Zoshchenko's style. It begins in his trademark comic manner with a sixteen-chapter, prefatory justification for addressing scientific matters in a literary work. From the narrator's point of view, the problems of aging and illness have been neglected in literature. He will therefore attempt to rectify this problem by relaying a "true" story of an acquaintance who has restored youthful vitality to his life and conquered the despair that often accompanies the onset of middle age. Referring to himself as "author," the narrator then presents his experience in this matter:

> Of course the author is no doctor, and his knowledge in this field is limited. All the same, since his childhood years he's had a deep and even extraordinary interest in medicine—even at one time treating his less valued relatives with various chemical remedies from around the house: iodine, tar, glycerine, grass that dogs chew when they're sick, and even psychological coercion. Such treatment, needless to say, sometimes turned out okay and didn't always end with the permanent departure of one or another of the wide-eyed relatives. (10–11)[16]

With these credentials on the table, he proceeds to discuss why people in their thirties lose the lust for life, waste away, or go insane and seek death. No doubt this weakness stems from some spirit of the times, and he offers various historical cases, anecdotes, and even legends to prove his point. Recognizing that the unconventionality of his approach might trouble readers, he hastens to add that this work should be considered a simple documentary on par with such educational films as "How Does a Human Being Differ from a Beaver?" "Why Does It Rain?" and "How Silk Stockings Are Made."

Preliminaries aside, the story proper begins in the seventeenth chapter. Volosatov, the protagonist, is an astronomer in his early fifties troubled by a melancholic disposition and skeptical of soviet ideals. Through exercise he reclaims some of the vigor of his youth and, at the instigation of the "villain" Kashkin, abandons his wife for an affair with a neighbor's "floozy" daughter. However, such youthful escapades are crushed when Volosatov finds his lover in the arms of another man. He suffers a heart attack and returns to his forgiving wife. In the end he is described as on a new path to recovery but still casting an occasional eye to his neighbor's apartment. Significantly, his improving health reflects and contributes to newfound optimism regarding soviet society.

If *Youth Restored* had ended with this story, then it would have been a successor (albeit a strange one) to the theme of an intellectual's reconciliation with the state, a topic that had received its most celebrated treatment a year before in Leonid Leonov's novel *Skutarevsky*, where an egocentric professor ultimately recognizes the need for a collective effort in all endeavors. But Zoshchenko was not so accommodating. His desire to provide factual support for his fiction got the better of him, leading him to append one hundred (!) pages of commentaries to the primary narrative.

Though the subject addressed is the same—how we should take control of our health—the language in the commentaries is qualitatively distinct. Absent are the comic absurdities, ironic asides, and usual gang of solecisms. In a matter-of-fact, direct tone, this Zoshchenko describes the origin of illness and the conclusions he has drawn from both research and personal observation. He mentions critics (such as Polonsky) and doctors with whom he has discussed this work and even cites the correspondence of actual readers to him. In a special move, he reserves the last commentary to resolve any confusion. Here he declares that all masks are "off" and delivers an accurate, up-to-date biography of himself. Important qualifications are made as well regarding the peculiar character of his treatise. It was all done to reach the "mass reader," and herein lies the difficulty of his work: manipulating syntax, language, and composition "so that it could be understood by everybody."

In tandem with Zoshchenko's prepublication comments, the weight of his biomedical ruminations falls on those individuals who have died at or before the forty-year threshold. In this unfortunate yet distinguished company we find, among others, Mozart, Schubert, Mendelssohn, van Gogh, Poe, Pushkin, Gogol, Dobroliubov, Byron, Lermontov, Mayakovsky, Griboedov, Esenin, London, and Blok. What can explain their premature passing, whether by accident, illness, or suicide? Zoshchenko cautions us that it is a fairly simple matter. Overwork and stress are the two demons that rob our bodies of vital energy and thereby directly cause or precipitate *all* kinds of death. The caprice of fate plays no role; everything, literally, is in our minds. We succumb to disease, kill ourselves, or intentionally place ourselves in dangerous situations (such as duels) only when the mind is exhausted and reason lost, and a kind of psychosomatic death wish takes hold. The effects not only are personal but can be global as well. What was the true reason for Napoleon's defeat in Spain? Bad nerves and overexertion. (Though in actuality the emperor did live to his fifties, Zoshchenko quickly notes that after "age thirty-nine Napoleon isn't really alive.")

With the cause of death clear, so is the cure. Rest and moderation keep rationality in charge and passions in check. The body should be tuned as one does a machine, letting it cool down after work. This lowers blood pressure and allows bodily fluids, primarily secretions of the endocrine glands, to achieve the proper balance. After all, we learn, the brain is easy to injure. As a relative newcomer to the organism, it lacks the fortitude that the stomach, heart, and lungs possess after having dwelled in our bodies for millions of years. Anything in the extreme, whether professional, creative, or even sexual in nature, puts it at risk. The above victims failed to respect the fragility of the harmony that keeps humans fit and alive. If their mental conditions had been sufficiently stable, if their bodies had not been subject to undue pressures, if, in sum, everything had been "in tune," then they should have defeated death at every turn.

Sometimes pedantic in the commentaries, Zoshchenko holds in low esteem historians and doctors who have failed to ascertain the "real truth" behind individuals' early demises. The case of Gogol, who died at age forty-two, is particularly distressing to him. Today, Zoshchenko informs us, we know that his neuroses most likely could have been cured by "careful psychoanalytical treatment and reeducation," though it would have required "extensive repairs to his entire organism." He definitely had "something wrong in the regulator that governs bodily rhythm and tempo," but close monitoring and proper intercession would have offset the destructive mood swings that led to his tortured, suicidal end. (That this was to describe Zoshchenko's own death remains the most stunning twist.) Of course, Gogol was not entirely blameless. "Completely ignorant" of himself, he failed to understand the "particulars of his not too healthy mind," and committed a "grave mistake," for example, when he traveled through Europe in his thirties seeking, of all things, a youth serum.

Equally comfortable passing out advice and accusations, Zoshchenko also turns his attention to his own readers. Part way through the commentaries, he includes two letters from readers complaining of depression. This gives him the opportunity to put in practice what he preaches and, at the same time, affirm the validity of his theories (a maneuver foreshadowing how the "real" Zoshchenko, outside the text, would publicly defend *Youth Restored* after its publication). His diagnoses are detailed and, so it seems, accurate. One reader writes back thanking Zoshchenko for his aid and notes that the doctors confirmed his analysis. Later, in the penultimate commentary, he mentions other readers who have written to him after the appearance of the first part of *Youth Restored*. An objection raised regarding his conclusions on Pushkin is given a curt but unyielding answer: "To be frank, I didn't think that there was anything to prove here. It all seemed to me that everything was quite clear."

Not content with just matters of health, Zoshchenko also takes the opportunity (and nine pages) to acquaint us with some of his other interests, primarily astronomy. He introduces us to the recent work of Sir James Jeans, *The Universe Around Us*, which he feels "reads like a fascinating novel." Providing substantial quotes so that we may see this for ourselves, he draws our attention to interesting points about the universe, such as the distances between stars, the planets' temperatures (where we learn that the closer a planet is to the sun, the hotter it is), the possibility of life on Mars, what future lies in store for our planet billions of years from now, and how it will meet its end.

CRITICISM AND COMMENDATION

Given Zoshchenko's complex approach to what he called a simple problem, it would have been surprising if *Youth Restored* had not met with confusion. However, no one could have foreseen the volume of response. In the short period from February to August of 1934 (after which the press was consumed with the First Writers' Congress), over eighteen separate articles, reviews, and reports (including two cartoons) appeared. But what was more striking than sheer numbers was the fact of who responded. Attention to Zoshchenko's new work quickly spilled beyond the literary community; doctors and scientists, including the former Commissar of Health, the ultra-orthodox Nikolai Semashko, saw fit to register their opinions. And no less than Ivan Pavlov, the distinguished physiologist, invited Zoshchenko to attend his weekly forums. Moreover, response was not just confined to the relative quiet of journals; public debates were devoted to *Youth Restored*, with Zoshchenko himself a frequent guest. With lecture halls packed, the audience crammed on the steps and windowsills, as one contemporary report tells us, he would personally be challenged, criticized, and praised by the scientific and literary world.[17] No other work gained such widespread fame and notoriety at this time—something Zoshchenko was no doubt to regret. As he wrote in April of that year, the speaking engagements, the flood of letters, and the number of people literally knocking at his door gave him no rest—an unfortunate twist of fate given that this very work pleads the importance of tranquility and peace of mind.[18]

Youth Restored was destined to engage so many different kinds of readers since its content and form united three key cultural issues. Thematically, as noted, it addressed the enduring question of what role intellectuals with a prerevolutionary (and thus suspect) education were to have in society. Were they to remain employed until genuine, soviet-educated specialists could take their place? What of their loyalty and unconscionable "bourgeois" behavior? Biologically, the idea of youth echoed the international euphoria following a technological revolution that promised a future of man-made paradise, with poverty, hunger, disease, and even age conquered. On soviet soil, belief in eternal youth became an explicitly patriotic metaphor, with marxism as its herald. From Mayakovsky's 1927 paean in "Everything's Great,"

A hundred years
         no aging
we
  will grow.
Year after year
         our joy
will show.
Hail,
     hammer
          and verse,
the land of youth.

to Olesha's declaration in 1934 at the Writers' Congress that under the graces of the Soviet Union his "youth had returned," the socialist future was one of long life and health.[19] Shaginian, in the midst of her social awakening while writing *Hydrocentral*, even felt that time had reversed itself. Returning to the "people," excising the vestiges of a feudalistic tradition through social and industrial transformation meant that one had conquered the past: "[I]t was a path not from youth to old age, but from old age to youth."[20] Finally, in generic terms *Youth Restored* would seem a spirited, if problematic, addition to the drive to erase functional distinctions in writing. As was proclaimed in 1930 on the pages of *Literaturnaia gazeta* (which presaged Zoshchenko's own declaration in the final commentary), a committed writer could not afford the luxury of specialization. The new soviet reader, a person of limited education yet great need, identified texts only in one way, their applicability:

> The commonly accepted division of prose into belles lettres and documentary is, for the marginally literate, inadmissible. Instead, every book intended for these readers should have a narrative quality that illustrates in a figurative way something practical to "use in life." Given this fact, documentary literature should, to a significant degree, be offered to the marginally literate reader in an artistic form.[21]

If there was something in *Youth Restored* to pique the interest of any critic, scientist, or "general" reader, then it stood an equal chance of disappointing just as many. The one obvious point that emerged from reviews and debates was that there was no consensus as to its meaning, value, or significance for contemporary literature. Was Volosatov to be welcomed as a reformed individual or rejected for offering a false path to salvation? Proponents of the former saw his reconciliation as a sign of Zoshchenko's own "rebirth," a turn from the despair and negativity that marked his earlier writing to a "life-affirming and joyful optimism." For the first time soviet readers could see in his work "the real sun, real emotion and real people."[22] Others were less favorable, arguing that even if Zoshchenko was trying to create a "positive hero," he was unsuccessful.[23] This would then be proof that he still "flounders in the cracks of his own moldy, noisome, louse-ridden world, into which the cheerful, luxuriant rays of socialist construction cannot penetrate."[24] For that matter, it was observed, could readers even be sure that Volosatov had truly regained his youth, or was the evidence deliberately vague? Still others countered that perhaps this failure was intentional. What if Volosatov was not a character to emulate but an obvious philistine who served as Zoshchenko's target? Would he not then be back on the solid ground of traditional satire?[25]

Decidedly more concern was voiced over the commentaries. Semashko took the claims made in them as a direct affront to contemporary science. Calling Zoshchenko "mechanistic" and "vulgar," he charged the writer with neglecting the influence of the social environment in determining one's health and longevity.[26] Coming from a decorated "old Bolshevik" who was currently chief editor of the *Great Medical Encyclopedia,* Semashko's opinion set the tone for other sociomedical objections. How dare Zoshchenko defame the likes of Belinsky and Pushkin, another fulminated, by seeing nothing in their tragic ends but neurasthenia? What of their heroism in the class struggle? Zoshchenko was "nihilistically naive to the highest degree." And why, for that matter, talk about aging when all knew that "the proletarian revolution had bestowed a new youth on the world"?[27] Alternately, at one public forum a Professor Lavrentev from, significantly, the All-Union Institute of Experimental Medicine heartily welcomed Zoshchenko's decision to write a scientific-medical work. It showed courage that, as a "layman," he undertook to address a subject in obvious demand.[28] Others commended Zoshchenko for bringing attention to the need for taking charge of one's life and keeping "expenditures of energy" within rational bounds.[29] Many, all the same, disagreed. Zoshchenko was clearly "out of his league," and the commentaries were "chaotic," nothing but a potpourri of simplistic, irrelevant items from history and science, which had no relation to one another or the story at hand.[30] Others were concerned that readers would misinterpret the commentaries,[31] or, more ominously, that the book might cause those who accepted it as established fact to stop going to doctors.[32] No, others countered, anyone who took the commentaries seriously had fallen victim to Zoshchenko's game. They were deliberately written in a simplistic manner, as if from the mind of an ignoramus, because they were meant to represent "philistine" thought. If Kashkin and the whole bag of fools and floozies from the story were to think about the subject of aging, these were the conclusions that *they* would draw.[33]

If there was serious disagreement as to what the parts of *Youth Restored* meant, what the whole represented was equally unclear. For all who proclaimed *Youth Restored* a worthy experiment in genre, one that synthesized fiction and documentary, a similar number saw it as an utter failure. Given efforts to "close ranks between science and literature," Boris Begak argued that one at first might be inclined to welcome Zoshchenko's unusual approach. "The whole point of the 'scientific-artistic' genre is that a convincing artistic format would emerge out of the scientific problem itself." However, he continued, in *Youth Restored*, confusion, not complementarity, reigned. In fact, the very presence of the commentaries proved that the project was flawed. If, in effect, Zoshchenko had done the job right in the first half, there would have been no need for an accompanying explanation; a successful fiction would not have required any additional baggage.[34] The result, another agreed, made Zoshchenko appear a "bungling encyclopedist."[35] As frustration spread, many cast doubt on Zoshchenko's intentions. What was he trying to do? Where was he "in the text"? Notably, such questions resurfaced in the West, as in Domar's apt conclusion, "he went into his work for edification and came out with mischief."[36] Today we still wrestle with these same issues. Though there is a final commentary, one ostensibly without a mask, does it really clarify all that precedes? Is Zoshchenko ironic, serious, or, for that matter, sane? A vulgar psychologist or visionary? Is it all a joke or a confession? Can it be an authentic sign of his reformation or do we catch the scent of Sinebriukhov peering through the cracks? In the end must we join company with Sats, who throws up his hands and says, "I just have to admit that I have no idea what this book is"?[37]

READING THE TEXT

In all fairness, it is not difficult to sympathize with Sats's exasperation. On the surface, Zoshchenko's use of footnoted commentaries would seem a logical move, an acknowledgment that his writing still constituted an interpretive puzzle. By convention, commentaries would fulfill an explicating role and, with pretensions to single-voiced authority, could be seen as a kind of cipher to the fiction. Keeping with the spirit of the times, they would surely present readers with sufficient guidelines to translate *Youth Restored* from its fictional postulates to real-life import. This addition would, for the first time, provide Zoshchenko the opportunity to answer *in the text* the question that had plagued so many of his contemporary critics: What do his works mean?

Yet what may have started as a reach for clarity, as an anticipatory hedge against objection, quickly became the most obfuscating point. No matter what Zoshchenko's declared intentions, *Youth Restored* is decidedly not the straightforward, easily digestible work that he envisioned. Bloated to one-half of the text, the commentaries far exceed any auxiliary capacity. They gain a narrative life of their own, and their size is subject to gross exploitation. The first five commentaries occur within just four sentences, and three of them in one sentence alone. Together, they inject over twenty pages of commentary into the space of four sentences in the primary narrative. The reader's experience of the text is maximally disrupted as the narrative's linear progression is continually turned on end by the vertical axis of commentary.

More important, however, is the qualitative tension this structure generates. The physical action of turning pages to access commentaries at the back becomes the least of our problems after we realize, which should not take too long, that the commentaries do not function in a traditional footnote sense. In reading the primary narrative, we get something of the familiar Zoshchenko, a Kolenkorovian performance in which, for example, the narrator declares that to save paper he will not speak of Volosatov's relatives but then expends half a page on the family cat. But upon reading the commentaries we get something contradictory, almost retrograde. They are devoid of the usual irony and, so it seems, comic exaggeration (especially if we come armed, unlike most of his contemporaries, with Zoshchenko's true feelings on this subject). This alone introduces a discordant tone since one would expect commentaries to match their parent text whether ironic-ironic or serious-

serious. Disturbingly, however, they seem to authenticate and legitimize the very propositions that are debunked or serve comic ends in the primary narrative. The beliefs of Kashkin, the resident idiot, curiously presage (or repeat) what can be found in the commentaries: the body, as determined by a person's mental state, governs susceptibility to illness.

> "Health," Kashkin said, "is not something you get for nothing. If somebody's got diseases all over, then he's just weak and can't deal with life." (Chapter 28, 68–69)
>
> Even death from an epidemic disease does not prove . . . the existence of chance. A normal, healthy organism would be able to offer sufficient resistance so as to conquer any illness.
> By this the author wants to say that chance deaths would seem not to occur. (Commentary 2, 98)

The coincidence between character and authorial speech puts us in an awkward position. That it is fiction predisposes us to reject Kashkin's words as part and parcel of the "philistine line."[38] Conversely, the commentaries, while essentially arguing the same point, seek authoritative ground. Should not health then be our primary concern? The commentaries seem to suggest yes. The answer is more ambivalent if we return to the fiction. In his introductory remarks, the narrator declares that "the single subject, which everyone thinks about, which is as familiar, close and important to us as water, food and the sun, is our life, our youth, our vigor and our ability to manage these valuable gifts" (17). But when we are introduced to characters whose thoughts are occupied by this very subject, the tenor fluctuates dramatically. Volosatov's neurasthenia is encoded in relatively neutral terms; it is the plot's motivating center and is designed to elicit (at least temporarily) compassion.[39] Yet with his other neighbor, Karetnikov, who believes that fleabites might be the cause of his own illnesses, preoccupation with one's health leads to the narrator's condemnation: "[Karetnikov was] completely impotent, a neurasthenic and psychopath who thought only about his diseases and sicknesses" (43).

To muddle the picture further, both the narrative and commentaries employ similar language and metaphors, usually of a machine-mechanistic nature. We remember Gogol's problem with his "regulator" and the ill effect it had on his "bodily rhythms," as described in the second commentary. In the narrative the same terminology infiltrates a description of those "scientists and professors" who have succeeded in avoiding the debilitating effects of aging. "[They] have figured something out, have perhaps discovered a secret, or maybe not a secret, but some kind of appropriate, perhaps *the* essential pattern of behavior and following it, have lived carefree, regulating their lives and organisms like, say, a worker or turner regulates his lathe" (15). Both have recourse as well to the same kinds of evidence, legends, and anecdotes, to corroborate theories regarding health. The discussion of health, alcohol, and sex in the narrative is peculiarly corroborated by its appended commentary (ellipses in the original):

> The author suspects that the health, or in any case, the nervous condition of all people of all categories and countries, of all classes and groups, has significantly depreciated over the last couple of centuries.
> The truth is that when you read those ancient books you sometimes can't help being surprised and awestruck when they describe the escapades of heroes coming from all sorts of classes and professions.
> They sure were rare specimens of health.
> They sure were strong and solid as rocks.
> They sure were the kinds of pigs and drunks like we've never seen.
> You always read something like: "He felt a great thirst but came round after polishing off two bottles of Anjou red. Hopped on his horse and then took off in a cloud of dust after the enemy . . ."
> Fine. Now say you put two bottles of Anjou in front of our guy, the one living in 1933. After that not only won't he be sitting on any horse but, money down, won't even be able to say m-a-m-a. (Chapter 10, 17–18)

> One could also cite another example, true, a bookish one, about changes in health.
> There exists the opinion that when the nervous condition deteriorates, the sexual instinct nevertheless does not diminish. However, it seems that that's not the case.
> We read in ancient books about such furious passion and the torture of unrequited love that is beyond anything we can imagine.
> We accept it as a case of literary exaggeration, like something exotic, without even suspecting that that's how it really was. In our modern books there's not anything even remotely similar. For us love and desire are looked on most of the time as something to be gratified if not in one place then in another. I can't even think of a single contemporary work that treats with the extreme suffering of someone in love.
> However, Apuleius for example compares a lover's suffering with, at the very least, the plague.
> Arab fairy tales talk of the physical changes an unrequited lover undergoes.
> "His face changed color and his body grew thin. He stopped eating, drinking and sleeping and looked just like a sick person who's been ill 20 years." (Commentary 7, 130–31)

An obviously valuable source, the same unidentified "fairy tales" also confirm the unusual consumption of alcohol in the past:

> By the way, something else concerning wine. There's one place in Arabic fairy tales about a man who was once a guest:
> "After drinking three riatls of wine, he was flushed with happiness and joy."
> Three riatls is about equivalent to 1½ liters, a portion not exactly normal for people with our health.

Fiction as Documentary

> In truth there's really no need to prove that nerves have taken a change for the worse in the past few centuries. It's patently clear. Only have to know how Seneca's death has been reported and the circumstances surrounding it. (Commentary 7, 128)

We are then treated to a lengthy discussion of Seneca's courage while facing a forced suicide: the coolness he evinced with wrists slashed is an upstanding illustration of how nerves were better "back then." Of course Zoshchenko omits the more contemporary—and famous—example of strength during death—that of Rasputin, who succumbed in 1916 only after a poisoning-shooting-drowning triple punch. Such a selective memory reflects Zoshchenko's favorite technique of substantiating arguments in the commentaries: make a generalization (in the past people were stronger), home in on a particular example (Seneca), then beef it up with literary allusions (the ubiquitous "Arabic fairy tales"). In and of itself the methodology is highly suspect since essentially any assertion can be validated by such so-called evidence. In *Youth Restored* it is even more problematic for an additional reason. The ironic preface, as we see above, follows the same procedure. What serves as a point of humor in the fiction "above" is, coversely, presumed to function as a factor of authenticity in the commentaries "below."

Such incongruity puts in relief why the text itself has generated such dissension. All voices, whether of narrator or author, claim equal authority with regard to the same subject matter, employ similar approaches, purport to fulfill the same function, and offer similar conclusions. Yet at the same time, they cannot logically be accepted as equivalent expressions. It should be kept in mind that the tension involved is not one of fiction versus fact. As noted, documentary inclusions in fiction were something to be expected at this time. The crucial difference comes in the fact that in the *ocherk* or production novel the two orientations did not operate at cross-purposes. This was precisely where Zoshchenko veered sharply from contemporary expectations. At a public debate, V. Raltsevich let it be known how he viewed this deviation:

> Contradiction runs through Zoshchenko's entire work—its genre, plot, language, the author's attitude to science, literature and the reader. Its ideas are fraught with ambiguity. In *Youth Restored* everything's split in two, even the author. It's not Zoshchenko but his double. Zoshchenko's somewhere outside the author of *Youth Restored*. It's a parody of himself. . . . It's unclear what his position is because you can't tell where he agrees with the author-narrator and where he doesn't.[40]

We may not agree with Raltsevich's censure, but his observations do point to the central dilemma that has continued to plague readers of *Youth Restored*: Zoshchenko wreaks havoc with the traditional contract between author and reader. Instead of one disposition—"this is generally ironic so read it with amusement and a sufficient grain of salt," *or* "though parts of the text are fictional and touched up for narrative effect, overall it is a serious treatment of a serious problem"—varying and generally incompatible contracts seem to be in force at different times. If just one dominated, even the "ironic" one, readers would not be so puzzled. Contemporary responses show that interpretive norms, even at this time, were flexible enough to accommodate either a straightforward or a tongue-in-cheek approach. The former would be evaluated in terms of its accessibility and accuracy (on a variety of ideological and medical grounds), the latter in terms of its success in satirizing the "philistine" who would take all this seriously. But both together? This is the semantic knot.

The sheer number and size of the commentaries ensure that the reader is tossed back and forth between contracts. The continual shifting of semantic gears means that the reader is not merely turning pages but is engaging and disengaging conflicting interpretive paradigms. Consequently, within the same text and often in the same *sentence* the reader is asked to perform a series of complex and contradictory maneuvers. This condition alone makes problematic the common assumption that the primary narrative and commentaries represent autonomous domains that can be treated separately. Seepage and mutual contamination of the two would be a more accurate description. This is apparent, no less, in what should arguably be the most authoritative context: the final commentary, where the author states he has taken off his mask and is speaking directly as "Mikhail Zoshchenko." After the declaration of intent (cited above) and a factual account of the writer's biography, "Zoshchenko" then slips back into the voice of the primary narrative and delivers the last lines of the text, speaking of Kashkin and other characters as if they existed outside the fiction:

> I'm finishing these last pages in Sestroretsk the 9th of August, 1933.
> I'm sitting on a bed by the window. The sun is shining in. Dark clouds swim by. A dog is barking. A child shouts as a soccer ball flies up in the air. An attractive woman in a colorful robe goes to take a swim.
> Kashkin is hurrying after her with his eyes on her luxuriant shoulders.
> He brandishes a stick while whistling a triumphant march.
> A gate screeches and a spindly *devchurka,* as my friend Olesha says, comes to visit my son.
> The familiar, bucolic nature of these eternal scenes for some reason is a comfort and makes me smile.
> I don't want to think any more and with that I cut short my story. (Commentary 18, 195)

By raising (lowering?) the author "Zoshchenko" and Kashkin to the same frame of reference, this final voice compromises the illusion (and authority) of speaking as oneself without irony. Incongruently, the narrative stance that the post-mask Zoshchenko attempts to exorcise reappears in the exorcism itself.

FIXING THE PROBLEM

As Raltsevich made clear, there is usually a limit as to how many twists and turns a given reader will perform. In the next edition of *Youth Restored* Zoshchenko included a disclaimer suggesting that for "the ease of reading," one should complete the novella first without interruption and only then access the commentaries. But this editorial addition hardly clarified the text or abated controversy. Why *Youth Restored* is not an easy work to understand has little to do with format. Rather, the heart of the problem is a clash of voices. To return to Bakhtin, we have a perplexing boggle of discourses: double-voiced parodic (as with the introductory prefaces and much of the story proper), double-voiced stylistic (the simplified languages, colloquial forms, and syntax of the commentaries presumed to match linguistic competency of the "common reader"), and single-voiced, direct authorial pronouncements. What form this melange takes is, for interpretive purposes, more or less irrelevant; footnotes only add some structural consistency to a preexisting discursive condition.

In fact, far from correcting the matter, Zoshchenko only exacerbated it with his second venture into a documentary-fiction hybrid, *The Blue Book*, which began to appear in 1934 while readers were still wrestling with *Youth Restored*. Here historical observations, anecdotes, and fictional stories (some being republications, with modification, of Zoshchenko's work of the 1920s) combined to map four governing principles of human behavior: money, love, treachery, and misfortune. Once again, as with prepublication claims made for *Youth Restored*, the project seemed straightforward. Stories would serve to illustrate and explicate factual data. There were, however, two notable changes: in *The Blue Book* no commentaries would confuse readers, and instead of waiting for the final lines to offer what he considered its interpretive key, Zoshchenko would step in at the very beginning.

The dedication takes the form of a personal letter to Gorky, the acclaimed founding father of socialist realism. Crediting him with personally inspiring *The Blue Book* (as well as the editorial decision on the commentaries in *Youth Restored*), Zoshchenko thus envelopes his composition with, for that time, the preeminent voice of cultural authority. Moreover, here Zoshchenko introduces the semantic principle by which to link the text's disparate genres. History, he claims, has provided the means to join the stories into a coherent "whole." The implication is that all interpolated narratives will work in tandem under one referential umbrella.[41]

The Politics of Reception

No doubt to the relief of many readers, a sizable portion of *The Blue Book* does just that, aligning stories with discussions of history that are mutually supportive and ideologically sound. The most prominent place where this occurs is the final chapter, "Amazing Events," which contrasts the four preceding sins with accounts of great achievements by soviets or other revolutionaries. Often mirroring the triumphant tone of official histories, Zoshchenko unceasingly accents the positive:

> A just and honorable cause combined with a heroic struggle and unbelievable courage—this is what brought about social revolution.
> It closed the past and brought forth the present age. We have told you about this past in our journey through history. Regarding the present, it is before your very eyes, and all of you can see what this means. Life has finally passed from the hands of factory owners, bankers and merchants, and from the hands of landowners into those of the people who work. And that is one of the most amazing events and changes time has ever known. (334)[42]

In order to aid the reader's assimilation of fiction and nonfiction, he underscores the thematic relevance between his stories and the historical component:[43]

> In any walk of life history knows of great actions of valor that are cause for joy and celebration.
> And we now invite your attention to several stories of such great events. I trust you will acknowledge these actions and understand that they also play a role in the creation of a new life and new people and that all of this is very commendable and worthy of respect too. (325)

Clarity is enhanced by the bulleted segments that make up the first half of each of the preceding chapters. Though these are often painfully dry, as with the litany of misfortune that has befallen famous writers, Zoshchenko shows that he can present the "facts" without ironic tampering:

- The famous historian Polybius was sold into slavery and stolen from his country. He perished from poverty and deprivation.
- Defoe, the author of *Robinson Crusoe,* was sentenced to prison in 1703 for a satiric article. He spent time in the stocks where passersby were obligated to spit at him. Defoe was then forty-two years old.[44]
- Cervantes, the author of *Don Quixote,* was captured by pirates and sold into slavery in Algiers. There his left hand was cut off. His relatives ransomed him. The last years of his life he worked around the country as a tax collector. He died in prison in 1616. (243)

It is a long trip, however, to Zoshchenko's single-voiced bullets. Immediately after the dedication to Gorky, he retreats into ludicrous banter over the work's title. "Blue," he reveals, has been chosen because most of the others were "already taken." Besides it, only gray, pink, green, and violet remained, and it simply would have been "strange and insulting to title our book with any of these dull and insignificant colors." A few pages later the

Fiction as Documentary

first historical exegesis treats us, of all things, to how an extraterrestrial might react to life on earth. In a similar vein, the favored topic of economics is given its due through the cartoon description of a capitalist and his mistress:

> Suddenly out of the car, head bent—just imagine—there pops this doll, a real looker, beautiful dame, sweet as any fantasy a guy can cook up. In one hand she's got this tiny little dog, a black fox terrier that's shaking around; in the other a bag of fruit—you know, whatever, peaches, pineapples and pears.
> So she jumps out of the car, letting on as if she's all helpless: "Oh, I'm going to fall!" or "Oh, Alexis, well where are you!"
> And then right after her, grunting, spitting, nonstop nose honking, out crawls Alexis with his game leg. Now here's a dirty old sack, whopper of a face. Nose all bent, cheekbone missing, pus coming out of his eye. He's got the clothes, real fashion. But anyone can see that it's hopeless. Only make him more ugly. (15–16)

The struggle to transmit all potential negatives—since these two are the resident villains—collapses in upon itself, and rather than pointing to Zoshchenko's newfound voice, this passage returns us to the erratic stories of the 1920s. Equally convoluted, with its redundancy-into-absurdity quotient, is the description of Hellenic rivalries:

> All in all, it was in the ancient times when the Dorians were up and at it. They were fighting with these Athenians. But Dorians, they're kinda like Greeks too. And the Athenians—Greeks again. Nothing, though, really to say about those Athenians. Especially since they were Greeks plain as day. Everyone knows that. Athens and all the rest. But still these Greeks could really wage war. In the ancient times these kinds of spats happened. It's a fact that they had this long war. Sparta and them. They really had it out. Who the hell knows what was going on. (229)

And the reported dialogue of Nero as he dreams of a trick ceiling to crush his mother borders on Sinebriukhovian extremes:

> Just imagine the conversation they had when the order was placed.
> "Pray, do not worry," said the contractor. "The ceiling, we'll make it a beaut! Ho-ho, you've really come up with a good one, your majesty!"
> "Just make sure you don't stuff it with hay," Nero said. "Make sure you put some weight in it. Something light like hay'll do her no good. You know the kinda mama I've got."
> "How could we not, your majesty? A typical old bag. But what's this about hay? Ho-ho, that's really a good one, your majesty. I guarantee that a nice little rock gets set right up there over the noggin of your venerable old mommy."
> "Okay, whatever," Nero said, "only so that—presto!—no more mommy."
> "Pray, do not be afraid. You may consider your mama no longer with us. One of these days soon she won't even have time to wake up when—thunk!—the ceiling'll be right on her. All and all, be like an accident, you know, an earthquake or something. No one's to blame and mommy, well, she won't be

squawking any more. Ho-ho, you've really come up with a good one, your majesty. A most natural cure-all, I must say, for the common mommy." (167)

With the exception of the last chapter and its "amazing stories," narratives in *The Blue Book* run back and forth between these poles. Just as *Youth Restored* circles around scientific treatise and sheer buffoonery, here history alternates with antihistory. Unsurprisingly, this pendulation guaranteed *The Blue Book* a fate similar to that of its predecessor: a split reception. In a series of articles and, again, at another public debate, we hear praise for Zoshchenko's innovativeness and, with critical attention on the more ideologically sound parts, learn that *The Blue Book* confirmed that Zoshchenko had overcome his earlier equivocation. In exemplary words, A. Dymshchits extended a warm welcome to Zoshchenko's newfound sense of purpose:

> The author of *The Blue Book* is already not the one who lacked a broad social vision. . . . This new work shows that Zoshchenko is an artist who clearly believes in the historical demise and defeat of philistinism. Just as before, he goes on the offensive, but this time he is not alone. His struggle with the petty vulgarian does not suffer from weak punches or ironic pessimism; many pages of his new book are filled with strength and optimism.[45]

Just as often, though, complexity bred contempt. The appearance of his "typically *skaz*" voice was construed as a trivialization of seminal historical events and personages. Writing about the Revolution in this manner only served the purposes of those who wished to discredit the Soviet Union. Ominously, A. Gurshtein sounded this alarm on the pages of *Pravda*: "No matter what he writes about—be it suffering, persecution, murder or poverty—Zoshchenko (his narrator?) cannot let it go by without a smirk on the side. What is so funny here? For some reason, Zoshchenko thinks laughter is appropriate."[46]

With the parenthetical aside—"narrator?"—Gurshtein raised an essential question regarding interpretive impediments in *The Blue Book*: the impossibility of distinguishing autonomous speech domains and, hence, the inability to demarcate Zoshchenko's true presence in the text. Here the pronominal potential of *skaz*, as described earlier by Vinogradov, again comes into full play. Any voice, one conforming to or confounding narrative standards, can appear as "author"; yet each claims the same referential domain and seeks to perform the same task: presenting a legitimate analysis of human behavior. For Gurshtein, however, referential authority was directly dependent on narrative clarity. Therefore, whether or not the "real" Zoshchenko could be found in the absurdist parts or the serious ones was for him irrelevant. Any confusion of voice boundary and hierarchy (especially of this quantitative and qualitative degree) was sufficient reason to reject the text: "Throughout his [narrator's] speech, Zoshchenko has sprinkled authorial irony. Passed through several stylistic prisms, it comes to us at some remove, often tripled and quadrupled. In order to track down the writer's true beliefs in all these layers, the reader has to expend much effort."[47]

THRESHOLD TEXTS

As might be expected, Zoshchenko claimed not to understand why his works met with such clamor. In "The Principal Questions of Our Profession," which appeared in August 1934, and coincided with the height of critical attention to *Youth Restored,* he acknowledged that fact-fiction hybrids entail certain "risks," but noted that they were clearly no anomaly for the times.[48] Echoing earlier dissatisfaction with traditional literary genres, he felt the novel in particular was "compromised." After all, of recent major successes in soviet literature, none were "typical products of belles lettres; instead we find in them new elements: history, chronicle, memoir, science and so forth." He singled out Vsevolod Ivanov, Mikhail Sholokhov, Aleksei Tolstoy, Iurii Tynianov, and Aleksei Novikov-Priboi for having given "new life to this form through their interest in facts." For this reason, he argued, *Youth Restored* and *The Blue Book* should be seen in this vein. Since he could not have addressed such subject matter "in obsolete forms," generic "experimentation" had become a necessity for him as well.

The company Zoshchenko chose should give reason for pause: dramatized autobiography (Ivanov's *The Adventures of Fakir*), critical realism (Sholokhov's *Virgin Soil Upturned*), historical fiction (Tolstoy's *Peter I*), dramatized biography (Tynianov's *Kiukhla*), and a dramatized autobiographical-historical treatise (Novikov-Priboi's *Tsushima*). Against the background of the classic nineteenth-century novel, these five do stand out as more factually oriented (so much so that in Novikov-Priboi's case, his firsthand account of Russia's 1905 naval defeat is classified by the Library of Congress as nonfiction). Yet equally true is that they are nothing like *Youth Restored* or *The Blue Book*. To put the latter and, say, Novikov-Priboi together as history requires a great leap of interpretive faith. In his sweeping comparison Zoshchenko too easily glossed over that the interpretive problems of his work were not a function of what went into the text but of how the material was presented. Individual elements of innovativeness notwithstanding, the other five place minimal demands on the reader in negotiating the fact-fiction spectrum and making sense of each text's overall semantics. They are compositionally uncomplicated: the authorial presence tends to be consistent; separate speech domains are observed; there are no ironic intrusions; and, most important, the fictional and factual components are well integrated and delivered through the same authorial frame. Readers of these five need not go through the semantic hoops that Zoshchenko continually tosses out. Indicatively then, no cry was raised as to their interpretive opacity. If anything, the contrary was true. Only two weeks before Zoshchenko's article and in the very same newspaper, who but Aleksei Tolstoy received incomparable praise from ever-present "mass readers" for the accessibility and value of *Peter I*. Declaring that "literature needs to explain, reflect and help us understand the great historical events that mankind has experienced," they bestowed the laurel that "not one textbook of history has given us as much knowledge about Russia's past as this novel has."[49]

For that matter, Zoshchenko was too simplistic as well in assuming that the "obsolete" novel could not support a distinct factual component. The novel has never been bound to pure invention in its choice of character, event, or geography. In Russian literature *War and Peace*, of course, jumps forth as the most clear-cut example, whether speaking of its attention to history or its closing essay. If we move to the "essay within the fiction" form, Melville has provided additional evidence that interpretive chaos need not result. In *Moby Dick* Ishmael's digressions and poetic waxings on cetology are ostensibly included as an aid to readers who may not fully appreciate the danger and importance of whaling and thus not fully respect it. To be sure, whether or not Ishmael is scientifically correct in his classification and description of whales is not the real point. His claim that readers need this aid only serves to motivate the discussion. Its actual relevance for the text is more a function of characterization, both for the title character (providing background on the sperm whale and thus adding to its awe) and for Ishmael himself (reinforcing his defensiveness and obsessive disposition, which is often humorous in its extremes). Hence, whether taken as scientific background, comic relief, or lyric digression, the cetology sections do not violate the narrative's overall tenor. The key is that they are properly motivated and that there is not a tremendous shift; essentially the same "Ishmael" is retained throughout.

This is precisely where *Youth Restored* and *The Blue Book* part company from the rest. They are strained, forced marriages of fictional and factual dispositions that are wrought with a highly variable and usually conflicting authorial-narrator presence. In *The Blue Book*, its appeal to Gorky notwithstanding, there is an acute absence of motivation within the text for integrating its disparate parts and for conjoining its simultaneous authoritative-absurdist orientation. With *Youth Restored*, its appeal to the mass reader notwithstanding, we face a mind-numbing play with form and voice marked by a similar absence of adequate motivation.

In contradistinction, then, to the work of Zoshchenko's contemporaries, *Youth Restored* and *The Blue Book* serve to illustrate an essential point: the combination of diverse content (whether in an ontological or discursive sense) can appear relatively natural *or* the differences can be played up. As the reception of these two works makes clear, the price to be paid for the latter course is often great. With attention—and tension—brought to bear on the seams, such a text necessarily defeats expectations for unilinearity. We find ourselves in the awkward position of trying to make sense of a text that reaches out in too many directions. In some places a certain proposition seems correct; elsewhere another does. Morson has introduced an apt term to describe this condition: "threshold text." The type relevant for Zoshchenko's work is defined as one that

> creates hermeneutic perplexity . . . by generic incompatibility, that is, by embedding or juxtaposing sections of radically heterogeneous material. The generic conventions governing individual sections may be clear, but the laws of their combination are not. Attempting to understand the entire text as a single literary work, the reader postulates hierarchical relations among its constituent parts, but discovers that the text sustains radically different hierarchies and therefore admits contradictory readings.[50]

What makes Morson's description particularly useful is its emphasis on the reader's dilemma. "Thresholdness" lies in the text's invocation of varying interpretive frames, none of which, however, alone seems adequate to embrace the whole text. It forces us simultaneously to entertain mutually exclusive reading strategies. The application of one dramatically and profoundly reshapes the text, often turning it into the polar opposite of what application of the other would do. Ultimately, in pursuing one strategy after another, we are caught in a kind of hermeneutic circle. This makes threshold texts exceedingly labor-intensive and, what is more maddening, without a foreseeable end, since the propositions—now serious, now ironic; now parodic, now authoritative—all find textual support and can be recycled indefinitely. This is why *The Blue Book* is as problematic as *Youth Restored* even though in the former the structural obstacle of bloated commentaries has been removed and the factual support entered directly into the main text. As underscored by Gurshtein's lament over "tripled and quadrupled" irony, the conflict of voices and, for the reader, the resulting clash of semantic propositions still remain. This is also why the work of Sholokhov, Tolstoy, and the others above is not threshold in nature; the potential to make qualitatively distinct interpretive demands on the reader is never exploited.

There is much then to be understood—especially in the 1930s—in Gurshtein's complaint concerning the reader's expenditure of energy. Threshold texts run counter to the need for referential coherency and thrust responsibility for relieving this tension into the reader's own hands. Given that the period's interpretive canon sought to relieve the reader of such obligations (accessibility and univalency above all else), the results of such collisions were usually dramatic and, in our case, stand at the forefront of how *Youth Restored* and *The Blue Book* were received. Either these two were rejected outright for their pronounced ambiguity (as Raltsevich does with the former and Gurshtein with the latter) or, more frequently, readers sought to reduce them to manageable size—in short, to divest them of their threshold quality.

It is this second course that sheds more light on the extant interpretive environment. Facing a cacophony where ideologically sound statements can appear alongside or embedded in ludicrous contexts, readers of this period, whether doctor, academician, or literary critic, generally shared a common purpose and pattern: divide and conquer. The text was broken into various domains (defined by either voice or structure), of which *one*, be it ironic, serious, comic, or whatever, was designated the "true" authorial disposition. With *The Blue Book* the focus tended to center on the text *either* as a vulgarization of history *or* as a celebration of soviet ideals. The first path necessarily committed the reader's attention to just the "joking aspects";[51] the second, to the final chapter and related statements, as we have seen with Dymshchits. Such a constricted view was necessary to turn an often cartoon version of history into a panegyric and vice versa.[52] With *Youth Restored* the tendency was to assume that the primary narrative and the commentaries were autonomous texts, either of which could be subject to separate analysis and evaluation on its own merits. This division underwrote all critical attempts to recover the text within some broader semantic purpose such as satire, a chronicle of the intelligentsia, or a medical guide. In order to advance *Youth Restored* as the story of Volosatov's reconciliation with the soviet state or, conversely, of his ironic defeat, opposite sides were taken as to the author's attitude toward his protagonist; here, depending on whether the attitude was accepted as "positive," the commentaries were either seen as factual illustrations of the fiction or dismissed. To claim the text as scientific essay, regardless of whether the advice was proclaimed sound or fraudulent, readers generally ignored the primary narrative as if it were an irrelevant addition to the "real message."

Each critical recovery of the text established univalency by negating its anomalous status. Coherency was thus preserved or, more accurately, created by reducing the text to a preconditioned, generic performance. In the end, critics could reassure themselves that they were on familiar ground: it was a satire on philistines, an analysis of the intelligentsia, a self-help book, a history of culture, and so forth. Each designation came with its own set expectations of what the text "meant," how it "performed," and what the reader was supposed to "learn" from it.

Of course every interpretive act assumes a form of condensation, a compression of narrative expanse into a cohesive unit of meaning that the reader identifies as "the work." But with a threshold text, the intended reader is forced to do sizable surgery. To make it simulate genre X or Y, one must cast out whole demons of recalcitrant data—in Zoshchenko's case often half the text. What readers felt he was doing was contingent on where they drew the line, where they saw the real text. If it was one of the parts, then which? If it was the whole, then how could the parts be integrated?

Ironically, readers' heightened efforts to keep Zoshchenko's work within normative bounds often came amid praise for his originality (*novatorstvo*). However, "original" cannot always be taken at face value. For most, even in the soviet context, it normally is a valued phrase. But threshold originality is not always welcome because it can all too easily upset a reader's desire for univocality. This was the motivation behind soviet critics' reduction of *Youth Restored* and *The Blue Book;* both texts did enter the nascent socialist realist canon but only on such restricted terms.

Unlike Zoshchenko's earlier work, *Youth Restored* and *The Blue Book* were not subjected to an ideological tug-of-war between East and West. The reason is quite simple. In the West, only with Hanson and Scatton has serious attention been paid to the two later works as authentic literary steps, a turning point in his development that looks backwards to his *skaz* roots while marking an increased effort at single-voiced didacticism. Previously the texts were mainly downgraded to an amusing joke or an obvious attempt on Zoshchenko's part to ingratiate himself with the state—both of which were expedient ways of delivering oneself from threshold ambiguity. The ideological push for clarity—whether manifest in a reader of the 1930s or 1960s—has rarely been tolerant of semantic openness.[53]

WRITER VERSUS TEXT

And, we should add, the same intolerance can be manifest in a writer as well. The strikingly odd but vital fact of Zoshchenko's artistic profile is that he actively worked outside his fiction to annul its threshold character. In numerous appearances, articles, authorial statements, and personal letters we hear only of his belief in the simplicity and clarity of his writing. Though ambiguity and dissonance might be the chosen venue of others, he declared that this did not describe his work. At one public forum, we are no doubt surprised to hear that in *The Blue Book* "I have successfully (*bez vreda*) combined literature with history and philosophy." Needless to say, claimed success comes at a heavy cost: deliberately closing his own eyes to a substantial part of the text. As with many positive reviews, he notably left out of his self-congratulatory pose any mention of those elements (the "alien" passages, excursus on Greek history, and so forth) that would put such a victory in doubt. Perhaps more astonishing was his description of *Youth Restored:* "I undertook the following task: to provide support in equal degree for the literary side and the serious commentaries. One complements the other, and, in the end, they provide a unified picture."[54] Zoshchenko's straightforward description of his straightforward writing effected an almost childlike tone of humility and nonbelligerence, as if to say, "it's all so simple, I don't understand why everyone's so troubled and confused."

The Politics of Reception

Of course, we would expect any author facing a backlash in difficult times to engage in such defensive maneuvers. (They culminated in Zoshchenko's specially crafted image of reader, which will be discussed in the next chapter.) We should not discount as well the influence of the contemporary cultural ethos. The persecution of fellow travelers, the excesses of the cultural revolution, the subsequent crackdown on RAPP, and the emerging call for socialist realism cannot have failed, with brutal clarity, to awaken every writer to the fact that artistic licenses of the 1920s had been rescinded. More and more, single-voiced clarity became the expected mode of expression. (Or irony, if present, was tolerable in limited doses and only if it did not seem to put in question the author's motives.)

Yet the heart of Zoshchenko's own response, his desire to impart a singular meaning to his work, cannot be attributed solely to external pressure. Where else but in the very commentaries to *Youth Restored* do we gain access to this other side of the writer? The objection may easily be made that the commentaries were written with the same reserve and distance that we find in his double-voiced *skaz*. Obviously some of his contemporaries felt this way. After all, the reasoning is often disturbing, and one might wish to separate Zoshchenko from such reductivism and simplistic generalizations. But we should not operate under the assumption that just because Zoshchenko is sometimes ironic, he is always ironic. We, with obvious but nonetheless relevant hindsight, cannot ignore the fact that the commentaries, his personal correspondence, and authorial testament to the world, *Before Sunrise,* speak one language. Often verbatim, the same evidence and conclusions, and, most important, the same righteous tone infiltrate all three.

So strong and pervasive does this voice become that one would suspect its source to be anything but the creator of Sinebriukhov and Kolenkorov. Notably on this account, we first meet it publicly in a nonfictional environment, Zoshchenko's roundtable with beginning writers at the Leningrad Publishing Center in 1930.[55] The advice offered by this most popular of authors must have caused something of a shock. In answer to the question what is the most important task for writers today, Zoshchenko unflinchingly responded that for the reader's sake they "need to write with clarity, concision and all possible transparency."[56] However, he cautioned, this is not a simple affair of the pen. Care needs to be taken of oneself as well. A proper balance should be maintained between pure inspiration and craft; oversight and control should preserve, too, the necessary "equilibrium" between mental and physical energy. With an eye to—whom else?—Gogol as a negative foil, Zoshchenko claimed that Gogol's failure to "give his head a rest" had led to a tortured end. The mistake need not be made again. Health, temperance, and lucidity should be the interlocking triangle of their literary faith. Only it could keep them on the right track, and only through it could they fulfill the principles of Zoshchenko's artistic credo: a work's contents should be logically apportioned, it should be presented accurately, and the narrative itself should be "smooth" and "seamless."[57]

Needless to say, this was the very credo that Zoshchenko discarded point by point that same year in "Lilacs in Bloom" and *M. P. Siniagin*. It was also the same credo he demolished three years later in *Youth Restored*. Significantly, the very distance between text and intention is unmasked in Zoshchenko's own citation of Sir James Jeans's *The World Around Us*. This is, arguably, the most revealing commentary because within the thematics of *Youth Restored* it is the most irrelevant. Why nine pages of astronomy tidbits à la *Reader's Digest*? Since the subject of Volosatov's profession plays no essential role in the plot (he could just as easily have been an engineer, chemist, biologist, or, God forbid, a doctor), it would be difficult to justify this length. If we turn, however, to Jeans's own preface, we find an interesting statement: "This present book contains a brief account, written in simple language, of the methods and results of modern astronomical research, both observational and theoretical. . . . My ideal, perhaps, never wholly attainable, has been that of making the entire book intelligible to readers with no scientific knowledge."[58] The coincidence with Zoshchenko's own declaration of intent cannot be ignored. Yet the very inclusion of Jeans in *Youth Restored* is self-defeating. The accessibility of Jeans's work, with no fictive amendments or madcap diversions, only highlights the difficulties inherent in Zoshchenko's. In no uncertain terms *The World Around Us* ironically shows—*pace* Zoshchenko—how to present science to the lay reader.

Look to what Zoshchenko says or to what he does? This is the paradox that emerges full force in the 1930s when we encounter an increasing number of his "faces," each with its own time on the page: humorist, absurdist, prophet, promethean. How to understand and reconcile these impulses has been an enduring chore for his readers. Volpe, writing only a year after the publication of *Youth Restored*, offered a key paradigm that, in variant form, has gained currency among many critics: Zoshchenko reveals two selves in his writing—the artist and the thinker-teacher.[59] For Volpe, what makes *Youth Restored* special is that here they are structurally divided, as if Zoshchenko is finally baring the compositional machinery that had been shielded in previous work. For descriptive purposes, Volpe's division is useful in giving us the vocabulary to outline the interpretive knot we face: the fiction seems a parodic reworking of the material treated seriously in the commentaries. For analytical purposes, it is more problematic. Underlying Volpe's argument is the premise that the two work in tandem, making *Youth Restored* a unique synthesis of dialectical halves. In his eyes, it is a "unity of contradictions" and an "unstable equilibrium."

No doubt the parodist and pedagogue are never far from each other in Zoshchenko's work. Yet coexistence does not necessarily yield complementarity. It is my contention—one that I believe is borne out by the critical legacy—that the two impulses form a competitive tension. Volpe attempts to integrate the two at a higher plane; however, the oxymoronic character of his metaphors already suggests the uneven ground we are on. The operative words would seem to be "contradiction" and "unstable" without reverse qualification. We can recognize that Volpe, like most, seeks to remove Zoshchenko from the traps of his own ambiguous writing. This is where the search for an all-explanatory, all-encompassing key (critics tend to stay in the singular) to the "Zoshchenko problem" originates. Is it in the evils of the Soviet Union and the desire to evade censorship, the philistine core of all humans, the linguistic chaos of postrevolutionary society, the rise of a newly literate and culturally distinct reader, or an artist's postrevolutionary angst, or, as advanced more recently, is it a guard against his own psychophysiological neuroses?

Yet these attempts to clarify the picture by making a single, final pronouncement—*this* is what Zoshchenko was doing—are exceedingly difficult to uphold against the whole of his legacy and life. The writer, his work, and his times suggest that both the environment and the self are to blame. And the more we learn from authorial declaration, archives, correspondence, response, and the texts themselves, the further we are from a single answer. His work always includes a countermanding backstep that immediately infects and impinges upon the authority of his writing, regardless of whether it appears in the guise of satire, fictional tale, moral instruction, self-help guide, historical exegesis, or autobiography. I call this his parodic (perhaps more appropriate would be Serapion) condition, and no matter how much he may have wished at certain times to suppress, dismiss, or disavow its self-compromising irony, its presence manifests itself—even in the most presumed univalent of texts.

Two of his postpublication comments regarding the commentaries in *Youth Restored* offer an appropriately oxymoronic dispensation of the conflict inherent in him. The first accords with his didactic side: "Every author has the right to append his own observations to a book. I believe, for example, that Sholokhov could have added documentary notes to his remarkable novel, *Virgin Soil Upturned.* No book will be ruined if an author adds his behind-the-scenes work to it."[60] The second marks the commentaries' aberrant, dislocating quality: "I simply added the material to the novella. You go figure it out yourself."[61] One seeks cooperation from its readers; the other repels it. Together they pull Zoshchenko and us in opposite directions.

Chapter Five

Authorizing Interpretation:
The Co-optation of the Mass Reader

> You of course won't get mad that we're writing to you. The point is that we've fallen madly for you (that is, for your work). We're just ticked off that our school library doesn't have your books.
> —Letter from "Raia" and "Tamara," both 17, written during their chemistry class, 1935

> Just what are you trying to accomplish with these hack-job stories. You want to make us laugh? . . . The content of your stories is so lame that after reading one or two, by the third, excuse me, I'm ready to lose it. Seriously!
> —From a 1930 postcard[1]

JUST WHAT WAS Zoshchenko doing? The question flared repeatedly as critical confusion reached its peak with the publication of *Youth Restored* and *The Blue Book*. Significantly, as Zoshchenko's own frustrated attempts to explain himself suggest, he too was at a loss to clarify his parodic treatment of contemporary literary motifs. It was at this point, as we have seen, that he introduced a third voice into the debate. Drawing from his widespread popularity, the thousands of letters he received from readers and, unknown for his time, their citation and select publication, Zoshchenko turned toward the mass reader for defense—precisely where the Party also claimed a monopoly of support. This extension of authorial-critical polemics into the domain of audience marked an acute departure from the typical conditions of disputes in soviet literary culture. By recourse to a third voice—one that nominally stood outside either the writer's or critic's control—Zoshchenko began to target the interpretive act itself and thus dramatically reshaped the stakes of his own unpredictable relationship with soviet critics. At the same time, through his challenge to institutional presumptions of where interpretive authority rested, he laid the groundwork for his later incarnation in the West and postsoviet Russia as mythic writer for the people.

THE OFFICIAL CAMPAIGN FOR THE MASS READER

In 1929, shortly into the cultural revolution, the journal *Na knizhnom fronte* published the following letter from a newly literate peasant, Sergei Vasiliev:

> I want a book about our land, about the sky and heavenly bodies, and about how the earth turns and whether it will end soon. And something too about where humans come from and how the world was created. And there is also the pressing question: does god exist? Can one travel through the sky or to the North? And what is on the other side of the Arctic Ocean? I would also like to be sent a small chart to mark down answers to these questions. Please don't ignore my request since these questions give me no peace.[2]

No mention was made as to whether Vasiliev's needs could be satisfied (indeed, who could venture a suggestion?). What remained from the letter's publication and, in fact, was underscored by the omission of an answer was the image itself of the nascent soviet reader, eager, voracious, and impatient. Not only was the sheer scope of his interests daunting—traversing cosmology, theology, physics, astronomy, anthropology, and geography—but their compression into a single query reflected an acute hunger for information, as if the introduction of the written word dictated that no facet of human knowledge should remain off limits. As exemplified by Vasiliev's additional request for a chart on which he could presumably visualize and plot his progress, each point of interest merged into a unified quest. Before his onslaught of questions, any notion of disciplines or boundaries collapsed, and concerns of epistemological viability disappeared. Of sole importance to him was the acquisition of concrete information, not postulations regarding its formulation or, for that matter, availability.

While today's librarian or bookseller might run from such a letter, in the soviet press requests like Vasiliev's served as a symbol, albeit hyperbolic, of new social conditions. Since the October Revolution had officially brought power to the people, an equivalent change was proclaimed in the literary environment, heralding a new identity for audience. Factors once governing the production and reception of literature—market forces, patronage of the wealthy and educated, and the consequent pandering to esoteric or "decadent" tastes—were deemed to have been swept away. The arbitration of artistic value now passed into the hands of the mass reader, who was canonized as the literary representative of the previously exploited proletariat and peasantry. With this readership at the fore, cultural intercourse would, for the first time in history, assume its proper form. Literature (and the same was pronounced for other media) would finally be oriented to and evaluated by those classes that constituted the majority of the population, but which in all other societies had been silenced or ignored.

The rise of a new class of reader made essential the identification of its needs. Summing up the spirit of the decade, the 1928 Party declaration

Authorizing Interpretation

"How the Book Should Be of Service to the Mass Reader" proclaimed that only by registering the nature and extent of readers' interests could soviet literature hope to keep pace with social change in the country.[3] Consequently, many officials, critics, librarians, and pedagogues conducted a variety of surveys in the army, libraries, schools, factories, and villages with the aim of determining what readers wanted. In this drive, which can be traced in journals like *On the Literary Front, Red Librarian,* and *The Bookpeddler,* Vasiliev-type letters provided a special impetus with their combined note of eagerness and frustration. Sometimes written on wrappers, used labels, or paper sealed with chewed bread, requests for printed material flooded publishing houses. The Revolution, as appearances would have it, had unleashed a previously unknown appetite for knowledge, and all kinds of texts were in demand: primers, fiction, newspapers, instruction manuals, technical guides. In fact, as one desperate youth wrote, *anything* would suffice since all he had was a Bible from which he rolled cigarettes.[4]

Yet for all the official attention to and celebration of the new reader, the attempt to reach individuals and communities identified as "mass" was gravely compromised. Primary documents of the postrevolutionary period highlight how the demand for written material often remained unsatisfied because of two related phenomena: the inadequacy and poor distribution of printed resources, as Jeffrey Brooks has shown,[5] and their relative inaccessibility to sometimes marginally literate segments of the population. In his 1923 account of a fact-finding trip in the Voronezh region, Iakov Shafir, a newspaper correspondent, demonstrated the marked difference between proclamation and reality.[6] Extensive interviews with people in whose name the Revolution had been conducted revealed to him that most official texts (state-printed books, newspapers, journals, and pamphlets) rarely penetrated to this region and, more pointedly, those that did were generally incomprehensible. A list of words compiled by Shafir that soldiers of the Red Army commonly misunderstood included some of the most important terms of contemporary political discourse: USSR, Sovnarkom, class enemy, territory, administrative order, communal home, authority, occupation, reparations. Likewise, in another survey the list of misunderstood words extended to such essential principles as marxism, socialism, imperialism, and democracy.[7] Moreover, letters to publishers were not limited to idealistic yet innocuous requests such as Vasiliev's. Often readers sought material on unsavory topics like the occult, magic, and witchcraft or asked for works that lay outside bounds of accepted literature. The contents of another letter, a plea that books be printed on paper unsuitable for smoking, suggest that even when available, texts (and not only the Bible) were liable to be consumed literally. And finally how is one to respond to the report that in a rural library a dissatisfied reader returned uncut one of Stalin's works because there were no pictures![8]

Understandably, such conditions alarmed Shafir. The communicative breakdown between the political center and general population constituted a threat to national security. Throughout his commentary ran the fear of losing control over the dissemination of information. He continually invoked a battle between the forces of "light and darkness" for the "people's minds" since the latter were all too frequent prey to rumors, specious thought, superstition, and the influence of the clergy and other "counterrevolutionary elements." His concerns, of course, were no small matter. They summed up what was essentially the third phase of the Revolution, one equal in importance to the political coup in October and to military victory in the civil war. Ultimately, the Revolution would fail if no progress was made in educating people as to the nature of their liberation—that is, to the very fact that the soviet state was not their enemy but their ally.

The collision of these two factors—Bolshevik glorification of the masses and the actual conditions of government-population communication—forms a necessary background to understand the position and, correspondingly, the function of the mass reader in the soviet literary environment. Significantly, the obvious tension between myth and reality was not lost on contemporary critics. The conclusion of one in the aptly titled 1927 article "The Sphinx Talks" highlighted the indecision and ambiguity surrounding this new audience:

> In the end, everyone argues over what the average reader needs, but this reader sits completely outside and from there dictates his own laws. Look at the request cards from workers' libraries, and you'll discover that they generally don't read those writers whom we are apt to praise and expound on. Instead, they are more likely to read those who are rarely mentioned in our press. In other words, the theory and practice of day-to-day literary activity are by far two different things. And this is true primarily because in the triad, writer-critic-reader, the unknown element is not the first or the second (hardly!) but precisely the third.[9]

The image of the common reader as a "sphinx," outside normal cultural channels, points to the dilemma faced by critics. Since doctrine could not allow for such conditions to continue, how could the claimed symbiotic relationship between state and mass readers be reified?

It was understood that to reconcile reality with ideological mandate, merely cataloging readers would not suffice. One needed to include them in the literary process and thereby make them active agents in the production and reception of texts. This effort reached a crescendo during the cultural revolution when an explosion of reader-oriented material—surveys, transcripts of reader-discussion groups, and letters from "mass/worker-readers"—appeared in major literary organs. With titles such as "The Readers Speak," "The Face of the Worker-Reader," "The Worker-Reader on the Language of Contemporary Prose," "The Readers' Tribune: the Reader in the Critic's Role," and "The Writer Before the Worker-Reader's Court," this near-crusade sought not only to identify but to mobilize and exhort the "sphinx." Prominent was the description of what evaluative criteria, in terms of language, plot, character, and theme, could be seen as innate to the worker-peasant reader, since the latter's opinion, henceforth, could serve as the basis for new direction in literature.[10]

Given the regularity and numbers in which such material was published, a new critical platform was established: commentary "from below" on contemporary literature. Consonant with the image of the soviet power structure as bottom-up, interpretations by mass readers were generally accorded more authority than those by literary critics. The latter were often dismissed as *spetsy* ("specialists"), a pejorative designating an exclusionary and antiegalitarian background. Without a hint of the irony inherent in this self-indictment of their own legitimacy, some critics welcomed mass criticism as more direct and socially relevant. One of the most strident treatises to this effect was A. M. Toporov's *Peasants on Writers*. Toporov, a teacher at a Siberian commune, held extensive readings of contemporary literature with peasants and afterwards engaged them in discussion and question-and-answer sessions. Publishing a record of their responses in 1930, he took the notable step of turning stereotypes about rural ignorance on end. If, as he argued, *spetsy* cultivated opacity, sophistication, and an arcane critical vocabulary, then any hints of "unrefinedness" or "coarseness" on the peasants' part only strengthened the authenticity and authority of their interpretations. "[The peasants'] criticism comes from the heart and is expressed simply, sincerely, figuratively and vividly. This makes it superior and more useful than professional criticism."[11] With this maxim held high, Toporov directly challenged the authority writers might presume to have over their own literary creations because "the people don't have time to waste on bad books." Writers, he believed, must labor to reach and understand their audience and not the reverse. Otherwise they would lose an already tenuous connection with the nation's true voice—that is, the class with which lay the path to a communist future.

It was this spirit that underlay the most dramatic manifestation of the mass critical platform: readers' conferences, or "evenings," dedicated to the discussion of a specific work or writer, often with the latter present. Held in conference halls, auditoriums, or even on the factory floor, these meetings aimed to show that literature could be subject to immediate criticism from the people. They, not critics, would be the arbiters of what should gain print, what should be destined for pulp. Their "collective decision," as one organizational brochure stated, carried far more weight than any other voice; it served as a stamp of legitimacy, a kind of ideological guarantee, for any work, fiction or nonfiction: "[O]nly after a text has gone through workers' control can a reader accept it with confidence."[12] Ideally, the brochure continued, all manuscripts would first be submitted for mass evaluation; only after the people's approval and the incorporation of any objections and criticism would a text be printed. The editorial power readers could be presumed to achieve at these conferences even reached a superhuman, X-ray ability to spot and destroy harmful books: "[Y]ou can't slip by the worker-critics' court with any hackwork; it will be blown away with one puff [from them]."[13] In the characteristic hyperbole of the cultural revolution, this was a warning to writers to mind their pens, but, more emphatically, it accorded mass readers an active role in shaping the creative process itself. From their participation at conferences, readers could truly make a book a collective work, one that began with writers but in its final form was the product of social input via the new channel of mass evaluation.

The newly proclaimed reader's role was sanctioned not only by many critics but also by writers themselves. One of the most popular authors among workers' circles, Aleksandr Serafimovich (pseudonym of Popov) welcomed the authority wielded by the reader at these meetings: "I suddenly was conscious of my reader; I sensed this connection. . . . I recognized his demands and the corrective that he introduces to my work . . . and this is invaluable to me." Indeed, when chided by one reader for overusing the metaphor "iron jaw" in his 1924 classic *The Iron Flood,* he respectfully hung his head in recognition of the verity of the objection: "Yes, it's true, in places I overdid it. . . . Now I wouldn't have done such a thing."[14] Extending this idea of the mass reader's influence to its orthodox conclusion, the writer Mikhail Karpov even assigned it a future role as coauthor/editor: "The writer will be under the overall control of the reading masses, which will give the writer general directives. . . . A work of literature is no longer created by the writer alone . . . but also by the reader, by means of his instructions [and] his criticism."[15] In Serafimovich's comments and Karpov's imagery one can sense the ideological value these forums held. They, more than anything, served as empirical proof of an organic connection between writers and readers in soviet literature. Literature would soon become a direct reflection of the proletarian's and peasant's needs, since writing in an authentic, or mass, way could be achieved only by recognizing and incorporating their demands beforehand.[16] Mass reader participation should begin, in effect, before the first words were committed to the page.

ZOSHCHENKO AND HIS READER

The scenario envisioned by Karpov mirrored Zoshchenko's assertions as to the reader's place in his own work. But whereas the former described a path for future collaboration, Zoshchenko presented himself as one of few who already served as an authentic bridge to the masses. On the basis of tremendous book sales and a deluge of letters from readers, he gave full voice to the image of a close, reciprocally beneficial relationship between artist and audience. His writing was the most accessible to newly literate readers; only in his *skaz* could be found an accurate reflection of the postrevolutionary linguistic farrago that dominated the streets; his narrators and characters were most endearing to the people; his themes spoke directly to their concerns. The cumulative weight of Zoshchenko's argument assigned readers the special role in the literary process that stood at the core of the readership campaign: they, not creative whim, governed the linguistic and compositional structure of his prose. It was their needs to which he subordinated his pen, and, consequently, it was only their responses to which he gave credence.

As noted in chapter 4, Zoshchenko introduced this position in the late 1920s in a series of interviews, speeches, and published statements that, significantly, represent the first time he publicly spoke or wrote as author without the ironic marks characteristic of Serapion pseudo-autobiographies. Admittedly, this self-promotion corresponded with official proclamation that in soviet literature the distance between writer and reader was being eliminated. At least since the beginning of the cultural revolution, recognition of the mass reader's positive influence in literary relations was de rigueur for writers,[17] and there can be no question that Zoshchenko was influenced by the contemporary ethos. At the same time, though, his stance cannot be reduced to a mere parroting of political rhetoric. What distinguishes his from other authorial statements about the reader is the use he made of this claimed connection. Reader response became a weapon against the critical establishment, as reflected in the following letter to him:

> I feel insulted on your behalf. It seems to me that for some reason your talent has been *consciously* devalued by someone. I read a lot of journals and newspapers and rarely see in them any recognition of your distinguished abilities. . . . Recently, I've come to this conclusion: I like whom the critic despises. Well, the hell with him, with this critic.[18]

Coming in 1929, these words could not have failed to encourage Zoshchenko. They surely confirmed a suspicion that for the better part of the decade his artistic output had been undeservedly attacked or inexcusably ignored by the literary hierarchy. Moreover, their source, a "common reader," furthered his belief that there nevertheless was a true audience for him. Yet undoubtedly for Zoshchenko, this letter was of most importance as an embodiment of how official and popular interpretations of literature often clashed. Against the background of official efforts to understand the needs of the soviet reader, what could be more incisive than this very same reader turning directly to one of the most popular writers and damning critics for their hostility and blindness to him?

How Zoshchenko exposed and exploited this gap is best illustrated in the reception of *Youth Restored*. As discussed before, the interest, ire and, in some circles, fear raised by the text's unusual content and mystifying structure led not only to a wave of articles and reviews, but also to public debates on its meaning and value. While scientists, academics, writers, and literary critics bandied this question among themselves, Zoshchenko faced a wave of reaction from the "other" soviet readers. For the most part, their letters replicated the range of published responses: from dissatisfaction with the fictional Volosatov story and criticism of a simplistic, naive approach to nervous disorders, to surprise at his apparent erudition or gratitude for addressing fundamental problems of health and aging. But the quantity and tone of positive evaluations in personal letters to him substantially outweighed and overshadowed anything that officially appeared in print.

> At just the right time you have opened up a hot topic, presented it in a fresh light through an interesting selection of material and framed it in the correct and necessary way.
>
> Dear writer, I thank you for a work which is for the people. What did I learn? I discovered the remedy for the illness that has tortured me for 15 years yet for which no doctor or professor could ever give me an answer.
>
> The book is tremendous. I must admit, I didn't expect that Zoshchenko was an exceptionally educated and well-read person.
>
> On the whole, the work is remarkable. After reading it, Zoshchenko [sic] rose before me like a great person, like a luminary of what is useful and healthy for the conduct of my life. . . . If only all books that were published gave such useful [information], then I would read without fail; I would devote 2–3 hours a day to reading literature.[19]

The superlatives here were unprecedented in Zoshchenko's reception. Voices gushing with praise, proclaiming near miracles and salvation from his pages, provided him with the recognition previously denied at the official level. Moreover, they raised his authorial profile from that of mere humorist or short-story writer to the lofty position of teacher, a "luminary"—a title of no small status in any cultural context, but one of heightened importance in this environment because of contemporary prescriptions on literature's edifying role.

Given the breadth of popular support he felt, Zoshchenko eschewed his customary insularity and entered the polemics surrounding *Youth Restored*. Armed with letters, he participated in debates and charged that the mass reader had validated his efforts. In an opening statement at a Leningrad literary club, he argued that despite the doubts others might have held, readers' responses had proved his approach sound:

> Perhaps [in *Youth Restored*] there will be found some sins against modern science. Scholars might think that my book is insufficiently developed and that the information given in it is [too] elementary for professional consideration. But, to repeat, I wrote this book for my own readers. And what they need I

know rather well. The great number of letters inspired by *Youth Restored* tells me that I have addressed questions of medicine in precisely the way which the reader requires.[20]

Zoshchenko's distinction of "my own readers" represented a crucial juncture in his relations with the critical establishment, for it suggested that responses from "above" (scientists, doctors, literary scholars), while perhaps of some interest, were in the end irrelevant. His picture of a reader gaining insight and edification from *Youth Restored* constituted a challenge to others' inability to do the same. It negated critics' avalanche of questions regarding textual coherency—that is, the confusion elicited by the text's complicated construction and seemingly contradictory messages. Since Zoshchenko asserted (and could prove) that he had matched readers' needs, he could show that critics' own indecision was a function of their distance from the reading habits and expectations of the general population. Any confusion or ambiguity in *Youth Restored* was consequently not the property of the text but was evidence of critics' own inadequacies. The voice of "his readers" had upheld Zoshchenko's claim that it was a clear, univocal work; textual complexity was present only if his readers experienced it; any mistakes, generalizations, or simplifications were valid only if his readers perceived them.

By claiming that the true value of *Youth Restored* lay with the mass reader, Zoshchenko directly opposed critics in the very terms and imagery deemed most legitimate in contemporary culture. In a direct illustration of the concurrent readership campaign, here we see the elevation of the mass reader over *spetsy*, the identification of textual meaning with the former's interpretation, and, especially, the author's acceptance of a subordinate, almost secondary role in the literary process as favored by Serafimovich, Karpov, and others. In his defense of *Youth Restored*, Zoshchenko was not just the compatriot of his readers; he acted more as their mouthpiece: "[W]hat drove me to write *Youth Restored* were the letters of my readers who complained about broken nerves and were seeking advice. I wanted to answer this [need] in an artistic form. And the letters which I've received after its publication show that I was on target."[21] By casting his readers as both the impetus for *Youth Restored* and the guarantors of its success, he surrounded the text with their authority and retreated into their hands, essentially effacing an active role.

A soviet writer's publicly dismissing the interpretations of a number of noted individuals because "they didn't get it" might seem like rash behavior for 1934. Therefore, one cannot discount that Zoshchenko's attribution of content and composition to the reader was a strategy to thwart critical objection—that is, to evade responsibility for the text by enveloping himself in the near sacred name of the mass reader. Yet it would be a mistake to reduce his defensive posture solely to a tactical ploy. Much of his personal correspondence and many colleagues' memoirs attest to the fact that he was sincerely and deeply affected by his popularity. The esteem with which he regarded his popular readers even reached, one could say, a somewhat unhealthy altitude, as in his declaration to Chukovsky, "Now I don't even listen if I'm criticized.... I know the public and have I made a mistake? No!"[22] As early as the 1920s Gruzdev saw in Zoshchenko's attachment to readers roots of the arrogance that would consume *Before Sunrise* two decades later.[23] Certainly Zoshchenko's repeated insistence that "he knows what the reader wants" and that his writing is "on target" betrays a heightened ego, brushing with presumptions of infallibility.

The kind of support his hubristic excursions could find with readers is vividly demonstrated by one of the more unusual letters appraising *Youth Restored*.[24] It was sent to his publishers, Sovetskii pisatel, after most of the controversy had abated but warrants attention because of its content and the use Zoshchenko made of it. Written by a certain Kotolevsky, who was appealing a death sentence for murder, the letter describes a vengeance broiling for fifteen years that finally exploded in blood. A neighbor, Sidorenko, harbored an unexplained hatred toward Kotolevsky's family. During the civil war, Sidorenko exploited the collapse of authority in order to kill Kotolevsky's brother, and, shortly after, the brother's wife died, presumably from grief. In the midst of the collectivization campaign ten years later, he intrigued to have Kotolevsky's other brother kicked out of the kolkhoz on false charges of hoarding bread. (Kotolevsky was working elsewhere at this time.) Still not satiated, Sidorenko, from a position of unidentified authority, then exerted pressure against the whole family. He demanded money and property in a time of extreme deprivation, an abuse that led to the death of Kotolevsky's second brother and father. In the end Kotolevsky, upon returning to what was left of his home, could not contain his rage and burst upon Sidorenko with an ax, killing him, his wife, their son, his bride, and their daughter.

The description of this gruesome conflict then switches unexpectedly to a note on literature. While imprisoned, Kotolevsky first became acquainted with Zoshchenko's work and was struck by the writer's discussion (primarily in *Youth Restored*) of how to temper excess emotion and energy through mind control. Only with this idea in hand did Kotolevsky finally realize what had driven him to murder: irrational blindness caused by the thirst for revenge. Recognizing that his inability to check these urges had led to crime, he came to a startling conclusion: had he known these facts before, he never would have chopped up his neighbor's family. Therefore, if his appeal met with success, he promised to devote his life to the propagation of this revelation, but—and a more successful bookselling promo has probably not been delivered—if the court were to refuse, it would mean that none of the judges had read Zoshchenko. (Kotolevsky's sentence was reduced, but we have no information as to whether this decision was due to the court's reading habits.)

Authorizing Interpretation

For all the, daresay, morbidly comic relief this letter may hold for us, it captures the impact Zoshchenko could have on certain readers. For some he became the bearer of a special wisdom or truth. The nature of Kotolevsky's praise, which was not lost on Zoshchenko, added a near spiritual dimension to the contemporary axiom that the writer should serve the reader. In 1941 he published a story based on this letter, "An Eye for an Eye," which modifies somewhat the details of the conflict between Sidorenko and Kotolevsky but preserves the central idea of tempering one's passions for the good of self and society.[25] This moralistic tale, however, spills beyond a fictional reworking of Kotolevsky's fate; it builds to a direct quotation from Kotolevsky's letter in which the verity of Zoshchenko's treatment of this topic is affirmed. "An Eye for an Eye" then closes with the author's comment that only with the lessons Kotolevsky has learned can we hope to advance to "life's higher stage," a state that remains undefined but which demonstrates the sometimes epiphanic colors in which Zoshchenko saw his own writing. And two years later, in the nonironic context of *Before Sunrise,* he cited this letter again with the exclaimer that its contents alone "have obligated me to impose upon people my own thoughts about the necessity of controlling oneself, about the necessity of directing one's feelings."[26] The spirit of reader-writer relations professed at workers' conferences had come full circle but with a decidedly different flavor.

THE SEARCH FOR ZOSHCHENKO'S TRUE READER

Whatever aim we attribute to Zoshchenko's citation of readers—clever stratagem or self-aggrandizement—we should be as cautious here as with his fictional projections of author. On one hand, as in debates with critics, he affected a position of equivalence with his reader: the writer serving as the unadorned mouthpiece for the latter. On the other, near Promethean claims that he was the exclusive fount of information and guidance upset the impression of a meek writer struggling to bring the truth to the average reader. Characteristically, Zoshchenko drew upon these competing impulses in his earliest, yet most illuminating, contribution to the mass reader polemics, the collection *Letters to a Writer,* which was published in 1929 and later became the sixth volume of his collected works.[27] Here, in both the contents and the accompanying editorial frame, vacillation between self-effacement and self-inflation vis-à-vis his own popularity was given full play.

As a whole, the compilation of over fifty letters to Zoshchenko (which, in answer to a question sometimes raised, are authentic as they can be verified in his archives) offers a broad portrait of reading habits and expectations among the general population. Some letters, marked by egregious mistakes in spelling and grammar, approach unintelligibility and typify the marginally literate reader of the 1920s. Many are devoid of any hint of Zoshchenko's official reception and are seemingly oblivious to the fact that his writing had been subject to vehement attack. Others, in turn, display what could be accepted as a proper marxist orientation and exemplify the mass reader celebrated in the contemporary press. And while voices of praise predominate, there is a curious mix of appeals for help that modify the picture of how Zoshchenko was received by the general population. A few ask for advice regarding personal problems in a kind of "Dear Abby" format; many offer him plot ideas, submit poetry (which Zoshchenko includes), or ask for professional guidance in their compositions. One even wishes to sell Zoshchenko his own stories since the writer's name would bring attention; another author-to-be wants to publish his work under the pseudonym "*Not*zoshchenko."

As could be expected at the height of the cultural revolution, critical opinion fractured over this slim volume and its bricolage of contributors. Guttered with a resounding "who needs this book and why was it published" or lauded as an authentic step to a truly proletarian literature, *Letters* left no reviewer neutral. A primary point of contention centered on readership identity and function: Who were these people and should they have a role in soviet literature? The most vociferous answer, under the expressive title "A Philistine's Letters," came from Arkady Glagolev, who dismissed any redeeming value for the collection: "In social terms the content of most of these 'letters to a writer' is shockingly pointless. It is far removed from what is of concern today to the literary culture of the advanced proletariat. The vitally important problem of intercourse between the reader and writer is reduced to mere triviality."[28] Likewise, Dmitri Maznin, mincing no words, castigated Zoshchenko for giving a forum to "counterrevolutionary" voices that contradicted how the true proletarian reader responded to literature.[29] On the other hand, some saw the publication of these letters as a useful exercise (albeit for reasons that discredited the respondents no less than Glagolev or Maznin). These critics welcomed Zoshchenko for exposing those readers who stood in the path of cultural advance and thus were deserving of ridicule. Such readers were identified as the flesh-and-blood embodiment of Zoshchenko's satiric targets. In this interpretation the "philistines," "money grubbers," and "ignoramuses" of Zoshchenko's fiction met their real-life counterpart in *Letters*, and the collection thereby became not propaganda for "worthless members of society" but a documentary attack against them.[30] Alternately, in a private letter to Zoshchenko, Gorky noted that these readers' responses had an affirmative value and their publication signified that "only in our country and in our time . . . the writer is becoming someone true and close to the reader."[31]

Dissension understandably came to a head on the question of Zoshchenko's attitude toward his correspondents: Sympathetic? Critical? Neutral? Speculation stemmed, quite legitimately, from his peculiar editorial stance. The opening lines of the preface are a veritable gauntlet cast at those displeased, to put it mildly, with his work to date: "It seems that the reader doesn't receive me in quite the same way as the critic. [So] I've decided to publish these letters." The suggestion that the contents therefore offer some empirical proof of Zoshchenko's true reputation in the country is reinforced by illumination of the text's documentary potential: "Of course I didn't have the slightest intention of making fun of my readers' illiteracy. I put this book together not for the sake of laughter. I put it together in order to show life authentic and uncovered, to present actual, living people with their desires, tastes and thoughts." The objective tones, which foreshadow Gorky's response, serve to bring Zoshchenko closer to "his reader" by intimating that in his popular reception can be found some real window, lacking in official culture, on life and literature in the Soviet Union.

The tendency, once again, to authorial effacement and solidarity with his popular audience is enhanced by Zoshchenko's commentary to certain letters. He gives the approving title "Sensible Criticism" to a collective letter from railroad workers who praise his simplicity, accessibility, and humor that exhibits proper contempt for "negative types," and follows it with the none-too-subtle note: "This is an exceptionally intelligent and interesting letter. True, it is flattering to me. But I try to stay above any mercenary feelings and accept it objectively. The letter is exceedingly interesting. I've read it several times and am still struck: where did such observant critics come from?" More emphatic words meet a reader who has championed the intelligibility and mimetic accuracy of Zoshchenko's *skaz* narratives:

> People usually think that for the sake of laughter I corrupt the "beautiful Russian language" by using words outside their normal context or that I purposely write in a sloppy language in order to amuse my most respected audience.
> This is not the case. I distort practically nothing. I write in that language in which the street now thinks and speaks. . . . [And] so it seems, I haven't made a mistake. This is clear from my book, from the letters which I receive every day.

This often-quoted commentary, the letter for which Zoshchenko arrantly entitles "It Came In Handy," encapsulates the pole of equivalency. Zoshchenko connects his accomplishments in fiction with his editorial role in *Letters* and circumscribes both in the domain of his reader. In effect, all three voices present in *Letters*—that of Zoshchenko, the writer of fiction; that of Zoshchenko, the editor of the collection; and that of his reader-contributor—are situated on an equal plane. Any hierarchical difference between fiction, commentary, and reader response is superseded by their congruence in intention and semantic orientation. After all, clarity and univocality, the two qualities on which the writer and this collective reader agree, were conspicuously absent from Zoshchenko's official reputation at this time.

Yet the spirit of equivalency is not the sole voice identifiable with Zoshchenko in *Letters*. Alongside cardinal statements of allegiance with his reader surfaces a second editorial stance, the chord of comic distance. Immediately following the steadfast declaration of showing life and people without shield or embellishment, the preface dissolves into absurd bantering where Zoshchenko counters imaginary critics on the charge that he might be "making money" off others' writings. After a page and a half trying to defend himself, Zoshchenko finally "gives in" with the offer to pay "market prices" for readers' verse submissions that have been published within and includes his address for inquiries concerning remuneration. Furthermore, the picture of him as sympathetic to the literary hopes and endeavors of new readers takes a curious turn with certain evaluations of their work. One youth, who includes her poetry, asks Zoshchenko if it would be possible for her to make a living as a writer. A representative stanza of her work follows:

> Amidst dreams of wealth and glory,
> I now sing only one tune:
> I would like to be a dog, big and furry,
> And sit and howl at the moon.

To this Zoshchenko appends a most astonishing comment:

> This poetry is really not that bad. Granted, they're not fully mature lyrics, but their author is only 16 years old. Even Pushkin was not the greatest of poets at that age. Of course I'm not an expert on verse . . . but I believe and am convinced that eventually the author will be an excellent poet. I asked the author's permission to print her name, but she didn't give it. Her refusal has since confirmed my opinion that this is the modesty of a true poet. They're very good poems!

However much Zoshchenko may have cultivated the image of a simple writer for the people, he was not the consummate naif these lines at first suggest. Clichés of a promising future that include comparison with the Poet of Russian literature leave little room for acceptance as serious appraisal. Instead, they seem to realize the potential irony of the line in the preface: "Of course I didn't have the slightest intention of making fun of my readers' illiteracy." Indeed, even if such unfounded hyperbole is taken as a humorous aside, the injection of levity gives us a second authorial profile, one manifestly at odds with the pretensions of documentary objectivity embodied in the first.

Ultimately, overt authorial intrusion interferes with the collection's original claimed function and underlies the confusion with which the critical field responded to Zoshchenko's turn to the reader. As evident in *Letters*, "Zoshchenko," the ostensible locus of authority, occupies two positions: (1) in his claims as spokesperson for popular audiences, in his role as mentor for new proletarian writers, and in his citation of letters that validate his work, Zoshchenko positions himself, his fiction and his publicistic writing in close proximity to mass readers—that is, where he appears in the guise of "one of them"; (2) alternately, comic exaggeration, ironic locutions, and the commentary and titles for some letters distance him from the thought and speech of his readers. It is important to keep in mind that given the number of letters Zoshchenko received, he could have published a specific type of response accompanied by a single editorial stance in order to secure the impression of either of these positions. Such an action certainly would have helped clarify authorial intention and thus have alleviated critical indecision. Instead, *Letters* intermixes the two potentials, and the problem is, of course, that they are antithetical. Much as has been the case with Zoshchenko's other quasi-documentary texts like *Youth Restored* and *The Blue Book*, *Letters* assumes a threshold status. It cannot be exclusively text 1 or text 2, yet neither can it simultaneously be both without one potential's compromising the other.

This anomaly is not just a problem for us today with our eye for textual instability and the like. Contemporary critics voiced their frustration and disapproval over *Letters*' unorthodox picture of readers. Glagolev, for example, tried to navigate editorial voices but could not resolve where the real Zoshchenko was. In the beginning of his review, where he attacked Zoshchenko's readers as society's refuse, he saw the writer as sympathetic to their concerns. Later, however, Glagolev reversed this insinuation by labeling the position taken in the foreword as ironic—that is, as a voice that could not be attributed directly to Zoshchenko and that would therefore problematize assumptions as to any editorial sympathy. Yet in the end, evidently unable to clarify this ambiguity, he threw up his arms and tossed the foreword out as the main culprit: "Strictly speaking, the foreword is the greatest failure of his book."[32] Similarly, though he favors *Letters,* Chumandrin foundered on the hope of locating an authoritative voice. At first he followed the path of identifying the readers as targets of Zoshchenko's satire. Yet in noting the latter's commentary to letters such as "It Came In Handy," Chumandrin immediately requalified Zoshchenko's alleged position: the writer and his readers should be seen as one.

> As is evident from a whole series of his remarks, Zoshchenko situates his work within the efforts to create a literature for the masses. Great events have occurred in the country, and literature should change with them. The masses demand a different literature, and therefore it is simply criminal not to write for the masses, for the millions. [In *Letters*] we can find as many comments as we wish in which Zoshchenko's positive attitude to the restructuring of our country is clearly evident.

The pomp of this statement, however, does not rescue him from the confusion that exasperated Gorelov, and Chumandrin unwittingly admitted his plight when he charged: "We are in full rights to demand from him [Zoshchenko] clarity and definition."[33]

Exacerbating this problem is Zoshchenko's ambiguous role as compiler. *Letters* gives not one profile of reader but a diffuse portrait that does not readily yield to the readership categories sanctioned by official institutions. By what criteria, motivation, or logic could one reconcile the inclusion of "Sensible Criticism" alongside the letter entitled "Drama on the Volga," which is from a woman who has been slighted on a cruise by an impostor passing himself off as Zoshchenko? She combines sentiment over lost romantic opportunity with reproach for "Zoshchenko's" excessive drinking yet all the while questioning the source of his "literary pessimism." And what place can one assign barely literate requests by infatuated readers for a photograph? Surely every artist can lay claim to a similar breadth of response ranging from the serious to the ridiculous. However, what is at stake here are Zoshchenko's decision to publish these voices back to back and, more important, the environment in which he did it. The orthodox inflection of one reader rebounds against the ludicrous stance of another.

Who, then, was the true soviet reader? This question, which nearly every page of *Letters* begs, necessarily placed critics in a quandary: how to accommodate diverse readers within critics' own expectations for a monofaced audience, whether positive ("mass") or negative ("philistine"). Understandably, we witness incompatible strategies to resolve the issue. Volpe, Messer, and Kriannikova, who saw the contributors as unknowing targets of Zoshchenko's satire, concentrated solely on the latter type of letter, ignoring the simultaneous presence of voices that fit the mass stereotype. Glagolev, on the other hand, hesitated: even if, as he contended, there were some "proper" readers, the efficacy of the latter as possible role models was undercut by the contaminating influence of responses fully at odds with the needs of contemporary literature. And Chumandrin tried to straddle both potentials: he accepted as fully authoritative those letters that coincided with his marxist principles and rejected as ironic targets those that did not. But the manner by which he made such distinctions was left only to his critical whim; the collection itself does not draw such clear boundaries.

As each critic tried to muster the contents of *Letters* into a cohesive picture of the soviet reader, there remained the stubborn knot that the text itself resisted wholesale incorporation in any one schema. To make it fit tightly within a given critical program required, as the above somersaults demonstrate, the selective citation of letters and accompanying commentary—in other words, a return to the paradox of either Text 1 or Text 2. In fact, the collection's inability, as it were, to project a unified reader, combined with the inconsistency and interplay of Zoshchenko's voice(s), makes it unique among contemporary reader documents. Unfortunately, this point has not been acknowledged in work on Zoshchenko; often the collection is ignored or reduced to an amusing curio. But *Letters* is a signature work of Zoshchenko inasmuch as it contravenes the period's norms for readership studies. Like his fiction, it leans to the parodic and, put bluntly, makes a mess of critics' search for a uniform image of the mass reader.

THE MASS READER IN SOVIET CULTURE

At the same time, not all messes are bad. By defying expectations for a single reader identity, *Letters* highlights two essentials of the mass phenomenon: the image's importance for contemporary culture and, for this very reason, its elasticity. Across the tortuous spectrum of early soviet arts—from the disjointed fighting among various avant-garde and proletarian factions during NEP, to the militant egalitarianism of the cultural revolution, to the hierarchical ethos of socialist realism—the mass reader could be called upon to champion new prescriptions for authoritative and accepted literature. Little did Zoshchenko know, therefore, that his own epistolary game would anticipate the climax of the critical debate over the identity of the "sphinx."

At the time of the publication of *Letters*, proletarian groups under the aegis of RAPP had increased efforts to secure their authority as the sole representatives of the mass reader. They discredited the likes of Toporov as too "elemental" (not exhibiting a proper party orientation) and attacked anyone who claimed to have captured the real voices of the masses. As Maznin declared in a characteristic broadside (which also included his attack on *Letters*), true understanding of the mass reader was given only to those who were themselves of the "correct" ideological mind-set:

> In connection with the increased activism of the worker-reader masses, the following question can be raised: but do we know this reader? Doesn't this reader remain a mystery for the proletarian writer? . . . This reader is a mystery only to those select specialists who, in studying the reader, stay in their offices without seeing or contacting him. For us, for RAPP—which subordinates all its work to the urgent tasks of the working class and which is always realizing its directives [through] the writer's connection with the practical work of this class—of course for us, our reader constitutes no such mystery.[34]

How RAPP solved this "mystery" is a monument to circularity. While Maznin, like others before, genuflected before the pedestal of the mass reader, he subtly yet definitively denied readers the right to speak for themselves. As their only true guardian, RAPP did not merely know and serve mass readers; it became the only vehicle for the expression of their demands. A question posed early in the article: "Do the mass readers' tastes differ from the principal theoretical and creative stance of our writers' organization?" received its expected answer by the end: "No, there is not one essential slogan of RAPP that has not met with the full support of advanced worker-readers."[35] In one breath, institution and reader became inseparable; the agenda, programs, and principles of one merged seamlessly, so it would appear, with the other's voice.

Unfortunately, however, chronology was not on Maznin's side. The claim he laid, one of RAPP's longest—and last—assertions of exclusive control over the reader, was published in 1932, a mere two months before RAPP's official liquidation. Eighteen months later his argument was stood on end at the First Congress of the Writers' Union, the single most impressive and authoritative expression of official cultural policy. Neither before nor after would there gather so many prominent political and literary figures to pronounce the what and wherefore of soviet art. For sixteen days and through twenty-six sessions of speeches, the likes of Zhdanov, Radek, Bukharin, and Gorky as well as select foreign guests championed the inauguration of socialist realism. (Zoshchenko was also there but did not speak.) Overseeing it all, metaphorically and literally, was, of course, Stalin, in whose name the congress was convened and concluded. Yet the show-stealer was not any of the big guns, but the humble soviet reader, who appeared en masse to consecrate the proceedings and offer proof that this was the first true meeting between socialist writers and the proletarian and peasant classes. Representing either the state's multinational character or its various mass professions (such as the military, collective farms, factories, mining, education, and even—to use the term of that time—the labor camp system), groups of readers paraded to the podium between sessions. The authenticity of their participation was presumably heightened by the fact that each group conducted itself in the full regalia befitting its position. Thus, for example, railroad workers entered to the sounds of a train whistle, and soldiers were accompanied by martial music. All identified themselves as the real audience for the new literature and presented their demands to the writers, including (since the pen is not always mightier than the sword) the request from a group of sailors that the literati learn how to shoot.

What occurred on stage was in full harmony with the postrevolutionary reversal of audience hierarchy. As declared by a Moscow engineer, readers were present so that writers could learn firsthand of their audience and its needs:

> Comrades, today's meeting is a first for us and you. We know and love you only through your books. Therefore, I would like to use this opportunity not only to offer praise but to present in the name of engineers a series of demands regarding your work. In your writing there is still little reflected of that tense struggle which we, technicians, are waging in the most advanced positions of [socialist] construction. Many of our great efforts in construction still are not included in soviet literature. . . .
>
> I, as a worker in aviation, would like to see masterful artistic canvases about our life and about the growth of soviet aviation. We are indeed surprised that such an exciting element of socialist construction still has not found its proper representation in fiction.[36]

It would be a truism to dismiss all this as mere show if Robin did not accord such appearances (and other mass reader documents of the period) a measurable degree of authenticity by implying that they were somehow spontaneously present and therefore representative of the population.[37] Two points should be made regarding this suggestion. First, readers who spoke at the Congress were by no means average soviet citizens. Across the board they were leaders of their respective groups or decorated members, with either position attesting to their ideological allegiance. Moreover, the fact that almost every one of them was the head or "most distinguished" member of his/her factory, farm, or unit demonstrates that selection was an honor and not reflective of a desire to present the typical reader. Second, their individual speeches exhibit near formulaic precision (something that is not true of the writers). Invariably readers praise the congress, pronounce the accomplishments of their group (thus establishing its worthiness to be represented), and welcome the progress of soviet literature. Next comes its sole deficiency, which, almost without fail, boils down to a "neglect" of their respective representation in literature.

At the same time the ritual behind their rhetoric—show us to ourselves; help us achieve more in our field through its favorable depiction—does not make readers' appearances meaningless. Here symbol tells us more than substance. The procession of readers literalized the declared harmony between soviet writers and their audience, and effectively put to rest any previous questions as to their identity. Socialist realism, regardless of RAPP's charges two years before, was to emerge from *this* reader's needs. The obvious question—how the mass reader's mandate for literature could change so radically in such a short period—was not posed. Instead, the Writers' Congress reasserted the organic thread of reader and writer in much the same spirit as before. As proclaimed by Demian Bedny, one of the more prolific orthodox poets, now writers and worker-readers could see themselves as one because, echoing the martial atmosphere of the congress, "the writers' front is the same as the workers'; only the weapons we employ are different."[38] Likewise, Gorky, chair of the newly formed Writers' Union and "first soldier of proletarian culture," closed the proceedings by reaffirming that the reader governed the writer; once again the first—"our reader, a reader-friend, who . . . lovingly surrounds us and teaches us how to work"—was to be the benevolent watchdog of the second.[39]

ARTIFICIAL INTERPRETIVE COMMUNITIES

The choreographed congress was certainly the most dramatic instance of official manipulation of the reader's image, but it was not the only one. Already in the 1920s, readership data were tainted by the contaminating hand of political need. In fact (holding to Maznin's assertion that ideological correctness confers infallibility), studies, surveys, and conferences often did little to hide this. Regarding the famous "workers' evenings," participants were usually screened,[40] and questions asked typically projected answers along predictable curves. Rooms were often equipped with exhibits of writers and works demonstrating "which are worthy to give opinions on," and walls were decorated with portraits of Lenin and Stalin extolling the "purpose of the Bolshevik press."[41] Most illuminating was the proud admission in contemporary guidelines that at the end of each conference an official should "summarize the debates and give a precise and correct evaluation of the work [under discussion]" since only in this way could allowances be made for "the correction of all inaccurate and mistaken comments"[42] (though as Shafir noted, the most expedient way to clean things up was to erase any dissension from the stenographic accounts).[43]

Critical intervention was motivated as much by the desire to present a flattering portrait of the reader as by suspicion of the very object of veneration. As with many symbolic orchestrations, celebrations of the mass reader were designed to contain its public identity within strict parameters.[44] It was not an open category; after all, literary, socioeconomic, or educational background alone did not ensure membership in its ranks—though the image was promoted primarily through this triad of criteria. Instead, what qualified one as a true mass reader was contingent on one's political orientation. "Mass" became more of a title, a mark of distinction, conferred upon specific kinds of *interpretations* rather than upon readers themselves.

A revealing illustration of the threat true breadth of response could pose can be found with Nikolai Rubakin, the bibliographer and prolix ambassador of popular science through such titles as *How and When People Appeared on Earth, What Are Comets,* and *How People Learned to Fly.* (We recall that Zoshchenko played with similar titles in *Youth Restored.*) On the wave of the psychoanalytic mania that spread through Russia in the first decades of the century, Rubakin floated the provocative (particularly for our post-structuralist ears) theory of "biblio-psychology."[45] Arguing that a text was basically an empty vessel awaiting interpretation, he attacked faith in fixed meanings. "We need to stop believing that words, phrases and books are like barrels filled with something set from their first appearance in this world." Only in a reader's perception was a text actually present; otherwise it was just marks on a page. "What meanings a book has are, more or less, as varied as the number of its readers." His advice to librarians, therefore, was to stop studying literature itself and concentrate instead on readers' individual psyches. Whether a work was good or bad, useful or harmful depended on how readers interpreted it and was not contingent on anything in the text.

Rubakin's enthusiasm for any and all readers was not just a challenge to critics; it was veritable heresy. To contend that a text lacked objective content and belonged to its reader was to embrace chaos or, as his attackers put it, "psychological debris."[46] But the censure of his iconoclasm provides a window onto the fear true reader autonomy could occasion and illustrates why, a short period later, Zoshchenko found himself under similar attack. Indeed, one could argue that in *Letters* Zoshchenko carried on the spirit of Rubakin (who was then abroad) by confronting critics with raw readers in all their (un)glory. His citation and publication of less-than-orthodox voices bypassed the normal channels by which soviet readers were generally granted entrance to public discourse and thus compromised critics' desired monopoly in this area. More to the point, he revealed empirically that official projections of the mass reader were not compatible with the notion of "common" reader—that is, with the broad majority of the reading public.

Critics' response was swift and enviously expedient. In 1930 Chumandrin let Zoshchenko know that audiences came in only two colors: "There is no such thing as simply 'a reader.' There is our kind, the worker-reader, and there is the enemy reader."[47] His warning was a logical outgrowth of the Manichaean vision best exemplified by Averbakh's dictum of a year before: "[O]ur times do not tolerate ambiguity."[48] If all events, peoples, classes, and writers could be classified as either "for" or "against" the Revolution, then why not readers? This is where the official identity of mass reader saw its greatest use, serving as an instrument of clarification through which to remove possible confusion or complexity from the field of textual response. In its name, the welter of interpretation that any text could occasion was reduced to accessible and easily enforceable antinomies of right versus wrong. In other words, though readers could differ, the text could have but one essential meaning (whether positive or negative), and one of the primary roles of the mass reader in official discourse was to produce it—that is, to secure the text in accordance with critical prescriptions over and above the interpretations individual readers might offer. As the Writers' Congress and other documents show, the mass reader performed handsomely in this capacity—in fact, perhaps too well. The power of its name was such that, as some have asserted, it led to the outright fabrication of readers. Officials themselves would pen letters identified as coming from the "common" soviet reader—a practice that recalls Zhdanov's own hand in orchestrating public attacks against Zoshchenko in the 1940s.[49]

The strict division between correct and mistaken readers necessarily committed all interpretations to a true-false polarity and placed writers in the tricky position of having to predict which camp their work would find itself in:

> An author, contemplating his future work, must first of all imagine his reader: Who is he? The worker-reader, the builder of a new life and existence with a new mentality forged in the years of the struggle for the Revolution . . . or is he the petty philistine born in NEP, with whom we must wage a "decisive, final battle" until his extermination is complete?[50]

Of course, the crux of the matter was that at the official level the audience publicly equated with an author was out of his/her hands. As the vicissitudes of Zoshchenko's reputation in the Soviet Union illustrate, the identity of one's readers—mass or not—was more often a function of one's official reputation: a writer for "our-kind" or a writer for the "enemy." In the 1920s, when his work was excoriated as a remnant of prerevolutionary sympathies or as an appeal to philistine elements, we find, as in the citation by Toporov, the voices of various mass readers (here a carpenter) enlisted against the writer:

> What kind of writer is Zoshchenko?! . . . It's surprising that his books are printed in such numbers. . . . What use to me are his stories like in [the 1928 collection] *Who Are You Laughing At?* Can I say anything good about them?! In them there isn't any useful guide or example for understanding life that I could use for some idea or plan. What are these stories of Zoshchenko?![51]

The power of this statement lies in its capacity as a protest "from the people" that Zoshchenko's success is somehow unfounded. At the same time, however, it refutes itself by acknowledging Zoshchenko's success in print. This contradiction speaks of the dilemma his popularity posed for critics: how to censure him in the very name of those who devoured him. As one critic regretfully admitted in a review of the phenomenally successful collection *Honored Citizens,* Zoshchenko was "inarguably the most popular, the most read author by the typical mass reader."[52] Notably, however, by the 1930s, after Zoshchenko had been accepted into the canon of approved writers, the problem disappeared; now his status among popular audiences could be cited as proof of his value for soviet culture. In fact, the sheer size of his readership led another critic in 1936 to proclaim Zoshchenko "the most democratic writer in the Soviet Union."[53] Yet in 1944, after the forced withdrawal from publication of the controversial *Before Sunrise,* the mass reader appeared in print once again to condemn the writer who had "spit in [our] eyes"—a pronouncement that with little variation remained in force until his death in 1958.[54]

The alacrity with which the mass reader (with or without its varying qualifiers as "proletarian," "worker," etc.) could change opinion points directly to the fact that, by and large, its *published* voice, identity, demands, and expectations constituted a projection of critical need. To expand Stanley Fish's formulation, we could argue that in official discourse the mass reader represented an artificial interpretive community.[55] This is not to discount the importance of surveys, discussion groups, and the like—in *The Formation of the Soviet Reader* Evgeny Dobrenko has demonstrated that they are invaluable in order to understand the origins of socialist realism—but to emphasize how institutions codified primary research and subordinated it to their interests. If a person's literacy, educational, or social status had no direct relation to the title of mass reader, then we can recognize how the identity of this

category was predicated, first and foremost, on the nature of its critical appropriation. The mass reader, in effect, demarcated and, by virtue of its status in the cultural hierarchy, privileged an exclusive set of interpretive practices. It became a critical category endowed with a specific ideological value whose functions consisted of (but were not necessarily limited to) the following:
- to propose and enforce institutional critics' interpretations of literary works
- to validate literary canons and critical doctrines
- to sanction as authentic the evaluative criteria of official literary culture
- to legitimize on ideological grounds critics' own practice
- to give authentic voice "from below" on the verity of cultural topoi

THE READER FUNCTION

We should not forget, of course, that the same intentions apply to Zoshchenko's own appropriation of the reader's image. The correspondence lies not in a similarity of ideological aims but in the need for a category of audience, whether in the broad terms of an interpretive community or in the form of Kotolevsky's lone voice, that would realize critical or authorial design. If for official culture the mass reader served to plant a fund of constancy ("the correction interpretation") amidst the webs of individual response, then for Zoshchenko his reader could cut through critical debates over his work and provide clear, concise support that it did have relevance and meaning for contemporary society.

Zoshchenko's need for this image was not only political but, as we have seen, deeply personal. As much as critics were confounded by puzzles like *Youth Restored,* Zoshchenko too was troubled by the enigmatic and often contradictory nature of his fictional endeavors. His anxiety is exemplified in a reported confession made to Chukovsky two years after the publication of *Letters* that he hated the complexity in himself and "would give several years of his life to become naive, ingenuous."[56] His inability to resolve this dilemma in the text itself shaped how he invoked his popular audience. For him the reader served as a vehicle to purge his writing and, by extension, his literary profile of any semblance of ambiguity. Through readers like Kotolevsky—no matter how hyperbolic, reductive, comic, or even profound their interpretations may be for us—Zoshchenko's fiction and his authorial persona were able to become that which critics denied and that which eluded the writer's own pen: simple, straightforward, and expressive. In their name he was able to "de-thresholdize" his most controversial works and thus bridge the gap between authorial pronouncement, critical expectation, and textual performance.

Given the depth of Zoshchenko's conviction, some perspective is necessary. When he dismissed the questions and objections of scientists, critics, and academics during the *Youth Restored* polemics by citing an approving

The Politics of Reception

letter of a common reader, we witness a bifurcation of audience—"those readers" v. "mine"—that unconsciously echoed Chumandrin's more militant distinction between "our kind" and the "enemy." By isolating one sphere of interpretation that was "correct," Zoshchenko engaged the same instrument of exclusion-privileging. Indeed, just like most of his contemporary critics, *this* Zoshchenko would have been equally intolerant of Rubakin's theories of biblio-psychology. And, symptomatically, Zoshchenko's claims only resurrect the same question as before: On what basis was the true mass reader to be identified?

That we can pose this question again suggests that once more the bestowment of title was contingent on confirmation of a particular agenda. Most indicative here would be Zoshchenko's argument in *Before Sunrise,* his most emphatic treatise on his status as writer for the people. In the vignette "A Public Appearance," he recounts a reading where members of the audience incessantly request that he give them something humorous. Their refusal to see the edifying message in his fiction dismays him, and he dismisses them with the retort, "I am at least comforted by the fact that these are not my readers."[57] The point is, of course, that these readers, however much their interpretation of Zoshchenko did not coincide with the writer's own impression of himself, were as much his readers as any of the ones invoked by him as his real audience. His comment illustrates and lays bare that for the writer the appellation "reader of Zoshchenko" was bounded and not given to any person holding one of his books. This differentiation of audience uncannily mirrors the beliefs held by critics opposed to him: only by reproducing a necessary interpretation could one enter the exalted ranks of "Zoshchenko's readers." If one did not or could not, then one effectively became a non-reader of him.

How then are we to reconcile competing official and authorial projections of the same mass reader? Mirrored methodology points to a special discursive function performed by the category of reader in textual hermeneutics and cultural polemics. In literary theory we have become accustomed to the image of author as distinct from actual writer. The former, a product of fiction, autobiography, and virtually any text projecting an authorial voice, has become an exceptionally fertile and useful concept for critical analysis. Through this image we readily gain a sense of unity and coherence at a number of levels, from identifying the perceived intent behind an individual work to assumptions of a writer's psychological disposition to a metaphor characterizing an artistic movement or age. By extension, from the practice described above we can posit in the construction of reader, whether by critic or writer, a similar move to closure, one that can resolve tension in the text, mask ambiguity, clarify purpose, validate intent, and legitimize product. A period, social group, or individual can invest any variety of identities with this function; for obvious political reasons, in the soviet context "mass" was the preferred title for the authoritative reader in culture. Here lies the source of its elasticity in soviet discourse. It displayed a chameleon-like ability to reconstitute itself across the shifts and conflicts of official doctrine, critical agendas, and writers' platforms. Yet in each position it (more accurately the group or person invoking its name) retained its semantic authority as both a metaphor and an agent of closure. Similarly, through his mass reader Zoshchenko was able to resolve questions of textual meaning that had exasperated both him and his critics and, in a reverse step, confirm the image of author that matched his personal beliefs.

The reader function is not a relative of implied readers or similar concepts that designate a postulated response formed within the text itself. The origin of this reader is in actual voices outside the text. But—just as with our distinction between the actual writer and the image of author—neither can this reader's voice, despite its extrinsic, empirical roots, be seen as identical to real readers. The latter do have a role in the formation of the reader function, but the role they play is not open-ended or subject to their control. Instead, in its interpolated state, the true, authentic voice of an actual reader is subject to codification by and subordination to an appropriating medium. In other words, readers in reader function are ontologically and functionally distinct from any empirical source.

The distinction between voice origin and voice appropriation is crucial, since what pervaded the rhetoric of the mass reader was a cloak of empirical validity that sought, unconsciously or not, to mask its constructed status. Claims of merely reflecting popular needs were intended to mute the subordination inherent in documenting the mass reader. To be sure, regardless of political motivation this is a problem in any effort to project one individual as representative of a larger entity; such is the bane of summation and generalization. But what we witness in the use of reader function for this period is decidedly different. The bifurcation of readerships, the reduction of multiplicity to an either-or possibility, in and of itself became the main goal. The preservation of this dualism, as noted, linked the succession of cultural orthodoxies during the first decades of the Soviet Union. In each phase we find a strict opposition between "right" and "wrong" readers. In fact, it could be argued that for any given period, out of thousands of potential responses only one was needed to uphold the requisite image of reader, since on the basis of one an authoritative reader function could be established if presented in proper ideological colors and if effective means of dissemination were employed.

While I may exaggerate, not all is hyperbole or hypothesis if we recall Toporov's condemnation of Zoshchenko through the voice of the Siberian peasant. One could, of course, marshal any number of readers' letters to demonstrate the opposite. But the point is not to subject Zoshchenko to an ad hoc popularity contest. Instead, it demonstrates an acute absence in mass reader documents of a willingness or even curiosity to explore how readers might have exhibited interpretive strategies, approaches, and expectations different from canonical ones. What was specifically not asked was that which was not accountable within ideological norms. What was missing, essentially, was supplied by two of Zoshchenko's contemporaries, Platonov and Pilniak, in "Che-Che-O," a tongue-in-cheek account, in part, of their search for the "soviet masses" in the Voronezh region (coincidentally where Shafir conducted his research). One character, Filipp Pavlovich, a peasant turned electrician, objects to having books and "culture" hurled at him "like bricks" from a bureaucracy "up there" that assumes to know what is right for him: "From up above it only seems that below there are the masses, but in truth down here there are individuals, people who have their own character and habits."[58] It is telling that this image appeared in a quasi-fictional guise, for it leaves open just how this individualism might have manifested itself in actuality. In the reader campaign, this potential was effectively erased through the propagation of the mass reader as one voice, one identity writ large.

CO-OPTING THE READER TODAY

The icon of the mass reader was not laid to rest after the polemics of the 1920s and 1930s. Its appeal has proven irresistible to Zoshchenko's champions in the cold war West and to the new quasi deification of him in Russia. Despite different political objectives, the more recent claims made upon the mass reader play along much the same lines as before. Rare is the critic who closes a discussion of Zoshchenko's language, satiric import, or didacticism without mention of the "common" or "simple" reader. Indeed, the writer's popularity makes it all the more tempting to anchor assertions as to his intentions and impact by invoking the reading public. Just as we have seen with realism earlier, the concept of the mass reader bears a special truth value—for who would dare speak against "the people"?

When a concept becomes canonical, the usual casualty is precision in usage. In Zoshchenko's case, no one has seen fit to question the contents or deployment of the image of reader. To use one of the more salient examples, in the whole of Chudakova's argument that his unconventional works were designed to match the soviet readers' needs, the reader makes an appearance in name only. Its identity is presumed self-evident, restricted to the realm of theoretical projection. This explains why it remains a supreme candidate for co-optation. For if we do not actively investigate and question reader-audience behavior, then we never lose the ability to hone its voice down to a single expression—one that can always be at our service.

In fact, it often seems that the more the reader is cited, the more we are destined to tread on the same problematic ground that bogged down RAPP and advocates of socialist realism. In the West, arguably the most prominent example of favoring a single, theoretical projection of audience coincided, importantly enough, with the expansion of the Russian-Slavic field after the Second World War. With the ghosts of Nazism and Stalinism still strong, "mass" often served as an all-purpose pejorative. Exemplary in this regard would be the Frankfurt School, in whose hands the term generally signified a debasement of aesthetic-intellectual norms. This, needless to say, did not bode well for the reputation of its consumers, who were invariably typed according to the assumed narcotic nature of mass culture. In the words of Theodor Adorno, automated products of intellectual Spam begat "children, largely robbed of autonomy and spontaneity"—in short, a malleability ripe for totalitarian manipulation.[59]

Such views found support among scholars who envisioned soviet citizens as pliable automatons. Yet, as is now commonly recognized, such prejudices ill served cultural studies by casting entities that lay outside "official" or "high" culture as deleterious and possibly threatening. The cure, however, has sometimes proven as self-serving as the initial problem. A decade ago in paradigmatic articles on "the popular," Stuart Hall and Tony Bennett sought to overcome the condescension of both Frankfurt-type approaches and their polar opposite, the "celebratory populism" of "utopian socialists." If the former compromised themselves by assigning an immanent, negative value to mass cultural forms and practices, the latter, with their inflated image of "the people," were too romantic in the belief that one can locate and then amplify an authentic, "autochthonous" popular voice uncontaminated by official culture. Largely via Gramsci's theory of hegemony, Hall and Bennett disqualified both tendencies by seeing popular culture not as a specific set of cultural texts, but as a dynamic field. Official (or "bourgeois") culture and "working-class/subordinate" culture do not oppose each other in separate vacuums. Instead, they meet in an "area of negotiation" where official ideology, in order to articulate and promulgate its interests, reorients itself to working-class culture. Simultaneously, the latter interprets and reshapes the products of official ideology for its own use. In this arena of continual interaction and struggle, "dominant, subordinate and oppositional cultural and ideological values and elements are 'mixed' in different permutations."[60] Consequently, neither side can be seen as an autonomous domain; each infiltrates the other. The contents of popular culture (and the same can be said of official culture) can never be reduced to a "fixed inventory." Depending on time, place, and the nature of social forces, it can manifest itself in myriad ways.

By acknowledging the dynamism inherent in meaning production, Hall and Bennett aptly point up the limitations of previous theories of mass/popular culture. Notably as well, these studies coincided with similar reformulations of soviet culture as given, for example, in the work of Robin. But in the need to tie an understanding of popular culture to a specific political end, Hall, Bennett, and lately John Fiske advance from one kind of determinism into another. For them the identity of the popular consumer is what is politically oppositional. Fiske provides a cogent picture of how response itself has become the new "fixed inventory" by differentiating possible interpretations of a text such as *Dallas:* "[I]f there are readings that fail to activate its [*Dallas'*] contradictions—that is, readings that consent to its hegemonic strategy—these are not part of popular culture: they are complicit with the interests of the power-bloc against which the formations of the people are variously situated."[61] If only that cultural response consonant with Fiske's position against the "power-bloc" is to be recognized as the location of the popular, have we truly escaped the pitfalls and self-compromising tactics employed by soviet critics of the 1930s? Of course, popular culture does show ample evidence of opposition to power blocs,[62] but we should not necessarily assume that "excorporation," Fiske's term for the construction of subversive meanings, is the only kind of response that can be popular. However much one may object to reactionary manifestations of popular culture (interpretations that do not oppose hegemonic strategies), they are there and cannot be dismissed or erased by restricting use of the appellation to that which an individual desires to see. Ironically, Fiske promotes his theory of the popular as liberating since it assigns a primary role to people outside power centers. Yet, paradoxically, it is reductive. It constrains the popular to responses delimited by him as truly representative, and by this limitation resurrects the previously condemned celebratory populism.

This more recent exchange illustrates how the reader/audience function readily lends itself to a variety of cultural polemics. Its deployment is relatively easy; its argumentative power is undeniable. At this level of abstraction no one can prove my "mass" (or "popular") consumer erroneous, insufficient, or nonexistent. Yet this is where we can locate the significance of Zoshchenko's *Letters*. However unintentionally on his part, the collection as a whole defeats attempts to promote a single reader as the authority for the "people." Alongside studies such as Janice Radway's analysis of women's reception of romance literature, these letters reveal that readers are not monoliths in either direction, whether as covert revolutionaries or as a blank-faced conglomerate whose tastes and expectations are predeterminable and unchanging.[63] To map these readers within the exclusive parameters of either "for" or "against" would mute their inherent diversity. If most of the popular responses to Zoshchenko are unconnected with and thus bypass the contemporary debates surrounding the writer at the official level, can we be secure in categorizing these responses in terms of an assumed political agenda? In short, Zoshchenko's legacy—that of a popular writer in a heavily politicized state—sheds light on how the responses of common readers (i.e., those outside critical/academic establishments) can be formed independent of a primary sense of political allegiance or opposition.

Authorizing Interpretation

The polemics over Zoshchenko's reader can also help us recognize that the production of meaning does not always match the clean-cut lines of "for" or "against" with which critics, whether then or now, tend to operate. Meanings generated may, at times, follow the general contours of theoretical debate, but they do not necessarily mirror or reproduce the black-and-white clarity through which such schemata construe the world. By this argument I in no way mean to imply that popular reception is impervious or unresponsive to political forces. However, the *potential* nature of popular response should not be taken as its sole or defining essence, since too often this strategy of identifying the popular effectively denies validity to those manifestations of it that fall outside a critic's given political needs. This, essentially, is what Maznin and others did. They imbedded the constitution-construction of the "authentic" audience in a verbal protocol of the "people," the "workers," and the "proletariat"—in short, terms that carried the tenor of infallibility in soviet discourse. Zoshchenko's response thus stands as an interrogative counter, demonstrating that the realm of the popular—what meanings are generated, what identities formed, what values communicated—is just as distinct, individual, and legitimate and as politically tame, orthodox, or subversive as any other sociocultural domain. This expanse, more readily, is the territory that the sphinx occupies, and it is terrain that cannot be adequately mapped or traversed by recourse to overarching, absolutist distinctions. The ambiguity that emerges from this realization can be unsettling, as we all, at times, presume to know who and where "the people" are. But for all its troubling implications, it saves us from the straitjacket of a plus/minus understanding of cultural intercourse and can serve as a tool by which to advance beyond increasingly worn ideological paths. For as Raymond Williams noted nearly four decades ago, within some political formula we all can be made part of "the masses."[64] Vasiliev, Kotolevsky—they are us.

Chapter Six

Writer as Reader:
The Paradox of Resolution in *Before Sunrise*

> Everything will be proven with mathematical precision.
> —Zoshchenko, 1943

THOSE OF US exasperated by Zoshchenko's literary twists and turns might find consolation in one place: the writer himself. His hyperbolic claims for *Youth Restored* and his crafting of a special image of reader reveal an acute need to mask textual anomalies, to pronounce interpretive closure on parody. This internal struggle brings him, in theoretical terms, close to the majority of his critics, both soviet and Western. In his longest and last major work, *Before Sunrise,* he took the next step and openly became his own reader. In content and format, it was designed to eclipse all his previous writing. Here Zoshchenko would reinterpret his past in order to reclaim himself from the vicissitudes of the critical eye. No longer would irony interfere. Equivocation was to be replaced by decision; inference by outright proclamation. It was intended to resolve all previous doubts and disputes. It achieved the opposite, precipitating the official opprobrium that would explode in 1946.

DESIGN AND CONTENT

Trouble came immediately. Just the first half of the text, primarily a series of memoiristic vignettes, saw print in the journal *Oktiabr* in 1943. Zoshchenko's declared need in reviewing past events was to uncover the source of his neurasthenia, the paralyzing depression we hear of from his colleagues and read in his own letters. But with publication abruptly ceased, *Before Sunrise* left readers ignorant of his final intentions. Ever-helpful critics quickly answered any questions by branding the work "crap," "a repulsive and harmful work," and "a contradiction of the beautiful traditions of Russian literature."[1] Introspection—"digging in one's own garbage" as an official put it[2]—did not seem to contribute to the war effort, and any hope that publication would be continued after the war was immediately extinguished by events of 1946.

Only in 1972, fourteen years after his death, was the second half of the book published under the title *A Story About Reason,* which gave no formal indication of its status as the conclusion to the chapters appearing in 1943. Nevertheless, readers familiar with the first half would likely have recognized its source. Here Zoshchenko continued the search and, through memory and recollected dreams, traced his psychological trauma to two events in his infancy: an operation without anesthesia and the fact that his mother, momentarily frightened while breast-feeding him during a storm, dropped him. These experiences induced in him a fear of hands, water, women, and food—four elements, needless to say, he would encounter every day of his life. Repeated contact meant that he had always been in the thrall of some, up until now unidentified, fear. Only with the completion of his search, only by abreacting these painful stimuli, could he declare himself healed of the past. A new Zoshchenko and a new writer were born.

His successful self-treatment further convinced him of the mind's role as both the cause and cure of essentially all illness—a conviction reflected in the triumphant titles of the last three chapters, "Reason conquers death," "Reason conquers suffering," "Reason conquers aging."[3] In them Zoshchenko launches into an excursus through literary history, presuming to uncover the origins of the psychophysiological disorders that plagued such seminal figures as Balzac, Poe, Nekrasov, and, no surprise, Gogol, to whom he devotes over eleven pages. Not content with the past, he also introduces people who have come to see him personally in hopes of curing themselves. Invariably Zoshchenko discovers that their conditions are psychosomatic in nature; an absence or neglect of reason has maimed their physical and psychological health. An appropriate dose of logical analysis, so it seems, is all that is needed to restore them to a full life.

Though we remember this argument from *Youth Restored, Before Sunrise* quickly outdistances its predecessor and, quite literally, reaches cosmic proportions. As a special force transcending the individual, reason is something to which we should yield all control. Why? Its opposite, the subconscious, occupies the "lower story" of the mind and is the province of irrationality, instinct, and urge. If people can only keep its "depraved," "base" influence under lock and key, they will undoubtedly infect others until the entire world is rid of evil and barbarity—here collectively represented by fascism. All that is good, just, healthy, and life-giving comes from our preservation and promotion of reason. Nothing can resist its healing power, neither Hitler nor, so it seems, the stars above. Every object emits energy, which means that even the earth is subject to cosmic rays. Our brains, our psyches, are therefore constantly being bombarded by external forces. What effect the physical environment exerts on our thoughts and behavior is not yet known. But if it is negative, then fortunately we already possess the best defense. "Human reason will liberate us" from any undue suffering.

Zoshchenko's speculation in this direction was by his own admission somewhat fuzzy, and he left concrete answers for future investigation. This appeal, however, has fallen on deaf ears. As far as his readers are concerned, many have instead pressed *Before Sunrise* into the service of autobiography. This is understandable since the memories collected here offer us the only inside picture of Zoshchenko's youth. They are brief, poignant narratives, "miracles of condensation" as McLean writes in one of the first reviews, that often conclude with a melancholic or meditative twist.[4] Critical opinion has generally favored their unexpected "Pushkinian clarity" and "Chekhovian depths."[5] Alternately, others with interests in psychoanalysis have been drawn to *Before Sunrise* as a covert (albeit unsuccessful) attempt to get around the Freudian taboo in soviet culture. Though of course Zoshchenko explicitly rejects Freudian approaches and couches his discussion in Pavlovian terms, consensus holds that this is an expected Aesopian maneuver. By the 1930s, one could mention Freud only to attack him, whereas Pavlov remained a hero in the soviet pantheon. Therefore, though the vocabulary of *Before Sunrise* might come from a safe source, the technique, diagnosis, and treatment outlined leave no doubt as to its true origin.[6]

As is generally the case with hybridlike texts, such readings prefer parts over the whole. The problem is, however, that while *Before Sunrise* might contain autobiographical data (always a tricky matter with Zoshchenko, as we will see again), it is not autobiography. Similarly, while psychoanalytic studies, as evidenced particularly in the work of Zholkovsky, have demonstrated an undeniable link between his earlier stories, real-life neuroses, and *Before Sunrise*, they cannot fully explain the fundamentals of his legacy: the popularity of and controversies generated by his writing.[7] For this reason I will treat *Before Sunrise* not as a key to his sub- and semiconscious fears, but rather as a guide to his (fully conscious) strategies of self-interpretation. Indeed, whatever his true psychological problems, whatever happened to him in his infancy, the text continually defines the "psychological" Zoshchenko in relation to the "artistic" one and vice versa. The nature of this interaction—how they complement and illuminate each other—offers a clearer picture of what, exactly, was to be "proven with mathematical precision."[8]

Interestingly, where such precision is not to be found is in those same areas where *Before Sunrise* has garnered so much attention. Given his unusually arcane biography, we very well may feel compelled to accept his reminiscences as an authentic reflection of his past. This, notably, is the spirit with which Zoshchenko offers them. Memories of war, trysts, family, student years, and writing weave in and out of each other, as if not bound to some underlying pattern. Such an unstructured appearance would be expected if the reader is to accept these episodes as windows onto the past. The language is commensurately dispassionate and reserved, "a unique style," in McLean's words, "pruned of all false rhetoric and sentimentality."[9] Extensive appeals to the infallibility of science, to the objectivity of his self-analysis, confirm that he has left for good the compromising hand of *skaz* and irony. For once we finally seem to be reading, as Bakhtin would term it, direct authorial discourse. Such would be the expected tenor if, as Zoshchenko tells us in the text, we have before us verbal "photographs" of his life.

However, the illusion is difficult to uphold. The very question that motivates the text—why the haunting images of storm and beast, why the terror and despondency—offers the most damning evidence. The filter this mystery imposes on the presented facts is severe. Obviously other events, pleasant or not, occurred in his past, but of these there is no mention. Nor should there be. Anything not contributing directly to the thematic axis would undercut his determined (and repetitive) attempt to evoke the reader's sympathy. The terms he uses to describe himself in third person as a traumatized child comprise an exemplary catalog of self-pitying locutions: "the small child," "the poor child," "the unhappy child," "the tiny being," "the tiny creature" with a "tiny, unhappy heart." The apogee of Zoshchenko-as-victim comes in two crescendo bursts. The first describes his shock upon realizing that the cause of his neuroses originates in his infancy: "What a tragic battle! What pain, what misfortune it ensured for me! What blows were predestined for my pitiable body!"[10] The second reconstructs a childhood operation that is unique in its reference to "castration"—a most unexpected insertion given the anti-Freudian campaign in the Soviet Union and the overt claims in the text (however unrealized) of repudiating Freud's theories:

> The poor little child couldn't even imagine why they were cutting into him. He lay with his tiny legs pulled up, felt the horrific pain and saw a hand with a knife—that familiar hand of the beggar, thief, predator and killer. [Referring to other memories and dreams described before.]
> What a shocking, fateful coincidence!
> What an affirmation of my trauma! What a psychological castration! (609)

The use of "affirmation" essentially lays bare the dilemma in which Zoshchenko finds himself: attempting to write objectively of the past yet all the time with his eye to the present. This leaves the unmistakable impression that autobiographical vignettes are important insofar as evidence in his search. Zoshchenko, of course, is not directly at fault since the paradox is not unique to *Before Sunrise*. As has long been recognized, any attempt to document one's own life, no matter how minimalist or broad, cannot escape the demands of the person's here and now.[11]

The same holds true for Zoshchenko's psychoanalytic methodology. The truth is his stated goal—one that leads him to speak of the "iron formulas" (452) that undergird his approach. Such insistence on empirical accuracy is to be expected given the analyst's role as mere translator of some preexisting event. As Roy Schafer notes, positivism is the standing tradition in the field, with Freud's own view of himself as an archaeologist being its classic formulation. The analogy is well chosen, Schafer continues, because it implies that the analysand's "reality is 'out there' or 'in there' in the inner world, existing as a knowable, certifiable essence."[12] Consequently, the proper approach would be to assume that a given trauma did happen, and it is up to the analyst merely to rediscover it in its original terms.

Yet this is exactly where we should retain a measure of caution.[13] As *Before Sunrise* makes clear, the further. Zoshchenko's own search extends into the past, the more his empiricism slides. With his conscious memory ostensibly exhausted and the mystery still unsolved, he realizes he must access his infant experiences. Paradoxically, the only means of penetrating this realm is through his dreams as an adult. Unfortunately, this need, as Zoshchenko curiously admits at times, has the tendency not just to uncover but to produce the desired data, with the result being that the difference between dream, conscious memory, and, to put it bluntly, wishful thinking quickly fades.

> But then, while thinking intensively about my childhood, I saw a weird kind of dream. (589)
>
> I probably wouldn't have remembered these scenes if I hadn't thought through what I'm thinking about now, trying to understand what caused this pain, happiness and sorrow. (593)
>
> So why then would a hand be associated with a tiger? Does it mean that something else happened as well? So it does. While studying the symbolic imagery of the tiger, I saw a dream that confirmed the accuracy and verity of that symbol. (608)
>
> I probably wouldn't have remembered that event if the conclusions [of my argument] didn't coincide with it. (637)
>
> I remembered a whole lot of events, and all of them convinced me of the credibility of my conclusions. (638)[14]

Essentially everything, no matter how, when, or why Zoshchenko may have thought of it, merges onto a single plane of reference that serves as a fund from which to draw the necessary proof. In short, what qualifies as evidence is what works in the overall narrative scheme. And once again he does not hide this from us. As the following lines suggest, for him ultimately there is no functional difference in the material that makes up this fund: "I remembered a dream from a long time ago. Maybe it wasn't even a dream. Maybe my memory preserved something that actually happened in real life but remained in my mind as if a dream" (607).

Zoshchenko is not, it should be noted, playing a game with factual representation, as might be expected from Kolenkorov. Instead, what we are witness to is, arguably, an indispensable component of the analysand's success in overcoming a presumed trauma. Donald Spence makes a useful distinction between "historical truth" (what actually happened in the patient's past) and "narrative truth" (what account of the past satisfies the patient's needs).[15] The two, needless to say, may sometimes coincide, but this can never be proven on the empirical grounds that Zoshchenko and others so desire. What the analysand can do—with the express aid of the analyst's questions and comments—is try to connect various thoughts, dreams, and memories within a single web of meaning. The web that is most coherent, that accommodates the most "evidence," and that offers the most efficient explanation is, Spence argues, what the patient may come to feel is the truth of what happened. As he notes (with no small relevance to Zoshchenko's own argument), "what the patient is saying about the past must be translated into what he is demanding of the present. If he needs to be pitied, for example, he might exaggerate the misery of his childhood."[16] This immediately opens the way for the intrusion of imagination, invention, and a host of other stimuli that would normally contradict any empirical intentions. Notably, Vera Vladimirovna, Zoshchenko's wife, has stated that some of his autobiographical vignettes are fictions in the literal sense of the word. If the charge is true, then his seemingly random "photographs" are not particularly random or photographic at all.[17] This would suggest that no matter what the claims of empirical fidelity, the real value of a psychoanalytic narrative lies elsewhere. After all, what is at stake, what is important, is the therapeutic benefit of a past recounted, not its true-to-form documentation. The former heals; the latter seeks to record.

Relevancy, then, is a central criterion for what constitutes evidence in psychoanalysis. It is, perhaps, the only one from the analyst's and analysand's point of view. Far from being an objective "fact-finding expedition," in Schafer's words, their dialogue is more an instantiation of the vocabulary and conventions inherent to psychoanalytical investigation: "At the very outset, each such expedition is prepared for what is to be found: it has its maps and compasses, its conceptual supplies, and its probable destination. This preparedness (which contradicts the empiricists' pretensions of innocence) amounts to a narrative plan, form or set of rules."[18] Such "preparedness" is exactly what we witness in *Before Sunrise,* where, it should not be forgotten, Zoshchenko is both analyst and analysand. The text is written backwards, after the mystery has been solved for him, and this hindsight cannot but impose a pregiven order on the presence and sequencing of evidence.

It is significant that studies of autobiographical and psychoanalytical narrative agree on similar points. Analysand, analyst, and autobiographer do not reconstruct "what was." Rather, they reconstruct a "what was" in terms of its function for today. With pretensions to both genres, *Before Sunrise* gives us a double dose of the effect. As a result, uncovering the truth so as to satisfy the historian in each of us becomes a troublesome task. McLean readily demonstrates that relying on the text as a primary source throws a number

The Politics of Reception

of obstacles in the biographer's way. Zoshchenko, we should remember, came from a large family; that this fact is absent from descriptions of his childhood leads McLean to comment:

> Seven brothers and sisters, two older, five younger! What a crucial fact about any child's environment! Yet except for fleeting references to two sisters, there is scarcely a mention of these siblings. There is lots about Mama and a good deal about Papa amidst all those beggars and tigers and black water; but no sibling rivals are allowed to obtrude their ugly heads. Now should this omission affect our judgment of the book?[19]

However we answer McLean's question, so substantial an omission does point to something else. If the influence of the present day cannot be avoided in the discussion of the past, if the demands of the analysand dramatically shape the evidence available, then we need to ask different questions of the text: in which direction these conditions pull the work and what the relevance is of such (un)conscious interference.

THE RHETORIC OF HEALING

Given the traditions inherent to both genres, the autobiographical and psychoanalytical model more easily allows Zoshchenko to produce what had essentially eluded him for two decades: a narrative of resolution. In content and style, *Before Sunrise* is an unequivocal break with the past. Uncommon simplicity and directness and an exceptionally repetitive argument have finally eliminated the back and forth of *Youth Restored* and the zigzag of *The Blue Book*. The expression of a thought or description of an event is generally restricted to a select number of syntactical and lexical invariants with the most prominent being the authorial "I," the center of attention in the text. Exemplary is a passage describing his depressed state upon leaving the army after the Revolution:

> I had fought in many battles, was wounded and had been gassed. I had ruined my heart. Nevertheless a cheerful state of mind almost never left me.
> At the beginning of the Revolution I returned to Petrograd.
> I didn't feel any nostalgia for the past. Quite the opposite. I wanted to see a new Russia, not the depressing one I had known. I wanted healthy, radiant people all around me—not the kind, like I was myself, prone to depression, melancholy and sadness. I didn't experience any of the so-called "social alienation." Nevertheless, I began to feel despair like before.
> I tried changing cities and professions. I wanted to run away from my terrible despair. I believed that it would destroy me. (455)

Similarly, an account of his early fears stands out for its un-Zoshchenkovian rhetorical discipline: "The reader shouldn't smile at these ideas. After all, we're speaking about a child. We're speaking about the beginning of his life when the light of reason is still absent, when there is no sense of logic, no consciousness. We're speaking about a tiny creature as it experiences the world around" (611–12).

Redundancy may not make for the most gripping of narratives, but it does place minimal demands on the reader in order to comprehend the what and wherefore. Of the many questions posed in the text, all are subject to on-the-spot resolution. (Only the big one, the why of psychological trauma, is obviously delayed.) No event, person, or phenomenon is left undefined or its relevance undetermined. In verifying the significance of his dream-infant imagery, Zoshchenko (now in the third person) leads us through a series of hypotheses, each of which receives immediate confirmation:

> The child saw a hand in the dream. This hand, judging by its outspread fingers, was going to take, seize him. Most likely, the dream did not repeat an event from during the day. In the daytime such fear would evidently have been less, otherwise there would have been no dream.
> What in this case happened during the day?
> Evidently, during the day a hand took, seized, grabbed something from the child. What could it have taken, seized or grabbed that would have so terrified him? Most likely, something valuable, important which was almost equal in value to the youngster himself.
> What could be so important in a child's life?
> A toy? A nipple? A mother's breast? Food?
> Undoubtedly food. Most likely his mother's breast. That breast which fed him, gave him life, nourishment and happiness.
> Undoubtedly that breast was removed by the hand. (607–8)

This sequence of questions is followed by four short paragraphs of additional suppositions with lead-ins such as "perhaps," "maybe," and so forth. Any doubt is removed, however, when Zoshchenko steps forth in the next lines and affirms all the above assumptions, verbatim, as fact: "And so it was the hand that took away the breast, the nourishment. The hand appeared behind the child in order to grab him, seize him and carry him away." With its teleology never hidden, the story of *Before Sunrise* thus reads well, seeking to relegate us to the status of observer, a position that, as per Zoshchenko's design, does not ask for interpretive energy or freedom.

The conviction Zoshchenko exhibits in *Before Sunrise* goes hand in hand with his choice of profession. It bears a striking resemblance to the case history approach as initially given by Freud and Breuer. By virtue of its theoretical premises—the key to unlock the analysand's mystery must be discovered—the analyst is necessarily endowed with remarkable powers of foresight and knowledge. In Case No. 4 of *Studies on Hysteria*, each of Freud's suppositions regarding "Katharina's" condition is immediately proven to be correct. As far as her physical complaints are concerned, he assumes: "This did not, at first sight, sound like a nervous symptom. But it soon occurred to

The Politics of Reception

me that probably it was only a description that stood for an anxiety attack: she was choosing shortness of breath out of the complex sensations arising from anxiety and laying undue stress on that single factor."[20] Remarkably, after four questions no doubt remains: "So it was in fact an anxiety attack and introduced by the signs of a hysterical 'aura'—or, more correctly, it was a hysterical attack the content of which was anxiety."[21] His ability in outlining the preliminary facts is matched by the instant verification he can offer us for each hypothesis:

> So I said, "If you don't know, I'll tell you how I think you got your attacks. At that time, two years ago, you must have seen or heard something that very much embarrassed you, and that you'd much rather not have seen."
> "Heavens, yes!" she replied, "that was when I caught my uncle with the girl, with Franziska, my cousin."[22]

Regardless of Freud's actual success rate in healing patients, what matters here is the image he projects of himself in the text. His voice stands as the sole locus of authority; it operates as the only legitimate frame of perception against which are arraigned all others. As patient-analysand, Katharina's speech by necessity is encoded as false, reflecting some pathological condition that conceals from her an essential secret to which only Freud possesses the answer. Such an ability, as reflected by the purported success of each case history, means that he is essentially bilingual; he alone can understand the latent meaning of her speech. This endows him with the right to insert retrospective comments that confirm the truth of what has occurred. This truth, notably, is expressed in a language decidedly different from Katharina's:

> "Fräulein Katharina, if you could remember now what was happening in you at that time, when you had your first attack, what you thought about it—it would help you."
> "Yes, if I could. But I was so frightened that I've forgotten everything." (Translated into the terminology of our "Preliminary Communication," this means: "The affect itself created a hypnoid state, whose products were then cut off from associative connection with the ego-consciousness.")[23]

The presumption that only Freud can provide the necessary closure-interpretation to his patient's narrative is reified when he informs her what she must have thought at the traumatic moment when she realized that her uncle had attempted to abuse her as he had her cousin. Solely through his intercession is the "riddle solved" and Katharina "transformed." Proof comes in the final "discussion" section of the case history, where her entire account is translated—literally speaking—into Freud's terminology, the language of finality that she herself can never attain within the text.

This image of author—confirming each textual postulate, filling in each gap for the reader, pronouncing who is right and wrong—defines the new Zoshchenko. No longer the paragon of ambiguity, he rises before us as one of the few individuals in the world who is aware of the forces that drive us as humans. Notably, in *Before Sunrise* his ascension begins with Freudian-type case histories where he describes healing others in the same manner as he healed himself. He suspects, for example, that a student who often comes for consultation has fallen in love with him. She later becomes disabled, hardly able to walk. Zoshchenko immediately recognizes that this infirmity is her body's response to the fear of betraying her husband and child through feelings for him:

> I immediately understood the reason behind her ailment. I said to her: "Get me out of your head, and you'll feel better this very instant. You became ill so as not to come see me. Your legs stopped obeying because you yourself said that it would be a catastrophe if you fell in love with anybody. Your ailment protected you. It chose the most vulnerable spot."
> The woman was smart. She listened to my words with half a smile. Then she began laughing. She laughed so hard that the cane fell out of her hands. Through her laughter she said:
> "That's amazing. That's exactly what it is."
> We parted on good terms. And when she left, she forgot her cane in my room. (636)

As a miracle worker, Zoshchenko feels comfortable lacing his descriptions with none-too-subtle reminders of the validity of his approach: "there is no doubt," "I am on the right path," "yes, it was exactly like that," "no doubt remained," "later events showed that in general I was not mistaken." As he continues in this vein, the quiet, unassuming tone of his autobiographical vignettes quickly disappears—a shift critics have been reluctant to emphasize presumably because it contradicts the favored impression of a meek, modest writer who would soon fall victim to Zhdanov's attacks. Nevertheless, the desire for control raises his voice to a decidedly shrill, petulant edge. Dispassion is replaced by outright aggression, and the exclamation point becomes his favored mark of punctuation. Put simply, his goal is to convince all present (and past) of his infallibility. In a discussion of Poe's idiosyncrasies, he declares that his investigative method alone can shed light on their origin: "In these circumstances, what other reasons could there have been except for those which we are discussing in our book?" (646). Though Zoshchenko does contemplate other scenarios to explain various human ills and to demystify the melancholy that has plagued famous people, alternate voices are introduced only to be attacked. Those who do not agree with his conclusions (whether dead or alive) are reduced to a crowd trapped in their own self-deception. He casts aside biographers' attempts to clarify Balzac's unusual behavior with one sweep: "What garbage! And what ridiculous reasons have been cited to explain his manias and fears!" (659) He delivers the same contempt to those (always unnamed) who would dare question his claims as to the necessity and power of mind control:

> I know that there are a number of opponents who revile, and will continue to do so, this method of control and even the very idea of control.
> What is the nature of such protest and what conclusions do they draw?
> Several of them feel that such control cannot be achieved. And even if it is, then [they will argue] that it is not really a form of control but rather self-hypnosis.
> That, of course, is ridiculous. (690)

And with one derisive breath he dismisses any intellectuals who assume that they might have something worthwhile to say:

> Here we find a typical mistake of philosophers, writers and poets. Too often they identify their own feelings and suppositions with "the whole of humanity."
> L. N. Tolstoy felt that "nonresistance to evil" would save people from a lot of misfortune. Maybe it saved Tolstoy but that idea was absolutely foreign to other people.
> Goncharov discovered Oblomovs among the Russian people. Maybe Oblomovism typified him but in no way did it characterize Russians.
> In his novel *The Wild Ass's Skin* Balzac held to the idea that life would dwindle and fade with each passing desire. Terrified of his own feelings and wants Balzac assumed that everyone should be terrified of them as well, scaring those who thought no with death.
> That was just a gross mistake. (661)

The bald hypocrisy of Zoshchenko's objection—for who else but he has attempted to define "all of humanity," indeed, the cosmos itself, as he did on the pages of *Before Sunrise*—betrays the hyperbolic reductionism into which text and author descend. If no explanations but his own can stand and if the authority of his assertions rests on the backs of those denounced, Zoshchenko leaves us no room, within the text itself, for refutation or even comment. His way is the only viable path since, unlike others, he has literally seen it all. If we dare believe that absolute devotion to reason might be harmful, then we only reveal our own ignorance.

PREDECESSORS AND PRECEDENTS

Before Sunrise marks a permanent shift from Serapion parody to uncompromising didacticism in Zoshchenko's writing. His great conversion has been traditionally attributed by the West to the unfortunate but inevitable pressures of socialist realism. Proof might be seen in the fact that the first unequivocal sign of Zoshchenko's turn from ironic *skaz* is his contribution, "The History of a Life," to *Belomor,* the collectively written 1934 volume that attempted to justify prison labor in the Soviet Union. To be sure, writing under the auspices of Yagoda, the head of the police, would likely have that straightening-out effect, and it cannot be denied that much of Zoshchenko's work does have a direct correspondence with official demands. Yet it cannot be denied as well that this change has internal roots too. As Chudakova and Scatton have argued, it would be too facile and one-sided to identify his new voice only as a reaction to the outside.[24] His advice to beginning writers, his planning and retrospective interpretations of *Youth Restored* and *The Blue Book,* and his special invocation of the reader all confirm Zoshchenko's inner frustration with his work and the contradictory ways in which he was read.[25] Moreover, all of these essential changes, it should be noted, coincided with or followed the self-treatment described in *Before Sunrise* (which took place in real life, Zoshchenko informs us, in the early 1930s). Its style is almost a predictable result of how he resolves this conflict. Indeed, his increasing use of mechanistic metaphors in the 1930s only paves the way for the imperious lecturing of *Before Sunrise*. Here would finally be achieved the synthesis that had been denied him by some critics of *Youth Restored* and *The Blue Book.* As Zoshchenko triumphantly declares in *Before Sunrise,* his earlier work had been written "with a blind hand" when "there was still much I did not understand." Now his eyes are open; "I am free to act as I choose."[26]

It is important not to forget the chain of works, maneuvers, confessions, and pronouncements that led to *Before Sunrise*. Without this background it is tempting to assume that Zoshchenko was out to dupe the state or us readers, as M. Keith Booker and Dubravka Juraga, on one hand, and Rachel May, on the other, have recently argued.[27] Both interpretations contend that Zoshchenko does not want his thesis taken at face value and is instead conducting a covert attack against Stalinism. For Booker and Juraga, proof of authorial intent lies in textual indeterminacies; May argues for the same and cites as further evidence the very absurdity of Zoshchenko's claims. Yet substantiating intent in this manner is highly problematic. Both approaches are silent on the wealth of information that confirms the legitimacy of Zoshchenko's faith in reason. Moreover, arguing that the presence of inconsistency or ambiguity equals antistate hostility can become a slippery slope. If the post-structuralist theory that Booker, Juraga, and May adhere to asserts that all texts are inherently unstable, then one is compelled to ask the obvious but necessary question: What work of soviet literature is not subversive? Coincidentally, Robin has argued from a similar theoretical position that the canonical works of socialist realism do reveal contradictions and inconsistencies. Dare we then extend the same logic and recast Nikolai Ostrovsky, Fyodor Gladkov, and Shaginian as closet subversives? One would think not, and there lies the catch. Many of the statements in *Before Sunrise* are ridiculous; but they are not necessarily ridiculous in a wink-wink, duplicitous sense. (We need only think of Gogol's *Selected Passages from a Correspondence with Friends* as a complementary illustration.) In fact, what May identifies as the "most absurd" claim (and thus the clearest proof of Zoshchenko's alleged ironic intentions) is his paean to Kotolevsky, the rehabilitated ax murderer. But this time, as his archives reveal, Zoshchenko is not pulling our leg. Unlike what he did with the photographs in *M. P. Siniagin*, he did not use his imagination with this one.

In short, the Zoshchenko who wrote *Before Sunrise* was not the writer whom we know from the 1920s. Both the content and style of his work had changed irrevocably, and it is significant in this regard that his first successful exercise in what can be termed a resolution narrative, the 1937 "Black Prince," has no overt political message and even less to do with the contemporary ethos.[28] Foreshadowing *Before Sunrise*, it presents us with a detective script as well: discovering the secret behind the legend of gold aboard the *Prince*, a British warship that sank in a gale off Balaklava during the Crimean War. As Zoshchenko comes to the conclusion that most likely the ship carried no gold, the text becomes for us a laboratory for narrative control. His argument is cadenced by uncharacteristic insertions marking the important points for the reader: "let us say again," "to repeat," "it is completely obvious," "and so, having checked everything over, we are inclined to think that," "please remember this [for later]," "we need to pause for a minute on this work since it is of importance later," "as we will see later on and prove via documents." The authoritative tenor is borne out by Zoshchenko's employment of nonfiction (archives, journals of the time, and so forth) without an ironic catch. He even includes bibliographic footnotes—a change indeed, in light of his previous play with interpolated texts. The voices of others are not subject to deformation but instead open to authorial commentary on their historical accuracy and trustworthiness. And when it comes time to present his conclusions, he reiterates and even numbers the evidence that has led him to the belief that ("65 percent sure") the *Prince* was not even the ship discovered by divers and that ("95 percent sure") it did not have any gold on board to begin with. Here clarity has finally triumphed over confusion. But so has formula over color. The first step toward "mathematical precision" had been made.

The fact that Zoshchenko came to repudiate overt polyvalency in favor of transparency should sound familiar. We meet the same with Gogol, whose shadow looms over the whole of Zoshchenko's legacy. No other person receives as much attention throughout his writing, and in *Before Sunrise* we learn better why this is. The relation extends beyond *skaz* or clichés of laughter through tears. Both actively sought to deny their celebrated reputations as figures of ambiguity. With equal conviction (and with similar bouts of self-doubt), each attempted in the last stage of his career to recover from his writing a stability and continuity that would defeat the multiplicity of faces that readers had imposed upon him during his life. Understandably, then, their efforts follow the same pattern: injecting coherency into an authorial image fraught with tension and incongruity.

The Gogolian equivalent of *Before Sunrise* is *An Authorial Confession,* written after widespread attacks on *Selected Passages* and published posthumously.[29] In this essay, Gogol places humankind at the center of his creative efforts: "[O]ur purpose is to serve; our entire life is service." All of his concerns are subordinated to discovering the "eternal laws" of humanity, and this mission functions as an interpretive key by which to impart meaning to those episodes of his life presented in the text. His prolonged absence from Russia and consequent separation from friends and family constitute a self-imposed exile, affording him a special post of observation from which to comprehend the totality of his nation and people ("to take up a position at that place from which I can see all peoples"). As could be anticipated, the search for these laws leads him spiritually to Christ and aesthetically to the doctrine "not to sin in any way against reality, against the age, or the epoch." Only if his writing achieves this authenticity can he offer the necessary moral nourishment to his reader.

As depicted here, Gogol's lifelong service is one of self-sacrifice, the very idea that frames *Before Sunrise.* For both writers, devotion to the good of all has brought suffering upon them. Gogol's renunciation of the expected pleasures of life endows his work with "monastic" piety. Likewise, seclusion abroad fills him with "sadness," but it is a necessary step that must be undertaken in order to maintain the range and profundity of his vision. It is this goal of making his writing as real and truth-imparting as possible that gives birth to the famous request in the second edition of *Dead Souls* for readers to supply him with letters of their experiences so that he may verify his representations: "I ask you, dear reader, to correct me. I cannot complete the last volumes of my work until that time when I know Russian life from all sides." While he acknowledges that these lines will bring him torment, this, too, is a duty that cannot be forsaken: "I well knew that many would laugh at this [appeal to readers], but I was prepared to withstand any ridicule."[30]

Zoshchenko picks up, as it were, where his predecessor has left off. Describing his reaction to Gogol's letters, he makes clear the common cause both share as promethean and martyr: "What horrific suffering did the great poet experience! And what pain do we feel because of this misery of his. It never would have been if only control had been exerted over the forces from below" (657). For only one other person—himself—does Zoshchenko reserve the same emotional register: "What a painful and sorrowful life I've had!" (619) The motif of suffering plays a critical role in symbolically uniting the young Zoshchenko, the hapless victim, with the adult, the writer who has sacrificed himself in order to teach people what they need to live a valued life. After all, if Pavlov studied animals, then Zoshchenko has directly engaged humans. Lest we underestimate his achievement, he makes it known (606) that his experiment was fraught with danger and therefore not one to be repeated by the mere mortal reader.

The ego in display here reveals the additional price, over and above claimed martyrdom, that both writers have paid: severe delusions of grandeur. Zoshchenko's inflated self-image parallels Gogol's belief in his own infallibility, especially in the period 1840–41, when he had recovered from a traumatic illness in which he sensed divine intervention. In his letters of that time we witness that arrogance that will fuel *Selected Passages* and be resurrected almost a century later in *Before Sunrise:*

> It is a sin, a most grievous sin, to distract me. [to S. T. Aksakov]
>
> My words are doubly sovereign over you and a curse to whoever does not heed them. . . . Without complaint, without question do my bidding! Not for yourself alone but for me you are doing a great, great thing. Do not try to understand what precisely the benefit is for it is beyond you. . . . Oh, believe my words for they are henceforth invested with a higher power! Everything [else] can disappoint, deceive and betray you, but never will they [to A. S. Danilevsky].
>
> Oh, believe my words! . . . I cannot say to you anything more but believe my words. I myself do not dare disbelieve them [to N. M. Yazykov].[31]

Zoshchenko, too, feels that his voice holds a special force over opponents: "Every page of my book will drive such people to fury. I can already hear their squealing voices" (690).

The writers' mirrored descent into megalomania is born not just in an overbearing ego. Their very efforts to control narrative and its meaning necessarily box them into an absolutist, imperious stance. In the end, closure can be pronounced only because each believes to have accessed the truth. To this degree the religious faith behind Gogol's "eternal laws" differs little from Zoshchenko's devotion to the "iron formulas" of his science. Both terms suggest that their writing is merely a direct transmission, divested of any distorting character, of some unimpeachable authority that prefigures the text itself. The result is to wed their words to an infinitely more powerful domain. This connection gives each the right, so to speak, to berate all critics and doubtful readers. After all, if *Before Sunrise* and *An Authorial Confession* are direct reflection-instantiations of the truth, then they are a priori impervious to outside questioning.

However, as Zoshchenko makes clear, one critical difference remains between them. Only he has actually succeeded in casting out the demons and achieving a state of perfect harmony. Gogol's salvation—religion—was a false one. Zoshchenko's is real. After the abreaction of his trauma, he is literally resurrected:

> I had been killed, crushed, beaten so as to rise anew from the ashes.
>
> I lay at death's door, expecting that once again my enemy [neuroses] would come back and then all would be over. But he did not return.
>
> At times the usual symptoms would reappear but they did not bring forth terror.

> Life began to return to me. And it returned with such speed and with such strength that I was shocked and even taken aback.
> I rose from the bed already not the one who I had been. I stood up full of health and strength, with immeasurable cheer in my heart.
> With every hour, every minute—joy, happiness, elation flowed into my life. I had not known this before. (626)

The healed Zoshchenko has passed from one world to another, from despair and negation to knowledge and vitality. Gogol's tortured end—the burning of the second volume of *Dead Souls* and his suicidal resignation—only proves that he, tragically, had never really been free. Yet his defeat, Zoshchenko would hasten to add, was not in vain. It gave him a century later the road map to health, as suggested by his comment to Chukovsky in 1927: "I have thoroughly studied Gogol's biography and now see what made him lose it. I've read a lot of medical texts and understand what I need to do in order to make myself a writer of optimistic, positive works. I have to train myself and, first of all, stop believing in my illness."[32]

For Zoshchenko this epiphany is professional as well. Breaking the chains of his childhood past has made him aware that art also occupies two contrasting realms: one of delusion versus one of truth and happiness. The distinction is not merely descriptive; the two are indexes of a writer's own health and the social milieu in which he or she lives. They form one continuum, are mutually dependent upon and mutually reflective of each other, and thus directly determine a writer's literary style and success. A degenerate psychological and/or social influence produces abstruse, complex, ironic, or ambiguous modes of writing. Conversely, the authentic, truthful narrative becomes the sole province of those who have exercised sufficient reason *and* who live in a just society.

Where this leads Zoshchenko is obvious: for him the Soviet Union takes care of the external, social side of the equation; he himself has provided the inner, psychological curative. The result, no surprise, is *Before Sunrise*, which presumably could only have been written after these two conditions had been met. It therefore marks his personal victory where the analyst and artist in him meet. For only by preserving or restoring one's health can one produce a true work of art: "Absolute health—that is the ideal for art. Only then can it truly be worthy" (661). It is through this axiom that Zoshchenko distinguishes himself from writers who have come before, especially poets of the preceding generation. In his vignettes and analytical discussion he includes numerous citations from and references to Briusov, Balmont, Soloviev, and Tiniakov (a minor poet who allegedly served as the model for Siniagin). Their work embodies the very forces that Zoshchenko himself has just conquered. Reading their "decadent" lyric poetry as mirror images of the writers' real-life mind-set, he concludes, as with Briusov: "I recognized that he's not at all a bad poet. But how uneven! What melancholy overcomes him at times! What hysterical notes we hear in his song and his thoughts! What devastation lurks in his heart! Without a doubt he did not consider himself to be healthy or in the best of shape" (600). He reserves exceptional opprobrium for Soloviev upon discovering that this poet's verse does not offer a positive portrait of life: "No, it's just unpleasant to read this poetry. It's impossible to listen to such wretched, infantile music. It's disgusting to see all this trumpery, all these pitiful, affected symbols" (601). Of course, we should keep in mind that symbolist poetry and the entire modernist movement were anathema to soviet art, and since Zoshchenko assumed *Before Sunrise* would be published, such disdain is to be expected. At the same time, however, Zoshchenko encodes their poetry not only within the clichés of socialist realism but in the same terms through which he describes the suffering caused by impotent reason—that is, when the "lower floor" of one's mind, the unconscious, is in control: "unhappy," "sad," "terrifying," "terrible," "unhealthy," "anguish," "melancholy," "pain," "cynicism." Art earning these epithets is therefore not merely obsolete but pernicious, since it thrives on "base" instincts.

It is nevertheless convenient that the line Zoshchenko draws between "healthy" and "corrupt" literature also coincides with the country's sociopolitical conversion following the October Revolution. What is more, the connection allows him to link his personal transformation with the national one. He openly renounces literature of the past and its social environment, thereby confirming that just as these currents have been eliminated in the Soviet Union, so too are they absent in him. "[This] poetry is repulsive," he declares; "I feel no regret for that world which I have lost" (601). The uncompromising tone portrays him not as a successor to anyone preceding but as someone wholly distinct, representing a completely new literature. Proof of his singularity lies in select memoiristic vignettes that project—retrospectively— a Zoshchenko who always recognized that the true future of art rested with the postrevolutionary reader. Two sketches, "Brie Cheese" and "Malarkey Once Again," which give snapshots of the beginning of his career, embody this disposition and, as might be expected, have gained much currency among critics who argue that Zoshchenko's sole intention in writing was always to meet the needs of the new reader. The first, depicting his rejection from *Krasnaia gazeta* for writing in a "refined" style, prompts the following comments:

> I can't believe my eyes. I'm shocked. Maybe they just didn't understand me? I begin to think back on what I wrote. No, it seems everything was written well, correctly, all tidied-up. A little affected, with some special touches and a citation from Latin. . . . My God! *Who* was I writing for? . . . Should one have really written like that? Old Russia is no more. Before me lies a new world, new people, a new language. (499)

The second, a reverse in circumstances, follows his rejection from a journal for writing in a purposely sloppy, raw manner. In arguing his case before the editor, he comes to this conclusion:

> "The hell with him," I think, "I'll do without the big journals. They want the business as usual stuff. They want things like the classics. That's what impresses them. That's something that's easy to do. But I don't intend to write for readers who no longer exist. The people have a different understanding of literature."
>
> I'm not upset. I know I'm right. (507)

Confirmation that he is right comes in his use of reader response, as discussed in the previous chapter. Here, on the pages of *Before Sunrise,* Zoshchenko is able to achieve, so he feels, that final symbiosis between readers' needs and his prose. For what makes this work more legitimate than all that has preceded is its absolute intelligibility combined with optimism and instruction.

The last should not be discounted no matter how much Zoshchenko argues that he does not intend to produce a book of "home remedies" (*lechebnik*). As he makes patently clear throughout, the "true writer" should also be maximally informative, something we are personal witness to in the second half with its flood of dicta that readers are pressed to follow in order to save their lives and the world. The utilitarian function of literature becomes for him its single, defining criterion. In one vignette he even divests himself of any connection with the assumed frivolity and waste of purely creative exercises. Describing his impressions of working as a bootmaker (an occupation in which he was actually employed after the Revolution), he writes: "I enjoy this work. I despise intellectual labor—it's just mental puttering that most likely leads to melancholy and depression" (492). This does not signify, I believe, a rejection of writing per se ("intellectual labor" par excellence) but reflects his desire to reencode his entire literary production as a model of universal accessibility and practicality. Since a boot is—as Pisarev assured us a century ago—an object that in itself presents no demands upon an interpreter as to its presumed use, it stands as a metaphor for the ultimate in simplicity and pragmatism.

Such declarations of anti-intellectualism invoke one of the dominant myths of the soviet ethos: the worker and artist laboring side by side on the path to communism. In spirit and deed Zoshchenko's words also reenact the other great conversion story of Russian literature: Tolstoy's. With its unrelenting assault against aesthetics, its copious citation of "decadent" poetry, its denigrating accounts of the theater and museums, "What Is Art" could not have failed to impress Zoshchenko. Both writers come to essentially the same conclusion: reducing literature to a finite set of expressions—true versus false—and wielding this stamp across the whole of history. He and Tolstoy seek to canonize an infallible axiological system with which to replace the capricious tastes of the aesthetes, theoreticians, artists, and all who support them. The only true literature is that which is an instrument of pedagogy, a maxim, both assure us, known intuitively by the people. A text's value is always and only a direct function of its communicability.

By ranking accessibility over aesthetics, message over medium, each necessarily assigns an ideological value to specific modes of expression. Narrative complexity, submerged meanings, and discordant language are all impediments on the road to truth and thus, as much as improper content, are decried as agents of falsification. As Tolstoy concludes, the requisite attributes of authentic literature are "clarity, simplicity, and brevity," a triad of evaluative criteria that reappears in Zoshchenko's repudiation of prerevolutionary literature and, by extension, defines the literary face of the "healthy" and "happy" writer.[33] This is art's "purpose" (*naznachenie*), and anything, therefore, that demands of the reader more than a surface interpretation of the text is suspect. (This is not to imply that either *Before Sunrise* or Tolstoy's postconversion work mirrors these dictates of textual clarity, as their writing is more dense than this.)

The postulated division between a true and false literature is further upheld by their mutual use of class-based definitions of art. Tolstoy distinguishes between the art of the ruling class (*gospodskoe*) and that of the people (*narodnoe*); Zoshchenko, between prerevolutionary and soviet. Axiomatically for both, the first in each polar distinction is the province of mendacity, corruption, and depravity, while the second constitutes the proper model for literature. For both, this opposition is expressed in terms of a revolution; the first in each case is to be overthrown precisely because it is based on exclusion. "False art" survives on the patronage of an extreme minority and is concerned with the propagation of beliefs specific to its interests, a value system held by Tolstoy and Zoshchenko to be inherently debased. For the former, Beethoven can never match the natural energy and power of peasants' singing;[34] for the latter, Briusov's work will never save Kotolevsky, the alleged inspiration for *Before Sunrise*. Each writer therefore feels qualified to present himself as reflecting the needs of the silent majority, and each presumes his own work to be a direct expression of this popular voice—evident in Tolstoy's celebration of the "people's way" of writing and conceptualizing experience and in Zoshchenko's doctrinaire pronouncement: "I don't intend to write for readers who no longer exist."

RESOLUTION

The Tolstoyan state of narrative transparency—what Gogol failed to achieve in Zoshchenko's eyes—is a logical extension of his increasingly mechanistic view of the body and mind. If a decade earlier Zoshchenko had described himself as a "machine," able to defeat all mental and physical ills through psychological coercion, in *Before Sunrise* he seeks to exert the same "iron" control over his writing. Since the triumph of reason ensures that one can plot a straight course in life with the element of chance eliminated or otherwise rendered impotent, then one should equally be able to construct a narrative that precludes the vagaries of response and interpretation. Meaning should be determinable so that what the artist believes he or she is putting into a work is what the audience will get out of it—nothing less and nothing more if the job has been done properly. *Before Sunrise* both addresses and, so he hopes, realizes this. Its subject is not Zoshchenko's neuroses or his past but, ultimately, Zoshchenko himself. It demonstrates his anxiety over and attempted resolution of the polyvalency inherent in all discourse. Just as there is only one answer to his psychological trauma, a text must have only one authoritative reading.

That Zoshchenko would reach this, hoping to bind the reader to a single, author-determined response, reflects not just a state of delusionary infallibility. *Before Sunrise* is also his response to the interpretive rigmarole to which he had been subjected all his career. It is a dogmatic attempt to set readers straight, both present and future. Even before 1946 Zoshchenko no doubt sensed that, like Gogol's, his legacy was destined to continue as a battlefield for critics.[35] *Before Sunrise* therefore creates a myth of Zoshchenko. And, as with every myth, it has a clear-cut purpose: to establish once and for all what he stands for in art and what his art stands for.

Before Sunrise thus fulfills a profoundly literary need in Zoshchenko. Chudakova argues that here he finally finds "his own voice," one uncompromised by equivocation and ambivalence.[36] Hanson likewise sees him breaking free of the "prison" of irony.[37] Yet this victory comes at no small cost. He overcomes frustration with aesthetic indeterminacy through the ultimate closure: the representation of self as bearer, like Tolstoy, of the Single Truth, of the one answer for all questions, of the one word for all people.[38] The discovery spells an end for literature: it imposes a finality of function and effect by freezing artistic expression to a preset, unchanging teleology. His entire past and literary output are reduced to the One Purpose, a maneuver that necessarily bleaches his writing of its own singularity. Taken to its logical end, the metaphor makes Zoshchenko into a mere transcriber of the world outside, the epitome of noncreative use of words. Machines, after all, are not known for initiative and innovation.

The machine is, in truth, an imagined state. No narrative matches the world it describes; no narrative can force the reader into a set response. Therefore, even at Zoshchenko's most "closed," we need not find ourselves in similarly narrow straits. No matter what its claimed value as the purveyor of complete knowledge, *Before Sunrise* does not necessarily constitute for us a literary terminus. We approach such an end, we become the quiescent, malleable reader that Zoshchenko desires, only if we accept the text without the critical apparatus that his initial foray into autobiography, "About Myself, Ideology and Some Other Stuff as Well," provides. Indeed, if, as Zoshchenko desired, his entire body of work leaves us with a lesson, it perhaps is not the power of reason, but an increased sensitivity to the inescapable contradictions and complexities of life and its representation.

In the end Zoshchenko's sentiments betray to us a dilemma inherent in his attempt to reclaim his name. By restricting his writing to a single effect, by trying to impose univalency onto earlier, openly ambivalent texts, Zoshchenko echoes what critics have sought to do. For this reason it would be shortsighted to speak of his reception without including his own effort to squeeze his work into a specific paradigm, whether in the construction of reader or, tangentially, in the construction of self. He follows, no less, the same path of constriction and closure—replete with the same selectivity and tendentiousness observable in his critical legacy. The irony is once again pointed and says more about Zoshchenko's work than about the author himself: even the writer could not escape the same problems that his readers have faced. The text always has the last word.

Conclusion

Reading Soviet Writers after Socialist Realism

> And they're still not writing anything about Zoshchenko
>
> —Ilf and Petrov

THE PAST SIXTY-FIVE YEARS have certainly made up for the neglect Ilf and Petrov first derided.[1] By now Zoshchenko's name has moved through many critics' hands, acquiring disparate and often irreconcilable colors along the way. For this reason his legacy at once captures the tortuous contours of the soviet literary experience with its alternating turns of praise and persecution. Yet, at the same time, it remains manifestly at odds with our traditional perception of what such a fate should signify. His writing resists the zero-sum/official-dissident axiology through which most critics, both then and now, have tried to pin him down. Why this anomaly arises, I have argued, is due to a constant of his work: a wide range of narratological, linguistic, characterological, generic, and other compositional motifs of both fiction and nonfiction are turned on end.

Here, I believe, lie the roots of contention in his legacy. Whether Zoshchenko is taken as pro- or antisoviet, most critics have sought to contain him within a realist-referential paradigm, yet it is precisely at this point that the tension between text and expectations snaps. Indeed, within all the efforts to make his literary texts function as an authoritative document of his person and society, there remains the sense that something prior impedes this process. His literary evasions confound and impinge upon the norms by which a coherent fictional world or documentary treatise could be formulated. Whatever form this obduracy takes—deformation of convention, authorial contradiction, narrative inconsistency, stylistic incompatibility—it resonates and is refracted through problems of *skaz* and genre, the representation of life and character, the image of writer, and the boundaries of fiction and nonfiction. These are the points that have alternately amused, bewildered, frustrated, and incensed readers, including Zoshchenko himself, driving him in the later stages of his life to a near repudiation of his earlier writing.

If the clash between what readers have needed and what his writing parodies has fueled dissension over intent and meaning, then it is not surprising that the first casualty in this conflict has been Zoshchenko himself, the victim of a reciprocal strategy on both sides of the Atlantic to cut his work down to ideologically sound and uniform proportions. In this respect his legacy echoes that of other contemporaries famous for ironic-absurdist approaches to literature. Exemplary here would be Platonov, whose writing, Thomas Seifrid ably demonstrates, also cannot be defined by standard linguistic or generic categories.[2] Notably, his reception shares many of the same features as Zoshchenko's: initial soviet hostility to unorthodox language and narrative ambiguity; a later tradition of realist interpretations seeking to understand him in conventional mimetic modes; a postsoviet rehabilitation that has made him clairvoyant in predicting a dire future for the Soviet Union. Such writers are indispensable to the field not only, of course, for their own literary merits but because the difficulties of their writing have much to say about what we do and have done as critics. For this reason, bringing to light the origin and effect of the interpretive surgery done on Zoshchenko has been only a preliminary goal. How he has been read affords essential insight into how we have sought to make sense of soviet-Russian literature and its representative writers and texts.

In this task we cannot escape the legacy of socialist realism. Today it may seem a matter of course to agree with the most recent survey of contemporary Russian literature, which declares that "socialist realism is a relic of the past."[3] Few mark its relevance anymore with capital letters. Most, especially in the former soviet and eastern bloc countries, have long since washed their hands of it. All seem to have thrown up their hands trying to understand its protean faces, with consolation, if any, resting in the fact that even its supporters have been known to retreat in frustration. Will we ever surpass the definition reportedly offered by Aleksandr Fadeev, once head of the Writers' Union: "The hell if I know what it is"?[4]

Yet however much we may celebrate its demise, socialist realism remains a part of our critical heritage. As the centerpiece and bête noire of the field, it still informs, consciously or not, our approach to writers like Zoshchenko. Put simply, we have found ample ground to answer Fadeev by concurring on "what the hell it is" at a more definitive level: the value accorded the system. Critical tradition informs us that the theoretical base of socialist realism was "self-contradicting," "incoherent," and "corrupt"; its methodology "schizophrenic" and "circular"; its demands "naive" and "stupid"; its ideas "pathetic and bewildering"; its effect "noxious"; and its application so political that it "lacked any real meaning as a literary term."[5] Nor have its soviet antecedents enjoyed a substantially better reputation. The pugilistic broadsides of marxist critics earlier in the 1920s were likewise "crude" and their impact "suffocating" and "deadening."[6] In Edward Brown's singular conclusion, they displayed little beyond "flatulent ignorance," an epitaph perhaps without precedent but which, physiologically speaking at least, marks the place where most would now consign their activity.[7]

The rhetoric that demonized socialist realism in the West is an inverse mirror of that which canonized Zoshchenko. For it is directly from within institutional aversion to socialist realism that he and others first gained international recognition and were enlisted in absentia as rebels against the soviet state. Though he was never imprisoned or exiled, his name could not be divorced from the Western critical tradition that, for the better part of five decades, sought to deny socialist realism's very authenticity, validity, and worth. Why this tradition took hold is not a contested point. If anywhere Twain's fear of "chloroform in print"[8] was to be realized, then surely from the West's point of view it was here, in both a metaphoric and a literal sense. Indeed, creativity and honesty, anesthetized by force, led Solzhenitsyn to provide one of the more concise and symbolic definitions of socialist realism: "a solemn pledge to abstain from truth."[9]

It would be wrong to deny the validity of Solzhenitsyn's charge. Nevertheless, contempt for the system placed a special task before the field: the search for responsibility and blame. Hence the *what* of socialist realism tended to give ground to a gnawing *why:* In which phenomena—political, aesthetic, social, or personal—could we find its source? The list of culprits, beginning of course with Stalin himself, quickly spread. If theoretical roots could be found in the marxist-proletarian prototypes of the 1920s, what then of civic-oriented fiction and literary criticism of the nineteenth century? Might not the original sin be with Belinsky or Chernyshevsky, two prerevolutionary critics who were canonized in the soviet pantheon? To some degree, such studies of an "organic" or "evolutionary" socialist realism demonstrated that cultural phenomena do not appear in isolation, thereby anticipating later theories of its negotiation and integration of competing aesthetic-political interests. Elsewhere, they traded accusations of who/what was guilty of this abomination. Ultimately, hints of the socialist realist virus could be found wherever the scholar looked—reflecting that particular problem of paternity-suit investigations. Depending on how it was defined (as a Party phenomenon, a literary doctrine, etc.), evidence could be unearthed in almost any Russian cultural tradition.

More important for our purposes was the methodological legacy of such searches. Given the undeniably confusing ground of early soviet literature, scholars tended to concentrate on big-gun statements: Lenin's 1905 declaration on Party literature, the ostensible compromise between literary factions authored by the Party in 1925, platform statements by officials or groups, the credo of the Writers' Union, and, of course, Zhdanov's 1946 attack. This primary reliance on decreelike sources to map the contours of soviet literature left a decisive impact on the field in two fundamental ways, both of which have shaped the tenor of Western interpretations of Zoshchenko. First, it circumscribed what meaning was perceived as operative in this environment. Literary phenomena were treated primarily as realizations and extensions of ideological-aesthetic platforms. Less consideration was given to how meaning might circulate contrary to or outside of the fixed lines of platform debate; the only voices that counted were those "up there." Second, it fed the impression of soviet culture as strictly a monolithic, top-down process. (This was generally commensurate with the reign of the totalitarian paradigm in the fields of history and political science, with their image of an atomized, passive society, helpless before the machinations of the Party.[10]) Few still adhere to this image, but a recent (1990) echo offers a concise illustration of how it served to deny the existence of complexity or plurality in soviet arts: "In 1934, Socialist Realism . . . terminated the aesthetic polymorphism of virtually all artistic expression in the USSR by imposing upon it a set of ideological dicta, thus inaugurating *l'art engagé* to a degree unparalleled in human history. Henceforth, thousands of writers, artists and composers in this multi-national empire have been reduced to one compliant voice, signature and quest."[11]

The smooth passage from "dicta" to "one compliant voice" yields a model of cultural intercourse that is not merely unidirectional or monologic but that constitutes a near zero-level of meaning production—in other words, where little meaning is recognized as culturally operative except that sanctioned or proclaimed by official sources. The impact this perception has had upon the field can be seen in the tendency of Western scholarship to operate within the terms and categories sanctioned by the Party; our early reliance on Zhdanov to define Zoshchenko's value is but one example of this kind of discursive seduction. Spokesperson, manifesto, decree, and other programmatic, policy-oriented voices always colored themselves as primary agents in meaning production, and, given our need for clear boundaries between good and evil in this environment, we unwittingly followed suit. Of course, while Zhdanov and Stalin may always have dreamed of such power to dictate meaning, it is no small irony that some Western critics have obliged them.

In the end, just as with the totalitarian paradigm as a whole, the stage was set for refutation. In 1986 Robin published *Socialist Realism: An Impossible Aesthetic,* which originated with a premise that the field had long resisted: soviet literature, whatever reputation it now enjoys, was not necessarily an abomination to its contemporary reader. It had validity and vitality for its time and arose from a synthesis of interests. Arguing as well against Western perceptions of a "controlled" literature, she enlisted Bakhtin to demonstrate that soviet novels resisted Party attempts to restrict textual meaning. Texts, as we are accustomed to hear, are slippery things: "they are tripped up somewhere, by the writing, by the novelistic space, by the alterity and the heterogeneity that undermine their discursive control."[12]

As evidenced by her title, Robin's parallel step was to turn this point onto the principles of socialist realism itself, which collapsed before the onslaught. Socialist realist intentions were unrealizable because they were "epic" in orientation, whereas the novel openly challenges such semantic impositions. Any attempt to combine or reconcile the two was therefore predestined for defeat:

> If every utterance is divided, if every utterance inevitably carries within itself the mark, the trace of words of others, if polyphony is already operative and is not simply a potentiality in language (all the more so in fiction), in the space the narration gives, in that space hollowed out for heterogeneity by the multiplicity of focalizations, viewpoints and voices, in that constitutive heteroglossia, then the dream of a full, homogeneous, smooth, and transparent discourse is utopian, unrealizable. Meaning cannot be congealed as doxa. Discourse cannot be simply concretized as doxa, as death of meaning, as preconstructions operating to efface the subject of enunciation, to universalize. Meaning always escapes and scatters itself, undetermines itself.[13]

Robin effectively wielded a double-edged argument, one aimed at soviet ideologues who would reduce literature to a single "compliant voice" and at critics in the West who would grant them the same. But the need to prove once again the fallibility of the system made her point of departure problematic. Having accepted the literature as having contemporary value, she then marked its doctrinal base as conceptually impossible and thus a failure—a closure that effectively halted any further inquiry into contemporary response and the dynamics of how readers may have understood the impossible. Recoding the usual target through a dense theoretical frame did not alter the fact that Robin, poised between validation and negation, made it clear which side we should again come down on. Her conclusion only brought us back to Andrei Siniavsky (writing, as Abram Tertz, in the late 1950s from inside the Soviet Union), who, in a still formidable analysis of socialist realism, pronounced it a "loathsome literary salad" for trying to combine the "uncombinable."[14]

Analyses of socialist realism that draw upon structuralist and poststructuralist ideas of textual instability have made the case for dismissing its precepts all the more convincing. Yet the continuing effort to prove the system's fallibility can lead us into a corner. Confidently armed with modern-day theory and its concomitant suspicion of all pretensions to authoritative discourse, we might find it easy to dismiss those systems that fail to admit our own dictum: "realism is a construct." The implied principle would then be that since socialist realism was not immersed in Bakhtin (far from it, as he was kept in exile!) it was blind to or ignored the requisite "heteroglossia," "hybridity," "plurilingualism," "dialogism," "confusion of accents," and so forth that are evident in all expression. But should sins against Bakhtin close the case? To answer affirmatively would risk descent into theoretical hubris. Viewed through the sophisticated critical lens available at the end of this century, what literary system, we might ask, does not display a certain naïveté, ignorance, myopia, or "utopianism"?

Before Robin, others were working to avoid this potential trap. Though doubt regarding socialist realism's claims of showing "reality in its revolutionary development" was never jettisoned, it became acceptable, especially through the work of Katerina Clark, to study the system's precepts on their own terms without need of qualification or denigration.[15] Here literary studies (always a little behind) followed the path of a new generation of Western historians and political scientists who had begun to argue that the Kremlin and the Party were not the be-all and end-all of the soviet experience. Life there was not so regimented or controlled as previous totalitarian models had assumed, and the very term, however poignant and compelling, had lost much of its explanatory authority. As David Joravsky has observed, totalitarianism had become so heavy with cold war freight that it seemed more "a missile in ideological combat rather than a concept in objective thought."[16] Crucial, then, to a broadened understanding of socialist realism was the push to integrate other voices into the debate on its origins and evolution; hence, following Robin's attention to soviet readers (upon which Zoshchenko's efforts in the same direction shed much light), Boris Groys incorporated the utilitarian orientation of certain avant-garde groups.[17]

Additional studies have continued to question the image of Stalinist culture as a monolithic giant and, by extension, of its literature as a direct reflection of official dictate. With an emphasis on overcoming a strict opposition among the avant-garde, intelligentsia, and Party, Clark's recent *Petersburg: Crucible of Cultural Revolution* offers a more complex understanding of the negotiated, problematic interaction of cultural forces.[18] More attention as well has been directed to the internal dynamics of socialist realism with the intent of accounting for its own peculiar logic and, pace Robin, the "possibility" of existence.[19] And, closer to home, David Shepherd's study of soviet metafiction (though Zoshchenko is curiously absent) questions our habit of dividing soviet literature into competing realms of "pure art" and "propaganda."[20]

As a result, the categories that underwrote the interpretation of socialist realism during the cold war no longer command the attention or authority of before. Yet the same cannot necessarily be said of individual writers. The urge to disqualify socialist realism bequeathed to the field a distinct vocabulary of "twos"—right/wrong, official/dissident, real/false, success/failure—that has proven difficult to relinquish. The impeccable clarity and concision of this inheritance would be the envy of other disciplines except for the cost, as Zoshchenko's legacy unequivocally illustrates, of making cultural phenomena conform to these antimonies. To this day Zoshchenko is held in place by our fixation, stated or not, with 1946. The ipso facto condition I described at the beginning—the writer who is attacked at any time by the state qualifies, by virtue of this, as being intentionally antisoviet—has not lost its centrality. Why this is so is not just a reflection of genuine concern over the tragedy of Zoshchenko's final years. As I have argued in the first three chapters, it also serves as an essential critical tool. It makes the soviet literary environment eminently accessible by providing transparent, morally sound categories to script writers into preset roles. Reducing the operative terms of evaluation to good-bad, enemy-ally, allows for the most efficient way to account for the whole of soviet culture. Zhdanov and the like can be packed to one side, Zoshchenko and the rest to the other.

This habit does not do justice to the field. As I have sought to demonstrate, soviet culture (especially in its early period) was immensely variegated at the level of both official and popular response. Despite the politicization of his name, despite his eventual persecution, how Zoshchenko's works were read was never a simple reflex of some "for or against the state" mentality. This condition alone should dispense with the facile yet expedient way that the reception of soviet writers is often handled in the West: what supported the establishment was accepted, what did not was rejected. The appropriation of the unorthodox *Youth Restored* and *The Blue Book* for the canon suggests that what a work came to mean was a complex affair. And it is in studying the strategies and processes of this meaning production—how in concrete ways a text could be read to fit or oppose a given agenda—that we can gain a more complete picture of soviet cultural praxis. Nothing less than the very chaos of Zoshchenko's legacy—the vagaries of his reception, the confused vacillation of critical opinion, the contradictory responses of "mass" readers—illustrates that the writing-production of literature and its reading-interpretation was, even in this most heavily ideologized context, an unpredictable phenomenon. Unfortunately, our traditional recourse, a priori, to bipolar definitions only boxes us into fixed conclusions. It flattens this picture, removing vital shades and nuances.

Nor does this tradition do justice to Zoshchenko. It is problematic, to say the least, to compartmentalize him in such terms, whether we are speaking of *skaz*, readerships, reference, or genre. That his parodies clashed with soviet interpretive norms of course should not be downplayed. Yet it would be premature to draw the line there. They compromise any attempt to extract some uniform semantic orientation. Western critical treatment of his texts demonstrates this condition no less than the soviet one. In fact, the problems *all* have faced suggest that his parodies transcend any single political orientation. They target instead the referential coherence that no doubt most readers, including myself, generally hope to find in literature. Here lies the value of Zoshchenko's own attempts to obtain it, especially as a projected reader in *Before Sunrise*. What are we to do if the author takes the greatest shortcut of all in the quest for univalency: declaring himself infallible? In the end, as we could say of Gogol, Zoshchenko's own frustrated efforts in trying to make his writing conform to a single orientation suggest that it would have upset, amused, or otherwise perplexed readers regardless of the time or context of its publication.

That Zoshchenko was aware of the problematic nature of his writing should not be forgotten. In 1928, during the first wave of critical hostility, Zoshchenko made the notable retort: "I am an artist and this quality, unfortunately, will never leave me."[21] The statement is quintessential Zoshchenko, with an assertion ("I am") immediately qualified by hesitation ("unfortunately"). This suggests an unwillingness to join or sanction the political labeling that had come to dominate critical discourse in the Soviet Union. Yet his words also speak to us as a warning against renewed Manichaean definitions of his literary work. To be sure, important exceptions exist. This book could not have been written without the penetrating analyses of Zoshchenko's verbal art produced by his formalist contemporaries (including here Vinogradov) and, later, by Titunik and Chudakova. Zholkovsky, Hanson, and Scatton as well avoid narrow typecasting in their recent studies of his psychological interests and evolutionary development, respectively.[22]

These studies notwithstanding, the impact of a bipolar vocabulary has not dissipated today. On the contrary, though the language of the cold war has run its course, a zero-sum image of Zoshchenko's literary achievement has gained new life in a changed political and theoretical climate. For Russia, as discussed in the introduction, Zoshchenko has proven an invaluable tool in castigating the Stalinist-socialist realist past. Likewise in the West, various post-structuralist readings, though insisting on ambiguity and indeterminacy, cannot do without the monochromatic image of Zoshchenko as implacable enemy of the state. May's addition to (and simultaneous criticism of) psychoanalytic readings (chapter 6) reveals many paradoxes and multivalencies in *Before Sunrise,* yet ultimately hitches them to a familiar mimetic paradigm: a fragmented text serves as subversive commentary on a fragmented soviet reality. Similarly Popkin's original deconstructive reading of Zoshchenko's "topoi of insignificance" (chapter 2) concludes on the same anticommunist tenor of decades before (and, characteristically, is limited in focus to the 1920s). A symbolic, if unintentional, allegiance with cold war predecessors can be found in her version of Zoshchenko's eight-point plan of "insurrection" against the "regime"[23]—a five-point jump, we recall, from Sven's three-pointer of 1958, but one that would have pleased Zhdanov nonetheless.

In effect, the politics of Zoshchenko have endured, reencoded in today's critical interests and language. The most emphatic resurrection of the old Zoshchenko in new theoretical clothes is Booker's and Juraga's 1995

Bakhtin, Stalin and Modern Russian Fiction,[24] where the writer, along with Ilf and Petrov, Vasily Aksenov, Sasha Sokolov, and others, is enlisted once more for the "assault" on socialist realism. (This reminds us of Heller's earlier use of a combat metaphor; as is evident here, the language has become distinctly more aggressive.) Bakhtin appears in the guise of a commander wielding strategies of dialogism and polyphony that are to be instantiated by the foot soldier-writers in order to thwart their nemesis. The stakes are nothing less than a good part of twentieth-century Russian literature, over which, we are reminded, Stalin hangs like a "specter." The results, to be sure, are never much in doubt; of more interest is how the battle is fought.

Booker and Juraga make the welcome claim that they avoid an "either-or" approach to the subject. Yet, as in the case of Zoshchenko, they immediately return us to familiar grounds. Applauding those critics who are "consistently on the look-out for anti-Soviet themes," they reduce Zoshchenko's interests in health, reason, and psychology to a uniform Aesopian ploy in order to attack socialist realism. Discursively, since *Youth Restored* and *Before Sunrise* are textbook incarnations of heteroglossia, they offer us a "subversive dialogic complexity." This quality makes them paradigmatic Bakhtinian "novels," which, in turn, makes them inherently antisoviet.

These conclusions are not difficult for Booker and Juraga to substantiate for a single reason. All the messy facts of what occurred then are quietly ignored; all evidence of subversive intent lies elsewhere, in Bakhtin's terminology. With *Youth Restored,* for example, they state that Zoshchenko's criticism of socialist realism is "quite clear." Yet there is no reference to how this text was actually read or how soviet critics dealt with its "subversion." No acknowledgment is made as to how the text, for all its anomalies and alleged transgressive parts, could be accommodated within existing norms—and this at the inaugural stages of socialist realism! Indeed, the very argument that a "generic mixture" was inherently subversive in the soviet environment would come as a surprise to most readers of the 1930s. After all, one of the most genre-bending discursive stews of the soviet canon was the aforementioned *Belomor,* the regrettable collective celebration of prison camp labor that mixed documentary, fictionalized history, *skaz* (Zoshchenko's contribution), autobiography, and lyric outburst with a whole host of official documents (citations of honor, letters, telegrams, orders, and so forth.)[25] If we came to Zoshchenko for the first time via Booker and Juraga, we no doubt would think that *Youth Restored* had been banned, he imprisoned, or worse. This was decidedly not the case.

Booker and Juraga's argument does include a necessary qualification: acknowledgment of the ambiguity of Zoshchenko's writing. In twenty pages they mention no fewer than four times that it is "susceptible to multiple interpretations." It is clear, however, that they themselves are not comfortable with this prospect. Each time openness of interpretation is quickly and invariably replaced by a single conclusion—Zoshchenko is attacking the precepts of the state. Regarding his *skaz,* Booker and Juraga rightfully argue that "depending on how one interprets subtle intonations in his language, the stories may be interpreted as anywhere from highly orthodox to extremely subversive." Here they hit upon the key to his unconventionality. Yet nowhere is this paradox left to stand; nowhere are we able to reflect on how such an intriguing language was actually received or how soviet critics may have manipulated its ambiguity to their own advantage. Any such questions are sacrificed on an altar of clarity as Booker and Juraga harness, a priori, all expressions of polyphony and ambiguity to an uncompromising antisoviet agenda.

I close with their study not only because of its contemporaneity, but because it encapsulates the principal issues of Zoshchenko's critical tradition. Stalin may be the "specter" plaguing modern Russian literature, but the field has also found it difficult to shake the same ghost. If earlier, realist readings of Zoshchenko have lost currency in today's theoretical climate, the push to retain the same ideological divisions has remained. Though Booker and Juraga do provide insight into increased possibilities of reading Zoshchenko through Bakhtin, in the end they and others maneuver Zoshchenko back onto the procrustean bed that attended his first appearance in Western Slavistics. Recognition of discursive complexity, multiplicity, and ambivalence has now become almost axiomatic; the hunt for subversion is also endemic. But here we see some of the problems of an all too hasty marriage between the two, of the assumption that where there is one, the other must be. With no provisions to register writer or voice outside a zero-sum, pro/anti stance, the terms in which soviet culture can be understood are restricted to the very same coda with which we began. The old agenda is made new with the addition of a more modern theoretical engine.

Leaving aside the reductionist reading of Bakhtin, we find here a continuing trend: the rule of a theoretical paradigm wherein its proof becomes the critic's primary goal. We certainly should welcome new approaches because they cause us to ask questions of texts we might not normally raise; they can open our eyes to facets and features of culture and expression whose existence we might not otherwise suspect. The benefit, nonetheless, is double-edged. They can just as well do the opposite, prematurely cutting off our horizons of inquiry out of deference to a paradigm's cohesion. This undoubtedly explains why in the whole of Booker and Juraga's discussion of Zoshchenko the only concrete references to the soviet environment itself are dates of publication. It also clarifies why there are none to Zoshchenko's own commentaries on his work, whether published or in correspondence. That side of the picture would surely muddy up the clean lines they have canonized in Bakhtin's name. Their silence is telling but, unfortunately, typical. It upholds the tradition of viewing Zoshchenko's work through one template and discarding anything that upsets the picture. Needless to say, the empirical conditions of meaning production and exchange—that is, the *actual* as opposed to the presumed cultural response—is certainly a more tangled, messy affair. It is for this very reason that we cannot afford to ignore it.

When the exercise of a theory comes at the expense of literally closing our eyes to substantial amounts of material—most of which, it should be kept in mind, was in Zoshchenko's case available before glasnost—then pause is needed. Paradoxically, the pursuit of subversion above all else can begin to work at cross-purposes. It is of course a necessary term, especially for the soviet context, but it has become problematically capacious and is cast about with a facility that weakens its potency for those times when its use is unquestionably called for. The all-too-casual dismissal of empirical questions and the overwillingness to substitute in these blank spots what theory or agenda says should be there again risk leaving us in an unhealthy position. If reluctant to recognize grayness, dissonance, or noise in the soviet literary environment, then we confine ourselves once more to select bodies of evidence in order to uphold a dominant myth. Once more we operate with a limited vocabulary of plus-minus, for-against. We surely may welcome the passing of socialist realism—ethically for its bloody legacy, aesthetically for its ideological reductionism—but we need not hold on to or resurrect the methodological and evaluative premises that were born in opposition to it.

Notes

INTRODUCTION

1. Andrei Zhdanov, "Doklad t. Zhdanova o zhurnalakh 'Zvezda' i 'Leningrad,'" *Zvezda* 7–8 (1946): 7–22. The August 14th Party Resolution was printed in a number of organs; in *Zvezda* it appears before Zhdanov's speech on pages 3–6.

2. This is a distillation of responses from the following: L. Dmitriev, "O novoi povesti Zoshchenko," *Literatura i iskusstvo*, 3 December 1943; "Na obsuzhdenii zhurnala 'Oktiabria,'" *Literatura i iskusstvo*, 11 December 1943; V. Gorshkov et al., "Ob odnoi vrednoi povesti," *Bol'shevik* 2 (1944): 56–58; N. Tikhonov, "Otechestvennaia voina i sovetskaia literatura," *Bol'shevik* 3–4 (1944): 25–40; A. Egolin, "Za vysokuiu ideinost' sovetskoi literatury," *Bol'shevik* 10–11 (1944): 39–49.

3. Gorshkov et al., "Ob odnoi vrednoi povesti," 57.

4. Zhdanov reportedly changed the title from "Concerning a Harmful Novel" to "Concerning *One* Harmful Novella." On this and Zoshchenko's defense at a December 1943 meeting of the Presidium of the Writers' Union, see Denis Babichenko, *Pisateli i tsenzory: sovetskaia literatura 1940-kh godov pod politicheskim kontrolem TsK* (Moscow: Rossiia molodaia, 1994), 72–81. In *Literaturnyi front: istoriia politicheskoi tsenzury, 1932–1946 gg.* (Moscow: Entsiklopediia rossiiskikh dereven', 1994), Babichenko has compiled a number of relevant documents relating to this and the 1946 incident, including an NKVD "conversation" with Zoshchenko in July 1944.

5. This fact sets the ground for the second traumatic event in Zoshchenko's last years: his public refusal in 1954 before a group of British students (the "enemy" no less) to accept the 1946 pronouncement. Though in a subsequent, "explanatory" speech Zoshchenko seems to have been protesting the specific vocabulary Zhdanov used, officials took it as a sign of continued defiance to the Party itself. Zoshchenko's apparent failure to repent guaranteed the continued suppression of both Zoshchenko and his work throughout the Thaw. The main source for this encounter with British students is Lidiia Chukovskaia. For reprinted sections of her diary see, M. Z. Dolinsky, "Dokumenty: materialy k biograficheskoi khronike," in Mikhail Zoshchenko, *Uvazhaemye grazhdane: parodii, rasskazy, feletony, satiricheskie zametki, pis'ma k pisateliu, odnoaktnye komedii*, ed. M. Z. Dolinsky (Moscow: Knizhnaia palata, 1991), 119–20. For a stenogram of Zoshchenko's

speech, see ibid., 120–23, and Iu. Tomashevskii, "'. . . Pisatel' s perepugannoi dushoi—eto uzhe poteria kvalifikatsii': M. M. Zoshchenko: pis'ma, vystupleniia, dokumenty, 1943–1958," *Druzhba narodov* 3 (1988): 181–84. See also Daniil Granin's account of Zoshchenko's speech in "Mimoletnoe iavlenie," *Ogonek* 6 (1988): 9–11, 29.

6. L. Plotkin, "Propovednik bezideinosti—M. Zoshchenko," *Zvezda* 7–8 (1946): 217–22. At this time Plotkin was the deputy director of the Institute of Russian Literature.

7. Stalin reportedly states this at a meeting with the Presidium of the Writers' Union. Benedikt Sarnov and Elena Chukovskaia, "Sluchai Zoshchenko," *Iunost'* 8 (1988): 70.

8. Mikhail Chumandrin, "Chei pisatel—Mikhail Zoshchenko," *Zvezda* 3 (1930): 210.

9. Tsesar' Volpe, "Dvadtsat' let raboty M. M. Zoshchenko: statia pervaia," *Literaturnyi sovremennik* 3 (1941): 129.

10. Evgeniia Zhurbina, "'Ikh sobstvennye melodii': o Mikhaile Zoshchenko," *30 dnei* 10 (1935): 81.

11. S. V., "Vecher Mikh. Zoshchenko," *Komsomol'skaia pravda*, 27 November 1932.

12. "Pisateliu M. M. Zoshchenko," *Krasnaia gazeta*, 13 November 1938.

13. "Ukaz Prezidiuma Verkhovnogo Soveta SSSR o nagrazhdenii sovetskikh pisatelei," *Literaturnaia gazeta*, 5 February 1939.

14. As compiled from numbers given by Iurii Tomashevskii in *Litso i maska Mikhaila Zoshchenko* (Moscow: Olimp, 1994), 346.

15. Zoshchenko's letters to Stalin are reprinted in Sarnov and Chukovskaia, "Sluchai Zoshchenko," 74; Denis Babichenko, "Delo ob 'otravlenii.' Mikhail Zoshchenko ob"iasniaetsia s nachal'stvom," in *Neizvestnaia Rossiia: XX vek*, ed. V. Kozlov, G. Bordiugov, S. Vakunov et al. (Moscow: Istoricheskoe nasledie, 1992), 1:140–42; Tomashevsky, "'. . . Pisatel,'" 173–74. An earlier letter to Stalin regarding *Before Sunrise* is reprinted in Tomashevsky, "'. . . Pisatel,'" 169. The letter to Zhdanov is reprinted in Babichenko, "Delo," 143–44. However, Tomashevsky (177) states that this letter was never sent. The letter to Ermilov (along with Ermilov's reply) is reprinted in Tomashevsky, "'. . . Pisatel,'" 184–86.

16. For more detail on publication of "The Adventures" in *Zvezda* without Zoshchenko's knowledge, see Linda Hart Scatton, *Mikhail Zoshchenko: Evolution of a Writer* (Cambridge, Eng.: Cambridge University Press, 1993), 43. For a reading of the story as an antisoviet tract, see Vasa Mihaslovich, "Zoshchenko's 'Adventures of a Monkey' as an Allegory," *Satire Newsletter* 4, no. 2 (1967): 84–89.

17. Written in 1955, this letter is excerpted in Sarnov and Chukovskaia, "Sluchai Zoshchenko," 80.

18. Kornei Chukovsky, diary entry for March 30, 1958, in *Dnevnik, 1930–1969* (Moscow: Sovremennyi pisatel', 1994), 267.

19. The Dostoevsky-as-lackey declaration was pronounced by Vladimir Ermilov in "F. Dostoevskii i nasha kritika," *Literaturnaia gazeta,* 24 December 1947; the "hyenas" statement was delivered by Alexander Fadeev at the World Congress of Intellectuals at Breslau. His speech appears in "Nauka i kul'tura v bor'be za mir, progress i demokratiiu," *Literaturnaia gazeta,* 29 August 1948.

20. "Soviet Reaction Decried," *New York Times,* 9 August 1949, 4. For other representative media reports of post-1946 soviet culture, see Drew Middleton, "Soviet Arts Trace Political Pattern," *New York Times,* 10 February 1948, 12; Brooks Atkinson, "In the Arts the Kremlin Line is Mid-Victorian," *New York Times,* 22 February 1948, sec. 6, pp. 12–13, 53–54; C. L. Sulzberger, "Communist Party Steers Russian Mental Processes," *New York Times,* 21 December 1948, 22; and Harrison Salisbury, "Russia Tightens the Curtain on Ideas," *New York Times,* 26 December 1948, sec. 6, pp. 9, 30–31.

21. Walter N. Vickery, "Zhdanovism (1946–1953)," in *Literature and Revolution in Soviet Russia, 1917–1962,* ed. Max Hayward and Leopold Labedz (London: Oxford University Press, 1963), 99.

22. Marc Slonim, *Soviet Russian Literature: Writers and Problems* (New York: Oxford University Press, 1964), 292.

23. Rebecca Domar, "The Tragedy of a Soviet Satirist: The Case of Zoshchenko," in *Through the Glass of Soviet Literature,* ed. Edward Simmons (New York: Columbia University Press, 1953), 201–43.

24. This is the title Slonim gives to his tenth chapter.

25. Vera Alexandrova, *A History of Soviet Literature,* trans. Mirra Ginsburg (Garden City: Doubleday, 1963), 108, 109.

26. Slonim, *Soviet Russian Literature,* 96.

27. Vera von Wiren, "Zoshchenko in Retrospect," *Russian Review* 21, no. 4 (1962): 361.

28. Viktor Sven, *Chei drug i chei vrag Mikhail Zoshchenko* (Munich: TSOPE, 1958), 7, 5.

29. Hector Blair, introduction to *Liudi,* by Mikhail Zoshchenko (London: Cambridge University Press, 1967), 5.

30 Cf. Sarnov and Chukovskaia, "Sluchai Zoshchenko"; Tomashevsky, "'. . . Pisatel'"; Denis Babichenko, "Zhdanov, Malenkov i delo leningradskikh zhurnalov," *Voprosy literatury* 3 (1993): 201–14.

31. See, for example, Vitalii Volkov, "Za kulisami," *Avrora* 8 (1991): 42–51.

32. Iu. Tomashevskii, "Rasskazy i povesti Mikhaila Zoshchenko," in Mikhail Zoshchenko, *Sobranie sochinenii v trekh tomakh,* ed. Iu. Tomashevskii (Leningrad: Khudozhestvennaia literatura, 1986), 1:5–24. For another

early glasnost—yet sufficiently less gushing—analysis of Zoshchenko's moral and philosophical sides as evidenced primarily in his early writing, see Galina Belaia, "Mikhail Zoshchenko—iumorist, satirik, moralist," in *Puteshestvie v poiskakh istiny: stat'i o sovetskikh pisateliakh* (Tbilisi: Merani, 1987), 28–56.

33. Stanislav Rassadin, "Srednie liudi," *Ogonek* 52 (1987): 14–16.

34. Dmitry Moldavsky, "Prevyshavshii obychnuiu meru," *Zvezda* 12 (1987): 179.

35. This reaches a peak in the sacral tones offered by N. Noskovich-Lekarenko in her contribution to *Vspominaia Mikhaila Zoshchenko* (Leningrad: Khudozhestvennaia literatura, 1990), which complements and extends a previous volume, A. Smolian and N. Iurgeneva, eds., *Mikhail Zoshchenko v vospominaniiakh sovremennikov* (Moscow: Sovetskii pisatel', 1981): "There was a tender kindness in him. I remember once when we were walking in the evening, a little boy, crying bitterly, came toward us on a deserted street. Mikhail Mikhailovich began to console him and, taking out some chocolate in a silver wrapper, he handed it to the boy. I then thought, is it possible that he carries chocolate in his pocket just for that reason? He probably did" (306–7).

36. Dolinsky, "Dokumenty," 17.

37. Ibid.

38. Representative of the first tendency would be Gleb Struve, *Russian Literature under Lenin and Stalin, 1917–1953* (Norman, Okla.: University of Oklahoma Press, 1971), 155–60; Mikhail Kreps, *Tekhnika komicheskogo u Zoshchenko* (Benson, Vt.: Chalidze, 1986); and Slonim, *Soviet Russian Literature;* of the second, Alexandrova, *A History of Soviet Literature,* and Sven, *Chei drug i Chei vrag;* of the third, Domar, "The Tragedy of a Soviet Satirist"; von Wiren, "Zoshchenko in Retrospect"; and Hugh McLean, introduction to *Nervous People and Other Satires,* by Mikhail Zoshchenko (Bloomington: Indiana University Press, 1963), vii–xxvii. The "spokesman" quote comes from Alexandrova, *A History of Soviet Literature,* 99.

39. This does not mean, however, that the reception of Solzhenitsyn does not have its own peculiar twists. See Michael Nicholson's article on the amusing and illuminating turns his reputation has taken in the West. "Solzhenitsyn: Effigies and Oddities," in *Solzhenitsyn in Exile: Critical Essays and Documentary Materials,* ed. John Dunlop, Richard Haugh, and Michael Nicholson (Stanford: Hoover Institute, 1985), 109–42.

40. Nikolai Aseev, Untitled review of *Rasskazy Nazara Il'icha, gospodina Sinebriukhova, Pechat' i revoliutsiia* 7 (1922): 316.

41. For key formulations of Zoshchenko's posthumous rehabilitation and the recanonization of the 1930s Zhurbina-type interpretation see L. Ershov, *Iz istorii sovetskoi satiry: M. Zoshchenko i satiricheskaia proza 20–40kh godov* (Leningrad: Nauka, 1973); A. Starkov, *Iumor Zoshchenko* (Moscow: Khudozhestvennaia literatura, 1974), and *Mikhail Zoshchenko: sud'ba*

khudozhnika (Moscow: Sovetskii pisatel', 1990); Dmitry Moldavsky, *Mikhail Zoshchenko: ocherk tvorchestva* (Leningrad: Sovetskii pisatel', 1977). Marietta Chudakova's analysis, *Poetika Mikhaila Zoshchenko* (Moscow: Nauka, 1979) is decidedly different from canonical views and is discussed in chapters 2 and 3.

CHAPTER ONE

1. Alter, *Partial Magic: The Novel as a Self-Conscious Genre* (Berkeley: University of California Press, 1975), x.

2. Régine Robin, *Socialist Realism: An Impossible Aesthetic,* trans. Catherine Porter (Stanford: Stanford University Press, 1992).

3. Marc Slonim, *Soviet Russian Literature: Writers and Problems* (New York: Oxford University Press, 1964), 92.

4. Viktor Sven, *Chei drug i chei vrag Mikhail Zoshchenko* (Munich: TSOPE, 1958), 9.

5. Glebe Struve, *Russian Literature under Lenin and Stalin, 1917–1953* (Norman, Okla.: University of Oklahoma Press, 1971), 157; see also Rebecca Domar, "The Tragedy of a Soviet Satirist: The Case of Zoshchenko," in *Through the Glass of Soviet Literature,* ed. Edward Simmons (New York: Columbia University Press, 1953), 210.

6. Roman Jakobson, "O khudozhestvennom realizme," in *Selected Writings* (The Hague: Mouton, 1981), 3:723–31.

7. Czeslaw Milosz, *The Captive Mind,* trans. Jane Zielonko (New York: Vintage, 1955), ix–x.

8. Leo Strauss, *Persecution and the Art of Writing* (Glencoe, Ill.: Free Press, 1952), 25.

9. Mikhail Heller, *Andrei Platonov v poiskakh schast'ia* (Paris: YMCA, 1982), 133.

10. Ibid., 134.

11. Ibid., 285–86.

12. Ibid., 402, 292, 270. The character in question is Shchekotulov from Platonov's *For the Benefit.*

13. Karl Marx and Frederick Engels, *Literature and Art: Selections from Their Writings* (New York: International Publishers, 1947), 42–43.

14. Roland Barthes, "The Reality Effect," in *The Rustle of Language,* trans. Richard Howard (Berkeley: University of California Press, 1989), 141–48. Of course, my definition of a referential condition can be compared with Barthes's statement in the same essay that "any discourse which accepts 'speech-acts' justified by their referent alone" constitutes "realism." I prefer "referential condition" to avoid confusion with nineteenth-century traditions. Much of Zoshchenko's writing is, if compared formally with nineteenth-century classics, antirealist.

15. See, especially, Iurii Tynianov, "Literaturnyi fakt" and "O literaturnoi evoliutsii," in *Arkhaisty i novatory* (1929; reprint Ann Arbor: Ardis, 1985), 5–47; and Jakobson, "The Dominant," in *Selected Writings*, trans. Herbert Eagle (The Hague: Mouton, 1981), 3:751–56.

16. Petr Bogatyrev, "Costume as a Sign (The Functional and Structural Concept of Costume in Ethnography)," trans. Yvonne Lockwood, in *Semiotics of Art: Prague School Contributions*, ed. Ladislav Matejka and Irwin R. Titunik (Cambridge, Mass.: MIT Press, 1976), 15.

17. Mikhail Zoshchenko, "O sebe, ob ideologii i eshche koe o chem," *Literaturnye zapiski* 3 (1922): 28–29.

18. Dolinsky provides information on the more obscure names in this piece and proposes as well that K. stands for Kaverin. M. Z. Dolinsky, "Dokumenty: materialy k biograficheskoi khronika," in Mikhail Zoshchenko, *Uvazhaemye grazhdane: parodii, rasskazy, feletony, satiricheskie zametki, pis'ma k pisateliu, odnoaktnye komedii,* ed. M. Z. Dolinsky (Moscow: Knizhnaia palata, 1991), 580. It should also be noted that the suggestion of his birthplace is incorrect; Zoshchenko was born in St. Petersburg, though his family roots were in Ukraine.

19. Andrei Zhdanov, "Doklad t. Zhdanova o zhurnalakh 'Zvezda' i 'Leningrad,'" *Zvezda* 7–8 (1946): 9.

20. Sven, *Chei drug,* 12.

21. Ibid., 31.

22. "About myself" is, in this sense, a classic example of what Gary Saul Morson calls a "threshold text." For a more detailed discussion of this concept and its implications for readers, see chapter 4.

23. David Bordwell, *Making Meaning: Inference and Rhetoric in the Interpretation of Cinema* (Cambridge, Mass.: Harvard University Press, 1989), 30; Iurii Lotman, *Struktura khudozhestvennogo teksta* (Moscow: Iskusstvo, 1970), 98–101.

24. Bordwell, *Making Meaning,* 245.

CHAPTER TWO

1. Richard Chapple, *Soviet Satire of the Twenties* (Gainesville: University of Florida Press, 1980), 7.

2. Mikhail Kreps, *Tekhnika komicheskogo u Zoshchenko* (Benson, Vt.: Chalidze, 1986), 147.

3. Viktor Sven, *Chei drug i chei vrag Mikhail Zoshchenko* (Munich: TSOPE, 1958), 21; A. B. Murphy, *Mikhail Zoshchenko: A Literary Profile* (Oxford: Willem A. Meeuws, 1981), 67.

4. Hugh McLean, introduction to *Nervous People and Other Satires,* by Mikhail Zoshchenko (Bloomington, Ind.: Indiana University Press, 1963), xvii.

5. For a representative but by no means exhaustive list of Ilf and Petrov's feuilletons and stories that address these topics, see "Velikii kantseliarskii shliakh," *Literaturnaia gazeta*, 5 May 1932; "Ideologicheskaia pena," *Literaturnaia gazeta*, 12 May 1932; "Otdaite emu kursiv," *Literaturnaia gazeta*, 29 May 1932; "Kak sozdavalsia Robinzon," *Pravda*, 27 October 1932; "Na zelenoi sadovoi skameike," *Literaturnaia gazeta*, 29 October 1932; "Ikh bin s golovy do nog," *Krokodil* 31 (1932), 5; "Razgovory za chainym stolom," *Pravda*, 21 May 1934. With the exception of "Ikh bin s golovy do nog," all have been reprinted in their collected works, *Sobranie sochinenii v piati tomakh* (Moscow: Gosizdat, 1961). "Ikh bin" has recently been republished in *Neobyknovennye istorii iz zhizni goroda Kolokolamska*, ed. M. Dolinksy (Moscow: Knizhnaia palata, 1989), 223–26.

6. Or, in the post-RAPP period, critics could cite the ubiquitous villain, "the bureaucrat," which was always a legitimate target in any period. For positive contemporary assessments of Ilf and Petrov's literary satire, see B. Grossman, "Zametki o tvorchestve Il'fa i Petrova," *Znamia* 9 (1937): 190–206; Evgeniia Zhurbina, "Ob Il'fe i Petrove," *Oktiabr'* 10 (1937): 171–78; S. Gekht, "Fel'etony Il'fa i Petrova," *Literaturnaia gazeta*, 26 August 1939. Grossman even makes a notable contrast between Ilf and Petrov and Zoshchenko, arguing that the former's "laughter" is better because it "leaves no doubt as to where it is directed."

7. Rebecca Domar, "The Tragedy of a Soviet Satirist: The Case of Zoshchenko," in *Through the Glass of Soviet Literature*, ed. Edward Simmons (New York: Columbia University Press, 1953), 208. For a breakdown of the thematic, plot, and narrative constants of Zoshchenko's "poetic world," see Iu. K. Shcheglov, "Mir Mikhaila Zoshchenko," *Wiener Slawistische Almanach* 7 (1981): 109–54, and "Entsiklopediia nekul'turnosti," in *Mir avtora i struktura teksta: stat'i o russkoi literature*, ed. A. K. Zholkovsky (Tenafly, N.J.: Hermitage, 1986): 53–84. For a complementary discussion focusing on Zoshchenko's *ostranenie-razoblachenie* and its relation to Tolstoy, see Zholkovsky, "Lev Tolstoi i Mikhail Zoshchenko kak zerkalo i zazerkal'e russkoi revoliutsii," *Sintaksis* 16 (1988): 103–28.

8. Cathy Popkin, *The Pragmatics of Insignificance: Chekhov, Zoshchenko and Gogol* (Stanford: Stanford University Press, 1993), 124. See also Chapple's affirmation of a subversive, reader-oriented motivation: "Zoshchenko's exaggerated treatment of violence in the streets effectively exposed the problem of the average citizen and public safety." *Soviet Satire*, 67.

9. "Gus'—ubiitsa" in the section, "Chto sluchilos' za den'," *Vecherniaia Moskva*, 17 April 1926.

10. Sergei Tomsky, "Obyvatel'shchina pered narsudom," *30 dnei* 9 (1928): 64–67.

11. Leon Trotsky, "Rol' pechati v kul'turnom stroitel'stve," in *Sochineniia* (Moscow: Gosudarstvennoe izdatel'stvo, 1927), 21:199.

Notes to Pages 34–38

12. Popkin is a notable exception. She affirms the complexity of cultural and literary trends of the 1920s; yet, curiously, she does not allow this fact to stand in the way of her insistence on a bichromatic image of the period: the Party versus the other.

13. V. Veshnev, "Komicheskie bliznetsy," in *Kniga kharakteristik: stat'i o sovremennoi literature* (Moscow-Leningrad: Gosudarstvennoe izdatel'stvo, 1928), 93. "Critical-social approach" comes from his other article on Zoshchenko, "Razgovor po dusham," where he states that the "trivialities of life" do have a place in literature but it is one that must be properly treated. *Na literaturnom postu* 11–12 (1927): 55–58.

14. Hugh McLean, "On the Style of a Leskovian *Skaz*," *Harvard Slavic Studies* 2 (1954): 300.

15. Mikhail Zoshchenko, *Rasskazy Nazara Il'icha, gospodina Sinebriukhova* (1922; reprint, with an introduction by Michael B. Kreps, Berkeley: Berkeley Slavic Specialties, 1982), 21, 9, 14 (hereafter cited as *RNIGS*).

16. Accurate conclusions as to what the stepdaughter actually says are inherently problematic because, as will be elaborated below, her speech is saturated with Sinebriukhov's own tags.

17. David Oulanoff, *The Serapion Brothers: Theory and Practice* (The Hague: Mouton, 1966), 79, 77. In his third chapter, "The Technique of *Skaz* in the Serapion Brothers' Works," he uses Sinebriukhov as his primary example.

18. Oulanoff, *Serapion Brothers*, 86 (emphasis added).

19. Boris Eikhenbaum, "Leskov i sovremennaia proza," *O literature* (Moscow: Sovetskii pisatel', 1987), 409–24; Ekaterina Mushchenko et al., *Poetika skaza* (Voronezh: Voronezhskii universitet, 1978); McLean, "On the Style"; Martin P. Rice, "On 'Skaz,'" *Russian Literature Triquarterly* 12 (1975): 409–24.

20. I. Sats, "Geroi Mikhaila Zoshchenko," *Literaturnyi kritik* 3 (1938): 156.

21. Erich Auerbach, *Mimesis: The Representation of Reality in Western Literature*, trans. Willard R. Trask (Princeton: Princeton University Press, 1991), 26.

22. Ibid., 26.

23. Ibid., 27.

24. Georgi Gorbachev, *Ocherki sovremennoi russkoi literatury*, 3d ed. (Leningrad: Gosizdat, 1925), 92.

25. See Evgeniia Zhurbina, "Mikhail Zoshchenko," the foreword to the first volume of his *Sobranie sochinenii* (Leningrad: Priboi, 1930), 1–20, which is continued in her later article "Ikh sobstvennye melodii: o Mikhaile Zoshchenko," *30 dnei* 10 (1935): 81–85. Her first discussion of the need to separate Zoshchenko from his narrator is the brief article "Mikhail Zoshchenko (v poriadke obsuzhdeniia)," *Krasnaia gazeta* (Vech. vyp.), 21 June

1927. Variations of this positive assessment can be found in the following comprehensive articles of Zoshchenko's work from the 1930s and early 1940s: Tsezar Volpe, "Zametki o sovremennykh pisateliakh (M. Zoshchenko, N. Tikhonov). Stat'ia pervaia," *Zvezda* 1 (1933): 177–82, and later in "Dvadtsat' let raboty M. M. Zoshchenko: stat'ia pervaia," *Literaturnyi sovremennik* 3 (1941): 128–48, and "Stat'ia vtoraia," *Literaturnyi sovremennik* 6 (1941): 125–43; Anna Beskina, "Litso i maska Mikhaila Zoshchenko," *Literaturnyi kritik* 1 (1935): 107–31; 2 (1935): 59–92; and I. Sats, "Geroi Mikhaila Zoshchenko," *Literaturnyi kritik* 3 (1938): 140–67.

26. Volpe, "Dvadtsat' let," part 1, 129, 130.

27. A. Faresov, *Protiv techenii: N. S. Leskov. Ego zhizn', sochineniia, polemika i vospominaniia o nem* (St. Petersburg: Publ. M. Markushev, 1904), 273–75 (emphasis in original). I have substantially abridged the quote to its essential points.

28. "Lefty" is an obvious and important exception to this.

29. McLean, "On the Style," 320.

30. This is, of course, a question of degree, and in no way am I suggesting that there is no "contamination" between narrating and renarrating contexts. Maria is prone, in certain instances, to slip in, as it were, her own "tag words" and the like.

31. Mikhail Bakhtin, *Problemy tvorchestva Dostoevskogo* (Leningrad: Priboi, 1929). In translating the title, I am following the argument of Gary Saul Morson and Caryl Emerson on the inappropriate and misleading use of "poetics" in conjunction with Bakhtin's theories. See *Mikhail Bakhtin: Creation of a Prosaics* (Stanford: Stanford University Press, 1990).

32. Bakhtin, 111.

33. Ibid., 111.

34. Beskina, "Litso i maska," 116.

35. Oulanoff, *Serapion Brothers*, 78 (emphasis in original).

36. Zoshchenko, *RNIGS*, 15–16 (ellipses in original).

37. Mikhail Kreps, "Introduction," in Zoshchenko, *RNIGS*, ix.

38. Zoshchenko, *RNIGS*, 10.

39. Volpe, "Zametki," 177.

40. "Lady with the Flowers" (*"Dama s tsvetami"*) first appeared in *Prozhektor* 38 (1929). References here are to its republication shortly thereafter in Zoshchenko's collected works, *Sobranie sochinenii*, 2nd ed., vol. 5 (Moscow-Leningrad, 1931), 31–39. This collection is hereafter cited as *SS* followed by volume number. A. K. Zholkovsky examines the intertextual resonance of "Lady" in light of Tolstoy, Ginzburg, Karamzin, Turgenev, and others in "Three on Courtship, Corpses and Culture: Tolstoj, 'Posle bal'—Zoščenko, 'Dama s cvetami'—E. Ginzburg, 'Raj pod mikroskopom,'" *Wiener Slawistischer Almanach* 22 (1988): 7–24.

41. Volpe, "Zametki," 177–78.

42. Titunik discusses in detail the nature and composition of these categories in "The Problem of *Skaz* (Critique and Theory)," *Papers in Slavic Philology*, vol. 1, ed. Benjamin Stolz (Ann Arbor: Michigan Slavic Publications, 1977), 294–95.

43. For the most recent emphasis on this point, see Benedikt Sarnov, "Razvivaia traditsii Prokrusta (Mikhail Zoshchenko i ego redaktory)," *Voprosy literatury* 2 (1994): 66.

44. See I. R. Titunik, "Mixail Zoščenko and the Problem of *Skaz*," *California Slavic Studies* 6 (1971): 88–93. Of course, the notion of an authorial "norm" is not guarded by some hermetic shield. Writers can freely color the authorial-reporting context with features more common to reported-speech contexts in order to impart certain effects. What we are dealing with here are degrees of penetration—that is, when the accumulation of reported-speech features dominates the authorial position so that, in Titunik's words, it "has the appearance of being reported."

45. Titunik, "The Problem of *Skaz*," 290.

46. Volpe, "Zametki," 178.

47. McLean, "On the Style," 322.

48. Zoshchenko, "Liubitel'," *SS*, 2:156. Titunik quotes this passage in "Mixail Zoščenko," 91.

49. Mikhail Zoshchenko, "Priskorbnyi sluchai," in *Sobranie sochinenii v trekh tomakh*, ed. Iu. Tomashevskii et al. (Leningrad: Khudozhestvennaia literatura, 1986), 1:348. (This collection is hereafter cited as *SS/86*.)

50. Zoshchenko, "Nervnye liudi," in *SS*, 2:83.

51. See, for example, Hans Günther, "Zur Semantik und Funktion des Skaz bei M. Zoščenko," *Von der Revolution zum Schriftsteller-kongreß*, ed. G. Erler et al. (Berlin: Osteuropa-Institut, 1979), 326–53.

52. Mikhail Zoshchenko, "Igra Prirody," in *Nad kem smeetes'*, 4th ed. (Moscow-Leningrad: Zemlia i fabrika, 1928), 127. The stories "Dushevnaia prostota" in the same collection (pp. 22–23) and "Proisshestvie" (*SS*, 5:40–44) offer similar patterns of repetition.

53. Marietta Chudakova, *Poetika Mikhaila Zoshchenko* (Moscow: Nauka, 1979). For additional commentary on how Zoshchenko turns over (and inside out) narrative conventions and expectations, see Shcheglov, "Entsiklopediia," 68ff.

54. Zoshchenko, "Priskorbnyi sluchai," in *SS/86*, 1:348.

55. Zoshchenko, "Zubnoe delo," in *SS/86*, 2:261.

56. Zoshchenko, "Svinoe delo," in *SS/86*, 1:124.

57. Zoshchenko, "Blednolitsie brat'ia," in *Nad kem smeetes'*, 112.

58. Zoshchenko, "Velikosvetskaia istoriia," in *RNIGS*, 17.

59. Recently Rachel May has also used the term "cacophony" to characterize his prose; see "Superego as Literary Subtext: Story and Structure in Mikhail Zoshchenko's *Before Sunrise*," *Slavic Review* 55, no. 1 (1996):

106–24. While upholding the view of Zoshchenko as antisoviet satirist, Victor Erlich, too, has given a colorful description of Zoshchenko's language, calling it "a virtual orgy of the 'mangled word,' or better, the mangled cliche." In *Modernism and Revolution: Russian Literature in Transition* (Cambridge, Mass.: Harvard University Press, 1994), 167. (He devotes his eighth chapter to Zoshchenko.) With regard to Zoshchenko's contemporary critics, there were few for whom this effect in and of itself was admirable; see the comments by his Serapion colleague Ilia Gruzdev, in "Vechera 'Serapionovykh brat'ev,'" *Kniga i revoliutsiia* 3 (1922): 110–11; Innokentii Oksenov's two reviews in *Kniga i revoliutsiia* 2 (1923): 63, and 3 (1923): 76–77; the review of *RNIGS* by "Vs. R." in *Kniga i revoliutsiia* 8 (1922): 41, and I. Fedorov's review of *Uvazhaemye grazhdane* in *Komsomol'skaia pravda*, 4 June 1927. However, with the exception of those by the formalists, most of the favorable words directed to Zoshchenko in the 1920s were guarded and generally replete with provisos and warnings. See, for example, the anonymous review of *RNIGS* in *Biulleten' knigi* 5–6 (1922): 49–50; Mikhail Mogilianskii, review of *Raznotyk*, *Kniga i revoliutsiia* 4 (1923): 69–70; V. F. Pereverzev, "Na frontakh tekushchei belletristiki," *Pechat' i revoliutsiia* 4 (1923): 127–33 (on Zoshchenko, 128–29); Ia. Braun, "Desiat' strannikov v 'osiazaemoe nichto,'" *Sibirskie ogni* 1 (1924): 201–40 (on Zoshchenko, 214–17); "O poshlosti," *Burevestnik* 4 (1924): 28–31; A. Menshoi, "Veselaia zhut'," *Zhizn' izkusstva* 41 (1924): 8–10; A. Pridorogin, review of *Veselaia zhizn'*, *Knigonosha* 48–49 (1924): 31; Ia. Shafir, "O iumore i iumoristakh," *Knigonosha* 8 (1926): 13–18.

60. Aleksandr Voronsky, untitled review of *Serapionovy brat'ia. Al'manakh pervyi*, *Krasnaia nov'* 3 (1922): 266. See also his review of *RNIGS* in *Krasnaia nov'* 6 (1922): 343–45.

61. For additional use of "Sinebriukhov," see "Ob ovoshchakh i prochem," *SS/86*, 1:454–55, and "Neskol'ko slov v zashchitu nachal'nikov," *Drezina* 4 (1923). He was also the signer along with "Semen Kurochkin" (another favorite pseudonym of Zoshchenko) and "Vasia Pushkin" in a letter to *Krasnyi voron* in 1924, which has been reprinted in *Voprosy literatury* 7 (1984): 256–57.

62. Viktor Vinogradov, "Problema skaza v stilistike," in *Izbrannye trudy: o iazyke khudozhestvennoi prozy* (Moscow: Nauka, 1980), 53. This article was first published in 1925. Regarding the discursive flexibility of Sinebriukhov's *skaz*, Vinogradov argued in a later study that it would not only be empirically impossible to find a single person possessing such a language capacity but, more important, it would necessitate muting the patent artificiality of Sinebriukhov's speech. See "Iazyk Zoshchenki," in *Mikhail Zoshchenko. Mastera sovremennoi literatury: stat'i i materialy*, ed. B. V. Kazanskii and Iu. N. Tynianov (Leningrad: Academia, 1928; reprint, Letchworth, Eng.: Prideaux, 1973), 58–69 (page citations are to the reprint edition). Edward

Brown comes to the same conclusion in *Russian Literature Since the Revolution* (Cambridge: Harvard University Press, 1982), 187.

63. Panteleimon Romanov, "Iz zapisnoi knizhki pisatelia," in *Utro. Literaturnyi sbornik,* ed. N. Fatov (Moscow-Leningrad: Publication by contributing authors, 1927): 197.

64. N. Popova, "Effekt otstranennosti i sostradaniia: satiricheskaia novellistika M. Zoshchenko," *Literaturnoe obozrenie* 1 (1995): 21–24.

65. Mushchenko et al., 254–55.

66. Beskina, "Litso i maska," 118. See also Sats's comments on the same, "Geroi," 156, and Kroichik, *Poetika skaza,* 232.

67. The most notorious instance is the addition of a more politically solid conclusion to the original ending of "Nervous People" so as to guide the reader into a "proper" (in an official soviet sense) response toward its represented world. See Mikhail Zoshchenko, *Rasskazy, fel'etony, povesti* (Moscow: Goslitizdat, 1958), 24.

68. And we should not forget that on occasion Zoshchenko openly taunts the reader who would accept his texts as referentially adequate. See the beginnings of "Rodnye liudi," *SS,* 1:75, and "Drova," *SS,* 2:34.

69. Iurii Tynianov, "Literaturnoe segodnia," originally published in *Russkii sovremennik* 1 (1924); reprinted in *Poetika. Istoriia literatury. Kino* (Moscow: Nauka, 1977), 160.

70. Postcard to Zoshchenko, dated 1928, *Fond 501, opis' 3, N. 96, Pushkinskii dom,* St. Petersburg.

71. Viktor Shklovsky, "O Zoshchenko i bol'shoi literature," in *Mikhail Zoshchenko. Mastera sovremennoi literatury,* 17. In the same volume, A. G. Barmin comes to a similar conclusion in his article "Puti Zoshchenki." For brief but more recent commentary on readers' tendency to entrap themselves and on the ambivalent nature of Zoshchenko's humor, see Vl. Novikov, "O meste Zoshchenko v russkoi literature," *Literaturnoe obozrenie* 1 (1995): 25–27.

CHAPTER THREE

1. K. Loks, "Sovremennaia proza," *Pechat' i revoliutsiia* 5 (1923): 86.

2. For Rose, see *Parody//Metafiction* (London: Croom Helm, 1979), and *Parody: Ancient, Modern and Post-Modern* (Cambridge, England: Cambridge University Press, 1993). For Hutcheon, see "Parody without Ridicule: Observations on Modern Literary Parody," *Canadian Review of Comparative Literature* 5, no. 2 (1978): 201–11; *Narcissistic Narrative: The Metafictional Paradox* (Waterloo, Ont.: Wilfred Laurier University Press, 1980), and *A Theory of Parody: The Teachings of Twentieth-Century Art Forms* (New York and London: Methuen, 1985). Coupling their names is not

meant to imply that Rose and Hutcheon share the same orientation. Rose takes a more socioideological view of parody and Hutcheon a more metafictional. More recently, however, in discussing parody as the primary enabling discourse of postmodernism's exploration of a thoroughly textualized world, Hutcheon allows for a more specifically ideological use for parody. See chapters 2 and 8 in *A Poetics of Postmodernism: History, Theory, Fiction* (New York: Routledge, 1988). Interestingly, this split mirrors the polemic over parody in the early Soviet Union. A precursor of Hutcheon would of course be Iurii Tynianov's seminal studies of parody, "Dostoevskii i Gogol' (k teorii parodii)," in *Arkhaisty i novatory* (1929; reprint, Ann Arbor: Ardis, 1985), 412–55; and "O parodii," in *Poetika. Istoriia literatury. Kino.* (Moscow: Nauka, 1977), 284–305. (This essay was written in 1929 but published only in 1977.) An antecedent of Rose would be E. Galperina, "K probleme literaturnoi parodii," *Pechat' i revoliutsiia* 12 (1929): 14–30.

3. Gary Saul Morson, *The Boundaries of Genre: Dostoevsky's "Diary of a Writer" and the Traditions of Literary Utopia* (Austin: University of Texas Press, 1981), 110. His study is a notable exception to critics' hesitancy in addressing the real problems readers have faced with parody.

4. Abram Lezhnev, review of *O chem pel solovei*, *Pechat' i revoliutsiia* 6 (1927): 221.

5. A. P. Palei, review of *O chem pel solovei*, *Novyi mir* 6 (1927): 205.

6. Vera Von Wiren, "Zoshchenko in Retrospect," *Russian Review* 21, no. 4 (1962): 353.

7. M. Olshevets, "Obyvatel'skii nabat. (O 'Sentimental'nykh povestiakh' M. Zoshchenko)," *Izvestiia*, 14 August 1927.

8. I. Zhiga, review of *Uvazhaemye grazhdane, Nervnye Liudi*, and *O chem pel solovei, Molodaia gvardiia* 9 (1927): 201.

9. Mikhail Gol'dshtein, review of *Vospominanie o M. L. Siniagine*, *Rezets* 13 (1931): 17. The title is misspelled ("M. L." instead of "M. P.") in the review.

10. Mikhail Chumandrin, "Chei pisatel—Mikhail Zoshchenko," *Zvezda* 3 (1930): 210.

11. Chumandrin, 216. A stenographic account of responses to Chumandrin follows his speech.

12. Evgeniia Zhurbina, "Mikhail Zoshchenko," foreword to volume 1 of *Sobranie sochinenii*, by Mikhail Zoshchenko (Leningrad: Priboi, 1930), 14.

13. I. Sats, "Geroi Mikhaila Zoshchenko," *Literaturnyi kritik* 3 (1938): 152.

14. Von Wiren, "Zoshchenko in Retrospect," 353.

15. Rebecca Domar, "The Tragedy of a Soviet Satirist: The Case of Zoshchenko," in *Through the Glass of Soviet Literature*, ed. Edward Simmons (New York: Columbia University Press, 1953), 209.

16. Hector Blair, introduction to *Liudi,* by Mikhail Zoshchenko (London: Cambridge University Press, 1967), 6.

17. The following abbreviations will be used for citing the contents of *Sentimental Tales,* "Lilacs in Bloom," and *M. P. Siniagin:* G ("The Goat"); AN ("Apollon and Tamara"); WNS ("What the Nightingale Sang"); TN ("A Terrible Night"); P ("People"); LB ("Lilacs in Bloom"); MPS (M. P. Siniagin). All citations of *Sentimental Tales* are from the fourth volume of Zoshchenko's collected works, *Sobranie sochinenii,* 2d ed. (Moscow-Leningrad: Goslitizdat, 1931). References to "Lilacs in Bloom" are from its original publication in the almanac *Zvezda: literaturno-khudozhestvennyi almanakh* (Leningrad: Priboi, 1930), 41–76. References to *M. P. Siniagin* are from its publication as a book (Leningrad: Izd. pisatelei, 1931); it first appeared in *Novyi mir* 12 (1930).

18. Chumandrin, 207–8.

19. Viktor Sven, *Chei drug i chei vrag Mikhail Zoshchenko* (Munich: TSOPE, 1958), 28.

20. Iulia Sazonova, "Kul'tura i zhizn'," *Sovremennye zapiski: Annales contemporaines* 34 (1928): 449.

21. Ibid., 445.

22. Ibid., 448.

23. Using church records, Tomashevsky has cleared up the (deliberate) confusion surrounding Zoshchenko's date and place of birth: 28 July (9 August, new style), 1894 in St. Petersburg. In Iurii Tomashevskii, *Litso i maska Mikhaila Zoshchenko* (Moscow: Olimp, 1994), 340.

24. Viacheslav Polonsky, *O sovremennoi literature* (Moscow-Leningrad: Gosizdat, 1929), 263–64.

25. Abram Lezhnev, review of the almanacs *Bagrianye l'dy, Kovsh, Krug,* and *Chet i Nechet, Pechat' i revoliutsiia* 5–6 (1925): 235. "A Terrible Night" appeared in the almanac *Kovsh.* Writing before the publication of the anthology, Lezhnev, of course, does not refer to Kolenkorov by name.

26. For additional commentary on the deliberate ambiguity inherent in these prefaces, see Linda Hart Scatton, *Mikhail Zoshchenko: Evolution of a Writer* (Cambridge, England: Cambridge University Press, 1993), 78–82; and Svetlana Boym, *Common Places: Mythologies of Everyday Life in Russia* (Cambridge, Mass.: Harvard University Press, 1994), 194–97.

27. Tsesar Volpe, "Dvadtsat' let raboty M. M. Zoshchenko: stat'ia pervaia," *Literaturnyi sovremennik* 3 (1941), 144.

28. Sven, 11.

29. Vera Alexandrova, *A History of Soviet Literature,* trans. Mirra Ginsburg (Garden City: Doubleday, 1963), 104.

30. Von Wiren, "Zoshchenko in Retrospect," 354.

31. Mikhail Zoshchenko, "O sebe, o kritikakh i o svoei rabote," in *Mikhail Zoshchenko. Mastera sovremennoi literatury: stat'i i materialy,* ed.

B. V. Kazanskii and Iu. N. Tynianov (Leningrad: Academia, 1928; reprint, Letchworth, Eng.: Prideaux, 1973), 10–11 (page citations are to the reprint edition).

32. On this point it should be noted that scholars generally do not speak of the vacillation that marks this declaration of intent. A half-page "Warning" precedes it in which he describes his impression of the public's response to his statement: "The article was a point of dispute, and now I myself am not in total agreement with it. However, at that time it seemed to me to be accurate."

33. The subject of classic plot motifs and characters in *Sentimental Tales* has dominated most studies of these texts. For detailed examinations of this side of Zoshchenko's parody, see Volpe, "Dvadtsat' let"; Marietta Chudakova, *Poetika Mikhaila Zoshchenko* (Moscow: Nauka, 1979); Jacqueline Cukierman, "Mikhail Zoščenko's *Povesti* and *Rasskazy* of the 1920s: A Study in Genre Evolution" (Ph.D. diss., University of Michigan, 1978); Sveta Le Fleming, "The Question of Narrator in Zoshchenko's *Mudrost'*," *Essays in Poetics* 6, no. 1 (1981): 67–85; and Scatton, *Mikhail Zoshchenko,* 83–101.

34. In a more recent article she places Zoshchenko's aspirations within the larger context of early Soviet literature; see "Bez gneva i pristrastiia: formy i deformatsii v literaturnom protsesse 20–30-x godov," *Novyi mir* 9 (1988): 240–60.

35. Later readers of Zoshchenko are less culpable in this silence because subsequent reprints of *M. P. Siniagin*, even in the postsoviet period, eliminated the photographs. One wonders if the reasons behind this editorial silence are similar to critics'.

36. Viktor Shklovsky, "Literatura vne siuzheta," in *O teorii prozy* (1929; reprint, Ann Arbor: Ardis, 1985), 226–45.

37. Ibid., 234.

38. N. F. Chuzhak, "Pisatel'skaia pamiatka," in *Literatura fakta*, ed. N. F. Chuzhak (Moscow: Federatsiia, 1929), 28.

39. Sergei Tretiakov, "Novyi Lev Tolstoy," *Novyi LEF* 1 (1927): 37.

40. Ibid., 38.

41. Osip Brik, "Blizhe k faktu," *Novyi LEF* 2 (1927): 32–34. Of course, when it came to putting theory into practice, the "factualists" could not help but show the author's hand is always present. See, for example, Tretiakov's play *Protivogazy* in *LEF* 4 (1923), and his two China chronicles, the travelogue "Moscow-Peking" in *LEF* 7 (1925), and the "bio-interview," "Den Sy-Khua" in *Novyi LEF* 7 (1927).

42. Miguel de Cervantes, *The Adventures of Don Quixote*, trans. J. M. Cohen (New York: Penguin, 1950).

43. Mikhail Levidov, "O piatnadtsati—trista strok," *LEF* 1 (1923): 246.

44. Ilia Gruzdev, "Litso i maska," in *Serapionovy brat'ia* (1922; reprint, Munich: Wilhelm Fink, Centrifuga Russian Reprintings and Printings, vol. 32, 1973), 217. This is the only essay in the Serapion almanac.

45. Lev Lunts, "Pochemu my serapionovy brat'ia," *Literaturnye zapiski* 3 (1922): 31.

46. See in particular Mikhail Bakhtin, "Iz predystoriia romannogo slova," in *Voprosy literatury i estetiki* (Moscow: Khudozhestvennaia literatura, 1975), 408–46.

47. David Shepherd, *Beyond Metafiction: Self-Consciousness in Soviet Literature* (Oxford: Oxford University Press, 1992), 12.

48. For a recent study on related critical efforts to contain parody that also draws from Bakhtin, see Mark Jones, "Parody and Its Containment: The Case of Wordsworth," *Representations* 54 (1996): 57–78.

CHAPTER FOUR

1. Vladimir Kirshon, "Rech' t. Kirshona," in *XVI S"ezd vsesoiuznoi kommunisticheskoi partii(b): stenograficheskii otchet*, 2d ed. (Moscow-Leningrad: Moskovskii rabochii, 1931), 280.

2. Ibid., 280.

3. Ibid. In a tragic twist of fate, it was Kirshon himself who was executed for being a "Trotskyist" in 1938.

4. Marietta Shaginian, "Puteshestvie po sovetskoi Armenii," *Sobranie sochinenii v deviati tomakh* (Moscow: Khudozhestvennaia literatura, 1972), 3:662.

5. These differences can be observed in the wide range of *ocherki* that appeared in the "Liudi i fakty" section of *Novyi Mir* for the years 1930–31.

6. Robert de Saint Jean, quoted in Harriet Borland, *Soviet Literary Theory and Practice During the First Five-Year Plan, 1928–32* (New York: King's Crown, 1950), 115.

7. Leopold Averbakh, "Kul'turnaia revoliutsiia i zadachi proletarskoi literatury," *O zadachakh proletarskoi literatury* (Moscow-Leningrad: Moskovskii rabochii, 1928), 15.

8. Anatoly Lunacharsky, "Rol' iskusstva v rekonstruktivnyi period (stat'ia vtoraia)," *Rost* 10 (1930): 14.

9. See, for example, A. Bek and L. Toom, *Litso rabochego chitatelia* (Moscow-Leningrad: Gosudarstvennoe izdatel'stvo, 1927), especially 19–20. In 1928 the Party gave official recognition to this new way of reading in the declaration "How books can be of service to the mass reader"; here all texts, historical and political tracts, science textbooks, and fictional works were defined according to the same functional goal: "guaranteeing the maximum accessibility (in both form and content) for the mass reader." KPSS resolution

of 28 December 1928. Reported in *O partiinoi i sovetskoi pechati: sbornik dokumentov* (Moscow: Pravda, 1954), 381.

10. Letter to Maksim Gorky, 8 September 1930, published in Gary Kern, "Letters from Zoshchenko," *Russian Literature Triquarterly* 6 (1973): 590.

11. Letter to Marietta Shaginian, 2 March 1931, published by Elena Shaginian in "Mikhail Zoshchenko—Mariette Shaginian: iz perepiski," *Tallin* 2 (1989): 92. Regarding concerns over health, Kornei Chukovsky's memoirs of Zoshchenko are also instructive. They are reprinted in *Mikhail Zoshchenko v vospominaniiakh sovremennikov*, ed. A. Smolian and N. Iurgeneva (Moscow: Sovetskii pisatel', 1981), 13–66. For detailed discussions of Zoshchenko's interests in this field, see von Wiren, "Zoščenko's Psychological Interests," *The Slavic and East European Journal* 11, no. 1 (1967): 3–22; and Krista Hanson, "Writing a Path to Health: Autobiography and Autotherapy in Zoščenko's Work" (Ph.D. dissertation, University of California, 1985). For a discussion of thematic precedents in Zoshchenko's work regarding health and aging, see Hanson, "Writing a Path," and Linda Hart Scatton, *Mikhail Zoshchenko: Evolution of a Writer* (Cambridge, Eng.: Cambridge University Press, 1993), 163–67. For additional insight into Zoshchenko's obsessive concerns over his health, see the memoirs of his wife, Vera Vladimirovna Zoshchenko, printed in G. V. Filippov, "Lichnost' M. Zoshchenko po vospominaniiam ego zheny (1916–1929)," *Mikhail Zoshchenko: materialy k tvorcheskoi biografii*, ed. N. A. Groznova (St. Petersburg: Nauka, 1997), 1:49–79.

12. Letter to Shaginian, 25 February 1934, "Mikhail Zoshchenko—Mariette Shaginian," 95 (emphasis in original).

13. Mikhail Gol'dshtein, review of *Vospominanie o M. L. Siniagine*, *Rezets* 13 (1931): 17.

14. P. Kazan, "Zoshchenko, Mikhail Mikhailovich," in *Literaturnaia entsiklopediia* 4 (1930) reprinted, American Council of Learned Societies Reprints: Russian Series no. 23 (J. W. Edwards: Ann Arbor, 1948), 376–78.

15. Vladimir Sobol', "Pisatel' za pukopis'iu," *Literaturnaia gazeta*, 23 April 1933, 7.

16. All references to *Youth Restored* are from the first edition (Leningrad: Izd. pisatelei, 1933).

17. Iu. Isakov, "Vozvrashchennaia molodost'," *Vecherniaia krasnaia gazeta*, 23 March 1934, 2.

18. Letter to Shaginian, 3 April 1934, "Mikhail Zoshchenko—Mariette Shaginian," 95.

19. Mayakovsky, *Polnoe sobranie sochinenii v tridtsati tomakh* (Moscow: Gosudarstvennoe izdatel'stvo, 1958), 8:328; Olesha, "Rech' t. Oleshi," in *Pervyi vsesoiuznyi s"ezd sovetskikh pisatelei, 1934: stenograficheskii otchet* (Moscow: Sovetskii pisatel', 1990), 236.

20. Shaginian, *Puteshestvie po sovetskoi Armenii,* 662.

21. L. I. Din, "Kakoi dolzhna byt' kniga," *Literaturnaia gazeta,* 25 August 1930. See as well Gorky's comments in "O neobkhodimosti sozdaniia nauchno-populiarnoi literatury dlia massovogo chitatelia, *Literaturnaia gazeta,* 11 September 1933, which, interestingly, coincided with the publication of *Youth Restored.* At certain points he and Zoshchenko seem almost to echo each other, a matter of interest, given their correspondence.

22. G. Munblit, "Kak vazhno byt' ser'eznym," *Literaturnaia gazeta,* 20 February 1934. The "rebirth" comment is from Evgeniia Zhurbina, "Variant sud'by intelligentnogo cheloveka," *Oktiabr'* 2 (1936): 256.

23. Boris Begak, "Povest' i kommentarii k nei," *Literaturnaia gazeta,* 18 March 1934.

24. A. Gorelov, "Omolozhenie dvunogogo sushchestva," *Literaturnyi Leningrad,* 31 May 1934.

25. See, for example, Anna Beskina, "Mikhail Zoshchenko v poiskakh optimizma," *Literaturnyi Leningrad,* 8 May 1934; B. Drugov, "Porazhenie geroia i pobeda avtora," review of *Vozvrashchennaia molodost', Kniga i proletarskaia revoliutsiia* 9 (1934): 99–102.

26. Semashko, N., "Mozhno li vozvratit' molodost'," *Literaturnaia gazeta,* 6 April 1934. Coincidentally, years before Semashko had published an article on the proper ways to rest using similar mechanistic language. For example, resorts are identified as "repair shops for the health of laborers." "Kak otdykhat'," *Tridtsat' dnei* 6 (1929): 28–31.

27. A. Gorelov, "V poiskakh formuly molodosti," in *Ispytanie vremenem* (Leningrad: Khudozhestvennaia literatura, 1935), 94, 98. This article was originally published in *Rezets* 3 (1934): 10. For other objections to the subject matter in the commentaries, see I. Lunts, "O povesti Zoshchenko," *Rabochii krai* 7 (1934): 24, and the reports of public disputes in Isakov and Rest.

28. Iu. Isakov, "Vozvrashchennaia molodost'," *Vecherniaia krasnaia gazeta,* 23 March 1934.

29. A. Orlova, "Volnuiushchaia povest'," *Rabochii krai* 6 (1934): 23.

30. A. Nemilov, "Mikh. Zoshchenko i problema omolozheniia," review of *Vozvrashchennaia molodost', Kniga i proletarskaia revoliutsiia* 9 (1934): 96. This review is immediately followed by Drugov's, "Porazhenie geroia," which takes the opposite view.

31. See, for example, the response of Professor Kupalov, reported in Iu. Isakov, "Vozvrashchennaia molodost'," *Vecherniaia krasnaia gazeta,* 23 March 1934, and B. Rest, "Pobeda ili porazhenie," *Literaturnaia gazeta,* 26 March 1934.

32. A. Olgina, "Sekret molodosti i krasoty," *Khudozhestvennaia literatura* 6 (1934): 18.

33. Anna Beskina, "V poiskakh optimizma," *Literaturnyi sovremennik* 5 (1934): 111–22.

34. Begak, "Povest' i kommentarii."

35. N. Oruzheinikov, "Na poliakh zhurnalov," *Literaturnaia gazeta*, 11 August 1933.

36. Rebecca Domar, "The Tragedy of a Soviet Satirist: The Case of Zoshchenko," in *Through the Glass of Soviet Literature*, ed. Edward Simmons (New York: Columbia University Press, 1953), 221.

37. I. Sats, "Geroi Mikhaila Zoshchenko," *Literaturny kritik* 3 (1938): 161.

38. See, for example, the characterization of Kashkin along the lines of a cartoon villain, 43.

39. See, for example, the description of Volosatov's neurasthenia, 60–61.

40. Cited by I. S., "Pisateli o 'Vozvrashchennoi molodosti,'" *Literaturnyi Leningrad*, 14 May 1934.

41. For corroborating statements by Zoshchenko himself, see "Mikhail Zoshchenko o svoei 'Goluboi knige,'" *Vecherniaia krasnaia gazeta*, 8 May 1934.

42. Parenthetical references are to *Golubaia kniga* (Leningrad: Sovetskii pisatel', 1935). The work first appeared in *Krasnaia nov'* 3, 10 (1934); 6, 7, 12 (1935). For an interesting account of the censorship of this text, see S. Pecherskii, "Tsenzorskaia pravka 'Goluboi knigi' M. M. Zoshchenko," *Minuvshee: Istoricheskii al'manakh* 3 (1987): 355–91.

43. Though I do not have the space to explore this in greater detail, it is along the lines of heightened referentiality that Zoshchenko modifies those stories from the 1920s reprinted in *The Blue Book*. This is most evident in the stories used for this section, "Amazing Events."

44. Defoe's stay in the stocks (for publication of *Shortest Way with Dissenters*) seems to have been the opposite of what Zoshchenko describes (in typical fashion he does not cite his sources). As James Sutherland notes, Defoe's popularity stood him in good stead: his health was drunk, his pillory garlanded, and his works sold from the spot. See *Defoe* (Philadelphia: Lippincott, 1938), 95–96.

45. A. Dymshchits, "O 'Goluboi knige" M. Zoshchenko," *Rezets* 6 (1936): 19. For other positive reviews, see Evgeniia Zhurbina, "Golubaia kniga," *Literaturnaia gazeta*, 20 September 1935; R. Messer, "Preodolenie formalizma," *Literaturnyi Leningrad*, 20 April 1936; L. Levin, "Zametki o satiricheskoi proze (Zoshchenko, Il'f i Petrov)," *Molodaia gvardiia* 9 (1939): 151–58; and the public debate where Fedin, Kaverin, Chukovsky, and Bergolts celebrated his originality, as reported by V. Rest, "Golubaia kniga: na dispute v Leningradskom diskussionom klube prozaikov," *Literaturnaia gazeta*, 15 March 1936. In "Golubaia kniga," *Vecherniaia krasnaia gazeta*, 8 March 1936, I. Eventov waits until the last chapter to express words of praise similar to those of Dymshchits. In the same vein see Iurii Tomashevsky's more recent response in which he declares that *The Blue Book* embodies

Zoshchenko's "moral code," an extended series of commandments that Soviet citizens should follow. From his "Rasskazy i povesti Mikhaila Zoshchenko," in *Sobranie sochinenii v trekh tomakh,* ed. Iu. Tomashevsky et al. (Leningrad: Khudozhestvennaia literatura, 1986), 1:22.

46. A. Gurshtein, "Po alleiam istorii," *Pravda,* 9 May 1936. For another negative response along the same lines, see Vladimir Mishchikhin, "Mikhail Zoshchenko—'Golubaia kniga,'" *Profrabotnik* 5–6 (1936): 54–55.

47. Gurshtein, "Po alleiam istorii."

48. Mikhail Zoshchenko, "Osnovnye voprosy nashei professii," *Literaturnyi Leningrad,* 14 August 1934.

49. V. Graboventskii et al., "Chego my khotim ot sovetskoi literatury," *Literaturnyi Leningrad,* 28 July 1934.

50. Gary Saul Morson, *The Boundaries of Genre: Dostoevsky's "Diary of a Writer" and the Traditions of Literary Utopia* (Austin: University of Texas Press, 1981), 50.

51. K. Zelinskii, "O novykh vkusakh narodakh," *Literaturnaia gazeta,* 27 March 1936.

52. For an alternate interpretation, focusing on the coherency of *The Blue Book* mainly along thematic and structural lines, see Scatton, *Mikhail Zoshchenko,* 181–207.

53. For a contrary view, see Jochen-Ulrich Peters, who argues that *The Blue Book* is an antisoviet tract in the Aesopian tradition. Zoshchenko "succeeded in formally abiding by the aesthetic and ideological postulates of Socialist Realism, while at the same time exposing them to ridicule through such favourite satirical devices as irony, parody and hyperbolic stylisation, thus revealing their absurdity." This statement, however, fails to take into account how many of his contemporary critics could accommodate the narrative's exaggerated, ironic side and account for it as pro-soviet satire. "Satire under Stalinism: Zoshchenko's *Golubaya Kniga* and M. Bulgakov's *Master i Margarita,"* in *The Culture of the Stalin Period,* ed. Hans Günther (London: Macmillan, 1990): 210–26.

54. Mikhail Zoshchenko, "Vstupitel'noe slovo Mikh. Zoshchenko na dispute o 'Vozvrashchennoi molodosti'," *Literaturnyi Leningrad,* 15 March 1934. In what could not have failed to surprise the audience present, because of "ill health" Zoshchenko did not deliver this speech himself but had it read publicly for him.

55. There are two versions of Zoshchenko's talk with "beginning writers" (*rabkory*); the one published under the title "Kak ia rabotaiu" in *Literaturnaia ucheba* 3 (1930): 107–13, is identified as an "abbreviated and corrected version" of his appearance at the Leningrad Publishing Center (*Dom pechati*). The same year, in an anthology of writers' appearances at the center, *Kak my pishem,* a second version appeared under the title "Mikh. Zoshchenko." Here Zoshchenko informs us that this is "a corrected and

somewhat extended" stenographic account of his very same conversation. The most notable distinction is that the journal edition excludes any mention of "sublimation," which is given much attention in the anthologized version. In 1989, the publishing house "Kniga" reprinted *Kak my pishem*. All references to the anthologized version are from this reprint.

56. "Mikh. Zoshchenko," 50.

57. Ibid., 44.

58. James Jeans, *The Universe Around Us* (New York: Macmillan, 1929), v.

59. Tsesar Volpe, "O 'Vozvrashchennoi molodosti' Mikhaila Zoshchenko," *Zvezda* 8 (1934): 161–71.

60. From Zoshchenko's opening words in I. S., "Pisateli o 'Vozvrashchennoi molodosti,'" *Literaturnyi Leningrad*, 14 May 1934.

61. Cited in Tsesar Volpe, "Dvadtsat' let raboty M. M. Zoshchenko: stat'ia pervaia," *Literaturnyi sovremennik* 3 (1941), 129.

CHAPTER FIVE

1. Letter of 2 March 1935, *fond* 501, *opis'* 3, N. 409; postcard of 21 September 1930, *fond* 501, *opis'* 3, N. 305. St. Petersburg: Institut russkoi literatury (Pushkinskii dom).

2. R. Grigor'eva, "Litso derevenskogo chitatelia po materialam 'knigapochtoi,'" *Na knizhnom fronte* 17–18 (1929): 25.

3. "Ob obsluzhivanii knigoi massovogo chitatelia (iz postanovleniia TsK VKP(b) ot 28 dekabria 1928 g.)," in *O partiinoi i sovetskoi pechati: sbornik dokumentov* (Moscow: Pravda, 1954): 380–82.

4. M. I. Slukhovsky, *Kniga i derevnia* (Moscow-Leningrad: Gosizd., 1928), 36.

5. Jeffrey Brooks, "The Breakdown in Production and Distribution of Printed Material, 1917–1923," in *Bolshevik Culture: Experiment and Order in the Russian Revolution,* ed. Abbott Gleason, Peter Kenez, and Richard Stites (Bloomington: Indiana University Press, 1985): 151–74.

6. Iakov. Shafir, *Gazeta i Derevnia* (Moscow: Krasnaia nov', 1923).

7. M. A. Smushkova, *Pervye itogi izucheniia chitatelia* (Moscow-Leningrad: Gosizd., 1926), 37–39; for further discussion of the problems posed by contemporary vocabulary, see Afanasii Selishchev, *Iazyk revoliutsionnoi epokhi* (Moscow: Rabotnik prosveshcheniia, 1928), especially chapter 8. The inaccessibility of Bolshevik language has also been noted by Brooks, "Breakdown," 164, and "Public and Private Values in the Soviet Press, 1921–1928," *Slavic Review* 1 (1989): 25.

8. Slukhovsky, 139.

9. Zel. Shteiman, "'Sfinks' govoriashchii (o rabochem chitatele)," *Novyi Mir* 6 (1927): 185.

10. Representative explications of these criteria can be found in Al. Isbakh, "Chto chitaiut: o roste rabochego chitatelia," *Na literaturnom postu* 2 (1928): 36–38; A. Meromskii, "Kriticheskoe chut'e derevni" *Na literaturnom postu* 3 (1928): 36–41; E. Korobkova and L. Poliak, "Rabochii chitatel' o iazyke sovremennoi prozy," *Na literaturnom postu* 14 (1929): 59–62; and in the book-length studies by A. Bek and L. Toom, *Litso rabochego chitatelia* (Moscow-Leningrad: Gosudarstvennoe izdatel'stvo, 1927); G. Brylov, N. Lebedev et al., eds., *Golos rabochego chitatelia: sovremennaia sovetskaia khudozhestvennaia literatura v svete massovoi rabochei kritiki* (Leningrad: Krasnaia gazeta, 1929); B. Bank and A. Vilenkin, *Krest'ianskaia molodezh' i kniga (opyt issledovaniia chitatel'skikh interesov)* (Moscow-Leningrad: Molodaia gvardiia, 1929). For an extensive discussion of readers' "horizon of expectations" and how it impacted the nature of socialist realism, see Evgeny Dobrenko, *Formovka sovetskogo chitatelia* (St. Petersburg: Akademicheskii proekt, 1997).

11. A. M. Toporov, *Krestian'e o pisateliakh* (1930; reprint, Moscow: Sovetskaia Rossiia, 1967), 27.

12. *Vechera rabochei kritiki* (Moscow: Gudok, 1927), 20.

13. *Vechera*, 18.

14. As quoted by N. P. Veis, "Obshchestvennaia i literaturnaia tsennost' vecherov rabochei kritiki," in *Pisatel' pered sudom rabochego chitatelia*, ed. G. Brylov, N. Veis, and V. Sakharov (Leningrad: Izdatel'stvo leningradskogo soveta profsoiuza, 1928), 17 (ellipses in original).

15. As quoted by Veis, 17 (ellipses in original).

16. For an illustration of this claim, see N. Prianishnikov, "Rassuzhdenie o chitatele i pisatele," *Na literaturnom postu* 8 (1930): 62–65.

17. See, for example, the compilation of writers' comments on readers in E. Korobkova and L. Poliak, "Pisatel' o chitatele," *Na literaturnom postu* 5–6 (1930): 100–103.

18. Letter of 25 October 1929, *fond* 501, *opis'* 3, N. 305.

19. Letters of 20 March 1934, 30 January 1935, 4 January (no year given), 31 May 1936, *fond* 501, *opis'* 3, N. 398. Some references to Zoshchenko are in third person because the letters were sent first to publishers and then passed on to him.

20. From "Vstupitel'noe slovo Mikh. Zoshchenko na dispute o 'Vozrashchennoi molodosti'," *Literaturnyi Leningrad*, 15 March 1934.

21. Evgeny Tank, "O knigakh M. Zoshchenko i pis'makh k nemu," *Literaturnyi Leningrad*, 20 October 1934.

22. Chukovsky, diary entry for 30 October 1927, in *Dnevnik, 1901–1929*, ed. by E. Chukovskaia (Moscow: Sovetskii pisatel', 1991), 422.

23. See his correspondence with Gorky in *Perepiska A. M. Gor'kogo s I. A. Gruzdevym. Arkhiv A. M. Gor'kogo XI*, ed. V. S. Barakhov et al. (Moscow: Nauka, 1966), 88–89.

24. Letter of 30 January 1935, *fond* 501, *opis'* 3, N. 398.

25. Mikhail Zoshchenko, "Oko za oko," in *Leningradskii al'manakh*, ed. P. O. Kapitsa, I. F. Kratt et al. (Leningrad: Sovetskii pisatel', 1941), 3–12.

26. Mikhail Zoshchenko, *Pered voskhodom solntsa*, in *Sobranie sochinenii v trekh tomakh*, ed. Iu. Tomashevskii et al. (Leningrad: Khudozhestvennaia literatura, 1986), 3:691.

27. Mikhail Zoshchenko, *Pis'ma k pisateliu* (1929; reprint, Ann Arbor: University Microfilms, 1961). The diverse style and content of these letters illuminate the genre of letter writing as discussed by Sheila Fitzpatrick, "Supplicants and Citizens: Public Letter-Writing in Soviet Russia in the 1930s," *Slavic Review* 55, no. 1 (1996): 78–105.

28. Arkady Glagolev, "Pis'ma meshchanina," review of *Pis'ma* in *Zhurnalist* 3 (1930): 88.

29. Dmitri Maznin, "Massovaia rabochaia kritika" (Part I), *Na literaturnom postu* 7 (1932): 17.

30. See R. Messer, review of *Pis'ma* in *Krasnaia gazeta*, 2 November 1929; Tsesar Volpe, "Dvadtsat' let raboty M. M. Zoshchenko: statia pervaia," *Literaturnyi sovremennik* 3 (1941): 147; Mikhail Chumandrin, "Chei pisatel—Mikhail Zoshchenko, *Zvezda* 3 (1930): 211; and Rud. Bershadskii, review of *Pis'ma* in *Pechat' i revoliutsiia* 9 (1929): 116–18. Kriannikova also sees letter writers as targets of Zoshchenko's satire but censures him for not being critical enough. "Vooruzhennyi solominkoi," *Rost* 8–9 (1930): 44–45.

31. Maksim Gorky, letter to Zoshchenko, 13 October 1930. Reprinted in *Literaturnoe nasledstvo: Gor'kii i sovetskie pisateli: neizdannaia perepiska* (Moscow: Akademiia nauk, 1963), 70:163.

32. Glagolev, 89.

33. Chumandrin, 212, 211.

34. Maznin, 12–13.

35. Ibid., 13, 15.

36. *Pervyi vsesoiuznyi s"ezd sovetskikh pisatelei, 1934: stenograficheskii otchet* (Moscow: Sovetskii pisatel', 1990), 61–62.

37. Régine Robin, *Socialist Realism: An Impossible Aesthetic*, trans. Catherine Porter (Stanford: Stanford University Press, 1992), 9, 183–90.

38. *Pervyi vsesoiuznyi s"ezd*, 63.

39. Ibid., 681.

40. See N. Poliak, "Vechera rabochei kritiki," *Kul'turnyi front* 24 (1926): 20–23; and V. Sakharov, "Vechera rabochei kritiki," *Kniga i profsoiuzy* 1 (1927): 8–10.

41. V. Berliner, "Chitatel'skie konferentsii v Rostove na Donu i Nakhichevani," *Krasnyi bibliotekar'* 6 (1927): 61.

42. V. Sakharov, "Kak provodit' vechera rabochei kritiki," in *Pisatel' pered sudom*, 38. See as well Boris K. "Chto pokazal opyt chitatel'skikh konferentsii v Rostove n/D," *Krasnyi bibliotekar'* 11 (1927): 33; M. Maizel, "O

rabochikh kriticheskikh kruzhkakh (iz opyta rukovodstva)," *Literaturnaia ucheba* 1 (1930): 101–14; E. Gopfengauz, "Rabota izdatel'stva na vechere rabochei kritiki," *Na knizhnom fronte* 32–33 (1929): 38–39. Problems in gaining accurate profiles of readers could be as much logistical as ideological. Libraries' lists of readers' preferences (which in the drive to identify popular taste received much print in the 1920s) could be skewed because of generally meager holdings, with the largest deficiency, predictably, being in contemporary literature. Availability was also circumscribed by the removal of "harmful books." How readers ranked literature, therefore, often had a tenuous relation with the literary environment as a whole. (Indeed, Zoshchenko's absence from most reader surveys is strong evidence against their purported accuracy.) Accuracy could also be compromised by the simple fact that readers did not understand the questions, would fill out forms quickly (sometimes library books would not be issued if readers did not hand in evaluations of previous selections), or would just copy their neighbors' answers. For comments on these problems, see Bek and Toom, *Litso rabochego chitatelia*, 3; Smushkova, *Pervye itogi*, 5–6; Iakov Shafir, *Ocherki psikhologii chitatelia* (Moscow-Leningrad: Gosudarstvennoe izdatel'stvo, 1927), 76; Toporov, *Krest'iane*, 23; Brylov et al., *Golos rabochego chitatelia*, 3; and Bank and Vilenkin, *Krest'ianskaia molodezh' i kniga*, 9–10. For a discussion of surveys and the problematic nature of their results, see Jeffrey Brooks, "Studies of the Reader," *Russian History* 9 (1982): 187–202, and Dobrenko, who in addition to the surveys and conferences also comments on police involvement and the forced correctness of readers' responses in *Formovka*, 37ff.

43. Shafir, 74.

44. For an open expression of this, see Mikhail Bekker, "Molodoi chitatel' v roli kritika," *Molodaia gvardiia* 11 (1933): 138. Similarly exclusive definitions of who constitutes the true worker-reader permeate Bek and Toom, *Litso rabochego chitatelia*, and Brylov et al., *Golos rabochego chitatelia*.

45. Rubakin's theories are presented in *Chto takoe bibliotechnaia psikhologiia* (Leningrad: Kolos, 1924), and "Rabota bibliotekaria s tochki zreniia biblio-psikhologii.—K voprosu ob otnoshenii knigi i chitatelia," in *Chitatel' i kniga: metody ikh izucheniia. Sbornik statei* (Khar'kov: Trud, 1925), 37–65.

46. See D. Balika, "Eshche o nauchnoi postanovke izucheniia chitatelia," *Krasnyi bibliotekar'* 11 (1925): 29–42, and the review of *Chitatel' i kniga: metody ix izucheniia* in *Krasnyi bibliotekar'* 10 (1925): 103–7. For further objections to Rubakin, see A. Bek, "Problema izucheniia chitatelia," *Na literaturnom postu* 5/6 (1926): 24.

47. Chumandrin, 219.

48. Averbakh's declaration appears, appropriately enough, in his discussion of Platonov's "Doubting Makar," a text as ambiguous and conten-

tious as Zoshchenko's work of the same period. See "O tselostnykh masshtabakh i chastnykh makarakh," *Na literaturnom postu* 21–22 (1929): 17.

49. See the roundtable discussion in Martin Dewhirst and Robert Farrell, eds., *Soviet Censorship* (Metuchen, N.J.: Scarecrow, 1973), 25.

50. A. Levitskaia, "Chitatel'skaia tribuna: chitatel' v roli kritika," *Na literaturnom postu* 6 (1929): 68. For similar comments see Shteiman, 187.

51. Toporov, "Literaturnye vechera v kommune 'Maiskoe utro,'" *Zemlia sovetskaia* 2 (1929): 59–60. In *Krest'iane* (p. 373), Toporov identifies the speaker, D. Shitikov, in model terms: a partisan in the civil war becomes a party member and now "gobbles up books like hotcakes. In each of them he discovers a lot and tries to put this newfound knowledge to practice in some way."

52. S. Okhitovich, review of *Uvazhaemye grazhdane*, *Na literaturnom postu* 4 (1928): 86.

53. R. Messer, "Preodolenie formalizma," *Literaturnyi Leningrad*, 20 April 1936.

54. Regarding writers or works that fell into disfavor, the invocation of mass reader's disapproval became the cultural norm, with one of the more notorious instances being the "people's letters" attacking Pasternak when he was awarded the Nobel Prize after the publication of *Doctor Zhivago*. See, for example, the letters from soviet readers (who never read the work) published in *Literaturnaia gazeta*, 1 November 1958.

55. Fish, *Is There a Text in This Class?: The Authority of Interpretive Communities* (Cambridge: Harvard University Press, 1980), 338–71. In "Socialist Realism in *Pravda:* Read All About It!" *Slavic Review* 53, no. 4 (1994): 973–91, Jeffrey Brooks also argues for the constructed image of the official reader, calling it an "invented" audience. An earlier and much abridged version of my argument has been published as "The Figure of the Mass Reader in Early Soviet Literature," *Critical Studies in Mass Communication* 12, no. 1 (1995): 1–22. Dobrenko's *Formovka* is the most recent and extensive analysis of readers and readerships in the early Soviet Union.

56. Kornei Chukovsky, "Iz vospominanii," in *Vspominaia Mikhaila Zoshchenko*, ed. Iu. V. Tomashevsky (Leningrad: Khodozhestvennai literatura, 1990), 70.

57. *Pered voskhodom solntsa*, 515.

58. Andrei Platonov and Boris Pilniak, "Che-Che-O," *Novyi Mir* 12 (1928): 257.

59. Theodor Adorno, "Freudian Theory and the Pattern of Fascist Propaganda," in *The Essential Frankfurt School Reader*, ed. Andrew Arato and Eike Gebhardt (New York: Urizen Books, 1978): 134. For a useful discussion of how mass has affected perceptions of text and audience, see Janice Radway, "Reading Is Not Eating: Mass-Produced Literature and the Theoretical, Methodological, and Political Consequences of a Metaphor" *Book Research Quarterly* 3 (1986): 7–29.

60. Tony Bennett, "Introduction," in *Popular Culture and Social Relations,* ed. Tony Bennett, Colin Mercer, and Janet Woollacott (Philadelphia: Open University Press, 1986), xvi.

61. John Fiske, *Understanding Popular Culture* (Boston: Unwin Hyman, 1989), 44; see also his *Reading the Popular* (Boston: Unwin Hyman, 1989).

62. An exemplary illustration of this would be Carlo Ginzburg's reconstruction of the reading habits and beliefs of Mennochio, the sixteenth-century miller and autodidact who was executed for heresy, in *The Cheese and the Worms: The Cosmos of a Sixteenth-Century Miller,* trans. John and Anne Tedeschi (New York: Dorset, 1989).

63. Janice Radway, *Reading the Romance: Women, Patriarchy, and Popular Literature* (Chapel Hill: University of North Carolina Press, 1984). For additional sampling of readers' letters to Zoshchenko from this period—including the memorable compliment "to me your stories are like wine to a drunkard"—see V. A. Prokofev, "'Zdes'. Pisateliu Zoshchenko.' Iz pisem chitatelei 30–x godov," in *Mikhail Zoshchenko: materialy k tvorcheskoi biografii,* ed. N. A. Groznova (St. Petersburg: Nauka, 1997), 1:193–220.

64. Raymond Williams, *Culture and Society, 1780–1950* (London: Chatto & Windus, 1960), 299–300.

CHAPTER SIX

1. In order, these are quotes from V. Gorshkov et al., "Ob odnoi vrednoi povesti," *Bol'shevik* 2 (1944): 57; L. Dmitriev, "O novoi povesti M. Zoshchenko," *Literatura i iskusstvo,* 3 December 1943; and "Na obsuzhdenii zhurnala 'Oktiabr','" *Literatura i iskusstvo,* 11 December 1943. For a behind-the-scenes account of official attacks against *Before Sunrise,* see Denis Babichenko, *Pisateli i tsenzory: sovetskaia literatura 1940-kh godov pod politicheskim kontrolem TsK* (Moscow: Rossiia molodaia, 1944), 72–81.

2. The words are of P. Iudin, quoted in Babichenko, *Pisateli,* 77.

3. In the foreword Zoshchenko states that he conceived of *Before Sunrise* right after finishing *Youth Restored.* He claims to have collected material for ten years but to have begun writing in August 1942, only a year before the book's publication. In 1937 he directly labeled it (at that time with a different title, *Keys to Happiness*) a "continuation" of *Youth Restored.* See "Moi plan," *Literaturnaia gazeta,* 5 January 1937. The thematic core of *Before Sunrise* also appears verbatim in an earlier, and decidedly wooden, story, "New Times," published in *Zvezda* 1 (1938), where the protagonist notes that reason is the key to overcoming undesirable instincts (here sexual). The ideal person of the future, it is suggested, will be the one who best exercises this control.

4. Hugh McLean, "Belated Sunrise: a Review Article," *Slavic and East European Journal* 18, no. 4 (1974): 409.

5. Dmitri Moldavsky, "Prevyshavshii obychnuiu meru," *Zvezda* 12 (1987): 182. For additional commentary on the stylistics of the vignettes and their structural relation to the rest of the text, see Gary Kern, "After the Afterword: The Genesis, Art and Theory of *Before Sunrise*," in Mikhail Zoshchenko, *Before Sunrise*, trans. Gary Kern (Ann Arbor: Ardis, 1974): 358–60.

6. For discussion of Zoshchenko's theories of the mind and the Pavlovian (primarily soviet) versus Freudian (Western) argument regarding their source, see in the Soviet Union, Ars. Gulyga, "'Povest' o razume' M. Zoshchenko," *Zvezda* 3 (1972): 141–44, and later in "Razum pobezhdaet (O nauchno-khudozhestvennykh povestiakh M. Zoshchenko)," in Mikhail Zoshchenko, *Sobranie sochinenii*, ed. Iu. Tomashevskii (Leningrad: Khudozhestvennaia literatura, 1986), 3:694–709; Dmitri Moldavskii, *Mikhail Zoshchenko: ocherk tvorchestva* (Leningrad: Sovetskii pisatel', 1977), 250–52; Iu. Tomashevskii, "Vera v razum," introduction to *Ispoved'* [which includes *Pered voskhodom solntsa*] (Moscow: Sovetskaia Rossiia, 1987), 5–22. In the West, see Vera von Wiren(-Garczynski), "Zoščenko's Psychological Interests," *Slavic and East European Journal* 11, no. 1 (1967): 3–22; and "Sud'ba 'Pered voskhodom solntsa': Freid ili Pavlov?" introduction to Mikhail Zoshchenko, *Pered voskhodom solntsa* (New York: Chekhov, 1973), 15–32; Kern, "After the Afterword," 345–57; Sigrid Nolda, "Zwischen Pavlov und Freud: Ammerkungen zu Michail Zoščenko's Autobiographie," *Die Welt der Slaven* 32 (1987): 78–100; Thomas Hodge, "Freudian Elements in Zoshchenko's *Pered voskhodom solntsa*," *Slavonic and East European Review* 67, no. 1 (1989): 1–28. For an extensive discussion of the text's imagery and thematics, see Irene Masing-Delic, "Biology, Reason and Literature in Zoščenko's *Pered voskhodom solntsa*," *Russian Literature* 8 (1980): 77–101. For a related discussion of Zoshchenko's new voice with attention to its expanded range, see Linda Hart Scatton, *Mikhail Zoshchenko: Evolution of a Writer* (Cambridge, Eng.: Cambridge University Press, 1993), 211 ff. She also provides the most detailed discussion to date on the text's structure and the aesthetic makeup of vignettes.

7. Of Zholkovsky's many articles on Zoshchenko, see in particular, "Ruka blizhnego i ee mesto v poetike Zoshchenko," *Novoe literaturnoe obozrenie* 15 (1995): 262–86; "K reinterpretatsii poetiki Mikhaila Zoshchenko," *Izvestiia akademii nauk: seriia literatury i iazyka* 54, no. 5 (1995): 50–60; "Zoshchenko iz XXI veka, ili poetika nedoveriia," *Zvezda* 5 (1996): 190–204; "'What Is the Author Trying to Say with His Artistic Work?': Rereading Zoshchenko's Oeuvre," *The Slavic and East European Journal* 40, no. 3 (1996): 458–74; "Food, Fear, Feigning and Flight in Zoščenko's 'Foreigners,'" *Russian Literature* 40 (1996): 385–404.

8. Quoted from a letter to L. A. Chalova, reprinted in Dmitri Moldavsky, "Ob odnoi povesti Mikhaila Zoshchenko," *Neva* 7 (1987): 165.

9. McLean, "Belated Sunrise," 406.

10. *Pered voskhodom solntsa, SS/86,* vol. 3, 587. All subsequent parenthetical page references will be to this edition.

11. See Roy Pascal, *Design and Truth in Autobiography* (Cambridge, Mass.: Harvard University Press, 1960); James Olney, *Metaphors of Self: The Meaning of Autobiography* (Princeton: Princeton University Press, 1972); Susanna Egan, *Patterns of Experience in Autobiography* (Chapel Hill: University of North Carolina Press, 1984).

12. Roy Schafer, "Narration in Psychoanalytic Dialogue," *Critical Inquiry* 7, no. 1 (1980): 49.

13. Paul Ricoeur's comments on the problematic nature of facts in psychoanalysis are particularly pertinent to Zoshchenko's "case": "[F]acts in psychoanalysis are in no way facts of observable behavior. They are 'reports.' We know of dreams only as told upon awakening; and even symptoms, although they are partially observable, enter into the field of analysis only in relation to other factors verbalized in the 'report.' It is this selective restriction which forces us to situate the facts of psychoanalysis inside a sphere of motivation and meaning." "The Question of Proof in Freud's Psychoanalytic Writings," *Journal of the American Psychoanalytic Association* 25, no. 4 (1977): 837.

14. For additional skepticism on the strength of Zoshchenko's argument and success of his claimed cure, see McLean, "Belated Sunrise," 409; Kern, "After the Afterword," 361–64; and Krista Hanson, "Autobiography and Conversion: Zoshchenko's *Before Sunrise*," in *Autobiographical Statements in Twentieth-Century Russian Literature*, ed. Jane Gray Harris (Princeton: Princeton University Press, 1990): 149–50.

15. Donald Spence, *Narrative Truth and Historical Truth: Meaning and Interpretation in Psychoanalysis* (New York: Norton, 1982).

16. Ibid., 95.

17. V. V. Zoshchenko, "Tvorcheskii put' Zoshchenko," in *Neizdannyi Zoshchenko* (Ann Arbor: Ardis, n.d.), 151. In fact, when confronted with his wife's objections over the portrayal of their relationship, Zoshchenko was forced to admit that passages in *Before Sunrise* were not "a true biography" but rather "literature" in which he needed to transmit "certain features of character." See his letter to her, dated 17 November 1943, reprinted by V. V. Buznik in "Iz pisem M. M. Zoshchenko k V. V. Zoshchenko (1941–1954)," *Mikhail Zoshchenko: materialy k tvorcheskoi biografii*, ed. N. A. Groznova (St. Petersburg: Nauka, 1997), 1:94–95.

18. Schafer, "Narration," 52.

19. McLean, "Belated Sunrise," 410. Scatton, *Mikhail Zoshchenko*, 11, also notes the problems inherent in treating the text as a biographical source. She has, notably, taken steps to answer our ignorance; her second chapter provides the most detailed account in English of Zoshchenko's life.

20. Josef Breuer and Sigmund Freud, *Studies on Hysteria*, trans. James Strachey and Alix Strachey (London: Hogarth, 1956), 126.

21. Ibid., 126.

22. Ibid., 127.

23. Ibid., 128.

24. In her analysis of Zoshchenko's authorial voice, Chudakova was the first to examine this narrative shift in detailed terms. See especially chapter 5 in *Poetika Mikhaila Zoshchenko*, "Literatura dolzhna byt' narodnoi" (Moscow: Nauka, 1979). Scatton, building off of Chudakova in *Mikhail Zoshchenko*, wittily entitles her first chapter "The Artistic Evolution Nobody (But the Artist) Wanted."

25. This inner confusion, no doubt combined with the influence of contemporary prescriptions of form, led Zoshchenko to make some incredible flip-flop pronouncements in the late 1930s and 1940s. See, for example, his articles "O negramotnosti," *Bol'shevitskaia pechat'* 12 (1938); reprinted in "Literatura dolzhna byt' narodnoi," *Literaturnoe obozrenie* 9 (1984): 100–8, and "O literaturnom iskusstve," *Literaturnyi sovremennik* 3 (1941): 124–27, where he castigates writers who indulge in verbosity, make deliberate grammatical-syntactic mistakes and create "chaos" in literature—the very sins of which Sinebriukhov, Kolenkorov, and company were most guilty!

26. *Pered voskhodom solntsa*, 612, 627.

27. M. Keith Booker and Dubravka Juraga, *Bakhtin, Stalin, and Modern Russian Fiction* (Westport, Conn.: Greenwood Press, 1995); they devote their fourth chapter to Zoshchenko. Rachel May, "Superego as Literary Subtext: Story and Structure in Mikhail Zoshchenko's *Before Sunrise*," *Slavic Review* 55, no. 1 (1996), 106–24. Recent publications from Zoshchenko's archives only confirm the sincerity of his beliefs, utopian and otherwise, in the power of science and technology. His notes regarding what has and could be done in the world often read as those of a wide-eyed child. See V. A. Shoshin, "Neizvestnyi Zoshchenko (po arkhivam materialam)," in *Mikhail Zoshchenko: materialy k tvorcheskoi biografii*, 172–92.

28. "Chernyi Prints," *Literaturnyi sovremennik* 3 (1937): 30–68. See also Chudakova's comments on this text in *Poetika*, 134–35. Scatton, too, notes the important role it plays in Zoshchenko's evolution. In addition, she sees a direct kinship between Zoshchenko's *Retribution*, a novella of 1937 chronicling the exploits of a revolutionary patriot, and *Before Sunrise*. See Scatton, *Mikhail Zoshchenko*, 113–27.

29. N. V. Gogol, *Avtorskaia ispoved'*, in *Polnoe sobranie sochinenii* (Moscow, 1952), 8:432–67.

30. N. V. Gogol, "Predislovie k vtoromu izdaniiu," in *Polnoe sobranie sochinenie*, 6:587, 589.

31. These citations are taken from the following three letters (nos. 192, 201, 205) dated 13 March 1841 (o.s.), 7 August 1841 (n.s.), 27 September 1841 (n.s.). All are in volume 11 of Gogol's *Polnoe sobranie sochinenii* (Moscow: Academiia nauk, 1952).

32. Kornei Chukovsky, diary entry for 23 August 1927 in *Dnevnik, 1901–1929*, ed. E. Chukovskaia (Moscow: Sovetskii pisatel', 1991), 409.

33. Lev Tolstoy, *Chto takoe iskusstvo*, in *Polnoe sobranie sochinenie* (Moscow: Gosudarstvennoe izdatel'stvo khudozhestvennoi literatury, 1951), 30:180.

34. Ibid., 144–45.

35. Instructive here is the colorful (and critical) contemporary response to Gogol's work and his troubled ways of dealing with it. See Paul Debreczeny, "Nikolay Gogol and His Contemporary Critics," *Transactions of the American Philosophical Society* 56, pt. 3 (1966). I am indebted to Alexander Zholkovsky for bringing this source to my attention. For Zoshchenko's own recognition of their shared fate, see his wife's comments in Filippov, "Lichnost' M. Zoshchenko po vospominaniiam ego zheny," 69.

36. See her chapter 6, "Svoim iazykom," in *Poetika*.

37. Hanson, "Autobiography and Conversion."

38. For Kern's comments as well on *Before Sunrise* as a "modern parallel" to Tolstoy's *Confession*, see "After the Afterword," 355. Tomashevsky even gives that title to a 1987 collection that includes *Before Sunrise* as its centerpiece: *Ispoved'* (Moscow: Sovetskaia Rossiia, 1987).

CONCLUSION

1. This is the refrain from Ilya Ilf and Evgenny Petrov, "Literaturnyi tramvai," in *Sobranie sochinenii v piati tomakh* (Moscow: Gosudarstvennoe izd., 1961), 3:172–75. The feuilleton was first published in *Literaturnaia gazeta*, 11 August 1932.

2. Thomas Seifrid, *Andrei Platonov: Uncertainties of Spirit* (Cambridge, Eng.: Cambridge University Press, 1992). For a recent discussion of the literary relation between the two, see N. Kornienko, "Zoshchenko i Platonov: vstrechi v literature," *Literaturnoe obozrenie* 1 (1995): 47–54.

3. N. N. Shneidman, *Russian Literature, 1988–1994: The End of an Era* (Toronto: University of Toronto Press, 1995), 204.

4. Fadeev's alleged statement was relayed by Mikhail Sholokhov in an interview with Czech writers while he was in Prague in April, 1958. See "Michail Šolochov beseduje s českými spisovateli," *Literární noviny*, 19 April 1958, 3.

5. In order, these citations are from John Fizer, "Has Socialist Realism Been Identical with Itself?" *Russian Literature* 28 (1990): 12; Victor Terras, "Phenomenological Observations on the Aesthetics of Socialist Realism," *Slavic and East European Journal* 23, no. 4 (1979): 448; Marc Slonim, *Soviet Russian Literature: Writers and Problems* (New York: Oxford University Press, 1964), 161; Eric Newton, "Art for Marx' Sake in Russia," *New York Times*, 19 October 1947, sec. 6, p. 8; Edward J. Brown, *Russian Literature*

Since the Revolution, rev. ed. (Cambridge: Harvard University Press, 1982), 15; John and Carol Garrard, *Inside the Soviet Writers' Union* (New York: Free Press, 1990), 169.

6. Herman Ermolaev, *Soviet Literary Theories, 1917–1934: The Genesis of Socialist Realism* (New York: Octagon Books, 1977), 32, 50.

7. Edward J. Brown, *The Proletarian Episode in Russian Literature, 1928–1932* (New York: Columbia University Press, 1953), 38.

8. Mark Twain, *Roughing It* (New York: Penguin Books, 1981), 146.

9. Aleksandr Solzhenitsyn, *The Oak and the Calf: A Memoir,* trans. Harry Willets (New York: Harper & Row, 1975), 8.

10. On the origin, impact, and legacy of this metaphor, see Abbott Gleason, *Totalitarianism: The Inner History of the Cold War* (New York: Oxford University Press, 1995).

11. Fizer, 20. At the end of his essay Fizer appends a statement to negate the monologic tones of his declaration. However, the weight of his argument, inhabiting solely the realm of theoretical proclamation, is manifestly in the other direction.

12. Régine Robin, *Socialist Realism: An Impossible Aesthetic,* trans. Catherine Porter (Stanford: Stanford University Press, 1992), 290.

13. Ibid., 282–83.

14. Andrei Siniavsky (Abram Tertz), *On Socialist Realism,* trans. George Dennis (New York: Pantheon, 1960), 90–91.

15. Katerina Clark, *The Soviet Novel: History as Ritual* (Chicago: University of Chicago Press, 1981). For a slightly earlier discussion of the theoretical implications of treating socialist realism-soviet literature on its own terms, see Gary Saul Morson, "Socialist Realism and Literary Theory," *The Journal of Aesthetics and Art Criticism* 38, no. 2 (1979): 121–33.

16. David Joravsky, "Communism in Historical Perspective," *The American Historical Review* 99, no. 3 (1994): 849. For an illustrative airing out of differences among historians regarding the "totalitarian paradigm," see the collection of articles in *The Russian Review* 45, no. 4 (1986).

17. Boris Groys, *The Total Art of Stalinism: Avant-Garde, Aesthetic Dictatorship and Beyond,* trans. Charles Rougle (Princeton: Princeton University Press, 1992). More than a decade earlier, Vera Dunham produced a pioneering work on how postwar changes in socialist realism reflected a negotiation of interests between the party and the new soviet bourgeoisie: *In Stalin's Time: Middlebrow Values in Soviet Fiction* (New York: Cambridge University Press, 1976).

18. Katerina Clark, *Petersburg: Crucible of Cultural Revolution* (Cambridge, Mass.: Harvard University Press, 1995). For another excellent study on the interrelation and conflict between Bolsheviks and the intelligentsia, see Sheila Fitzpatrick's collection of articles (most originally published in the

1970s and 1980s) in *The Cultural Front: Power and Culture in Revolutionary Russia* (Ithaca, N.Y.: Cornell University Press, 1992).

19. See Evgenii Dobrenko, *Metafory vlasti: Literatura stalinskoi epokhi v istoricheskom osveshchenii* (Munich: Verlag Otto Sagner, 1993); he also comments on the organic growth of socialist realist principles from both the left and the right. See also the collection of articles in Thomas Lahusen and Evgeny Dobrenko, eds., *Socialist Realism Without Shores*, a special issue of *The South Atlantic Quarterly* 94, no. 3 (1995). "Possibility" comes from Dobrenko's contribution, "The Disaster of Middlebrow Taste." Recently, Jeffrey Brooks has argued for the impossibility of understanding socialist realism outside the contradictions of its 1930s discursive context in "Socialist Realism in *Pravda:* Read All About It!" *Slavic Review* 53, no. 4 (1994): 973–91.

20. See especially his conclusion, "Rewriting Literary History," in *Beyond Metafiction: Self-Consciousness in Soviet Literature* (Oxford: Oxford University Press, 1992).

21. Mikhail Zoshchenko, "O sebe, o kritikakh i o svoei rabote," in *Mikhail Zoshchenko. Mastera sovremennoi literatury: stat'i i materialy,* ed. B. V. Kazanskii and Iu. N. Tynianov (Leningrad: Academia, 1928; reprint, Letchworth, Eng.: Prideaux, 1973), 7 (page citations are to the reprint edition).

22. In his structural-psychoanalytic readings of Zoshchenko, Zholkovsky also comes out expressly against, though in terms different from my argument here, the ideological, anti-soviet dominant in Zoshchenko's critical legacy.

23. Cathy Popkin, *The Pragmatics of Insignificance: Chekhov, Zoshchenko and Gogol* (Stanford: Stanford University Press, 1993), 122.

24. M. Keith Booker and Dubravka Juraga, *Bakhtin, Stalin, and Modern Russian Fiction* (Westport, Conn.: Greenwood Press, 1995).

25. I have discussed how socialist realism could accommodate the text's generic hybridity in "Genre in Socialist Realism," *Slavic Review* 53, no. 4 (1994): 992–1009.

Bibliography

WORKS BY ZOSHCHENKO

Rasskazy Nazara Il'icha, gospodina Sinebriukhova. 1922; reprint, Berkeley: Berkeley Slavic Specialties, 1982.
"O sebe, ob ideologii i eshche koe o chem." *Literaturnye zapiski* 3 (1922): 28–29.
"O sebe, o kritikakh i o svoei rabote." In *Mikhail Zoshchenko. Mastera sovremennoi literatury: stat'i i materialy,* edited by B. V. Kazanskii and Iu. N. Tynianov, 5–11. Leningrad: Academia, 1928. Reprint, Letchworth, Eng.: Prideaux, 1973.
Nad kem smeetes'. 4th ed. Moscow-Leningrad: Zemlia i fabrika, 1928.
Pis'ma k pisateliu, 1929. Reprint, Ann Arbor: University Microfilms, 1961.
"Kak ia rabotaiu." *Literaturnaia ucheba* 3 (1930): 107–13.
"Mikh. Zoshchenko." In *Kak my pishem,* 42–50. 1930. Reprint, Moscow: Kniga, 1989.
M. P. Siniagin (Vospominaniia o Mishele Siniagine). Leningrad: Izd. pisatelei, 1930.
"Siren' tsvetet." In *Zvezda: literaturno-khudozhestvennyi almanakh.* Leningrad: Priboi, 1930, 41–76.
Sobranie sochinenii. 2d ed. 6 vols. Moscow-Leningrad: Goslitizdat, 1931.
Vozvrashchennaia molodost'. Leningrad: Izd. pisatelei, 1933.
"Vozvrashchennaia molodost'." *Literaturnyi Leningrad,* 5 September 1933.
"Vstupitel'noe slovo Mikh. Zoshchenko na dispute o 'Vozvrashchennoi molodosti' v stolovoj lenkublita." *Literaturnyi Leningrad,* 15 March 1934.
"Mikhail Zoshchenko o svoei 'Goluboi knige.'" *Vecherniaia krasnaia gazeta,* 8 May 1934.
"Osnovnye voprosy nashei professii." *Literaturnyi Leningrad,* 14 August 1934.
Golubaia kniga. Leningrad: Sovetskii pisatel', 1935.
"Moi plan." *Literaturnaia gazeta,* 5 January 1937.
"Chernyi prints." *Literaturnyi sovremennik* 3 (1937): 30–68.
"O negramotnosti." *Bol'shevitskaia pechat'* 12 (1938). Reprinted in "Literatura dolzhna byt' narodnoi." *Literaturnoe obozrenie* 9 (1984): 100–108.
"Oko za oko." In *Leningradskii al'manakh,* edited by P. O. Kapitsa, I. F. Kratt et al., 3–12. Leningrad: Sovetskii pisatel', 1941.
"O literaturnom iskusstve." *Literaturnyi sovremennik* 3 (1941): 124–27.

Bibliography

Rasskazy, fel'etony, povesti. Moscow: Goslitizdat, 1958.
"Literatura dolzhna byt' narodnoi." *Literaturnoe obozrenie* 9 (1984): 100–8.
Sobranie sochinenii. 3 vols. Edited by Iu. Tomashevskii. Leningrad: Khudozhestvennaia literatura, 1986.
The Mikhail Zoshchenko Archive. *Fond* 501. St. Petersburg: Institut russkoi literatury (Pushkinskii dom).

OTHER WORKS CITED

Adorno, Theodor. "Freudian Theory and the Pattern of Fascist Propaganda." In *The Essential Frankfurt School Reader*, edited by Andrew Arato and Eike Gebhardt, 118–37. New York: Urizen Books, 1978.
Alexandrova, Vera. *A History of Soviet Literature.* Translated by Mirra Ginsburg. Garden City: Doubleday, 1963.
Alter, Robert. *Partial Magic: The Novel as a Self-Conscious Genre.* Berkeley: University of California Press, 1975.
Aseev, Nikolai. Review of *Rasskazy Nazara Il'icha gospodina Sinebriukhova. Pechat' i revoliutsiia* 7 (1922): 316.
Atkinson, Brooks. "In the Arts the Kremlin Line Is Mid-Victorian." *New York Times,* 22 February 1948, sec. 6, pp. 12–13, 53–54.
Auerbach, Erich. *Mimesis: The Representation of Reality in Western Literature.* Translated by Willard R. Trask. Princeton: Princeton University Press, 1991.
Averbakh, Leopold. *O zadachakh proletarskoi literatury.* Moscow-Leningrad: Moskovskii rabochii, 1928.
———. "O tselostnykh masshtabakh i chastnykh makarakh." *Na literaturnom postu* 21–22 (1929): 10–17.
Babichenko, Denis. "Delo ob 'otravlenii.' Mikhail Zoshchenko ob"iasniaetsia s nachal'stvom." In *Neizvestnaia Rossiia: XX vek,* vol. 1, edited by V. Kozlov, G. Bordiugov, S. Vakunov, et al., 129–46. Moscow: Istoricheskoe nasledie, 1992.
———. "Zhdanov, Malenkov i delo leningradskikh zhurnalov." *Voprosy literatury* 3 (1993): 201–14.
———. *Literaturnyi front: istoriia politicheskoi tsenzury, 1932–1946 gg.* Moscow: Entsiklopediia rossiskikh derevenʹ, 1994.
———. *Pisateli i tsenzory: sovetskaia literatura 1940-kh godov pod politicheskim kontrolem TsK.* Moscow: Rossiia molodaia, 1994.
Bakhtin, Mikhail. *Problemy tvorchestva Dostoevskogo.* Leningrad: Priboi, 1929.
———. "Iz predystorii romannogo slova." In *Voprosy literatury i estetiki.* Moscow: Khudozhestvennaia literatura, 1975: 408–46.
Balika, D. Review of *Chitatel' i kniga: metody ix izvcheniia,* edited by Ia. V. Rivlin, N. A. Rubakin, and B. O. Borovich. *Krasnyi bibliotekar'* 10 (1925): 103–7.

———. "Eshche o nauchnoi postanovke izucheniia chitatelia." *Krasnyi bibliotekar'* 11 (1925): 29–42.
Bank, B., and A. Vilenkin. *Krest'ianskaia molodezh' i kniga (opyt issledovaniia chitatel'skikh interesov)*. Moscow-Leningrad: Molodaia gvardiia, 1929.
Barthes, Roland. *The Rustle of Language*. Translated by Richard Howard. Berkeley: University of California Press, 1989.
Begak, B. "Povest' i kommentarii k nei." *Literaturnaia gazeta*, 18 March 1934.
Bek, A. "Problema izucheniia chitatelia." *Na literaturnom postu* 5–6 (1926): 24.
Bek, A., and L. Toom. *Litso rabochego chitatelia*. Moscow-Leningrad: Gosudarstvennoe izdatel'stvo, 1927.
Bekker, Mikh. "Molodoi chitatel' v roli kritika." *Molodaia gvardiia* 11 (1933): 138–43.
Belaia, Galina. "Mikhail Zoshchenko—iumorist, satirik, moralist." In *Puteshestvie v poiskakh istiny: stat'i o sovetskikh pisateliakh*. Tbilisi: Merani, 1987: 28–56.
Bennett, Tony, Colin Mercer, and Janet Woollacott, eds. *Popular Culture and Social Relations*. Philadelphia: Open University Press, 1986.
Berliner, V. "Chitatel'skie konferentsii v Rostove na Donu i Nakhichevani." *Krasnyi bibliotekar'* 6 (1927): 60–63.
Bershadskii, Rud. Review of *Pis'ma k pisateliu*. *Pechat' i revoliutsiia* 9 (1929): 116–18.
Beskina, Anna. "Mikhail Zoshchenko v poiskakh optimizma." *Literaturnyi Leningrad*, 8 May 1934.
———. "V poiskakh optimizma." *Literaturnyi sovremennik* 5 (1934): 111–22.
———. "Litso i maska Mikhaila Zoshchenko." *Literaturnyi kritik* 1 (1935): 107–31; 2 (1935): 59–92.
Blair, Hector. Introduction to *Liudi*, by Mikhail Zoshchenko. London: Cambridge University Press, 1967.
Bogatyrev, Petr. "Costume as Sign (The Functional and Structural Concept in Ethnography)" (1936). Translated by Yvonne Lockwood. In *Semiotics of Art: Prague School Contributions*, edited by Ladislav Matejka and I. R. Titunik, 13–19. Cambridge, Mass.: MIT Press, 1976.
Booker, M. Keith, and Dubravka Juraga. *Bakhtin, Stalin, and Modern Russian Fiction*. Westport, Conn.: Greenwood Press, 1995.
Bordwell, David. *Making Meaning: Inference and Rhetoric in the Interpretation of Cinema*. Cambridge, Mass.: Harvard University Press, 1989.
Borland, Harriet. *Soviet Literary Theory and Practice During the First Five-Year Plan, 1928–32*. New York: King's Crown Press, 1950.
Boym, Svetlana. *Common Places: Mythologies of Everyday Life in Russia*. Cambridge, Mass.: Harvard University Press, 1994.

Braun, Ia. "Desiat' strannikov v 'osiazaemoe nichto.'" *Sibirskie ogni* 1 (1924): 201–40.
Breuer, Josef, and Sigmund Freud. *Studies on Hysteria.* Translated by James Strachey and Alix Strachey. London: Hogarth, 1956.
Brik, Osip. "Blizhe k faktu." *Novyi Lef* 2 (1927): 32–34.
Brooks, Jeffrey. "Studies of the Reader in the 1920s." *Russian History/ Histoire Russe* 9 (1982): 187–202.
———. "The Breakdown in Production and Distribution of Printed Material, 1917–1923." In *Bolshevik Culture: Experiment and Order in the Russian Revolution,* edited by Abbott Gleason, Peter Kenez, and Richard Stites, 151–74. Bloomington: Indiana University Press, 1985.
———. "Public and Private Values in the Soviet Press, 1921–1928." *Slavic Review* 1 (1989): 16–35.
———. "Socialist Realism in *Pravda:* Read All About It!" *Slavic Review* 53, no. 4 (1994): 973–91.
Brown, Edward J. *The Proletarian Episode in Russian Literature, 1928– 1932.* New York: Columbia University Press, 1953.
———. *Russian Literature Since the Revolution.* Rev. ed. Cambridge: Harvard University Press, 1982.
Brylov, G., N. Lebedev et al., eds. *Golos rabochego chitatelia: sovremennaia sovetskaia khudozhestvennaia literatura v svete massovoi rabochei kritiki.* Leningrad: Krasnaia gazeta, 1929.
Brylov, G., N. Veis, and V. Sakharov. *Pisatel' pered sudom rabochego chitatelia.* Leningrad: Izdatel'stvo leningradskogo soveta profsoiuza, 1928.
Buznik, V. V. "Iz pisem M. M. Zoshchenko k V. V. Zoshchenko (1941–1954)." *Mikhail Zoshchenko: materialy k tvorcheskoi biografii.* Ed. N. A. Groznova. St. Petersburg: Nauka, 1997. 1:80–106.
Carleton, Greg. "Genre in Socialist Realism." *Slavic Review* 53, no. 4 (1994): 992–1009.
———. "The Figure of the Mass Reader in Early Soviet Literature." *Critical Studies in Mass Communication* 12, no. 1 (1995): 1–22
Cervantes, Miguel de. *The Adventures of Don Quixote.* Translated by J. M. Cohen. New York: Penguin, 1950.
Chapple, Richard. *Soviet Satire of the Twenties.* Gainesville: University of Florida Press, 1980.
Chudakova, M. O. *Poetika Mikhaila Zoshchenko.* Moscow: Nauka, 1979.
———. "Bez gneva i pristrastiia: formy i deformatsii v literaturnom protsesse 20–30-x godov." *Novyi mir* 9 (1988): 240–60.
Chukovsky, Kornei. "Iz vospominanii." In *Mikhail Zoshchenko v vospominaniiakh sovremennikov,* edited by A. Smolian and N. Iurgeneva, 13–66. Moscow: Sovetskii pisatel', 1981.
———. *Dnevnik, 1901–1929.* Edited by E. Chukovskaia. Moscow: Sovetskii pisatel', 1991.

———. *Dnevnik, 1930–1969.* Edited by E. Chukovskaia. Moscow: Sovremennyi pisatel', 1994.

Chumandrin, Mikhail. "Chei pisatel'—Mikhail Zoshchenko." *Zvezda* 3 (1930): 206–19.

Chuzhak, N. F., ed. *Literatura fakta.* Moscow: Federatsiia, 1929.

Clark, Katerina. *The Soviet Novel: History as Ritual.* 2d ed. Chicago: University of Chicago Press, 1985.

———. *Petersburg: Crucible of Cultural Revolution.* Cambridge, Mass.: Harvard University Press, 1995.

Cukierman, Jacqueline. "Mixail Zoščenko's *Rasskazy* and *Povesti* of the 1920s: A Study in Genre Evolution." Ph.D. diss., University of Michigan, 1978.

Debreczeny, Paul. "Nikolay Gogol and His Contemporary Critics." *Transactions of the American Philosophical Society* 56, pt. 3 (1966).

Dewhirst, Martin, and Robert Farrell, eds. *Soviet Censorship.* Metuchen, N.J.: Scarecrow, 1973.

Din, L. I. "Kakoi dolzhna byt' kniga." *Literaturnaia gazeta.* 25 August 1930.

Dmitriev, L. "O novoi povesti M. Zoshchenko." *Literatura i iskusstvo.* 3 December 1943.

Dobrenko, Evgeny. *Metafory vlasti: literatura stalinskoi epokhi v istoricheskom osveshchenii.* Munich: Verlag Otto Sagner, 1993.

———. *Formovka sovetskogo chitatelia: sotsial'nye i esteticheskie predposylki retseptsii sovetskoi literatury.* St. Petersburg: Akademicheskii proekt, 1997.

Dolinsky, M. Z. "Dokumenty: materialy k biograficheskoi chronike." In Mikhail Zoshchenko, *Uvazhaemye grazhdane: parodii, rasskazy, fel'etony, satiricheskie zametki, pis'ma k pisateliu, odnoaktnye komedii,* edited by M. Z. Dolinsky, 33–143. Moscow: Knizhnaia palata, 1991.

Domar, Rebecca. "The Tragedy of a Soviet Satirist: The Case of Zoshchenko." In *Through the Glass of Soviet Literature,* edited by Edward Simmons, 201–43. New York: Columbia University Press, 1953.

Drugov, B. "Porazhenie geroia i pobeda avtora." Review of *Vozvrashchennaia molodost'. Kniga i proletarskaia revoliutsiia* 9 (1934): 99–102.

Dunham, Vera. *In Stalin's Time: Middlebrow Values in Soviet Fiction.* New York: Cambridge University Press, 1976.

Dymshchits, A. "O 'Goluboi knige' M. Zoshchenko." *Rezets* 6 (1936): 18–19.

Egan, Susanna. *Patterns of Experience in Autobiography.* Chapel Hill: University of North Carolina Press, 1984.

Egolin, A. "Za vysokuiu ideinost' sovetskoi literatury." *Bol'shevik* 10–11 (1944): 39–49.

Eikhenbaum, Boris. "Leskov i sovremennaia proza." In *O literature,* 409–24. Moscow: Sovetskii pisatel', 1987.

Erlich, Victor. *Modernism and Revolution: Russian Literature in Transition.* Cambridge, Mass.: Harvard University Press, 1994.

Ermilov, Vladimir. "F. Dostoevskii i nasha kritika." *Literaturnaia gazeta.* 24 December 1947.

Ermolaev, Herman. *Soviet Literary Theories, 1917–1934: The Genesis of Socialist Realism.* New York: Octagon Books, 1977.

Ershov, L. *Iz istorii sovetskoi satiry: M. Zoshchenko i satiricheskaia proza 20–40-kh godov.* Leningrad: Nauka, 1973.

Eventov, I. "Golubaia kniga." *Vecherniaia krasnaia gazeta,* 8 March 1936.

Fadeev, Aleksandr. "Nauka i kul'tura v bor'be za mir, progress i demokratiiu." *Literaturnaia gazeta,* 29 August 1948.

Faresov, A. *Protiv techenii: N. S. Leskov. Ego zhizn', sochineniia, polemika i vospominaniia o nem.* St. Petersburg: Publ. M. Markushev, 1904.

Fedorov, I. Review of *Uvazhaemye grazhdane. Komsomol'skaia pravda,* 4 June 1927.

Filippov, G. V. "Lichnost' M. Zoshchenko po vospominaniiam ego zheny (1916–1929)." *Mikhail Zoshchenko: materialy k tvorcheskoi biografii.* Edited by N. A. Groznova. St. Petersburg: Nauka, 1997, 1:49–79.

Fish, Stanley. *Is There a Text in This Class?: The Authority of Interpretive Communities.* Cambridge, Mass.: Harvard University Press, 1980.

Fiske, John. *Reading the Popular.* Boston: Unwin Hyman, 1989.

———. *Understanding Popular Culture.* Boston: Unwin Hyman, 1989.

Fitzpatrick, Sheila. *The Cultural Front: Power and Culture in Revolutionary Russia.* Ithaca, N.Y.: Cornell University Press, 1992.

———. "Supplicants and Citizens: Public Letter-Writing in Soviet Russia in the 1930s." *Slavic Review* 55, no. 1 (1996): 78–105.

Fizer, John. "Has Socialist Realism Been Identical with Itself?" *Russian Literature* 28 (1990): 11–22.

Galperina, E. "K probleme literaturnoi parodii." *Pechat' i revoliutsiia* 12 (1929): 14–30.

Garrard, John, and Carol Garrard. *Inside the Soviet Writers' Union.* New York: Free Press, 1990.

Gekht, S. "Fel'etony Il'fa i Petrova." *Literaturnaia gazeta,* 26 August 1939.

Ginzburg, Carlo. *The Cheese and the Worms: The Cosmos of a Sixteenth-Century Miller.* Translated by John and Anne Tedeschi. New York: Dorset, 1989.

Glagolev, Arkady. "Pis'ma meshchanina." Review of *Pis'ma k pisateliu. Zhurnalist* 3 (1930): 88–89.

Gleason, Abbott. *Totalitarianism: The Inner History of the Cold War.* New York: Oxford University Press, 1995.

Gogol', N. V. *Polnoe sobranie sochinenii.* Moscow: Akademiia nauk, 1952.

Gol'dshtein, Mikh. Review of *Vospominanie o M. L. Siniagine* [sic]. *Rezets* 13 (1931): 17.

Gopfengauz, E. "Rabota izdatel'stva na vechere rabochei kritiki." *Na knizhnom fronte* 32–33 (1929): 38–39.

Gorbachev, Georgii. *Ocherki sovremennoi russkoi literatury*. 3d ed. Leningrad: Gosizdat, 1925.

———. *Sovremennaia russkaia literatura*. Moscow-Leningrad: Priboi, 1928.

Gorelov, Anatolii. "Omolozhenie dvunogogo sushchestva." *Literaturnyi Leningrad*, 31 May 1934.

———. *Ispytanie vremenem*. Leningrad: Khudozhestvennaia literatura, 1935.

Gor'kii, Maksim. "O neobkhodimosti sozdaniia nauchno-populiarnoi literatury dlia massovogo chitatelia." *Literaturnaia gazeta*, 11 September 1933.

———. "Gorky–Zoshchenko: Perepiska." In *Literaturnoe nasledstvo: Gorky i sovetskie pisateli: neizdannaia perepiska*. Moscow: Akademiia nauk, 1963. 70:157–68.

———. *Perepiska A. M. Gor'kogo s I. A. Gruzdevym. Arkhiv A. M. Gor'kogo XI*. Edited by V. S. Barakhov et al. Moscow: Nauka, 1966.

Gorshkov, V. et al. "Ob odnoi vrednoi povesti." *Bol'shevik* 2 (1944): 56–58.

Graboventskii, V. et al. "Chego my khotim ot sovetskoi literatury." *Literaturnyi Leningrad*, 28 July 1934.

Granin, Daniil. "Mimoletnoe iavlenie." *Ogonek* 6 (1988): 9–11, 29.

Grigor'eva, R. "Litso derevenskogo chitatelia po materialam 'knigapochtoi.'" *Na knizhnom fronte* 17–18 (1929): 25–26.

Grossman, B. "Zametki o tvorchestve Il'fa i Petrova." *Znamia* 9 (1937): 190–206.

Groys, Boris. *The Total Art of Stalinism: Avant-Garde, Aesthetic Dictatorship and Beyond*. Translated by Charles Rougle. Princeton: Princeton University Press, 1992.

Groznova, N. A., ed. *Mikhail Zoshchenko: materialy k tvorcheskoi biografii*. Vol. 1. St. Petersburg: Nauka, 1997.

Gruzdev, Ilia. "Vechera 'Serapionovykh brat'ev.'" *Kniga i revoliutsiia* 3 (1922): 110–11.

———. "Litso i maska." In *Serapionovy brat'ia*. 1922. Reprint, Munich: Wilhelm Fink, 1973: 205–37.

Gulyga, Ars. "'Povest' o razume' M. Zoshchenko." *Zvezda* 3 (1972): 141–44.

———. "Razum pobezhdaet (o nauchno-khudozhestvennykh povestiakh M. Zoshchenko)." In Mikhail Zoshchenko, *Sobranie sochinenii*, vol. 3, edited by Iu. Tomashevskii, 694–709. Leningrad: Khudozhestvennaia literatura, 1986.

Günther, Hans. "Zur Semantik und Funktion des Skaz bei M. Zoščenko." In *Von der Revolution zum Schriftstellerkongreß*, edited by Gernot Erler et al., 326–53. Berlin: Osteuropa-Institut, 1979.

———, ed. *The Culture of the Stalin Period*. London: Macmillan, 1990.

Gurshtein, A. "Po alleiam istorii." *Pravda*, 9 May 1936.

"Gus'—ubiitsa." *Vecherniaia Moskva*, 17 April 1926.

Hanson, Krista. "Writing a Path to Health: Autobiography and Autotherapy in Zoščenko's Work." Ph.D. diss., University of California, Berkeley, 1985.

———. "Autobiography and Conversion: Zoshchenko's *Before Sunrise.*" In *Autobiographical Statements in Twentieth-Century Russian Literature,* edited by Jane Gray Harris, 133–53. Princeton: Princeton University Press, 1990.

Hayward, Max, and Leopold Labedz. *Literature and Revolution in Soviet Russia, 1917–1962.* London: Oxford University Press, 1963.

Heller, Mikhail. *Andrei Platonov v poiskakh schast'ia.* Paris: YMCA, 1982.

Hodge, Thomas. "Freudian Elements in Zoshchenko's *Pered voskhodom solntsa.*" *Slavonic and East European Review* 67, no. 1 (1989): 1–28.

Hutcheon, Linda. "Parody without Ridicule: Observations on Modern Literary Parody." *Canadian Review of Comparative Literature* 5, no. 2 (1978): 201–11.

———. *Narcissistic Narrative: The Metafictional Paradox.* Waterloo, Ont.: Wilfred Laurier University Press, 1980.

———. *A Theory of Parody: The Teachings of Twentieth-Century Art Forms.* New York: Metheun, 1985.

———. *A Poetics of Postmodernism: History, Theory, Fiction.* New York: Routledge, 1988.

Ilf, Ilya, and Evgenny Petrov. *Sobranie sochinenii v piati tomakh.* Moscow: Gosudarstvennoe izd., 1961.

———. *Neobyknovennye istorii iz zhizni goroda Kolokolamska.* Ed. M. Dolinsky. Moscow: Knizhnaia palata, 1989.

Isakov, Iu. "Vozvrashchennaia molodost'." *Vecherniaia krasnaia gazeta,* 23 March 1934.

Isbakh, Al. "Chto chitaiut: o roste rabochego chitatelia." *Na literaturnom postu* 2 (1928): 36–38.

Jakobson, Roman. "O khudozhestvennom realizme" (1921). In *Selected Writings.* The Hague: Mouton, 1981. 3:723–31.

———. "The Dominant." Translated by Herbert Eagle. In *Selected Writings.* The Hague: Mouton, 1981. 3:751–56.

Jeans, James. *The Universe Around Us.* New York: Macmillan, 1929.

Jones, Mark. "Parody and Its Containments: The Case of Wordsworth." *Representations* 54 (1996): 57–77.

Joravsky, David. "Communism in Historical Perspective." *The American Historical Review* 99, no. 3 (1994): 837–57.

K., Boris. "Chto pokazal opyt chitatel'skikh konferentsii v Rostove n/D." *Krasnyi bibliotekar'* 11 (1927): 25–37.

Kazan, P. "Zoshchenko, Mikhail Mikhailovich." In *Literaturnaia entsiklopediia.* Vol. 4. Moscow: Izd. Kommunisticheskoi akademii, 1930. American Council of Learned Societies Reprints: Russian Series No. 23, 376–8. 1948.

Kazanskii, B. V., and Iu. N. Tynianov, eds. *Mikhail Zoshchenko. Mastera sovremennoi literatury: Stat'i i materialy.* Leningrad: Academia, 1928. Reprint, Letchworth, Eng.: Prideaux, 1973.

Kern, Gary. "Letters from Zoshchenko." *Russian Literature Triquarterly* 6 (1973): 586–606.

———. "After the Afterword." In Mikhail Zoshchenko, *Before Sunrise.* Translated by Gary Kern, 345–64. Ardis: Ann Arbor, 1974.

Kirshon, Vladimir. "Rech' t. Kirshona." In *XVI S"ezd vsesoiuznoi kommunisticheskoi partii(b): stenograficheskii otchet.* 2d ed., 277–82. Moscow-Leningrad: Moskovskii rabochii, 1931.

Kornienko, N. "Zoshchenko i Platonov: vstrechi v literature." *Literaturnoe obozrenie* 1 (1995): 47–54.

Korobkova, E., and L. Poliak. "Rabochii chitatel' o iazyke sovremennoi proze." *Na literaturnom postu* 14 (1929): 59–62.

———. "Pisatel' o chitatele." *Na literaturnom postu* 5–6 (1930): 100–103.

Kreps, Mikhail. *Tekhnika komicheskogo u Zoshchenko.* Benson, Vt.: Chalidze, 1986.

Kriannikova. "Vooruzhennyi solominkoi." *Rost* 8–9 (1930): 44–45.

Lahusen, Thomas, and Evgeny Dobrenko, eds. *Socialist Realism Without Shores.* Special Issue of *The South Atlantic Quarterly* 94, no. 3 (1995).

Le Fleming, Sveta. "The Question of Narrator in Zoshchenko's *Mudrost'*." *Essays in Poetics* 6, no. 1 (1981): 67–85.

Levidov, Mikhail. "O piatnadtsati—trista strok." *LEF* 1 (1923): 246.

Levin, L. "Zametki o satiricheskoi proze (Zoshchenko, Il'f i Petrov)." *Molodaia gvardiia* 9 (1939): 151–58.

Levitskaia, A. "Chitatel' v roli kritika." *Na literaturnom postu* 6 (1929): 66–68.

Lezhnev, Abram. Review of *Bagrianye l'dy, Kovsh, Krug,* and *Chet i Nechet. Pechat' i revoliutsiia* 5–6 (1925): 229–38.

———. Review of *O chem pel solovei,* 1927. *Pechat' i revoliutsiia* 6 (1927): 220–21.

Loks, K. "Sovremennaia proza." *Pechat' i revoliutsiia* 5 (1923): 86.

Lotman, Iurii. *Struktura khudozhestvennogo teksta.* Moscow: Iskusstvo, 1970.

Lunacharsky, A. "Rol' iskusstva v rekonstruktivnyi period (stat'ia vtoraia)." *Rost* 4 (1930): 24–26; 10 (1930): 14–16.

Lunts, I. "O povesti Zoshchenko." *Rabochii krai* 7 (1934): 24.

Lunts, Lev. "Pochemu my serapionovy brat'ia." *Literaturnye zapiski* 3 (1922): 30–31.

McLean, Hugh. "On the Style of a Leskovian *Skaz.*" *Harvard Slavic Studies* 2 (1954): 297–322.

———. Introduction to *Nervous People and Other Satires,* by Mikhail Zoshchenko, edited by Hugh McLean, vii–xxvii. Bloomington: Indiana University Press, 1963.

Bibliography

———. "Belated Sunrise: A Review Article." *Slavic and East European Journal* 18, no. 4 (1974): 406–10.
Maizel, M. "O rabochikh kriticheskikh kruzhkakh (iz opyta rukovodstva)." *Literaturnaia ucheba* 1 (1930): 101–14.
Marx, Karl, and Frederick Engels. *Literature and Art: Selections from Their Writings*. New York: International Publishers, 1947.
Masing-Delic, Irene. "Biology, Reason and Literature in Zoščenko's *Pered voschodom solnca*." *Russian Literature* 8 (1980): 77–101.
Matejka, Ladislav, and Irwin R. Titunik, eds. *Semiotics of Art: Prague School Contributions*. Cambridge, Mass.: MIT Press, 1976.
May, Rachel. "Superego as Literary Subtext: Story and Structure in Mikhail Zoshchenko's *Before Sunrise*." *Slavic Review* 55, no. 1 (1996): 106–24.
Mayakovsky, Vladimir. *Polnoe sobranie sochinenii v tridtsati tomakh*. Vol. 8. Moscow: Khudozhestvennaia literatura, 1953.
Maznin, Dmitri. "Massovaia rabochaia kritika" (Part I). *Na literaturnom postu* 7 (1932): 8–17.
———. "O massovoi rabochei kritike" (Part II). *Na literaturnom postu* 8 (1932): 1–9.
Menshoi, A. "Veselaia zhut'." *Zhizn' iskusstva* 41 (1924): 8–10.
Meromsky, A. "Kriticheskoe chut'e derevni." *Na literaturnom postu* 3 (1928): 36–41.
Messer, R. Review of *Pis'ma k pisateliu*. *Krasnaia gazeta*, 2 November 1929.
———. "Preodolenie formalizma." *Literaturnyi Leningrad*, 20 April 1936.
"Michail Šolochov beseduje s českými spisovateli." *Literární noviny*, 19 April 1958.
Middleton, Drew. "Soviet Arts Trace Political Pattern." *New York Times*, 10 February 1948, 12.
Mihaslovich, Vasa. "Zoshchenko's 'Adventures of a Monkey' as an Allegory." *Satire Newsletter* 4, no. 2 (1967): 84–89.
Milosz, Czeslaw. *The Captive Mind*. Translated by Jane Zielonko. New York: Vintage, 1955.
Mishchikhin, Vladimir. "Mikhail Zoshchenko—'Golubaia kniga.'" *Profrabotnik* 5–6 (1936): 54–55.
Mogiliansky, Mikhail. Review of *Raznotyk*. *Kniga i revoliutsiia* 4 (1923): 69–70.
Moldavsky, Dmitri. *Mikhail Zoshchenko: ocherk tvorchestva*. Leningrad: Sovetskii pisatel', 1977.
———. "Ob odnoi povesti Mikhaila Zoshchenko." *Neva* 7 (1987): 161–65.
———. "Prevyshavshii obychnuiu meru." *Zvezda* 12 (1987): 177–84.
Morson, Gary Saul. "Socialist Realism and Literary Theory." *The Journal of Aesthetics and Art Criticism* 38, no. 2 (1979): 121–33.
———. *The Boundaries of Genre: Dostoevsky's 'Diary of a Writer' and the Traditions of Literary Utopia*. Austin: University of Texas Press, 1981.

Morson, Gary Saul, and Caryl Emerson. *Mikhail Bakhtin: Creation of a Prosaics*. Stanford: Stanford University Press, 1990.

Munblit, G. "Kak vazhno byt' ser'eznym." *Literaturnaia gazeta*. 20 February 1934.

Murphy, A. B. *Mikhail Zoshchenko: A Literary Profile*. Oxford: Willem A. Meeuws, 1981.

Mushchenko, E. G., V. P. Skobelev, and L. E. Kroichik. *Poetika skaza*. Voronezh: Izd. voronezhskogo univ., 1978.

"Na obsuzhdenii zhurnala 'Oktiabria.'" *Literatura i iskusstvo*, 11 December 1943.

Nemilov, A. "Mikh. Zoshchenko i problema omolozheniia." Review of *Vozvrashchennaia molodost'*. *Kniga i proletarskaia revoliutsiia* 9 (1934): 95–98.

Newton, Eric. "Art for Marx' Sake in Russia." *New York Times,* 19 October 1947, sec. 6, pp. 8, 38, 40.

Nicholson, Michael. "Solzhenitsyn: Effigies and Oddities." In *Solzhenitsyn in Exile: Critical Essays and Documentary Materials*, edited by John Dunlop, Richard Haugh, and Michael Nicholson, 109–42. Stanford: Hoover Institute, 1985.

Nolda, Sigrid. "Zwischen Pavlov und Freud: Ammerkungen zu Michail Zoščenkos Autobiographie." *Die Welt der Slaven* 32 (1987): 78–100.

Novikov, Vladimir. "O meste Zoshchenko v russkoi literature." *Literaturnoe obozrenie* 1 (1995): 25–27.

O partiinoi i sovetskoi pechati: sbornik dokumentov. Moscow: Pravda, 1954.

"O poshlosti." *Burevestnik* 4 (1924): 28–31.

Okhitovich, S. Review of *Nad kem smeetes'*. *Na literaturnom postu* 4 (1928): 86–88.

Oksenov, Innokentii. Review of *Al'manakh arteli pisatelei; 'Krug'; Kniga 1-aia. Kniga i revoliutsiia* 2 (1923): 63.

———. Review of *Rasskazy. Kniga i revoliutsiia* 3 (1923): 76–77.

Olesha, Yurii. "Rech' t. Oleshi." In *Pervyi vsesoiuznyi s"ezd sovetskikh pisatelei, 1934: stenograficheskii otchet*, 236. Moscow: Sovetskii pisatel', 1990.

Olgina, A. "Sekret molodosti i krasoty." Review of *Vozvrashchennaia molodost'*. *Khudozhestvennaia literatura* 6 (1934): 16–19.

Olney, James. *Metaphors of Self: The Meaning of Autobiography*. Princeton: Princeton University Press, 1972.

Olshevets, M. "Obyvatel'skii nabat. (O 'Sentimental'nikh povestiakh' M. Zoshchenko)." *Izvestiia*, 14 August 1927.

Orlova, A. "Volnuiushchaia povest'." *Rabochii krai* 6 (1934): 23.

Oruzheinikov, N. "Na poliakh zhurnalov." *Literaturnaia gazeta*, 11 August 1933.

Oulanoff, David. *The Serapion Brothers: Theory and Practice*. The Hague: Mouton, 1966.

Palei, A. P. Review of *O chem pel solovei*. *Novyi mir* 6 (1927): 205.
Pascal, Roy. *Design and Truth in Autobiography*. Cambridge, Mass.: Harvard University Press, 1960.
Pecherskii, S. "Tsenzorskaia pravka 'Goluboi knigi' M. M. Zoshchenko." *Minuvshee: Istoricheskii al'manakh* 3 (1987): 355–91.
Pereverzev, V. F. "Na frontakh tekushchei belletristiki." *Pechat' i revoliutsiia* 4 (1923): 127–33.
Pervyi vsesoiuznyi s"ezd sovetskikh pisatelei, 1934: stenograficheskii otchet. Moscow: Sovetskii pisatel', 1990.
Peters, Jochen-Ulrich. "Satire under Stalinism: Zoshchenko's *Golubaya Kniga* and M. Bulgakov's *Master i Margarita*." In *The Culture of the Stalin Period*, edited by Hans Günther, 210–26. London: Macmillan, 1990.
"Pisateliu M. M. Zoshchenko." *Krasnaia gazeta*, 13 November 1938.
Platonov, Andrei, and Boris Pilniak. "*Che-Che-O*." *Novyi Mir* 12 (1928): 249–58.
Plotkin, L. "Propovednik bezideinosti—M. Zoshchenko," *Zvezda* 7–8 (1946): 217–22.
Poliak, N. "Vechera rabochei kritiki." *Kul'turnyi front* 24 (1926): 20–23.
Polonsky, Viacheslav. *O sovremennoi literature*. 2d ed. Moscow-Leningrad: Gosizdat, 1929.
Popkin, Cathy. *The Pragmatics of Insignificance: Chekhov, Zoshchenko and Gogol*. Stanford: Stanford University Press, 1993.
Popova, N. "Effekt otstranennosti i sostradaniia: satiricheskaia novellistika M. Zoshchenko." *Literaturnoe obozrenie* 1 (1995): 21–24.
Prianishnikov, N. "Rassuzhdenie o chitatele i pisatele." *Na literaturnom postu* 8 (1930): 62–65.
Pridorogin, A. Review of *Veselaia zhizn'*. *Knigonosha* 48–49 (1924): 31.
Prokofev, V. A. "'Zdes'. Pisateliu Zoshchenko.' Iz pisem chitatelei 30–x godov." In *Mikhail Zoshchenko: materialy k tvorcheskoi biografii*. Edited by N. A. Groznova. St. Petersburg: Nauka, 1997. 1:193–220.
R., Vs. Review of *Rasskazy Nazara Il'icha gospodina Sinebriukhova*. *Kniga i revoliutsiia* 8 (1922): 41.
Radway, Janice. *Reading the Romance: Women, Patriarchy, and Popular Literature*. Chapel Hill: University of North Carolina Press, 1984.
———. "Reading Is Not Eating: Mass-Produced Literature and the Theoretical, Methodological, and Political Consequences of a Metaphor." *Book Research Quarterly* 2 (1986): 7–29.
Rassadin, Stanislav. "Srednie liudi." *Ogonek* 52 (1987): 14–16.
Rest, B. "Pobeda ili porazhenie: leningradskie uchenye o povesti M. Zoshchenko 'Vozvrashchennaia molodost'.'" *Literaturnaia gazeta*, 26 March 1934.
———. "'Golubaia kniga': na dispute v Leningradskom diskussionnom klube prozaikov." *Literaturnaia gazeta*, 15 March 1936.

Review of *Rasskazy Nazara Il'icha gospodina Sinebriukhova*. *Biulleten' knigi* 5–6 (1922): 49–50.

Rice, Martin P. "On 'Skaz.'" *Russian Literature Triquarterly* 12 (1975): 409–24.

Ricoeur, Paul. "The Question of Proof in Freud's Psychoanalytic Writings." *Journal of the American Psychoanalytic Association* 25, no. 4 (1977): 835–71.

Robin, Régine. *Socialist Realism: An Impossible Aesthetic*. Translated by Catherine Porter. Stanford: Stanford University Press, 1992.

Romanov, Panteleimon. "Iz zapisnoi knizhki pisatelia." In *Utro. Literaturnyi sbornik*, edited by N. Fatov, 197–207. Moscow-Leningrad: Publication by contributing authors, 1927.

Rose, Margaret. *Parody//Metafiction*. London: Croom Helm, 1979.

———. *Parody: Ancient, Modern, and Post-Modern*. Cambridge, Eng.: Cambridge University Press, 1993.

Rubakin, N. A. *Chto takoe bibliotechnaia psikhologiia*. Leningrad: Kolos, 1924.

———. "Rabota bibliotekaria s tochki zreniia biblio-psikhologii.—K voprosu ob otnoshenii knigi i chitatelia." In *Chitatel' i kniga: metody ikh izucheniia. Sbornik statei*, 37–65. Khar'kov: Trud, 1925.

S., I. "Pisateli o 'Vozvrashchennoi molodosti.'" *Literaturnyi Leningrad*, 14 May 1934.

Sakharov, V. "Vechera rabochei kritiki." *Kniga i profsoiuzy* 1 (1927): 8–10.

———. "Kak provodit' vechera rabochei kritiki." In *Pisatel' pered sudom*, edited by G. Brylov, N. Veis, and V. Sakharov, 38. Leningrad: Izdatel'stvo leningradskovo soveta profsoiuza, 1928.

Salisbury, Harrison. "Russia Tightens the Iron Curtain on Ideas." *New York Times*, 26 December 1948, sec. 6, pp. 9, 30–31.

Sarnov, Benedikt. "Razvivaia traditsii Prokrusta (Mikhail Zoshchenko i ego redaktory)." *Voprosy literatury* 2 (1994): 45–91.

Sarnov, Benedikt, and Elena Chukovskaia. "Sluchai Zoshchenko." *Iunost'* 8 (1988): 69–86.

Sats, I. "Geroi Mikhaila Zoshchenko." *Literaturnyi kritik* 3 (1938): 140–67.

Sazonova, Iu. "Kul'tura i zhizn'." *Sovremennye zapiski* 34 (1928): 442–51.

Scatton, Linda Hart. *Mikhail Zoshchenko: Evolution of a Writer*. Cambridge, Eng.: Cambridge University Press, 1993.

Schafer, Roy. "Narration in Psychoanalytic Dialogue," *Critical Inquiry* 7, no. 1 (1980): 29–53.

Seifrid, Thomas. *Andrei Platonov: Uncertainties of Spirit*. Cambridge, Eng.: Cambridge University Press, 1992.

Selishchev, Afanasii. *Iazyk revoliutsionnoi epokhi*. Moscow: Rabotnik prosveshcheniia, 1928.

Semashko, N. "Kak otdykhat'," *Tridtsat' dnei* 6 (1929): 28–31.

———. "Mozhno li vozvratit' molodost'." *Literaturnaia gazeta*, 6 April 1934.

Shafir, Ia. *Gazeta i Derevnia*. Moscow: Krasnaia nov', 1923.

Bibliography

———. "O iumore i iumoristakh (M. Zoshchenko)." *Knigonosha* 8 (1926): 13–18.

———. *Ocherki psikhologii chitatelia.* Moscow-Leningrad: Gosudarstvennoe izdatel'stvo, 1927.

Shaginian, Elena. "Mikhail Zoshchenko—Mariette Shaginian. Iz perepiski." *Tallin* 2 (1989): 89–104.

Shaginian, Marietta. *Sobranie sochinenii v deviati tomakh.* Moscow: Khudozhestvennaia literatura, 1972.

Shcheglov, Iu. K. "Mir Mikhaila Zoshchenko." *Wiener Slawistische Almanach* 7 (1981): 109–54.

———. "Entsiklopediia nekul'turnosti." In *Mir avtora i struktura teksta: stat'i o russkoi literature,* edited by A. K. Zholkovsky, 53–84. Tenafly, N.J.: Hermitage, 1986.

Shepherd, David. *Beyond Metafiction: Self-Consciousness in Soviet Literature.* Oxford: Oxford University Press, 1992.

Shklovsky, Viktor. *O teorii prozy.* 1929. Reprint, Ann Arbor: Ardis, 1985.

Shneidman, N. N. *Russian Literature, 1988–1994: The End of an Era.* Toronto: University of Toronto Press, 1995.

Shoshin, V. A. "Neizvestnyi Zoshchenko (po arkhivnym materialam)." In *Mikhail Zoshchenko: materialy k tvorcheskoi biografii.* Vol. 1. Edited by N. A. Groznova. St. Petersburg: Nauka, 1997: 172–92.

Shteiman, Zel. "'Sfinks' govoriashchii (o rabochem chitatele)." *Novyi mir* 6 (1927): 184–89.

Simmons, Edward, ed. *Through the Glass of Soviet Literature.* New York: Oxford University Press, 1964.

Siniavsky, Andrei (Abram Tertz). *On Socialist Realism.* Translated by George Dennis. New York: Pantheon, 1960.

Slonim, Marc. *Soviet Russian Literature: Writers and Problems.* New York: Oxford University Press, 1964.

Slukhovsky, M. I. *Kniga i derevnia.* Moscow-Leningrad: Gosizd., 1928.

Smolian, A., and N. Iurgeneva., eds. *Mikhail Zoshchenko v vospominaniiakh sovremennikov.* Moscow: Sovetskii pisatel', 1981.

Smushkova, M. A. *Pervye itogi izucheniia chitatelia.* Moscow-Leningrad: Gosizd., 1926.

Sobol, Vladimir. "Pisatel' za rukopis'iu." *Literaturnaia gazeta,* 23 April 1933.

Solzhenitsyn, Aleksandr. *The Oak and the Calf: A Memoir.* Translated by Harry Willets. New York: Harper & Row, 1975.

"Soviet Reaction Decried." *New York Times,* 9 August 1949, 4.

Spence, Donald. *Narrative Truth and Historical Truth: Meaning and Interpretation in Psychoanalysis.* New York: Norton, 1982.

Starkov, A. N. *Iumor Zoshchenko.* Moscow: Khudozhestvennaia literatura, 1974.

———. *Mikhail Zoshchenko: sud'ba khudozhnika*. Moscow: Sovetskii pisatel', 1990.

Strauss, Leo. *Persecution and the Art of Writing*. Glencoe, Ill.: Free Press, 1952.

Struve, Gleb. *Russian Literature under Lenin and Stalin, 1917–1953*. Norman, Okla: University of Oklahoma Press, 1971.

Sulzberger, C. L. "Communist Party Steers Russian Mental Processes." *New York Times*, 21 December 1948, 22.

Sutherland, James. *Defoe*. Philadelphia: Lippincott, 1938.

Sven, Viktor. *Chei drug i chei vrag Mikhail Zoshchenko*. Munich: TSOPE, 1958.

Tank, Evgeny. "O knigakh M. Zoshchenko i pis'makh k nemu." *Literaturnyi Leningrad*, 20 October 1934.

Terras, Victor. "Phenomenological Observations on the Aesthetics of Socialist Realism." *Slavic and East European Journal* 23, no. 4 (1979): 445–52.

Tikhonov, N. "Otechestvennaia voina i sovetskaia literatura." *Bol'shevik* 3–4 (1944): 25–40.

Titunik, I. R. "Mikhail Zoščenko and the Problem of *Skaz*." *California Slavic Studies* 6 (1971): 83–96.

———. "The Problem of *Skaz* (Critique and Theory)." In *Papers in Slavic Philology*. Vol. 1, edited by Benjamin Stolz, 276–301. Ann Arbor: Michigan Slavic Publications, 1977.

Tolstoy, Lev. *Polnoe sobranie sochinenie*. Vol. 30. Moscow: Gosudarstvennoe izdatel'stvo khudozhestvennoi literatury, 1951.

Tomashevsky, Iurii. "Vera v razum." In Mikhail Zoshchenko, *Ispoved'*, 5–22. Edited by Iurii Tomashevsky. Moscow: Sovetskaia Rossiia, 1987.

———. "'. . . Pisatel' s perepugannoi dushoi—eto uzhe poteria kvalifikatsii': M. M. Zoshchenko: pis'ma, vystupleniia, dokumenty, 1943–1958," *Druzhba narodov* 3 (1988): 168–89.

———. "Rasskazy i povesti Mikhaila Zoshchenko." In Mikhail Zoshchenko, *Sobranie sochinenii v trekh tomakh*, edited by Iu. Tomashevskii, vol. 1, 5–24. Leningrad: Khudozhestvennaia literatura, 1986.

———. *Litso i maska Mikhaila Zoshchenko*. Moscow: Olimp, 1994.

———, ed. *Vspominaia Mikhaila Zoshchenko*. Leningrad: Khudozhestvennaia literatura, 1990.

Tomsky, Sergei. "Obyvatel'shchina pered narsudom." *30 dnei* 9 (1928): 64–67.

Toporov, A. M. "Literaturnye vechera v kommune 'Maiskoe utro.'" *Zemlia sovetskaia* 2 (1929): 59–60.

———. *Krest'iane o pisateliakh*. 1930. Reprint, Moscow: Sovetskaia Rossiia, 1967.

Tretiakov, S. "Novyi Lev Tolstoi." *Novyi LEF* 1 (1927): 34–38.

Trotsky, Leon. *Sochineniia.* Vol. 21. Moscow: Gosudarstvennoe izdatel'stvo, 1927.

Twain, Mark. *Roughing It.* New York: Penguin Books, 1981.

Tynianov, Iurii. *Poetika. Istoriia literatury. Kino.* Moscow: Nauka, 1977.

———. *Arkhaisty i novatory.* 1929. Reprint, Ann Arbor: Ardis, 1985.

"Ukaz Prezidiuma Verkhovnogo Soveta SSSR o nagrazhdenii sovestkikh pisatelei." *Literaturnaia gazeta,* 5 February 1939.

V., S. "Vecher Mikh. Zoshchenko." *Komsomol'skaia pravda.* 27 November 1932.

Vechera rabochei kritiki. Moscow: Gudok, 1927.

Veis, N. P. "Obshchestvennaia i literaturnaia tsennost' vecherov rabochei kritiki." In *Pisatel' pered sudom rabochego chitatelia,* edited by G. Brylov, N. Veis, and V. Sakharov, 17. Leningrad: Izdatel'stvo leningradskogo soveta profsoiuza, 1928.

Veshnev, V. "Razgovor po dusham." *Na literaturnom postu* 11–12 (1927): 55–58.

———. "Komicheskie bliznetsy." In *Kniga kharakteristik: stat'i o sovremennoi literature,* 85–96. Moscow-Leningrad: Gosudarstvennoe izdatel'stvo, 1928.

Vickery, Walter N. "Zhdanovism (1946–1953)." In *Literature and Revolution in Soviet Russia, 1917–1962,* edited by Max Hayward and Leopold Labedz, 99. London: Oxford University Press, 1963.

Vinogradov, Viktor. "Problema skaza v stilistike." In *Izbrannye trudy: o iazyke khudozhestvennoi prozy,* 42–54. Moscow: Nauka, 1980.

Volkov, Vitalii. "Za kulisami." *Avrora* 8 (1991): 42–51.

Volpe, Tsezar'. "Zametki o sovremennykh pisateliakh (M. Zoshchenko, N. Tikhonov). Stat'ia pervaia." *Zvezda* 1 (1933): 177–82.

———. "O 'Vozvrashchennoi molodosti' Mikhaila Zoshchenko." *Zvezda* 8 (1934): 161–71.

———. "Dvadtsat' let raboty M. M. Zoshchenko: stat'ia pervaia." *Literaturnyi sovremennik* 3 (1941): 128–48. "Stat'ia vtoraia." *Literaturnyi sovremennik* 6 (1941): 125–43.

Voronsky, Aleksandr. Review of *Serapionovy brat'ia. Al'manakh pervyi. Krasnaia nov'* 3 (1922): 265–68.

———. Review of *Rasskazy Nazara Il'icha gospodina Sinebriukhova. Krasnaia nov'* 6 (1922): 343–45.

Williams, Raymond. *Culture and Society, 1780–1950.* London: Chatto & Windus, 1960.

Wiren, Vera von. "Zoshchenko in Retrospect." *Russian Review* 21, no. 4 (1962): 348–61.

———. "Zoščenko's Psychological Interests." *Slavic and East European Journal* 11, no. 1 (1967): 3–22.

———. "Sud'ba 'Pered voskhodom solntsa': Freid ili Pavlov?" In Mikhail Zoshchenko, *Pered voskhodom solntsa*, 15–32. Edited by Vera von Wiren. New York: Chekhov, 1973.

———, ed. *Neizdannyi Zoshchenko*. Ann Arbor: Ardis, n.d.

Zelinskii, K. "O novykh vkusakh narodakh." *Literaturnaia gazeta*, 27 March 1936.

Zhdanov, Andrei. "Doklad t. Zhdanova o zhurnalakh 'Zvezda' i 'Leningrad.'" *Zvezda* 7–8 (1946): 7–22.

Zhiga, I. Review of *Uvazhaemye grazhdane, Nervnye Liudi*, and *O chem pel solovei*. *Molodaia gvardiia* 9 (1927): 201–2.

Zholkovsky, A. K. "Lev Tolstoi i Mikhail Zoshchenko kak zerkalo i zazerkal'e russkoi revoliutsii." *Sintaksis* 16 (1988): 103–28.

———. "Three on Courtship, Corpses and Culture: Tolstoj, 'Posle bal'—Zoščenko, 'Dama s cvetami'—E. Ginzburg, 'Raj pod mikroskopom.'" *Wiener Slawistischer Almanach* 22 (1988): 7–24.

———. "K reinterpretatsii poetiki Mikhaila Zoshchenko." *Izvestiia akademii nauk: seriia literatury i iazyka* 54, no. 5 (1995): 50–60.

———. "Ruka blizhnego i ee mesto v poetike Zoshchenko." *Novoe literaturnoe obozrenie* 15 (1995): 262–86.

———. "Food, Fear, Feigning and Flight in Zoščenko's 'Foreigners.'" *Russian Literature* 40 (1996): 385–404.

———. "'What Is the Author Trying to Say with His Artistic Work?': Rereading Zoshchenko's Oeuvre." *The Slavic and East European Journal* 40, no. 3 (1996): 458–74.

———. "Zoshchenko iz XXI veka, ili poetika nedoveriia." *Zvezda* 5 (1996): 190–204.

Zhurbina, Evgeniia. "Mikhail Zoshchenko (v poriadke obsuzhdeniia)." *Krasnaia gazeta* (Vech. vyp.), 21 June 1927.

———. "Mikhail Zoshchenko," foreword to *Sobranie sochinenii* by Mikhail Zoshchenko. Vol. 1, 1–20. Leningrad-Moscow: Priboi, 1930.

———. "Golubaia kniga." *Literaturnaia gazeta*, 20 September 1935.

———. "'Ikh sobstvennye melodii': o Mikhaile Zoshchenko." *30 dnei* 10 (1935): 81–85.

———. "Variant sud'by intelligentnogo cheloveka." *Oktiabr'* 2 (1936): 246–57.

———. "Ob Il'fe i Petrove." *Oktiabr'* 10 (1937): 171–78.

Zoshchenko, V. V. "Tvorcheskii put' Zoshchenko," 151. *Neizdannyi Zoshchenko*. Ann Arbor: Ardis, n.d.

Index

Absurdism, 17, 74–75, 102
Acmeism, 2, 4
Adorno, Theodor, 137
Aesopian tradition, 142, 169, 191n53
"Agitlit," 83
Akhmatova, Anna, 1, 2, 4, 7
Aksakov, S. T., 154
Aksenov, Vasily, 170
Alexandrova, Vera, 72, 174n25, 175n38
All-Union Institute of Experimental Medicine, 93
Alter, Robert, 15
Aseev, Nikolai, 175n40
Atkinson, Brooks, 174n20
Auerbach, Erich, 41; *Mimesis,* 37–38
Averbach, Leopold, 86, 131; "The Cultural Revolution and the Mission of Proletarian Literature," 84–85

Babel, Isaak, 71
Babichenko, Denis, 172n4, 173n15, 174n30, 197n1
Bakhtin, Mikhail, 46, 80, 164–70 *passim,* 187n46; and discourse, 40–41, 75, 99, 143; exiled, 165; and *skaz,* 54, 57; *Problems of Dostoevsky's Creative Art,* 40
Balika, D., 195n46
Balmont (poet), 155
Balzac, Honoré de, 141, 149; *Comédie Humaine,* 19; *The Wild Ass's Skin,* 150
Bank, B., 193n10
Barmin, A. G., 73
Barthes, Roland, 20, 29
Bedny, Demian, 129
Beethoven, Ludwig van, 158
Begak, Boris, 93, 189n23
Bek, A., 187n9, 193n10
Bekker, Mikhail, 195n44
Belinsky, Vissarion, 2, 93, 163

Belomor (collectively written volume, 1934), 150, 169
Bely, Andrei, 70, 74
Bennett, Tony, 137
Bergolts (in public debate), 190n45
Berliner, V., 194n41
Bershadskii, Rud., 194n30
Beskina, Anna, 38, 41, 55–56, 189nn25, 33
"Biblio-psychology," 130, 134
Blair, Hector, 62, 174n29
Blok, Alexander, 74, 89
Bogatyrev, Petr, 21, 62, 177n16
Bolshevik (journal), 3
Bolshevik Revolution, 61, 74, 131; education as third phase of, 114; Zoshchenko depicts, 16, 31, 62, 102; Zoshchenko during, 146; Zoshchenko honored during twenty-first anniversary of, 5. *See also* October Revolution
Booker, M. Keith, 151; *Bakhtin, Stalin and Modern Russian Fiction* (with Juraga), 168–70
Bookpeddler, The (journal), 113
Bordwell, David, 28, 29
Boym, Svetlana, 185n26
Braun, Ia., 182n59
Breuer, Josef, 147
Brik, Osip, "Closer to the Facts," 77–78
Briusov (poet), 155, 158
Brooks, Jeffrey, 113, 195n42, 196n55
Brown, Edward J., 162–63, 183–84n62
Brylov, G., 195n42
Bukharin (speaks before Writers' Union, 1934), 128
Bulgakov, Sergii, 16, 70
Bureaucrat as target, 178n6
Buznik, V. V., 199n17
Byron, George Lord, 89
Byt (details of soviet life), Zoshchenko's depiction of, 32–34, 56, 68, 74

221

Index

Capote, Truman, 84
Censorship, 17, 19, 56, 110, 190n42, 196n49
Cervantes, Miguel de, *The Adventures of Don Quixote,* 66, 75–79 *passim,* 100, 186n42
Chapple, Richard, 31, 178n8
Chekhov, Anton, 142
Chernyshevsky, N. G., 2, 163
Chudakova, Marietta, 136, 151, 159, 168, 173n7, 176n41, 200n28; *The Poetics of Mikhail Zoshchenko,* 52, 74
Chukovskaia, Lidiia, 172n5
Chukovsky, Kornei, 7, 120, 133, 155, 188n11, 190n45
Chumandrin, Mikhail, 31, 61, 69, 79, 87, 173n8; and the mass reader, 125, 126, 131, 134; "Whose Writer Is Mikhail Zoshchenko," 25, 67–68
Churchill, Winston, 3
Chuzhak, N. F., 186n36
Clark, Katerina, *Petersburg: Crucible of Cultural Revolution,* 165
Clothing, significance ("reading") of, 21, 62
Cold war, 1, 7, 9, 136, 166
Collectivization, 9, 85
Communism, Zoshchenko on harmful effects of, 31
Communist Party: denounces Zoshchenko, 1; intolerance of and restrictions on writers, 81, 164; literary declaration of, 112–13, 163; *ocherk* recognized by, 187n9; resolutions of, 3, 7; Sixteenth Congress of (1930), 81; support claimed by, 111. *See also* Soviet Union
Crimean War, 152
Cukierman, Jacqueline, 186n33
Cultural revolution, 7, 108, 122, 127; intolerance toward writers, 81, 116; reader's influence emphasized, 117; workers and peasants promoted to rank of writer, 84; writers experience "socialist construction," 82–83

Dallas, possible interpretations of, 138
Danilevsky, A. S., 154
"Dark Ages," 7
Debreczeny, Paul, 201n35
Defoe, Daniel, 100
De Saint Jean, Robert, 84
Din, L. I., 189n21

Dmitriev, L., 172n2
Dobrenko, Evgeny, *The Formation of the Soviet Reader,* 132, 193n10, 195n42
Dobroliubov, early death of, 89
Dolinsky, M. Z., 10, 177n18
Domar, Rebecca, 32, 62, 72, 93; "The Case of Zoshchenko," 11; "The Tragedy," 8, 174n23
Dostoevsky, Fedor Mikhailovich: denounced, 7; "Mr. Prokharchin," 74
Double-voiced narrative. *See* Language and speech
Drugov, B., 189n31
Dymshchits, A., 102, 106

Egan, Susanna, 199n11
Egolin, A., 172n3
Eikhenbaum, Boris, 37, 40
Eliot, T. S., denounced, 7
Emerson, Caryl, 180n31
Encyclopedia of Literature (1930s), 86
Engels, Frederick, 19
Erlich, Victor, 182n59
Ermilov, Vladimir, 5, 6, 174n19
Ermolaev, Herman, 203n6
Ershov, L., 175n41
Esekin, early death of, 89
Eventov, I., 190n45

Fadeev, Aleksandr, 162, 174n19
Faresov, A., 180n27
Fedin (in public debate), 190n45
Fish, Stanley, 132
Fiske, John, 137–38
Fitzpatrick, Sheila, 194n27
Five-Year Plan, 81
Fizer, John, 201n5, 202n11
Frankfurt School, 137
Freud, Sigmund, 142, 143, 144, 147–48, 149; *Studies on Hysteria,* 147

Garrard, John and Carol, 202n5
Gatskevich, Zoia, 24
Gekht, S., 178n6
Ginzburg, Carlo, *The Cheese and the Worms,* 197n62
Gladkov, Fedor, 151; *Energy,* 83
Glagolev, Arkady, 125, 126; "A Philistine's Letters," 122
Glasnost, 1, 9, 13, 17, 171
Gleason, Abbott, 202n10

Index

Gogol, Nikolai, 66, 152, 158, 159; Zoshchenko compared to, 7, 95, 168; Zoshchenko on illness of, 89–90, 108, 141; *An Authorial Confession*, 153, 154; *Dead Souls*, 153, 155; "The Overcoat," 74; *Selected Passages from a Correspondence with Friends*, 151, 153, 154
Gol'dshtein, Mikhail, 184n9, 188n13
Goncharov, Ivan, 150
Gopfengauz, E., 195n42
Gorbachev, Georgii, 38
Gorelov, A., 125, 189nn24, 27
Gorky, Maksim, 5, 6, 123, 128, 129, 189n21; *Blue Book* dedicated to, 99, 100, 104; Zoshchenko's correspondence with, 4, 85, 122, 193n23
Gorshkov, V., 172n3, 197n1
Graboventskii, V., 191n49
Gramsci, Antonio, 137
Great Medical Encyclopedia, 91
Griboedov, Alexander, 89
Grigor'eva, R., 192n2
Grossman, B., 178n6
Groys, Boris, 165
Gruzdev, Ilia, 79, 120, 182n59
Guber (literary scholar), 24
Guchkov (head of Octobrist party), 22, 24, 27
Günther, Hans, 181n51
Gurshtein, A., 102, 105

Hall, Stuart, 137
Hanson, Krista, 29, 107, 159, 168, 188n11, 199n14
Heller, Mikhail, 18–20, 169
Hodge, Thomas, 198n6
Hutcheon, Linda, 59–60, 80

Ilenkov, Vasily, *The Driving Axle*, 83
Ilf, Ilia, 32, 35, 161, 169
Ilin, Iakov, *The Great Conveyor*, 83
Isakov, Iu., 188n17, 189n31
Isbakh, Al., 193n10
Iudin, P., 197n2
Ivanov, Vsevolod, *The Adventuress of Fakir*, 103; *The Tales of Brigadier-leader M. N. Sinitsyn*, 57, 83
Izvestiia, 70; "Philistine Alert," 61

Jakobson, Roman, 16, 19, 177n15
Jeans, Sir James, *The Universe Around Us*, 90, 109

Jones, Mark, 187n48
Joravsky, David, 165
Juraga, Dubravka, 151; *Bakhtin, Stalin and Modern Russian Fiction* (with Booker), 168–70

Karpov, Mikhail, 116
Kataev, *Time, Forward!* 83
Kaverin, Veniamin, 24, 190n45
Kazan, P., 188n14
Kern, Gary, 198n5
Khorun (quartermaster), 23, 24
Kirshon, Vladimir, 81–82, 86
Kolenkorov, I. V. (character created by Zoshchenko). See Zoshchenko, Mikhail, works: *Youth Restored*
Komsomol'skaia pravda, 173n11
Korobkova, E., 193nn10, 17
Kotolevsky case, 120–21, 133, 139, 152, 158
Krasnaia gazeta (journal), 33, 156, 173n12
Krasnaia nov' (journal), 24
Kreps, Mikhail, 29, 31, 43, 175n38
Kriannikova, 126, 194n30
Kroichik, Lev, 37, 55, 56

Language and speech, 49–53; Bolshevik, inaccessibililty of, 113, 192n7; directed to worker-peasant reader, 115; in double-voiced narrative, 40–43, 46–47, 49–50, 57; inconsistency of style, 51, 54, 68–69; Leskov on, 39; of reading public, 121, 123–24; Zoshchenko's style rejected, 156–57
Lavrentev, Professor, 93
LEF (journal), 77, 78, 79, 84
Le Fleming, Sveta, 186n33
Lenin, Vladimir Ilyich, 2, 10, 61, 130, 163
Leningrad literary club, 118
Leningrad Publishing Center, 108
Leningradskaia pravda, 33
Leonov, Leonid, *Skutarevsky*, 87
Lermontov, Mikhail, 89
Leskov, Nikolai, 37, 39–40, 42, 49; "At the Edge of the World," 39; "Night Owls," 39, 40; "The Sealed Angel," 39, 42
Levidov, Mikhail, 79
Levin, L., 190n45
Levitskaia, A., 196n50
Lezhnev, Abram, 60, 71
Libedinsky, Iurii, 61, 87
Library of Congress, 103

Index

Literature of Fact (LEF anthology), 77
Literaturnaia gazeta, 32, 92, 173n13
Literaturnye zapiski (*Literary Notes*), 22, 24
Loks, K., 59
London, Jack, 65, 89
Lotman, Iurii, 28
Lunacharsky, Anatoly, 24, 85
Lunts, I., 189n27
Lunts, Lev, 79

McLean, Hugh, 13, 29, 31, 35, 43, 175n38, 199n14; analysis of *Before Sunrise*, 142, 145–46; analysis of Leskov, 37, 40, 49
Mailer, Norman, 84
Maizel, M., 194n42
Mandelshtam, Osip, 2
Marx, Karl, 176n13
Masing-Delic, Irene, 198n6
"Mass" as pejorative term, 137
Mass reader, the: accuracy of profiles of, 195n42; "collective decision" of, 115–16; language of, 121, 123–24; official campaign for, 112–16; official manipulation of image of, 129–33; present day, 136–39; seen as "sphinx," 114–15, 127; in Soviet culture, 127–29; Zoshchenko and, 111, 116–21, 133–36; Zoschenko's response to, 117, 121–27, 132; Zoschenko's special image of, 140
May, Rachel, 151, 168, 181n59
Mayakovsky, Vladimir, 87, 89; "Everything's Great," 90
Maznin, Dmitri, 122, 127–28, 130, 139
Melville, Herman, *Moby Dick*, 104
Mendelssohn, Felix, 89
Mennochio, 197n62
Menshoi, A., 182n59
Meromskii, A., 193n10
Messer, R., 126, 190n45, 194n30
Middleton, Drew, 174n20
Mihaslovich, Vasa, 173n16
Milosz, Czeslaw, 18, 19; *The Captive Mind*, 17
Mogiliansky, Mikhail, 24, 182n59
Moldavsky, Dmitry, 10, 176n41, 198n5
Molodaia gvardiia (marxist journal), 61; "Life today" section, 33
Morson, Gary Saul, 80, 105, 177n22, 180n31, 202n15; *The Boundaries of Genre*, 60

Mozart, Wolfgang Amadeus, 89
Munblit, G., 189n22
Murphy, A. B., 31, 72
Murzilka (children's magazine), 5
Mushchenko, Ekaterina, 37, 56, 183n65

Na knizhnom fronte (journal), 112
Napoleon, 89
Narrative principles (in *skaz*). See Skaz effect
Nazism, 137
Nekrasov, Nikolai, 141
Neldikhen (poet), 24
Nemilov, A., 189n30
NEP (New Economic Policy), 127, 131
Nero, 101
New Age, 85
New Journalism (1950s and 1970s), 84
Newton, Eric, 201n5
Nicholson, Michael, 175n39
Nobel Prize, 74, 196n54
Nolda, Sigrid, 198n6
Noskovich-Lekarenko, N., 175n35
Novikov-Priboi, Aleksei, *Tsushima*, 103

Ocherki, 83–84, 85, 97
October Revolution, 64, 112, 113, 114, 156. See also Bolshevik Revolution
Octobrist party, 24
Okhitovich, S., 196n52
Oksenov, Innokenty, v
Oktiabr (journal), 3, 140
Olesha (at Writers' Congress, 1934), 91
Olgina, A., 189n32
Olshevets, M., 61, 70, 72
On the Literary Front (journal), 113
Order of the Red Banner of Labor, 5, 6
Orlova, A., 189n29
Oruzheinikov, N., 190n35
Ostrovsky, Nikolai, 151
Oulanoff, David, 37, 42

Palei, A. P., 184n5
Pascal, Roy, 199n11
Pasternak, Boris, 8; *Doctor Zhivago*, 196n54
Pavlov, Ivan, 90, 142, 153
Pecherskii, S., 190n42
Perestroika, 10, 13
Pereverzev, V. F., 182n59
Peters, Jochin-Ulrich, 191n53

Index

Petronius, *Satyricon,* 37
Petrov, Evgeny, 32, 35, 161, 169
Photographs in *M. P. Siniagin,* 76–77, 78, 152
Pilniak, Boris, 12, 67, 84; "Che-Che-O" (with Platonov), 136; as "villain," 81–82; *Mahogany,* 83; *The Volga Flows to the Caspian Sea,* 83
Pisarev, D. I., 157
Platonov, Andrei, 18, 19, 162, 195n48; "Che-Che-O" (with Pilniak), 136
Plotkin, Lev, "Preacher of Immorality," 3
Poe, Edgar Allan, 89, 141, 149
Poetics of Skaz, The (Mushchenko et al.), 37, 56
Poliak, L., 193nn10, 17, 194n40
Polonsky, Viacheslav, 70, 89
Polybius, 100
Popkin, Cathy, 33, 168, 179n12
Popova, N., 54
Prague School, 21
Pravda, 32, 102
Prianishnikov, N., 193n16
Pridorogin, A., 182n59
Prince (British warship), 152
Prokofev, V. A., 197n63
Protokol, literary preference for, 78
Provisional Government, 24
Psychoanalysis, 89–90, 142–49
Pushkin, Aleksandr, 22, 93, 124; death of, 87, 89, 90; Zoshchenko's style compared to, 142; *Eugene Onegin,* 74

Quixote, Don. *See* Cervantes, Miguel de

Radak (speaks before Writers' Congress, 1934), 128
Radway, Janice, 138, 196n59
Raltsevich, V., 97, 99, 105
RAPP, 127–28, 129, 136; attack against, 32, 108
Rasputin, Grigori, 97
Rassadin, Stanislav, 10
Reader, the. *See* Mass reader, the
Realism: polemics over (1920s), 77, 79; pursuit of, 15–20; reality effect, 20; socialist, *see* Socialist realism; Western obsession with, 17; Zoshchenko as antirealist, 176n14; Zoshchenko as "true" realist, 4, 62
"Recalcitrant data," 28, 106

Red Army: misunderstanding of words by, 113; Zoshchenko in, 5, 23, 146
Red Librarian (journal), 113
Referential condition, 20
Rest, B., 189n31, 190n45
Revolution. *See* Bolshevik Revolution; Cultural revolution
Rice, Martin, 37
Ricoeur, Paul, 199n13
Robin, Régine, 15, 129, 137, 151, 166; *Socialist Realism: An Impossible Aesthetic,* 164–65
Romanov, Panteleimon, 54
Rose, Margaret, 59–60
Rozanov, Vasily, 77; *Fallen Leaves,* 76; *Solitaria,* 76
Rubakin, Nikolai, 134; popular science titles by, 130–31
Russia: Zoshchenko as viewed by postsoviet, 9–11, 20, 31, 55, 111, 136. *See also* Soviet Union

Sakharov, V., 194nn40, 42
Salisbury, Harrison, 174n20
Sarnov, Benedikt, 173n7, 181n43
Sats, I., 38, 62, 94, 179n20
Sazonova, Iulia, 68–69, 72
Scatton, Linda Hart, 29, 107, 151, 168, 173n16, 199n19, 200nn24, 28
Schafer, Roy, 143–44, 145
Schubert, Franz, 89
Seifrid, Thomas, 162
Selishchev, Afanasii, 192n7
Semashko, Nikolai, 90, 92
Seneca, 97
Serafimovich, Aleksandr (Popov): *The Iron Flood,* 116
Serapion Brothers, 4, 24, 38, 57, 61, 79, 110, 182n59; Serapion almanac, 59; Serapion "autobiographies," 22, 64, 70, 79, 117; Serapion parody, 150; "Serapion" as pejorative, 4
Shafir, Iakov, 113–14, 130, 136, 182n59
Shaginian, Marietta, 82, 151; Zoshchenko's letters to, 86; *Hydrocentral,* 83, 91–92
Shakhty affair (1928), 81
Shcheglov, Iu., 178n7
Shepherd, David, 80, 166
Shitikov, D., 196n51
Shklovsky, Viktor, 48, 73; "Literature Outside the Plot," 76–77

Index

Shneidman, N. N., 201n3
Sholokhov, Mikhail, 105, 201n14; *Virgin Soil Upturned*, 103, 110
Shteiman, Zel., 192n9; "The Sphinx Talks," 114
Sinebriukhov, Nazar Ilich (character created by Zoshchenko). See Zoshchenko, Mikhail, works: *The Stories of Nazar Ililch, Mr. Sinebriukhov*
Siniavsky, Andrei (Abram Tertz), 165
Sixteenth Party Congress (1930), 81
Skaz effect, 35–40, 83; early studies of, 37, 54; narrative discourse, 40–49, 53, 56; peculiarities of, 40–49; "realistic," 39; suspicions of use of, 38; Zoshchenko and, 36–58 *passim*, 102, 108, 123, 169, 170
Skobelev, Vladislav, 37, 56
Slonim, Marc, 16, 174nn22, 24, 26, 175n38, 201n5; "The Condemned Humorist," 8
Slukhovsky, M. I., 192n4
Smena (marxist journal), 33
Smushkova, M. A., 192n7
Sobol', Vladimir, "The Writer at His Manuscript," 86
Socialism, Soviet Union moves toward, 81
"Socialist construction," 82–83
Socialist realism, 85, 107, 132, 136; Gorky as founder of, 99; inaugurated (1984), 7, 108, 128, 164; legacy of, 162–67; Milosz defines, 17; Zoshchenko satirizes, 191n53
Sokolov, Sasha, 169
Soloviev (poet), 155, 156
Solzhenitsyn, Alexander, 9, 12, 163
Sovetskii pisatel (publishers), 120
Soviet Union: anti-Freudianism in, 142, 143; artistic expression quashed, 1, 164; corruption of, 19; critical discourse in, 168; cultural revolution in, *see* Cultural revolution; descriptions of life in, 123; descriptions of life in and *ocherki*, 83–84, 85, 97; descriptions of life in and social conditions, 32–35; descriptions of life in by Zoshchenko (*byt*), 11, 32–34, 56, 68, 74; discoveries and inventions claimed by, 7; dissolution of, 9; dualism during first years of, 135; Five-Year Plan, 81; forbidden topics in, 34; nationalism of, 1, 7; in 1920s, 12, 34; in 1930s and 1940s, 4, 6, 9; postwar standing of, 2, 9; prison labor justified, 150; reading public in, *see* Mass reader, the; "true," 69; Western view of literature in, 7, 13, 30; writers distanced from, 82; Zoshchenko's reception/reputation in, 12, 132; Zoshchenko seen as slandering, 3, 102; Zoshchenko's view of, 72–73, 155, 156, 162. *See also* Russia
Spence, Donald, 144–45
Spetsy, 119; as pejorative, 115
"Sphinx." *See* Mass reader, the
Stalin, Joseph, 10, 32, 128, 130, 164; death of, 1, 3; denounces Zoshchenko, 3, 4, 9; legacy of, 9; as "specter" over modern Russian literature, 169, 170; and Stalinism, 1, 34, 137, 168; and Stalinism, attacked by Zoshchenko, 151; writings of, 113; Zhdanov as spokesperson for, 1; Zoshchenko's letters to, 5
Starkov, A., 175n41
Sterne, Laurence, 76, 79
Strauss, Leo: *Persecution and the Art of Writing*, 18
Struve, Gleb, 16, 175n38
Sulzberger, C. L., 174n20
Sutherland, James, 190n44
Sven, Viktor, 16, 27–28, 31, 69, 72, 168, 174n28, 175n38; "Whose Friend and Whose Enemy Is Zoshchenko," 25–26, 68

Taboo, idea of, 31–35
Tagore, Rabindranath, 73, 74
Talese, Gay, 84
Tank, Evgeny, 193n21
Terras, Victor, 201n5
Terror, the, 9
Tertz, Abram (Andrei Siniavsky), 165
Thaw, the, 2, 7, 172n5
"Threshold text," 105–7, 177n22
Tikhonov, N., 172n3
Tiniakov (poet), 155
Titunik, I. R., 46, 47, 49, 57, 168
Tolstoy, Aleksei, 105; *Peter I*, 103, 104
Tolstoy, Lev, 150, 159, 178n7; "epic" literature as personified by, 33; "Red," 73, 77, *War and Peace*, 104; "What Is Art," 157–58
Tomashevsky, Iurii, 9, 173n14, 185n23, 190n45; 201n38
Tomsky, Sergei, 178n10

Index

Toom, L., 187n9, 193n10
Toporov, A. M., 127, 132, 135, 195n42;
 Peasants on Writers, 115
Travlia, 8, 9
Tretiakov, Sergei, 77
Trotsky, Leon: quoted on social disorder, 34; "Trotskyists" executed, 187n3
Twain, Mark, 163
Tynianov, Iurii, 58, 177n15, 184n2;
 Kiukhla, 103

Van Gogh, Vincent, 89
Vasiliev, Sergei, 112, 113, 139
Vecherniaia Moskva (newspaper), 33;
 "Justice and Daily Life" section, 35
Veis, N. P., 193n14
Veshnev, V., 34
Vickery, Walter N., 174n21
Vilenkin, A., 193n10
Vinogradov, Viktor, 54, 57, 73, 87, 102, 168
Volkov, Vitalii, 174n31
Voloshinov, Valentin, 46
Volpe, Tsezar, 38, 61, 74, 173n9; analyzes *skaz*, 43–49 *passim*; seeks clarity, 72, 109–10, 126
Von Wiren, Vera, 60, 62, 72–73, 174n27, 188n11
Voronsky, Aleksandr, 22, 24, 53–54

Williams, Raymond, 139
"Workers' evenings," 130
World War I, 64
World War II, 2, 137; Zoshchenko during, 4, 5
"Writers' brigades," 82
Writers' Union, 6, 162, 163, 172n4, 173n7;
 First Congress of (1934), 90, 91, 128–29, 131; Zoshchenko expelled from, 8

Yagoda (head of police), 150
Yazykov, N. M., 154

Zamiatin, Evgeny, 12, 16, 61, 70, 81; *We*, 19
Zelinskii, K., 191n51
Zhdanov, Andrei, 4, 6, 10, 20, 128, 164, 167; death of, 2, 3; denounces Zoshchenko, 1, 2–3, 7–12 *passim*, 24–30 *passim*, 149, 163; and Zhdanovism, 7, 9; Zoshchenko's letter to, 5
Zhiga, I., 184n8

Zholkovsky, Alexander, 29, 168, 178n7, 180n40, 201n35
Zhurbina, Evgeniia, 38, 61, 87, 173n9, 178n6, 189n22, 190n45
Ziv, "Olenka," 23, 24
Zola, Emile, 62
Zoshchenko, Mikhail: as antirealist, 176n14; as "antisoviet," 1, 2, 16; as "antisoviet," in Western and postsoviet Russian view, 11–12, 25, 30, 55, 62, 68, 72–73, 167–68, 182n59, 191n53; birthplace, 177n18; British students meet with (1954), 172n5; canon of his writing, 28–30; death of, 2, 7, 9; denounced in 1920s, 34, 38, 59, 61, 70–71, 72, 79; denounced in 1930s, 87, 92–93, 122, 135; denounced in 1944, 132; denounced in 1946, 1, 2–3, 7–11 *passim*, 24–30 *passim*, 140, 149, 163, 167; denounced, then regains reputation, 12–13; describes details of social life (*byt*), 32–34, 56, 68, 74; health advice given by, 88–91, 93, 108, 141, 149; health of, *see* melancholy ("neurasthenia") of, *below*; as icon of dissidence, 30; joins writers' trip (1933), 82; kindness of, 175n35; letters of, 4, 5, 85, 86, 122, 193n23; as martyr, 9; melancholy ("neurasthenia") of, 6, 60–61, 71–72, 85–86, 87, 155; melancholy ("neurasthenia") of, and psychological trauma in infancy, 141–47 *passim*; melancholy ("neurasthenia") of, and suicidal behavior, 7, 23; output diminishes, 6–7; as parodist, 59–60, 69, 73–77, 80, 109–10, 111, 140; as parodist, shift from, 150; praised/supported, 4–6, 86, 142; praised/supported in 1920s–1940s, 61–62, 87, 132; praised/supported in postsoviet era, 9–11, 136; praised/supported by Western critics, 16, 136; and psychoanalysis, 142–49; and the reading public, *see* Mass reader, the; in Red Army, 5, 23, 146; Russian interpretation of work in 1930s, 41, 55; Russian interpretation of work in postsoviet era, 9–11, 20, 31, 55, 111, 136; Russian interpretation of work and Zoshchenko's rebuttal, 5, 172n5 (*see also* denounced, *above*); self-ordained "task" of, 31; as shoemaker, 6, 157; *skaz* of,

Index

36–58 *passim,* 102, 108, 123, 169, 170; stories rewritten, 56; style of, *see* Language and speech; Western view of, 16, 20, 22, 29, 41, 52, 93, 107, 163–64; Western view of as icon for fate of soviet literature, 7, 8–9, 13; Western view of as writer for the people, 111, 136–37 (*see also* as "antisoviet," *above*); work rejected, 156–57; works derived from other authors, 74; works repressed, 3; works reprinted (1991), 10; during World War II, 4, 5

Zoshchenko, Mikhail, works: "About Myself, Ideology and Some Other Stuff as Well," 22–28, 73, 160; "The Adventures of a Monkey," 1–2, 4, 5, 24; "Apollon and Tamara," 60, 67, 74; *Before Sunrise,* 52, 85, 108, 134, 168, 169; *Before Sunrise,* arrogance displayed in, 120, 121, 150, 151; *Before Sunrise,* as break with past, 146, 152; *Before Sunrise,* conception of, 197n3; *Before Sunrise,* denounced, publication ends, 3, 132, 140; *Before Sunrise,* favorably received, 5, 10; *Before Sunrise,* Gogol's equivalent to, 153–55; *Before Sunrise,* seen as autobiographical, 142, 143, 159; *Before Sunrise,* self-interpretation of, 14, 141; *Before Sunrise,* writer as reader, 140–60; "Black Prince," 152; *The Blue Book,* 10, 14, 99–102, 103–6 *passim,* 111, 125, 146, 151, 167; *The Blue Book,* "Amazing Events" as chapter in, 100; *The Blue Book,* public response to, 102, 105, 107; "Brie Cheese," 156; "An Eye for an Eye," 121; "A Fluke of Nature," 51; "The Goat," 60, 66, 74; "A Happy Adventure," 60, 66; "The History of a Life" in *Belomor,* 29, 150, 169; *Honored Citizens,* 132; "The Lady with the Flowers," 44–45, 47; *Letters to a Writer,* 121–27, 131, 133, 138; "Lilacs in Bloom," 60, 67, 71, 109; "Malarkey Once Again," 156; "Monkey Language," 33; *M. P. Siniagin,* 60, 74, 75–76, 79, 86, 109, 155; *M. P. Siniagin,* photographs in, 76–77, 78, 152; "Nervous People," 33, 50, 183n67; "New Times," 197n3; *Notes of a Former Officer,* 23, 27; "People," 60, 62, 65, 70, 80; "Philistinism before the People's Court," 33; *Poking Around,* 23; The Principal Questions of Our Profession," 103; "A Public Appearance," 134; *The Stories of Nazar Ilich, Mr. Sinebriukhov,* 12, 23, 27; *The Stories of Nazar Ilich . . . ,* Sinebriukhov as character in, 36–43 *passim,* 53, 59, 94, 102, 108, 200n25; *A Story About Reason,* 141; *Tales,* 54; "A Terrible Night," 60, 66, 74; "A Tragic Event," 50; "Viktoria Kazimirovna," 59; "What the Nightingale Sang," 60, 64; *What the Nightingale Sang: Sentimental Tales,* 60, 61–62, 67–74 *passim,* 78, 79, (Kolenkorov as character), 63–72 *passim,* 74–81 *passim,* 86, 94, 108; "Who Are You Laughing At?" 132; "Wisdom," 60, 66; *Youth Restored,* 6, 10, 14, 81, 86–88, 102–10 *passim,* 125, 141, 146, 151, 167, 169, 197n3; *Youth Restored,* commentaries on, 94–98, 99, 108, 110; *Youth Restored,* critics puzzled by, 29, 111, 133; *Youth Restored,* Kashkin as character in, 93, 95, 98, 144, 200n25; *Youth Restored,* public response to, 90–94, 97, 104–7 *passim,* 117–20; *Youth Restored,* Zoshchenko defends, 119, 140

Zoshchenko, Vera Vladimirovna, 145, 188n11, 201n35

Zvezda (journal), 1, 5, 10, 43, 197n3